THE LOGIC AND DESIGN OF COMPUTER PROGRAMS

THE LOGIC AND DESIGN OF COMPUTER PROGRAMS

by

James Messinger

Scott/Jones Inc.
P.O. Box 696
El Granada, California 94108
Voice: 650-726-4693
Facsimile: 650-726-4693
e-mail: scotjones2@aol.com
Web page: www.scottjonespub.com

The Logic and Design of Computer Programs
James Messinger, Weatheford College

ISBN: 1-57676-130-4

The publisher wishes to acknowledge the memory and influence of James F. Leisy. Thanks, Jim. We miss you.

Production Manager:
Mario M. Rodriguez

Copyediting:
Judith Wilson

Composition and Text Design:
Tolman Creek Design

Proofreading:
Fran Eastman

Cover Design:
Nicole Clayton

Book is printed in the USA

Scott/Jones Publishing Company

Editorial Group:
Richard Jones, Denise Simon,
Leata Holloway, and Patricia Miyaki

Production Management:
Mario M Rodriguez

Business Operations:
Michelle Robelet, Cathy Glenn,

Marketing and Sales:
Victoria Judy, Leata Holloway

Additional Titles of Interest from Scott/Jones

Extended Prelude to Programming, Concepts and Design, 2/e
by Stewart Venit

Web Developer Foundations Using XHTML
by Terry Felke Morris

Focus on Excel 2003
by Julie Hayward Spooner

Excel 2003: Volume I, Core Concepts in Excel, 5/e
Excel 2003: Volume II, Advanced Concepts in Excel, 5/e
by Karen Jolly

Starting Out with C++, 4/e
Starting Out with C++ Brief, 4/e
Starting Out with C++ Alternate, 4/e
Starting Out with Java
Starting Out with Java Alternate
Stating Out with Visual Basic.Net, 2/e
by Tony Gaddis

Third Edition
Starting Out with C++,
Third Alternate Edition
by Tony Gaddis

C by Discovery,
Third Edition
by L.S. and Dusty Foster

Assembly Language for the IBM PC Family, Third Edition
by William Jones

The Visual Basic 6 Coursebook, Fourth Edition
QuickStart to JavaScript
QuickStart to DOS for Windows 9X
by Forest Lin

Advanced Visual Basic.Net,
Third Edition
by Kip Irvine

HTML for Web Developers
Server-Side Programming for Web Developers
by John Avila

The Complete A+ Guide to PC Repair
The Complete Computer Repair Textbook, Third Edition
by Cheryl Schmidt

Windows 2000 Professional Step-by-Step
Windows XP Professional Step-by-Step
by Leslie Hardin and Deborah Tice

The Windows 2000 Professional Textbook
Prelude to Programming: Concepts and Design
The Windows XP Textbook
by Stewart Venit

The Windows 2000 Server Lab Manual
by Gerard Morris

Contents

BIOGRAPHY

The author received his doctorate in Mathematical Sciences from the University of Texas at Arlington in December 2003. He received the Master of Science in Management Science at the University of Central Texas in Killeen, TX in 1994. He received his Bachelor of Science in Mathematics and a Bachelor of Science in Education the same year at Midwestern University in Wichita Falls, TX in 1974. He received an Associate in Arts degree in 1971 from Thornton Jr College in Harvey, IL.

He was a programmer in Dallas, Texas in 1974 – 1976 with primary languages of FORTRAN and ASSEMBLER. He also programmed in COBOL and RPG and later taught BASIC (and variations), PASCAL, and C++.

The author was born in Geneva, Illinois, was married in Mineral Wells, Texas and has three daughters. His primary areas of interest are computer science, mathematics and business. His hobby is building the National Vietnam War Museum in Parker County, Texas.

Preface

Any instructor who has taught logic design knows that it is a very challenging task. So is finding a good textbook for it. After I was unable to find a textbook that both covered the material and was student friendly, I decided to write my own book. This book was intended to be a textbook for the Texas Academic Course COSC 1309 Logic Design; however, it can be used for a variety of courses and applications because of its general nature. The course is a disciplined approach to problem solving with structured techniques and a representation of algorithms using pseudocode and graphical tools. The book does not rely on a programming language or a specific hardware set. It is intended to capture the generic portions of programming logic, because we cannot predict which programming languages students will need in the future.

Tools

The graphical tools in this book are the hierarchy chart and the flowchart, because they are extremely prevalent in the business and technology communities. Flowcharts and hierarchy charts are not just for programmers and systems analysts. It is difficult to open a book about business, information systems, or management that does not contain one or both of those tools. The primary purpose of my logic design course is to teach beginning students the techniques of solving problems with a computer using the above tools.

Pseudocode vs. Flowcharts

Two distinct kinds of teaching styles appear in this area. Many believe that students should learn pseudocode and not flowcharts. Many others believe that students should learn flowcharts and not pseudocode. This book attempts to find a balance between those polar views and provides both flowcharts and pseudocode. The pseudocode is generally contained in a special enrichment section so that instructors can choose to add the pseudocode to the lesson plan if they wish. Pseudocode is a text-based solution to a given problem, while the flowchart is a graphic-based solution. A flowchart is not just pseudocode written inside special symbols. Pseudocode is more detailed than the flowcharts found in this text and should be more concise. Pseudocode should be translatable to a programming language on a line-for-line basis. Flowchart symbols, on the other hand, may require many lines of programming, depending on the programming language used, because some flowchart symbols (predetermined process, for example) represent entire modules. In simple algorithms there is normally a line-for-line correspondence among pseudocode, flowcharts, and completed programs.

Task Lists

A special tool called a task list has been provided to help students discover the solution to a problem in an informal manner. Students enrolled in this course typically cannot solve the sample problems using paper and pencil, so writing a computer program to solve the problem is impossible for those students. The task list attempts to identify the steps involved in solving a problem. Once a student sees the individual tasks involved in a solution, they can generally be expected to determine the proper sequence of steps. The hierarchy chart is used to depict the correct sequence of steps. Armed with the steps of the solution and the correct sequence, the student should be able to draw a flowchart that depicts a solution to the given problem. For the text-based user, it may be possible to proceed from the hierarchy chart to the pseudocode; however, the visual representation of the solution is often easier to "debug" than the pseudocode solution.

Procedural vs. OOP

This book contains a section on the object-oriented paradigm and the visual paradigm, but the emphasis of the text is on solving the procedural part of a program. Both object-oriented and visual programs contain procedural sections, so the students complete the course with a capability that is used in all paradigms.

Module on Arithmetic: Flexible Placement

This book provides a special module on computer arithmetic and number conversions that does not obey the standard chapter numbering system. The reviewers of the text have requested that this module be in a wide variety of places in the book, so it was given a unique designation to help the reader avoid thinking of it in a specific sequence. The material is appropriate in many different sections of the text and can be taught first, last, or in the middle, depending on the instructor.

Module on Subprograms: Flexible Placement

A second module is included that covers subprograms. Like the arithmetic module, there was general agreement that this module was necessary, but no consensus was reached as to where in the course it belonged. The module technique allows the instructor the freedom to place this material at any point in the course work.

Sorting

The chapter on sorting may appear extensive, but it includes only the three most basic sorting algorithms: selection, exchange, and insertion. Experience has shown me that students who study three algorithms are better able to grasp the sorting concept than students studying less than three.

"Table" terminology from spreadsheet courses

Much thought was given to the section on tables. Many of us prefer the term "array," but my students seem to be more comfortable talking about tables. With the pervasive use of spreadsheet software, the term "table" is becoming common to most beginning computer students. Indeed the spreadsheet is a classic example of a three-dimensional table and is taught without reference to the term "array." Multiple workbooks of multiple spreadsheets can be combined to form a four-dimensional table. The spreadsheets begin with a table of rows and columns (two dimensions) and provide a natural progression to the four-dimensional case.

Case Study

A case study was invented for a fictitious bowling league in an effort to show the student an entire project and how it can be addressed through each of the techniques in the text. The project begins with the simplest of solutions and expands through the chapters until it encompasses most of the material in the text.

Exercises

The end-of-chapter exercises are organized by chapter objectives. At the end of the exercises there are sections that include Softskills and research assignments.

Acknowledgements

This book would be incomplete without recognizing the contributions of other people to its contents. The complete list of contributors is too long to be included, but some special people need to be mentioned.

Weatherford College

Dr. Sue Casey, who is primarily responsible for the book being published. She encouraged me to present the concept at the ACET Conference in Dallas in 1999, and it was there that it attracted the attention of a publisher.

Ken Logan, Department Chair, Computer Science, who encouraged the book and even taught from it in its infancy.

Marilyn St. Clair, Department Chair, Office Systems Technology, who proofread the draft and is the only person that I know personally, besides myself, who has read every word.

My students (and other students) who took this course and insisted that it be done better. They believed that I could write a better textbook than we had been using and I keep trying. It gets better every semester because the students provide more input.

I also want to thank Dr. Don Huff, Weatherford College President; Arleen Atkins, Vice President for Instruction; and Dr. Richard Bowers, Dean, Math, Science, and Technology; for their administrative support throughout the many years that I have worked on this project.

Scott Jones Publishing

Richard Jones and his crew of reviewers, production managers, copyeditors and compositors. Many professors provided me excellent feedback in the development of this text. I would like to thank them here: Joyce Welby, San Jacinto Community College; Carol Grimm, Palm Beach Community College; Patty Santoianni, Sinclair Community College; Daniel Terrian, Indian Hills Community College; Steve Smith, El Paso Community College; Naser Heravi, Community College of Southern Nevada; Marty Cronlund, Anne Arundel Community College; Marg Chauvin, Palm Beach Community College- Boca Raton; Susan Thrall, Community College of lake City; Cindy Mortensen, Truckee Meadows Community College; David Parker, St Charles Community College.

Personal

Last, and most critical, my wife, who permitted me to devote several summer vacations to the book.

INTRODUCTION AND TERMINOLOGY

What you do ahead of time is what counts most.
(Harold J. "Si" Seymour)

OBJECTIVES

After completing this chapter, you will be able to:

1. Prepare an informal logic plan (task list) for a given problem.
2. Explain the difference between a variable and a constant.
3. Define counters and accumulators.
4. Explain an assignment statement.

Introduction

This course is designed to challenge the way that you think. To learn to program a computer, you need to learn to think like the computer thinks. You also need to think in terms of generalities—yet be specific. Are there 12 months in a year? Yes. Have there always been 12 months in a year? No. Are there 365 days in a year? Have there always been 365 days in a year? Will there always be 365 days in a year? What is pi (π)? These questions and their answers are more complex than most people realize; yet they have "answers" that have been available to generations.

In the early days of computer programming, computer programmers were free to create any set of instructions that would solve a problem. Programmers that could program a computer to do something were successful, and they were free to choose which programming language they would use to program, regardless of business efficiency. Typically, a programmer could enjoy a lifetime career while only knowing one computer language. With the advent of the PC and the downsizing of corporate personnel, many programmers found their jobs in jeopardy or lost entirely. In many cases programming jobs were available, but they were available in the newest language on the market or a language unknown by the programmer. In today's computer programming market, we expect programmers to learn several computer languages in a career.

Our challenge in education becomes one of trying to determine which language to teach students so that they are ready to enter the marketplace with the correct set of programming skills. If we knew which language you were going to use to program, we would introduce you to that language. Each of you is likely to program in a different language, and all of you will change languages during your career. This course is designed to teach the common skills used by all programmers in all programming languages. The *flowchart* is the primary tool we will use in this course; we will explain this tool in great detail in later chapters. *Pseudocode* is a substitute for flowcharts and is another tool that we will describe in this book.

We begin by establishing some ground rules and some standard definitions. First, we need to agree on the definition of a computer. In this book a *computer* is an electronic device that is capable of receiving input (data), processing the input to produce output (information), and providing auxiliary storage (floppy disk, hard disk). A *computer program* is a set of instructions to a computer that will cause the computer to perform a desired task. A *computer programmer* is a person who creates the set of instructions that exist as a computer program.

Occupations

Three primary occupations use the skills presented in this course. The job descriptions provided here are simplistic but provide a starting point for understanding their relationships with business. A computer programmer, as mentioned above, is a person who writes computer programs. To be more specific, a programmer translates a process into a computer program that can be run on a computer. A systems analyst is a person who analyzes a system and designs a process that can be used to develop a computer program to perform the system tasks on a computer. Many times a systems analyst is a programmer as well, and quite often programmers become systems analysts; but these are not necessary requirements. In large software design projects, we would find software engineers in charge of a project with systems analysts doing the design work and passing the design on to the computer programmers to do the actual programming. A software engineer is a person who applies engineering techniques to the design of software. For small projects, the software engineer, system analyst, and programmer could be the same person. For purposes of this text, we will assume that you are all three people. You will, of course, be in charge of your projects: you will analyze the problem, and then develop a flowchart that could be used to write a computer program that would solve the problem with a computer. In this course you will not write the computer program, but you may find that the solutions you develop in this class will be useful in later programming classes.

Many other occupations that use the techniques described in this course are available. Web page designers are sometimes considered programmers depending on the language level they use to design their web pages. Managers of information systems, network administrators, and database administrators often use these techniques. Anyone who is interested in a method for analyzing and solving problems can use these techniques to help solve a variety of problems.

Methodology

Currently, computers cannot solve problems that they have not been programmed to solve. This means that a person must solve the problem, translate the solution into a computer program, and install the program on the computer so that the program can be run and the problem solved "by" the computer. This process is not intuitive and is often not easy. If it were easy, all of us would be programming our computers to solve most of our problems. Solutions to very simple problems can be easily translated into a computer program without using the methods shown here. However, many problems that appear to be very difficult will become easy when using the procedures and methods described in this course.

This course translates real-life problems into visual or text depictions of solutions. To do this work, we will use three general tools; *task list*, *hierarchy chart* (Chapter 2), and *flowchart (visual)* or *pseudocode (text)* (Chapters 3–13). We begin with a problem. The first step in arriving at a solution is to create a *task list*. The task list is

1. Informal.
2. Written.
3. The steps needed to solve the problem.
4. Composed of statements, not questions.
5. Not necessarily in the proper sequence.

A *task* is a simple statement like a formula (or equation) or an assignment statement. For this course a task is also one line of printing or one line displayed on a monitor. A task is also getting one value from either input devices or storage devices. The task list is a list of all the tasks necessary to solve a problem. Given a problem, you will determine which tasks are necessary to arrive at a solution.

Task List

In order to solve a problem, you must have a plan. For very easy problems, the plan is simple; and the problem, in many cases, can be solved more quickly than the plan can be made.

EXAMPLE 1: Solve the equation $x + 1 = 5$. The plan is to subtract 1 from both sides of the equation, which will leave the result $x = 4$. The tasks would look like this:

1. Subtract one from the left-hand side of the equation
2. Subtract one from the right-hand side of the equation
3. State the answer, $x = 4$

Compare that to the problem $2x^2 - x + -3 = 0$. Here we need a more sophisticated plan, and the solution is not so obvious. You might be aware that there are at least two valid plans for solving this problem[1].

EXAMPLE 2: Calculate how much your total pay was last month. Assume that you are paid weekly and that all months have 4 weeks. Compare your plan for solving that problem to the plan for solving the problem of calculating the net pay for all IBM employees for a year.

1 If you have memorized the general formula for solutions to the quadratic equation ($\frac{-b \pm \sqrt{b^2 - 4ac}}{2a}$), you could substitute the values 2, 3, and 1 into the formula for a, b, and c and obtain the solution $x = 3/2$ or $x = -1$. If you forgot the quadratic formula but remember how to factor, you might factor the equation to get the same answers.

No one designs a complex program without giving it some thought. Great novels are not written in one draft. Great buildings are not built without blueprints, and so it goes with computer programs. Very simple programs can be coded directly into the computer with little thought. That type of program is not the kind of program that we are considering. But we will use some simple illustrations to show how the process works. The process can then be applied to any problem with any level of difficulty. To begin our planning we use the task list.

As an example, assume that you want to design a computer program that will calculate the miles per gallon of gas that your car travels on a trip. Let's suppose that we are driving from Chicago to New Orleans. When we get to New Orleans, we will enter some data into a computer, and the computer will print out our car's fuel consumption (miles per gallon used) for this trip. Before reading the task list below, write down some of the things that you think will be required to solve this problem. Remember, it's an informal plan and need not be in proper sequence at this time. To solve this problem, we need to know:

1. How much gas did we have to start?
2. How much gas did we have when finished?
3. How to calculate how much gas we used?
4. What was the starting mileage on the odometer?
5. What was the ending mileage on the odometer?
6. How to calculate how many miles we drove?
7. How to calculate miles per gallon?

To put these questions into a task list, we would rewrite them in statement form:

1. Determine how much gas we have at the beginning of the trip.
2. Look at the odometer, and write down the number of the starting mileage.
3. Record the amount of gas added during the trip.
4. Determine the amount of gas left at the end of the trip.
5. Calculate the amount of total gas used:
   (Total Gas Used = Starting Gas + Gas Added – Gas Remaining).
6. Look at the odometer, and write down the number of the ending mileage.
7. Calculate how many miles that we drove.

   (Miles Driven = Ending Odometer Reading – Beginning Odometer Reading).

8. Calculate miles per gallon:
   (Miles Per Gallon = Miles Driven / Total Gas Used).
9. Display (or print) the miles per gallon.

Desk Checking

We now have an informal logic plan to solve our problem. Are the items in the proper sequence? Are there other sequences that will work as well? Does this solution work? The greatest difficulty students seem to encounter in this course is looking for the "right" solution. As you can see from the example above, there could be several ways to solve the problem; and all could be equally right. This course allows for some creativity as long as the creativity does not result in a "wrong" answer. By wrong answer, we mean that the answer itself is incorrect. If your car achieved 25 miles per gallon of gas and your computer solution said that the car achieved 250 miles per gallon, we would assume that your program was incorrect, regardless of how you designed the program. To ensure that our logic plan is correct, we should perform *desk checking.* Desk checking means that we will produce some sample data and work through the solution by hand to see if we get the right answer. Let's look at our plan using some real data and see if the plan will produce a correct answer.

1. **Determine how much gas we have at the beginning of the trip.** How is this done? Can we look at a car's fuel gauge and determine how much gas is in the tank? I know that I can't; so we need a method to determine our starting fuel level. The easy way to do this is to fill the tank before starting the computations. By filling the tank, we will still not know how much is in the tank, but we can refill the tank in the same manner at each stop and have a very good idea of how much gas has been added. At this point we need to modify our task list somewhat. Our first task has now changed to:

   1. Fill the gas tank

      We can also see that filling the gas tank is really *not* a task. It's a collection of tasks. There are actually several steps involved in filling a gas tank. For our purposes, we will break this step into three tasks:

      A. Park at the gas pump
      B. Turn off the ignition
      C. Pump the gas

2. Continue checking our task list with **record the starting mileage on the odometer** (for discussion purposes assume a reading of 24,688).
3. **Record the amount of gas added during the trip.** This step would be conducted at each fuel stop by reading the amount on the gas pump and recording it. At the end of the trip we could add the amounts to get the total used. Or we could save receipts and add the amounts at the end of the trip. A third method would be to keep track of the amounts at each stop so that we have the total when we finish the trip. Let's suppose that we stopped for gas three times and added fuel according to Table 1.1 shown here. The third column shows our total accumulation.

Table 1.1 Gas Used

Stop Number	Gas Added	Accumulated Gas Used
1	3.3	3.3
2	17.2	20.5
3	15.6	36.1

4. **Determine the amount of gas left in the tank at the end of the trip.** This is similar to the problem we faced at the beginning of the trip, and we can solve it by filling the tank one more time. So we end up with the data in Table 1.2.

Table 1.2 Gas Used Continued

Stop Number	Gas Added	Accumulated Gas Used
1	3.3	3.3
2	17.2	20.5
3	15.6	36.1
Last	5.1	41.2

So we have again modified our task list. This is the advantage of checking our work. As we work through a sample problem, we examine our task list to see if it works or should be modified.

5. **Calculate the total gas used.** Since we have been keeping track of the gas added as the trip proceeded, we see that we have already completed this step. So we have another change for the task list.

6. **Record the ending mileage on the odometer.** Let's assume a reading of 25,617.

7. **Calculate how many miles driven.** Using the formula we have:
   25,617 - 24,688 = 929

8. **Calculate miles per gallon.** Using the formula we have:
   929 miles/41.2 gallons = 22.5 miles per gallon.

9. **Display the miles per gallon.**

From this example, we can see how desk checking allowed us to find difficulties within the task list and modify the task list so that the solution was improved. Here is our redesigned task list:

1. Park at the gas pump.
2. Turn off the ignition.
3. Pump the gas.
4. Look at the odometer, and write down the starting mileage.
5. Calculate the total amount of gas added during the trip.
6. Fill the tank at the end of the trip, and add this amount to the amount from step 5.
7. Look at the odometer, and write down the ending mileage.
8. Calculate how many miles that we drove:
   Miles Driven = Ending Odometer Reading – Beginning Odometer Reading.
9. Calculate miles per gallon:
   Miles Per Gallon = Miles Driven / Total Gas Used.
10. Display (or print) the Miles Per Gallon.

With a more complex problem, we might want to recheck the task list with some new data to see if there are other changes we can make. This process should continue until the designer is satisfied that the task list is correct.

Now that we have an informal logic plan, we can proceed to develop a *formal logic plan*. Many standard techniques are available to create formal logic plans: *hierarchy chart*, *flowchart*, *pseudocode*, and *computer program*, to name a few. We will focus on using the hierarchy chart and flowchart in this course; but each chapter will include a special section for demonstrating pseudocode, and pseudocode can be used in addition to, or in lieu of, the flowchart.

The formal logic plan takes the informal logic plan and arranges the steps into the "proper" sequence so that when the problem is solved, we get an accurate answer. The formal logic plan is something you can show to the boss or the customer. A formal plan should look professional and produce the desired result. Chapter 2 will look at hierarchy charts, while Chapters 3, 4, and 5 are devoted to flowcharts and pseudocode. Before we move on, let's look at our miles per gallon problem one last time and see how to explain "correct" and "proper." The "correct" answer to our example is 22.5 miles per gallon. We determined that answer by working through the problem by hand. When this process is solved by a computer, we will know the programming is correct if the computer produces the answer of 22.5 miles per gallon. One "proper" sequence was produced already. Other sequences are left for the reader to find. The following is one improper sequence:

1. Determine how much gas we have at the beginning of the trip.
2. Record the amount of gas added during the trip.
3. Determine the amount of gas left at the end of the trip.
4. Calculate the total gas used:

   Total Gas Used = Starting Gas + Gas Added – Gas Remaining
5. Record the starting mileage on the odometer.
6. Record the ending mileage on the odometer.
7. Calculate how many miles that we drove:
   Miles Driven = Ending Odometer Reading – Beginning Odometer Reading
8. Calculate miles per gallon:
   Miles Per Gallon = Miles Driven / Total Gas Used.
9. Display the miles per gallon.

In this task list, we are recording the starting mileage after the trip is complete, so we're going to get the same mileage for starting and ending the trip. The resulting calculations will tell us that we traveled zero miles per gallon of gas.

Solutions can be "right" or "wrong." An infinite number of right and wrong solutions are probably available, and a fascinating field of study in computer science analyzes "right" solutions to determine which solutions are better. Usually no best general solution exists because the best general solution depends on which computer you are using and which computer language you are using. Given a specific computer, a specific computer language, and a specific set of data, you may be able to find a "best" solution.

The following key points can summarize the concept of a task list:

1. A task list is an informal plan to use in solving a problem.
2. The task list needs to be written.
3. The task list does not need to be in sequence.
4. Many task lists can be created to solve a given problem; you don't have to spend time trying to determine the "right" task list.

In creating a task list, you can solve the problem first by hand and then record the steps that you took to solve the problem.

As an example, suppose that you are asked to compute the average score for a bowler. Let's assume that the bowler has bowled three games and scored 150, 165, and 174. To calculate the average score we add the three games (150 + 165 + 174) and then divide by three, yielding an answer of 163. Our task list then would look something like this:

1. Get bowler's first game score.
2. Accumulate total score.
3. Get bowler's second game score.
4. Accumulate total score.
5. Get bowler's third game score.
6. Accumulate total score.
7. Calculate average, total score/3.
8. Display average.

This solution to the bowler's problem assumes an interactive solution. We enter scores as they are received and accumulate them.

Terminology

Before moving on to the next chapter, we need to discuss more terms. The definitions given here are for the purposes of this course and may be used differently in other courses you take.

Order of operations The computer processes calculations in a specific order known as the *order of operations*. This order is the same one used in mathematics, so it is not unique to the computer. The order is: parentheses, exponents, multiplication and division, addition and subtraction. Given a mathematical statement containing the operations, the statement is processed by first performing any calculations inside parentheses. After the parentheses have been removed any exponentiation is completed. After exponentiation is completed, multiplication and division are processed working from left to right in the statement. Finally, all addition and subtraction is performed working from left to right in the statement.

Example: Find the value of the statement $4*(8+1)/3-(6-4)^2 *3 + 8$

1. Evaluate the parentheses to give the intermediate result: $4*9/3-2^2 *3 +8$

2. Perform the exponentiation giving the intermediate result: 4*9/3-4*3 +8

3. Perform multiplication and division working from left to right.

   A. 36/3-4*3 + 8

   B. 12-4*3 + 8

   C. 12-12 + 8

4. Finally, perform the addition and subtraction, working from left to right.
   A. 0 + 8
   B. 8 is the answer

Relational operators There are six basic relational operators shown here with their symbols as used in this text:

1. Equal to (=)
2. Less than (<)
3. Greater than (>)
4. Not equal to (≠)
5. Less than or equal to (≤)
6. Greater than or equal to (≥)

Algorithm An *algorithm* is a step-by-step procedure to solve a problem.

As an example of an algorithm, consider the steps necessary to sort a list of numbers into ascending sequence. The steps might be:

1. Find the smallest number in the list.
2. Move the smallest number to the output area.
3. Repeat steps 1 and 2 until all numbers have been moved.

These three steps constitute a sorting algorithm.

Notice the similarity between an algorithm and a task list. The differences are significant and perhaps not obvious. The algorithm steps must be in the correct sequence to solve the problem. For our purposes, you can think of an algorithm as a formal task list.

Programming language A *programming language* is a computer language that is a collection of symbols used by a computer programmer to create a set of instructions for a computer. The program is processed through an interpreter, or compiler, which is software that translates the instructions into the machine language that the computer can understand. The interpreter, or compiler, is also capable of telling the programmer where syntax[2] errors have occurred in the programmer's instructions.

Currently hundreds of different programming languages are available. Selecting the appropriate language to solve a problem can make the difference between the success and failure of a project. Languages that are common today include JAVA, XML, LISP, C, C++, COBOL, FORTRAN, Basic, Visual Basic, SQL, and Assembler. Computer languages are constantly being invented, hence the need for programmers to learn new languages.

2 The syntax of a programming language refers to the spelling, punctuation, and structure of the statements in the program

Pseudocode *Pseudocode* means literally "false code." It is a fake programming language. It looks like a programming language, and some authors provide a set of rules for their pseudocode that exceeds the rules for some real computer languages. But pseudocode will not run on any computer today. Indeed, if pseudocode did run on a computer, it would not be pseudocode.

Pseudocode is intended to be a formal logic plan that looks like a computer program. It can be easily translated into a computer language. Pseudocode can be used as a substitute for the flowchart. It is a text-based logic plan, whereas the flowchart is a graphic-based logic plan.

Variable A *variable* is a value that may change during the course of the procedure that is used to solve the given problem. In flowcharts, pseudocode, and computer programs, variables are given names. Variable names should be assigned so that they are meaningful to the person who will be reading the flowchart, pseudocode, or program. Variable names represent a location in computer memory that stores the value of the variables.

Mathematicians like to use X as a variable name, but it has little meaning. In our earlier example of calculating miles per gallon, we might use X to designate the answer. A more meaningful name would be "answer." An even more meaningful name might be "miles_ per_gallon." As systems become more complex, variable names become more complex; and using meaningful names becomes more important. Imagine 10 programmers generating the code for one program. What if they all used different names for the same thing? Big mess! To avoid that kind of problem, we use a *data dictionary*, which is a list of all the names used and their meanings. Each programming language has its own customs for naming variables. COBOL programmers are taught to use long variable names with each word separated by hyphens, like miles-per-gallon in our earlier example. Visual Basic programmers use the convention of capitalizing successive words like MilesPerGallon. C programmers use the underscore, so you would see Miles_per_gallon as their variable name. The reason for these techniques is that most programming languages do not allow blank spaces in variable names. In this text we will use a variety of methods to name variables. Variable names should be assigned to variables before the flowchart is begun. Once the task list is developed, the variable names can be assigned as needed. It is critically important that you be consistent with the variable names that you use. If you decide to use the name miles_per_gallon to stand for the number of miles a car drove for each gallon of gas used; then whenever that name is used, it must stand for the number of miles a car drove for each gallon of gas used.

Constant A *constant* is a value that doesn't change during the course of the procedure.

The number 5 is an example of a constant. The letter "a" is also a constant. Constants can be assigned names in a manner similar to the way that variables are assigned names. Since the value doesn't change during the procedure, you might wonder why we would assign a name to a constant. Suppose that you are writing a very long computer program that uses the value of pi for many computations. You could simply type 3.14 in every place where the value for pi was required. However, the value of pi is not exactly 3.14, and there is a possibility that you would want to change that value at a later time. The program could use the constant identifier name "pi" in all of the places that pi was needed and have an assignment statement at the beginning of the program that stated pi = 3.14. If you later decided to use the value 3.14159 for pi, you could update the program to this new value by changing only that assignment statement in the beginning of the program. The rest of the program would continue to operate with the new value.

Another example of using a name for a constant is in a case where you want to maintain some generality in the program, in case values change after the program is completed. Some business computations use a year length of 360 days and some that use 365 days. If you were uncertain of which year length to use, you might use a constant name of "days_in_a_year" to stand for that value. Once that value was known, the program could be adjusted by setting days_in_a_year = 360 or days_in_a_year= 365.

Data dictionary A *data dictionary* is a dictionary of variable names used in a computer program. The dictionary is begun during the analysis portion of the project and is continued with terms added until the project is completed. The data dictionary includes all the variable names, the constant names, and the meaning for those names in the context of the program.

Data types (character and numeric) This text will be concerned with only two data types, character and numeric.

Numeric data *Numeric* data consists of any data that is entirely composed of numbers. Numbers can be used for calculations.

Character data This text restricts the *character data* to the characters contained in the ASCII data set (see Appendix B). A character is any data that can be entered from the keyboard[3]. You can see that the keyboard also has the capability to enter numbers, which permits some confusion between numbers used for calculation and numbers used as characters or text. To distinguish between the two types of numbers, this book uses quotation marks around numbers that are intended to be characters. Character data are not normally used in mathematical calculations. Each programming language has a convention that is used to make the distinction between numeric and character data.

3 Data can be entered into a computer in a variety of ways. The keyboard is used as an example only and not intended to restrict input.

Assignment statement The *assignment statement* assigns a value to a variable name. Pi = 3.14 is an example of an assignment statement. Notice that the value is on the right-hand side of the equal sign, and the result is on the left-hand side. This is an important procedure to remember. In our assignment statements we will always put the result on the left-hand side of the equal sign.

Correct assignment statements:

Total Gas Used = Starting Gas + Gas Added – Gas Remaining

Net Pay = Gross Pay – Deductions

Gross Hourly Pay = Hours worked * Hourly Pay

Gross Pay = Regular Pay + Special Pay

Incorrect assignment statements:

Starting Gas + Gas Added – Gas Remaining = Total Gas Used

Gross Pay – Deductions = Net Pay

Hours worked * Hourly Pay = Gross Hourly Pay

Regular Pay + Special Pay = Gross Pay

In general, the assignment statement does not have the same meaning as a mathematical sentence. The assignment statement pi = 3.14 tells the computer to assign the label pi to a memory location and put the value 3.14 in that memory location. This is similar to the mathematical sentence pi = 3.14. However, the assignment statement x = x + 1 is a valid assignment statement, but impossible as a mathematical sentence. This statement tells the computer to go to the storage location called x, get the value stored there, add 1 to that value, and store the result at the storage location called x.

Imagine that we start the program with the value 0 (zero) stored in the location identified by variable name x. The computer will get the zero and add one, which results in a value of 0 + 1, which is 1. The computer then stores the resulting value of 1 at location x. If we repeat the process, the computer will go to location x, pick up the 1 and add 1 to it and store the result, which is 2. Table 1.3 illustrates this procedure for three iterations.

Table 1.3 Assignment Statement

Starting value stored at location x	Resulting value of x=x+1 Assignment statement	New value stored at location x
0	1=0+1	1
1	2=1+1	2
2	3=2+1	3

Understanding the logic of the assignment statement x = x + 1 is a key to understanding how to program computers and design programs. You will use this type of logic in most programs you design.

Counter A *counter* is a logical series of instructions that cause a value to increase (or decrease) in a regular manner, normally by one. When a counter increases by a value, we call that value an increment. If we increase a counter by 1, we increment the counter by 1. If we decrease a counter by a value, we decrement the counter by that value[4]. Counters normally start at zero or one. Table 1.3 depicts the results of a counter process that begins at zero and continues to three.

The process would look like this: counter = counter + 1

Accumulator An *accumulator* is a generic form of a counter that counts in irregular increments.

The simplest example of an accumulator is found in most accounting software and is known as a total. Let's assume that we want to know our total income for a year, and we receive income monthly. Here's our informal logic plan for calculating total income:

1. Start total at zero.
2. Increment total by monthly income.
3. Repeat step 2 until all monthly incomes have been added.
4. Display total.

The formula that makes this work looks like this:

Total Income = Total Income + Monthly Income

Table 1.4 shows the results of the accumulation.

Table 1.4 Income Accumulator

Month	Income	Total Income Starting Value	Total Income Ending Value
		0	0
January	2226.10	0	2226.10
Febuary	2226.10	2226.10	4452.20
-	-	-	-
-	-	-	-
-	-	-	-
December	2226.10	24487.10	26713.20

4 Counters can be incremented using negative numbers, which is equivalent to decrementing by positive numbers.

The computer gets the value from the storage location called Total Income, adds the value from storage location Monthly Income, and then stores the answer back into the location called Total Income. After all months have been processed, the storage location Total Income contains the total income for the year.

Our final definitions are for terms used mainly for making decisions. *Switches, indicators,* and *flags* are variables that we use to control the "direction" of a process.

Switch Generally speaking, a computer can only decide between yes and no (on or off, true or false, and so on). Sometimes it is convenient to set a variable value equal to 0 (zero) when one decision is to be made and to change that value to 1 when the other decision is to be made. This variable sounds like an on/off switch; hence the name switch. The switch could also have the values 1 and 2 or 5 and 7 or any other values that could be reduced to the equivalent of true or false.

Indicator *Indicator* means switch (zero **indicates** off, where one **indicates** on). Your car probably has a low oil indicator that causes a red light to illuminate when your car's engine is low on oil. The light illuminates when current flows to it and stays off when current does not flow.

Flag A *flag* is related to flagging of data. It is similar to flagging in car races where the flag tells you to take a specific action, and no flag tells you the opposite. Typically in a computer, the flag is on when it is 1 and off when it is zero. In car races, there are a variety of flags: yellow, white, checkered, and so on. Each of these could be represented in a computer by an appropriately named variable and could be set to 0 or 1 to indicate to the computer program the state of the car race.

In this book, we will use the terms switch, flag, and indicator interchangeably. As we develop more complex programs, you will understand these operations more thoroughly.

Summary

In this chapter you were given some fundamental definitions and were also introduced to some occupations appropriate to our study. Next you were presented with information about the informal task list and how to use it in the first step toward solving a problem with a computer. And finally, some terms were described that you will need in the succeeding chapters. Many of the terms introduced in Chapter 1 will be explained in greater detail in the succeeding chapters.

Key Terms

Each number in parentheses indicates the page where the term first occurs in the chapter.

accumulator (15)
algorithm (11)
assignment statement (14)
compiler (9)
computer (2)
computer program (2)
computer programmer (2)
constant (12)
counter (15)
data dictionary (13)
data types (13)
desk checking (6)
flag (16)
flowchart (2)
hierarchy chart (4)
formal logic plan (8)
indicator (16)
order of operations (10)
programming language (11)
pseudocode (2)
software engineer (3)
relational operators (11)
switch (16)
systems analyst (3)
task (4)
task list (4)
variable (12)

Chapter 1
Exercises

Some of the following exercises are more difficult than others. They have not been classified by difficulty because some problems are easy for some people and hard for others. Some exercises have tricks and errors built into them because students need practice finding errors and correcting them. Being able to find the errors in computer programs is what separates programmers from ordinary people. If everything worked as it was supposed to, everyone would be a programmer.

Objective 1 Prepare an informal logic plan (task list) for a given problem.

1. Create a task list to calculate and display one employee's net pay for one week.

   Some of the formulas that you need are the following:

   net pay = gross pay – deductions
   gross pay = regular pay + special pay

2. Create a task list that will calculate and display a college student's grade point average. Desk check your task list with the following data: a 4-credit-hour course with a grade of A and a 1-credit-hour course with a grade of C. Assume a 4-point grading system, and state the grade point average that you calculated.

   Some formulas that you need are the following:

   grade point average = total honor points/total credit hours

   honor points = numeric grade * credit hours

3. Create a task list to model checking out at a retail store. Assume a customer arrives at the cash register and wants to pay for his purchases and get a receipt. Show all the tasks that are accomplished to process the customer, assuming he is purchasing two or three items.

4. Create a task list to calculate and display the batting average of a baseball player. The formula for batting average is:

   batting average = number of hits/number of times at bat * 100

5. Create a task list for processing a bowling team's statistics. Assume four members per team, and calculate each player's average and the team average. Display all the statistics.

6. Create a task list to calculate and display the value of an investment of $10,000 after 10 years, placed at 6% annual interest. Assume that the interest is compounded monthly. A formula for calculating the value of an investment is: ending amount = investment (1 + interest rate/compounding frequency)Number of years*Compounding frequency)

7. Assume that you have borrowed $5,000 at an annual interest rate of 8% simple interest. Create a task list that will determine how many months it will take to pay off the loan, assuming a monthly payment of $300.00. Formulas you need:

   interest = interest rate * amount owed
   balance due = balance due + interest – payment

8. Create a task list for finding the area of a regular hexagon. The formula for the area of a regular polygon with n sides is:

   area = $\frac{1}{4}$ n *length of one side * cotangent 180°/n

Objective 2 Explain the difference between a variable and a constant.

1. Select the variables from the following list:

   A. pi
   B. ?
   C. Months in a year
   D. X
   E. 768.95
   F. Net pay

2. Select the constants from the following list:

   A. pi
   B. ?
   C. Months in a year
   D. X
   E. 768.95
   F. Net pay

3. Assign variable names to the following items:

   A. A variable name for the radius of a circle.
   B. A variable name for the height of a triangle.
   C. A variable name for the total deductions from an employee's pay.
   D. A variable name for a picture of a clown.
   E. A variable name for tax Form 1040.

4. Examine the list of variable or constant names below and decide which are meaningful and which are not. If the name is meaningful, give its value or describe it in some detail.

   A. e
   B. p
   C. x
   D. *i*
   E. Annual_income

5. You are designing a program that deals with college students and decide to use a student's first and last name as the variable name associated with his or her grade point average. Give two or three reasons why this is a good idea. Then give two or three reasons why this is a bad idea.

6. Select three programming languages, and examine how they create variables. Report on the syntax and rules for variables of each of the three languages. Compare and contrast the syntax and rules.

7. A programmer friend is designing a program and is having difficulty creating variable names. He has the following names in his data dictionary: Variable_1, Variable_2, Variable_3, A, Q. Write a short paper on his choices of variable names.

Objective 3 Define counters and accumulators.

1. State the value of the variable named "counter" after each step in the algorithm below. Also state when the algorithm is finished.

   A. Counter is set to zero.
   B. Counter is incremented by one.
   C. Repeat step B until counter is 5.

2. Show how the value of the variable named "accumulator" changes in the following algorithm:

   A. Accumulator is set to zero.
   B. Accumulator is incremented by 15.
   C. Accumulator is incremented by 37.
   D. Accumulator is incremented by 29.
   E. The value of the accumulator is printed.

3. State the value of the variable named "counter" after each step in the algorithm below. Also state when the algorithm is finished.

   A. Counter is set to zero.
   B. Counter is incremented by one.
   C. Repeat steps A and B until counter is **5**.

4. State the value of the variable named "counter" after each step in the algorithm below. Also state when the algorithm is finished.

   A. Counter is set to zero.
   B. Counter is decremented by one.
   C. Repeat step B until counter is **5**.

5. Explain what happens to the value of the variable named "counter" in the following algorithm:

   A. Counter is incremented by one.
   B. Repeat step A until counter is 5.

6. State the value of the variable named "counter" after each step in the algorithm below. Also state when the algorithm is finished.

   A. Counter is set to zero.
   B. Counter is decremented by minus one.
   C. Repeat step B until counter is 5.

7. State the value of the variable named "counter" after each step in the algorithm below. Also state when the algorithm is finished.

   A. Counter is set to zero.

   B. Counter is incremented by minus one.

   C. Repeat steps A and B until counter is 5.

8. State the value of the variable named "counter" after each step in the algorithm below. Also state when the algorithm is finished.

   A. Counter is set to zero.

   B. Counter is decremented by minus one.

   C. Repeat steps A and B until counter is -5.

Objective 4 Explain an assignment statement.

1. Examine the assignment statements below and explain what each of them means.

   A. total = total + monthly income

   B. square = number * number (assuming that number = 3, what value is assigned to Square)

   C. sum = total + square

2. You want to calculate average monthly income and you are given total annual income. Here are three statements that do the required calculation.

   average monthly income = total annual income / 12

   average monthly income = total annual income / months in a year

   x = y / 12

   Discuss the three statements, explaining how they differ. Which (if any) is right, wrong, or best.

Note!

Are there always 12 months in a year? Has it ever been different? Could it be different in the future?

3. Assume that a memory location named "answer" contains the value 37. State what value is in "answer" after each of the following statements. Each statement follows the previous statement(s).

   A. answer = 2 * answer + 1

   B. display answer

   C. answer = answer –17

   D. answer = answer/2

4. Show an assignment statement that would assign the value for the number of weeks in a year to some memory location.

5. Show how you would assign the following values to memory locations. Use variable names of your own choosing.

   A. 1735
   B. 29
   C. 17

6. Identify the incorrect assignment statements below.

   A. 7 = sum
   B. variable = variable
   C. accumulator = accumulator + X
   D. X + Y + z = Total

7. Describe an assignment statement that would assign the value for the number of months in a year to the memory location labeled Months_in_a_year.

Other Assignments

SoftSkills

Select one problem from Objective 1 or from the Internet/library research projects below. Prepare and give an oral report to the class on your solution.

Internet/library research projects

A. What is "the" algorithm to determine when Easter occurs?

B. How is leap year determined?

C. What is a leap second?

D. Find a calendar that did not have 12 months.

E. How is daylight savings time determined?

F. What is a doomsday? How is it used?

STRUCTURED DESIGN AND THE HIERARCHY CHART

Every seeming equality conceals a hierarchy.
(Mason Cooley)

OBJECTIVES

After completing this chapter, you will be able to:

1. Read a hierarchy chart.
2. Relate and assign tasks from a task list to modules in a hierarchy chart.
3. Draw a hierarchy chart from a given task list.
4. Draw a hierarchy chart to display a solution for a given problem.

Introduction

Chapter 1 introduced the task list as a first step in designing a solution to a problem. In this chapter we will learn to take the task list and incorporate it into a hierarchy chart. In order to do that, we'll first need to study the hierarchy chart and the design process.

Structured Design

In this course structured design refers to the principle of designing a solution to a problem using a structured approach. This book employs a three-step approach. First, develop an informal logic plan (the task list described in Chapter 1). Next develop a general, formal, logic plan, the *hierarchy chart.* And finally, develop a detailed, formal, logic plan, the *flowchart.* We will attempt to obey three basic design principles:

1. Top-down approach.
2. Modular design.
3. Use of three structures: sequence, selection, and iteration. These structures will be discussed in detail in later chapters.

The *top-down* approach is an intuitive way to attack a problem. Begin at the beginning (top) and proceed to the end (bottom). Many students believe that this is the only way to solve problems, but other popular methods exist: the *reverse sequence* method, and the "normal" programming method - *output, input, process.* There are others, but we will explain just these two.

The *reverse sequence* method is also intuitive, and it requires that the problem be solved in reverse sequence. We start at the end and backtrack until we arrive at the beginning. This is a common method employed in the logistics field.

For example, suppose that you want to build a house. You will need to know how much lumber (bricks, sheet rock, nails, and so on) it will take to build the house so that you can buy the lumber. You can also buy more if you miscalculate, but it might be difficult to return excess lumber. As a builder, you want to minimize the number of trips to the lumberyard, so it's fairly important to know how much lumber you want before you actually start building. You begin building from a plan that describes the finished house (end). If you didn't know what the house was supposed to look like, you would be very challenged trying to build it.

The *output, input, process* method is similar to reverse sequence in that we start at the end (output) of a program and determine exactly what the output will look like. Once we know the finished product, we look for the input data that we will need to obtain in order to produce the desired output. Then, we design the process that will take the input data and provide the output information.

A simple example might help. Suppose you wish to calculate the area of a circle. The output would be something like this: The area of the circle is *144 square feet.* What input do we need to calculate the area of a circle? We will certainly need π (pi). We could use 3.14 or 3.14159 or something more precise, depending on our needs. Do we need the radius of the circle? Could we use the diameter instead? Depending on the answer to these questions, we would need different statements to solve the problem. If we input the radius, we use the statement[1]: *area = pi x radius*^{2}. If we input the diameter, then our statements could be: *radius = diameter/2 and area = pi x radius*^{2}, or combined into the single statement: *area = pi x (diameter/2)*^{2}. Can you think of a reason for selecting the use of two statements instead of the use of one statement? Is one more correct than the other?

Modules

Modular design refers to the technique of using modules to develop a solution. A *module* is a collection of related tasks. A module will always contain two or more tasks. Modules have one entry point and one exit point. They are used to separate complex problems into solvable components. Several advantages for using modules exist. A program can be designed more quickly using modules because each does not have to be developed in detail before continuing the design. We establish modules that describe the "big picture" solution and then develop the details of the modules independently. Each module can be assigned to a separate programmer; and as the modules are completed, they can be assembled into the final program.

Modules that become complex can be subdivided. A *sub-module* is a component of a module.

As an example, think of a car as a program. Its modules could be the engine, transmission, and body. Sub-modules of the engine could be the fuel system, ignition system, and exhaust system. Sub-modules are controlled by modules. Modules invoke (call) sub-modules. This system of modules and sub-modules creates a hierarchy of control that can be pictured as a hierarchy chart.

Cohesion

The instructions internal to a module need to be closely related. The measure of how well the instructions are related is the measure of cohesion of the module. Modules with instructions that are very well related have high cohesion. High cohesion is a desirable quality for modules.

Coupling

This is a measure of the strength of association between two modules. High coupling is undesirable. High coupling is an indication of an overly complicated system and/or a large amount of information shared between (or among) modules.

1 Notice how we use the meaningful variable names "area" and "radius" instead of the abbreviated algebraic notation of "a" and "r."

Hierarchy Chart

The hierarchy chart is a pictorial representation of a solution to a problem, which shows the relationship to the solution's parts. The hierarchy chart is a general plan because it does not provide details of what is being accomplished. The task list gives more details than the hierarchy chart. The hierarchy chart is composed of modules, and each module can be expected to contain several tasks from the task list. Since the hierarchy chart is a formal plan, it is expected to look professional.

Hierarchy Chart Procedures

Hierarchy charts are drawn using three symbols: rectangles, straight-line segments, and solid triangles. Each rectangle in the chart represents a module. Remember that a module consists of two or more tasks. Words are inserted into the rectangles to describe what happens inside the module. Hierarchy charts are best drawn on paper in landscape mode (printed sideways) and normally will fit on one piece of paper. Module numbers are inserted into the rectangles to use as references. Modules are connected with straight-line segments. The straight-line segments depict the flow of logic and the control of modules. Finally, the solid triangle is used to show that a module is reused within the same hierarchy chart. Hierarchy charts do not depict loops or decisions. No symbols are available for those items in a hierarchy chart even though that logic may be contained within the modules.

Figure 2.1 shows a sample of a completed hierarchy chart. Using the figure, let's examine the details of hierarchy charts before moving on to a discussion of modules. Hierarchy charts are arranged in levels. Level one will only have one module and that rectangle will contain the name of the program/system that we are designing. The level one module will normally be labeled as the 1000 module. Use of the number 1000 as the label for the first module is a convention or tradition, and the module could just as easily be labeled 100 or 10 or even 1. (It could be numbered 2000 as well, but we are generally more comfortable starting with 1 when numbering.) Modules are numbered in sequence from top to bottom and left to right using a pattern that identifies the major module that controls each submodule. Eventually, the number 1000 began to be commonly used so that a number of sub-modules could be developed. Moving down the sheet of paper, you should discover that in the next row all rectangles have module numbers starting with 2. These are the level 2 modules. The convention here is to use numbers across the levels that would leave room for sub-modules to be added at the same level without re-numbering the hierarchy chart. If you move down to the next row of rectangles, you shouldn't be surprised to see that these modules all start with 3, designating level 3 modules. As we move down the hierarchy chart, the level numbers increase and the labels in the rectangles follow the pattern established. Notice that the numbers in the modules tend to increase as we read from left to right on each level. That is intentional and required unless a module is re-used. This numbering system is an aid to the hierarchy chart developer and reader as a reminder of the processing sequence of the modules.

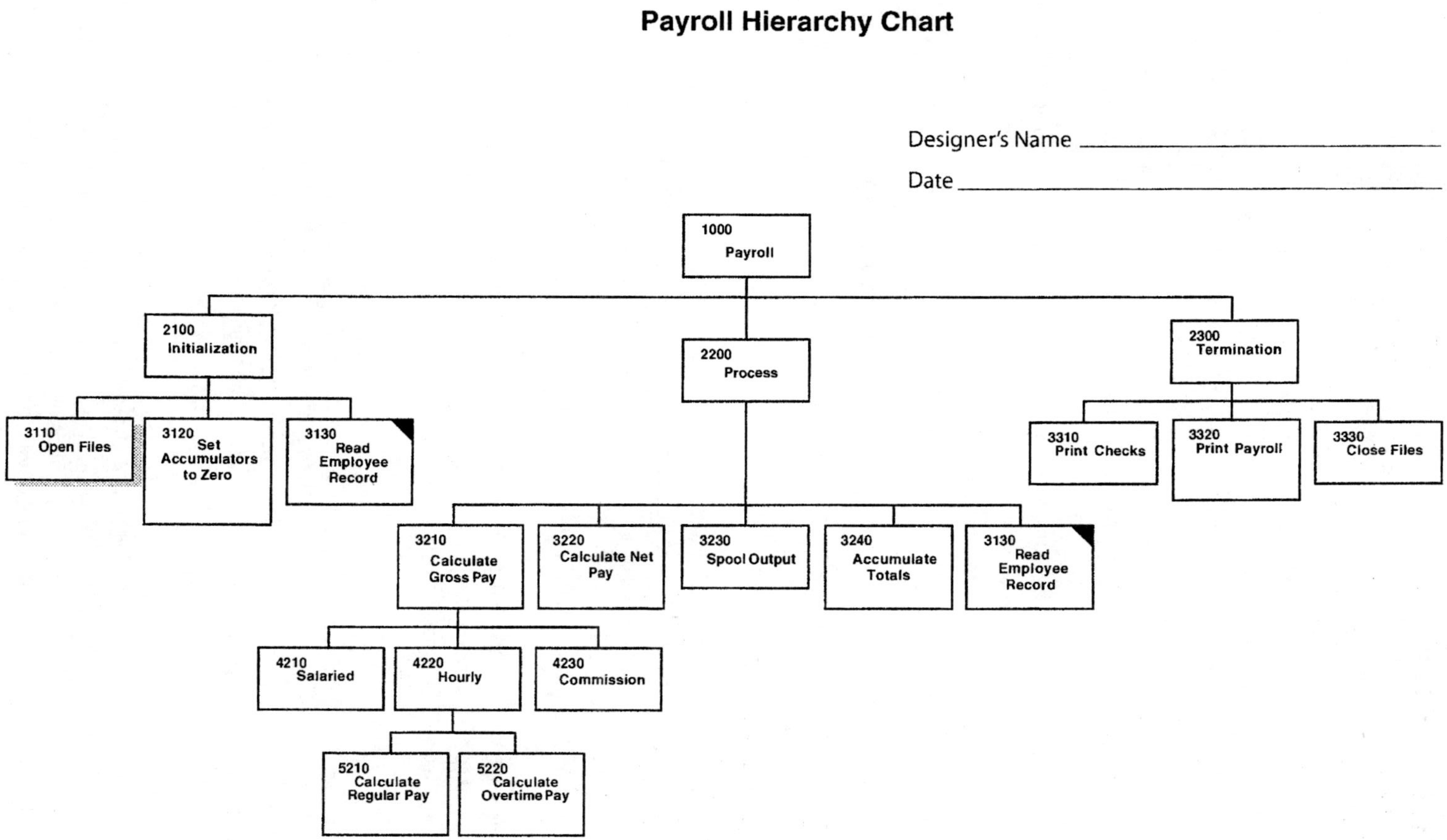

Figure 2.1 Sample Hierarchy Chart

We will process the modules in a hierarchy chart by starting at the 1000 module and passing control to the lowest leftmost module. Then move to the right. If the next module has a lower level, we proceed down to the lowest leftmost sub-module and continue processing until reaching a right sub-module that does not connect to the right. If there is no module to the right, then move back up the hierarchy chart one level and repeat the process. Look at Figure 2.1, and note the flow. Control begins with module 1000. Because there is a module below it, control is passed down to the next level (level 2) and to the leftmost module (module 2100).

Because there is a module below 2100, control passes down and left again to sub-module 3110. Module 3110 is processed, then module 3120 is processed, and then module 3130[2]. At this point control passes back to module 2100, and its instructions are completed before passing control to module 2200. At 2200 control is passed down to level 3, module 3210, and down to level 4, module 4210. Module 4210 is processed, control passes to module 4220, and then down to module 5210. Module 5210 is processed, followed by module 5220, then module 4220, and followed by 4230. Control passes back up to complete 3210, followed by modules 3220, 3230, 3240, and 3130[2]. Control moves back up to 2200 and across to 2300. The final three modules are processed as 3310, 3320, and 3330, and control returns to module 2300 where the program stops.

Span of Control

Another feature of hierarchy charts with which you need to be familiar is called *span of control.* Span of control is a number associated with the number of sub-modules controlled by a module. It is the number of sub-modules under a module at the next level. Looking at Figure 2.1 again, we see that the span of control for module 1000 is three. The span of control for 2100 is three, 2200 is five, and 4220 is two.

Tip!

A rule of thumb[3] for span of control in hierarchy charts is "the span of control for a module should be three to seven sub-modules[4]." Notice that module 4220 violates this "rule."

Many exceptional circumstances occur where the span of control is violated. Drawing a hierarchy chart is as much art as science. The modules of a hierarchy chart can be easily combined by just changing the description of a module. Similarly, modules can be created by removing a task from a large module and making a separate

2 Notice that module 3130 contains a shaded triangle. That triangle indicates that module 3130 is used more than once in this hierarchy chart. You will find it under module 2100 and again under module 2200.

3 Rule of thumb can be formally defined as "some method or procedure that comes from practice or experience, without any formal basis." As used here, the rule of thumb represents a rule that is not always followed. There is an old saying that rules can not be broken, but a rule of thumb is a rule that can be broken.

4 A shorthand notation for this is 5 ± 2 sub-modules.

module. The goal of a hierarchy chart is to produce a one-page "big picture" description of the solution to our problem. The hierarchy chart should look professional. It must be a complete description and usable to show a customer (or the boss) that the problem has been analyzed, and a solution has been developed. It is the designer's job to be sure that the customer finds it easy to read. If the customer asks where specific tasks are performed, the designer needs to have answers. If the tasks are not performed in the hierarchy chart, then the chart needs modification.

Hierarchy Chart Module Contents

The first module is considered to be the title for the program, which does not contain any instructions. For hierarchy charts in this course, the 1000 module is documentation only and will not contain instructions or tasks. Under the 1000 module we will always draw three, level 2 modules: Initialization, Process and Termination. This tripartite division is not a convention or a rule, and you will find many hierarchy charts drawn with more than three modules at the second level. In this book, we will use 2100 as the initialization module, 2200 as the process module, and 2300 as the termination module. This makes task assignment relatively easy because initialization tasks will go into or under module 2100, processing tasks go into or under module 2200, and termination tasks go into or under module 2300.

If files are opened in a program, they will be opened in the initialization section of the hierarchy chart. Normally this will be a single module. Occasionally, we may have multiple files with each file having its own module.

If files are closed in a program, they will be closed in the termination section of the hierarchy chart (*if files are opened, they must be closed).*[5]

Report headings are printed in the initialization section. The report body is printed in the processing section, and the report summary is printed in the termination section[6].

These rules and some others are summarized for you in Table 2.1. As you work through the problems in this course, or in real life, you should be able to add to the list. After several years' experience, you may have a fairly good list, but it's doubtful that anyone can provide you with a complete list. Think in terms of initialization, process, and termination and then try to establish the task in the correct section.

5 This example describes one of the most common types of applications — that of processing a batch file to produce a report. Although this type of application is used in examples, the core principles taught will apply equally well to modern interactive application design.

6 The table shows that printing occurs at three different times. The actual print to paper will probably occur only once. This type of application will probably save the printing to a disk file while the program is running, and you will not see the printed paper until after the termination. However, this does not mean that the printing is done under the termination module. The body of a report must be captured during the process module so the "printing" is shown under that module. The summary statistics cannot be calculated until the detail processing is complete, so the summary data are "printed" in the termination section. The operation of the printer is not directly tied to the printing task in the hierarchy chart.

Table 2.1 Generic Instructions for Creating Hierarchy Chart Modules

Initialization Section—all modules controlled by module 2100

1. Initial values of variables are set[1].
2. Constants are established[2].
3. Files are opened.
4. The first opportunity to enter a help module is given.
5. Report title and headings are printed.

Process Section—all modules controlled by module 2200

1. Data is processed.
2. The body of a report is printed (Detail Area).
3. End of file indicator gets changed to "yes" because no more records are found.

Termination Section—all modules controlled by module 2300

1. The last opportunity to enter the help module is given.
2. Report totals are printed.
3. Files are closed.
4. The program terminates and releases control to the operating system.

[1] "Total" variables or accumulators would be set to zero. Indicators are types of variables. End of file indicator should be set to "no".
[2] Examples: Interest Rate = 7%; pi =3.14.

Now that you have some idea how to read a hierarchy chart and what it provides, let's look at some examples.

In Chapter 1, we prepared a task list for calculating the miles driven per gallon of gas used on a car trip. How would we put this into a hierarchy chart?

We draw[7] module 1000 and assign it a title, as shown in Figure 2.2.

1000 Miles per gallon

Figure 2.2 Title Module

7 Today's computer software comes with a variety of drawing tools. Several general drawing programs, like Microsoft Paint™, are available. You can use these programs to draw anything. Special programs like Visio™, Edge™, and Smart Draw™ can draw special-purpose drawings like flowcharts and organizational charts. Some word processing programs have incorporated a limited drawing ability that will satisfy most requirements for a short period of time. Select whichever method you like for this course. If you don't have a computer, or don't have the software, or don't like drawing with a computer, then use a template or ruler and pencil.

Next, add the three modules for initialization, process, termination, and connect the modules with straight-line segments. Figure 2.3 illustrates this.

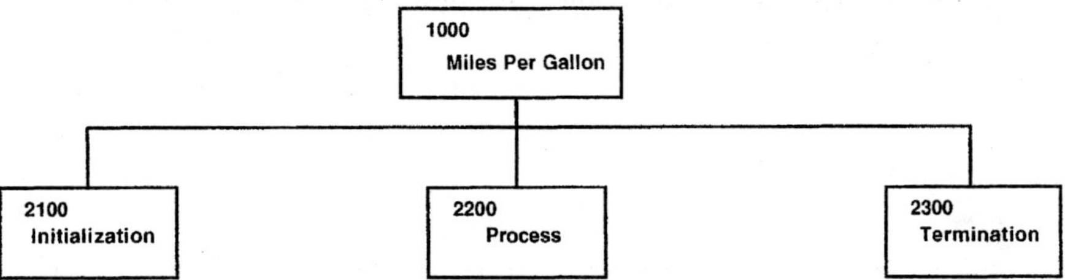

Figure 2.3 Major Module

Next, we examine our task list from Chapter 1 and determine where the tasks fit into the hierarchy chart.

1. Park at the gas pump.
2. Turn off the ignition.
3. Pump the gas.
4. Record the starting mileage on the odometer.
5. Accumulate the total amount of gas added during the trip.
6. Fill the tank at the end of the trip and add this amount to the total.
7. Record the ending mileage on the odometer.
8. Calculate how many miles that we drove:
   (miles driven = ending odometer reading – beginning odometer reading).
9. Calculate miles per gallon: (miles per gallon = miles driven / total gas used).
10. Display the miles per gallon.

Tasks 1, 2, 3, and 4 are initialization tasks. Tasks 5, 6, and 7 are processing tasks. Tasks 8 and 9 are summary statistics that only occur at the end of the program, so they are placed in the termination section. Task 10 displays the results from task 9, so it is in the termination section.

Next, we need to ask which of these tasks should be combined into modules, because we really don't need to show all the details in our hierarchy chart. Tasks 1, 2, and 3 are concerned with filling the gas tank, so they would make a good module. Task 4 is not related to filling the gas tank, so it needs to go into a different module. We might notice now that recording the mileage actually consists of two steps: first we get the odometer reading, and then we record it (or enter it). So we see now that our initial task list was incomplete, and we listed a module as a task.

Now is the time to repair that and identify the new tasks while creating the module to contain them. Tasks 5 and 6 are about calculating gas used, but they cannot be combined because they occur at different times. Task 5 occurs several times during the trip, but task 6 occurs only at the end. Notice also that we can't determine the gas added without filling the gas tank again. So we need to repeat tasks 1, 2, and 3 at this point. Tasks 7 and 8 calculate miles driven; these tasks are similar to the gas processing above. It appears now that we need to check the odometer after we fill the gas tank so that we will always have the mileage accumulated and handy to use when the trip ends. Other ways exist to solve this problem, but this solution provides two modules for processing: one module handles the gas calculations, and the other handles the miles calculations. At the end of the trip, we only need to calculate the miles per gallon and display the answer. The calculation of miles per gallon is a task. Displaying the result really should be a module as well so that we can provide an explanation in addition to the numeric answer. As a result of these changes, our task list now looks like this:

1. Park at the gas pump.
2. Turn off the ignition.
3. Pump the gas.
4. Record the starting mileage on the odometer.
5. Drive.
6. Park at the gas pump.
7. Turn off the ignition.
8. Pump the gas.
9. Read the gallons of gas added.
10. Read the odometer.
11. Record the gallons of gas added.
12. Record the odometer reading.
13. Accumulate the miles driven.
14. Accumulate the gallons of gas.
15. Calculate miles per gallon: (miles per gallon = miles driven / total gas used).
16. Display "The miles per gallon on this trip was:".
17. Display miles per gallon.

Now that we have a more complete task list, we can assign the tasks to modules and place the modules on the hierarchy chart. The outline below provides module names and lists each task that is contained in the module.

A. Fill gas tank module. Notice that this is the same as tasks 6, 7, and 8.

1. Park at the gas pump.
2. Turn off the ignition.
3. Pump the gas.

B. Record mileage module.

1. Get the odometer reading.
2. Record the starting mileage on the odometer.

C. Drive.

D. Accumulate gas used module.

1. Read the gallons of gas added.
2. Record the gallons of gas added.

E. Accumulate miles driven.

1. Read the odometer.
2. Record the odometer reading.

F. Display miles per gallon.

1. Calculate miles per gallon: (miles per gallon = miles driven / total gas used).
2. Display "The miles per gallon on this trip was:".
3. Display miles per gallon

Our hierarchy chart for the task list would look like Figure 2.4.

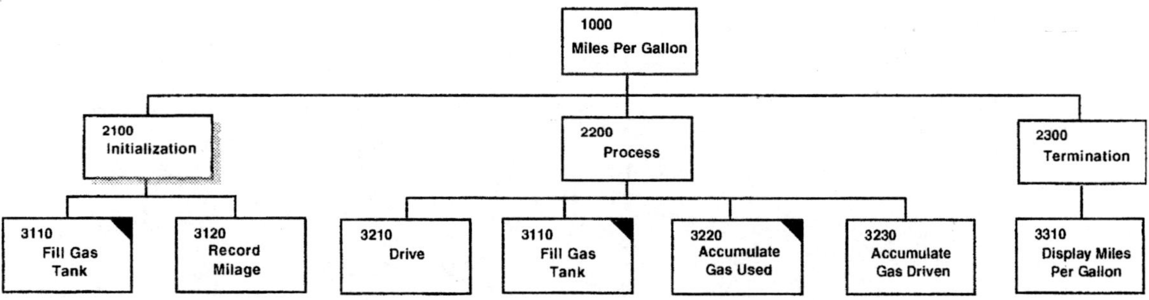

Figure 2.4 Hierarchy Chart

Now let's look at a more computer-friendly problem. Suppose we wish to design an application that will calculate the compound interest earned on an investment. We know that our hierarchy chart begins with a 1000 module and the title of the program. The sub-modules 2100 initialization, 2200 process, and 2300 termination follow this module, so we can draw the first portion of our hierarchy chart without much effort. Figure 2.5 illustrates this chart.

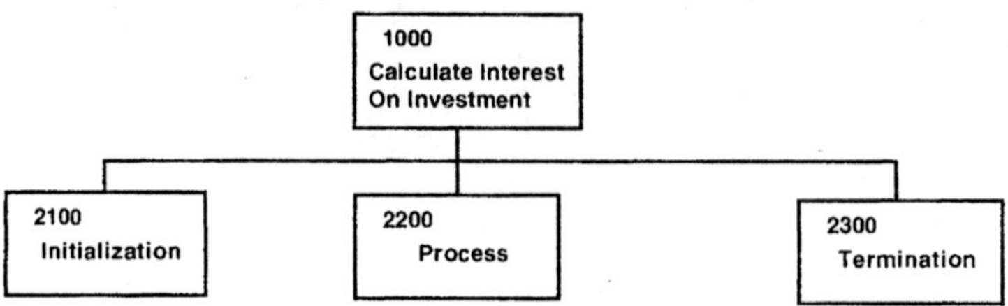

Figure 2.5 Investment Major Modules

But we're not ready to draw the remainder of the hierarchy chart because we don't have a task list to work with.

Let's look at an example of what we want to accomplish. Suppose that we are going to invest $10,000; and we are to accumulate interest on our investment at a rate of 6% compounded monthly. We want to know how much money we will have in the investment account at the end of each year.

To determine our account balance, we will first determine the monthly rate of compounding. The interest rate of 6% is an annual rate, so our monthly rate is .06/12 or .5%. At the end of the first month, we will receive an interest payment of $50. Our account balance will become $10,050, which will be used to calculate our next month's interest. Table 2.2 shows the first seven months of calculations.

Table 2.2 Compound Interest

Intitial Investment= $10,000

At the end of Month	Interest	Account Balance
1	$50.00	$10,050.00
2	$50.25	$10,100.25
3	$50.50	$10,150.75
4	$50.75	$10,201.50
5	$51.01	$10,252.51
6	$51.26	$10,303.77
7	$51.52	$10.355.29

Now let's prepare a task list, keeping in mind that we want the tasks to be generic so we will avoid using the numbers from the example.

1. Determine the rate of interest (input).
2. Initialize total investment accumulator.
3. Determine the frequency of compounding (input).
4. Calculate the compounding rate (compounding rate = Annual rate/frequency).
5. Determine the amount of the investment (input).
6. Print headings for the report.
7. Calculate the amount of interest earned during a compounding period.
8. Add the interest calculated in step 7 to the investment amount to get a new total investment.
9. Display the total investment.
10. Repeat steps 7 through 9 until termination is requested.

Evaluating the above task list to determine which tasks need to be combined and where they belong in the hierarchy chart, we find that tasks 1, 2, 3, 4, 5, and 6 are initialization tasks, even though task 4 is a calculation. Tasks 7, 8, and 10 are processing tasks. Task 9 is part of the termination section. Task 6 is really a module and is shown here as a task only to reinforce the printing concept. Our hierarchy chart could look like Figure 2.6.

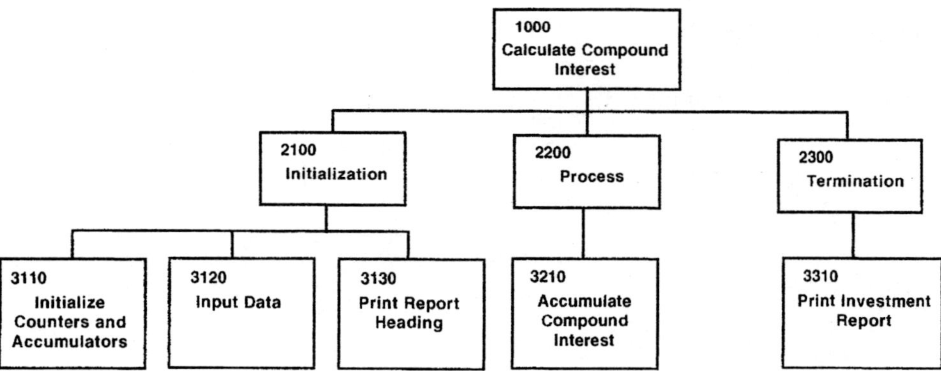

Figure 2.6 Compound Interest Hierarchy Chart

As a final example, let's complete a hierarchy chart for the bowling average in Chapter 1. The task list is repeated here for simplicity.

Task List for bowling average:

1. Get bowler's first game score.
2. Accumulate total score.
3. Get bowler's second score.
4. Accumulate total score.
5. Get bowler's third score.
6. Accumulate total score.
7. Average = total score/3.
8. Display average.

First, we'll need a title for our hierarchy chart. We'll keep it simple and call it Bowler's Average.

Next we'll look for initialization tasks. There don't appear to be any, but there is an accumulator used, so we know that it needs to be initialized to zero. We might also add a counter to this task list so that we can count the number of games entered. The counter will be set to zero initially, so we have two initialization tasks. These two tasks can be combined into a module that sets the counter and accumulator to zero.

Now we examine the process and see that we need to input a score, accumulate the total, and finally calculate the average. Here we can see that there are some tasks that should be added as well. Before having the user input a score, we should print a message asking for the score. After accumulating the total, it might be nice to interact with the user and print out the summary information so that the user can see what is happening. Before continuing, let's update the task list.

1. Set Counter to zero.
2. Set accumulator to zero.
3. Print message: "Input score for game 1".
4. Get bowler's first game score.
5. Accumulate total score.
6. Print message: "Total for 1 game is".
7. Print total score.
8. Print message: "Input score for game 2".
9. Get bowler's second game score.
10. Accumulate total score.

11. Print message: "Total for 2 games is:".
12. Print total score.
13. Print message: "Input score for game 3".
14. Get bowler's third game score.
15. Accumulate total score.
16. Print message: "Total for 3 games is:".
17. Print total score.
18. Average = total score/3.
19. Display average.

Now we can see that the process section of the hierarchy chart should contain two modules: one for getting a score and one for accumulating the total. Each of those two modules contains two tasks.

Finally we decide that the average should be displayed as part of the termination module; because it is a summary statistic, we will calculate and display the average in a final module. Here's the finished hierarchy chart in Figure 2.7.

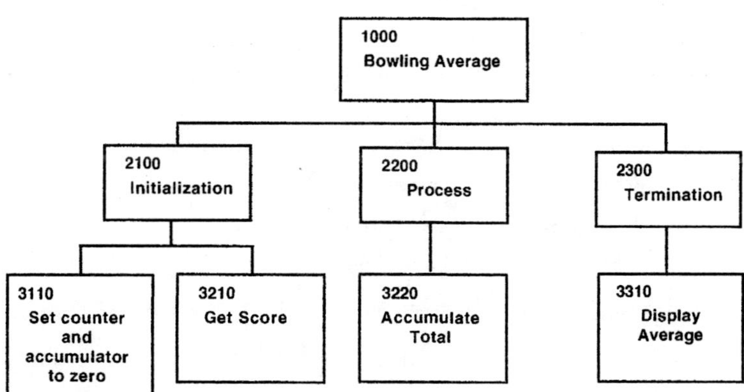

Figure 2.7 Bowling Average Hierarchy Chart

Summary

In this chapter you were introduced to the hierarchy chart and the procedures for reading and drawing hierarchy charts. You were also shown how to create modules from a task list and place those modules into a hierarchy chart. Table 2.1 provided a partial listing of some generic instructions for placing modules into a hierarchy chart.

Key Terms

Each number in parentheses indicates the page where the term first occurs in the chapter.

cohesion (25)	modular (25)	structured design (24)
coupling (25)	module (25)	sub-module (25)
flowchart (24)	reverse sequence (24)	top-down (24)
hierarchy chart (26)	span of control (28)	

Chapter 2 Exercises

Objective 1 Read a hierarchy chart

1. Use the hierarchy chart depicted in Figure 2.1 to answer the following questions about hierarchy charts.

   __________ Which module(s) have a span of control equal to 3?

   __________ Which module executes immediately after module 3110?

   __________ Which module is used more than once?

   __________ Which module tells the name of the program?

   __________ How many levels does the hierarchy chart have?

2. Refer to the hierarchy chart in Figure 2.1 and list the module numbers of the modules that have sub-modules.

3. Refer to the hierarchy chart in Figure 2.1 and list the order in which each module would be processed. Use the module numbers for the list.

4. Refer to Figure 2.1 and comment on the rule of "span of control."

5. If a level were added to the hierarchy chart in Figure 2.1, what number(s) would you expect the modules to have in that new level?

6. Use the hierarchy chart depicted in Figure 2.7 to answer the following questions about hierarchy charts.

   __________ Which module(s) have a span of control equal to 3?

   __________ Which module executes immediately after module 3110?

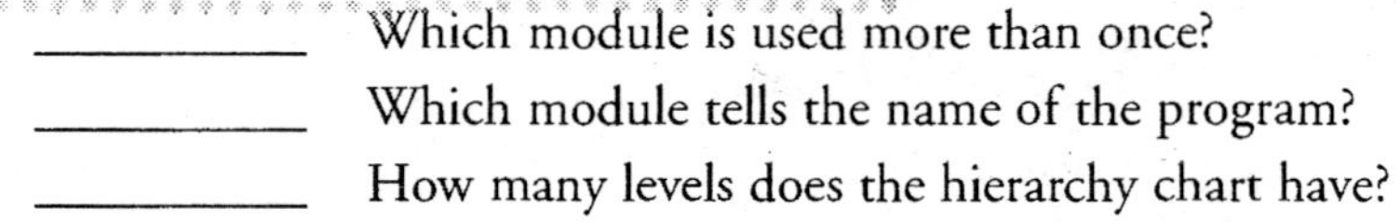

__________ Which module is used more than once?
__________ Which module tells the name of the program?
__________ How many levels does the hierarchy chart have?

7. Refer to the hierarchy chart in Figure 2.7 and list the module numbers of the modules that have sub-modules.

8. Refer to the hierarchy chart in Figure 2.7 and list the order in which each module would be processed. Use the module numbers for the list.

9. Refer to Figure 2.7 and comment on the rule of "span of control."

10. If a level were added to the hierarchy chart in Figure 2.7, what number(s) would you expect the modules to have in that new level?

11. Use the hierarchy chart depicted in Figure 2.8 below to answer the following questions about hierarchy charts.
    __________ Which module(s) have a span of control equal to 3?
    __________ Which module executes immediately after module 3110?
    __________ Which module is used more than once?
    __________ Which module tells the name of the program?
    __________ How many levels does the hierarchy chart have?

12. Refer to the hierarchy chart in Figure 2.8 and list the module numbers of the module(s) that have sub-modules.

13. Refer to the hierarchy chart in Figure 2.8 and list the order in which each module would be processed. Use the module numbers for the list.

14. Refer to Figure 2.8 and comment on the rule of "span of control."

15. If a level were added to the hierarchy chart in Figure 2.8, what number(s) would you expect the modules to have in that new level?

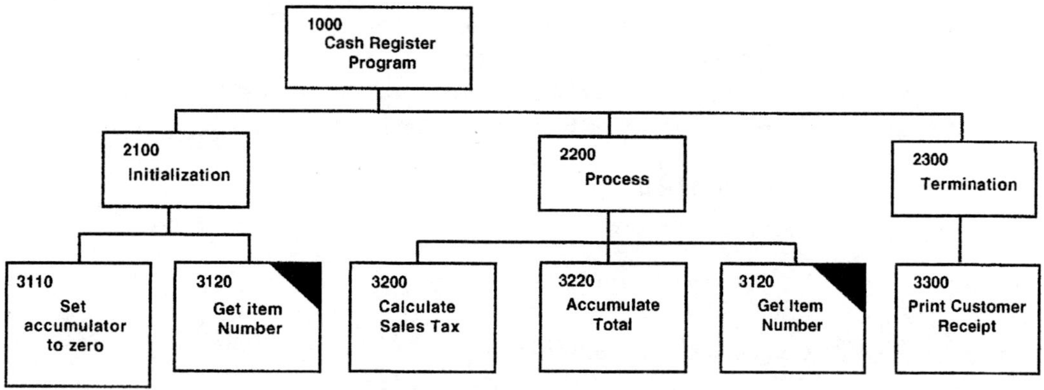

Figure 2.8 Cash Register Hierarchy Chart

Objective 2 Relate and assign tasks from a task list to modules in a hierarchy chart.

1. A list of tasks to be performed by an application to process point of sale transactions is given below. (Assume that you are a customer in a store and you are going to purchase some items.) Use the hierarchy chart shown in Figure 2.8 in conjunction with the task list. Assume that the hierarchy chart is drawn correctly. Don't change the chart.

   Determine which module contains each task. Enter the module number in the space provided. Some tasks may be in more than one module, and some modules do not contain any tasks. Some tasks may not need to be represented in the hierarchy chart. For these tasks enter 9999 in the space provided.

   ___________1. Total sales for the day are printed.

   ___________2. Accumulator(s) are set to zero.

   ___________3. Customer name is entered.

   ___________4. Determine when all of a customer's purchases have been processed.

   ___________5. The customer is provided with a record of the purchase.

   ___________6. The total owed by the customer is calculated.

2. Read the task list below and determine to what section of a hierarchy chart they should be assigned. Use I for initialization, P for processing, and T for termination section.

   ___________1. Close the customer file.

   ___________2. Calculate the sub-total.

   ___________3. Initialize the counters.

   ___________4. Process the payroll file.

   ___________5. Print the headings.

3. Read the list of tasks below and determine if any of them should be grouped into a module or kept as their own module. Also indicate in what section of a hierarchy chart they would appear using the method described in problem 2. If they should be modules, then identify some of the tasks that would be found in the module.

   ___________1. Read sales data.

   ___________2. Calculate sales tax.

   ___________3. Reorder inventory item.

   ___________4. Initialize sub-totals.

   ___________5. Get a customer's record.

Objective 3 Draw a hierarchy chart from a given task list.

1. Draw a hierarchy chart for the following list of modules that represents starting a car:

   A. Find the car key.
   B. Find the car.
   C. Unlock the driver's door.
   D. Put the ignition key in your hand.
   E. Open the driver's door.
   F. Sit in the driver's seat.
   G. Close the door.
   H. Fasten the seat belt.
   I. Put the key in the ignition switch.
   J. Turn the key to the start position.
   K. Release the key when the engine starts.

2. Draw a hierarchy chart for the following task list that represents calculating a college student's grade point average.

   A. Set grade point average to zero.
   B. Set total honor points to zero.
   C. Set total credit hours to zero.
   D. Get student record.
   E. Extract course number.
   F. Extract course grade.
   G. Determine credit hours for this course.
   H. Convert letter grade to numeric equivalent.
   I. Calculate honor points for this course.
   J. Accumulate honor points.
   K. Accumulate credit hours.
   L. Calculate grade point average (GPA = total honor points/total credit hours)
   M. Display GPA.

   After drawing the hierarchy chart, identify which modules contain each of the tasks above. Make an outline using the modules as major headings and place the tasks contained in each module under that major heading.

3. Draw a hierarchy chart for the following task list that represents estimating the cost of a job for a construction contractor.
   A. Get customer name.
   B. Get customer address.
   C. Get customer tax code (tax code indicates whether or not the customer is charged tax).
   D. Print the report heading.
   E. Get an item number of an item that the customer ordered.
   F. Retrieve the inventory record for this item number (Inventory record contains the price of each item).
   G. Get the quantity of the item ordered.
   H. Calculate the cost of each item.
   I. Accumulate the total material cost.
   J. Print the item on the report.
   K. Repeat steps E through J until all items have been processed.
   L. Calculate the sales tax.
   M. Estimate the labor cost.
   N. Calculate the total project cost (total project cost = labor cost + material cost).
   O. Print the total project cost.

Objective 4 Draw a hierarchy chart to display a solution for a given problem.

1. Develop a task list and draw a hierarchy chart for the following problem:

   You have charged $1,000 on a credit card at 18% annual interest rate compounded monthly. The monthly interest rate will be the annual rate divided by the number of months in a year. You plan to pay $200 each month until the credit card balance is zero. Design the program that will determine how many months it will take to pay off your credit card debt.

2. Develop a task list and draw a hierarchy chart for the following problem:

   A teacher wishes to print a report of test results for her class. She plans to enter 3 grades for each student into the computer and wants the computer to total the grades for each student, compute an average for each student, and calculate a class average for each of the three tests and for the overall score. She has 20 students in the class.

3. Develop a task list and draw a hierarchy chart for the following problem:

   A friend wishes to have a program that he can use to help balance his checkbook. The program should show a starting balance and a balance after each check is posted.

4. Develop a task list and draw a hierarchy chart for the following problem:

   You bought a car and borrowed $10,000 to help pay for it. The interest rate is 12% simple interest annually. Develop a task list and draw a hierarchy chart that shows how to determine how many months it will take to pay off the loan if you pay $500 per month.

5. Develop a task list and draw a hierarchy chart for a program that would allow 4 players to play poker in a computer game.

6. Develop a task list and draw a hierarchy chart for the following problem:
   A satellite is in earth orbit, and your boss wants a program that will print out (or display on the screen) the expected position of the satellite at a given future time.

Other Assignments

SoftSkills

Select one problem from Objective 4 or from the Internet/Library Research Projects below. Prepare and give an oral report to the class on your solution.

Internet/library research projects

A. Research the history of hierarchy charts and write a short report describing the development of the hierarchy chart.

B. Find a hierarchy chart that describes a solution not presented in the textbook, and write a report on it.

FLOWCHARTS, PSEUDOCODE, AND SEQUENCES

Do not become paralyzed and enchained by the set patterns which have been woven of old. No, build from your own youthful feeling, your own groping thought and your own flowering perception.

(Lotte Lehmann)

OBJECTIVES

After completing this chapter, you will be able to:

1. Read a flowchart containing sequence logic structures.
2. Draw and revise a flowchart using sequence logic structures for a given problem.
3. Read pseudocode containing sequence logic structures.
4. Write pseudocode using sequence logic structures for a given problem.

Introduction

The primary difference between a hierarchy chart and a flowchart is that the flowchart gives details. Pseudocode provides those details as well. A flowchart is a graphic tool for providing a solution to a problem; pseudocode is a text description. To draw a flowchart we use a hierarchy chart and describe each of the hierarchy chart's modules in sufficient detail to provide a design plan that can be directly translated into a programming language. The emphasis is on detail; the biggest pitfall to avoid is not giving enough specifics in the flowchart. We'll need some flowcharting symbols and rules for flowcharts, and we'll need some pseudocode rules for pseudocode.

Arithmetic Symbols

To aid in writing shorter sentences, we will employ the following mathematical symbols: + (addition), - (subtraction), * (multiplication), / (division), = (equal or equals), < (less than), and > (greater than). These symbols will be used in both flowcharts and pseudocode statements.

Flowchart Symbols

Flowcharts are drawn using special symbols. A set of flowchart symbols is shown in Figure 3.1[1]. The size of each symbol is arbitrary. Draw the symbol big enough so that the text being used fits inside the symbol. The shape of each symbol is unique and important. The shape tells the reader the definition of the symbol.

We will not need all of these symbols for this course. Instead we will concentrate our efforts on applying a limited number of symbols to design solutions to problems.

Flow Lines

Flow lines are used to connect flowchart symbols together. The lines should have arrowheads whenever the direction of flow is not down or anytime the direction of flow could be unclear.

Terminal

All flowcharts will start with this symbol and end with this symbol, thus ensuring that the flowchart user knows where and when to start and stop. In sub-modules, the word *return* will be used at the end of the module to indicate that control is passing back to a calling module. The start symbol will contain the module's name or title and should be descriptive of the function performed by the module. The ending symbol will contain the word *end.*

1 A standard set of symbols and definitions for flowcharts is maintained by ANSI (American National Standards Institute), but almost all organizations add to or modify the ANSI set of symbols.

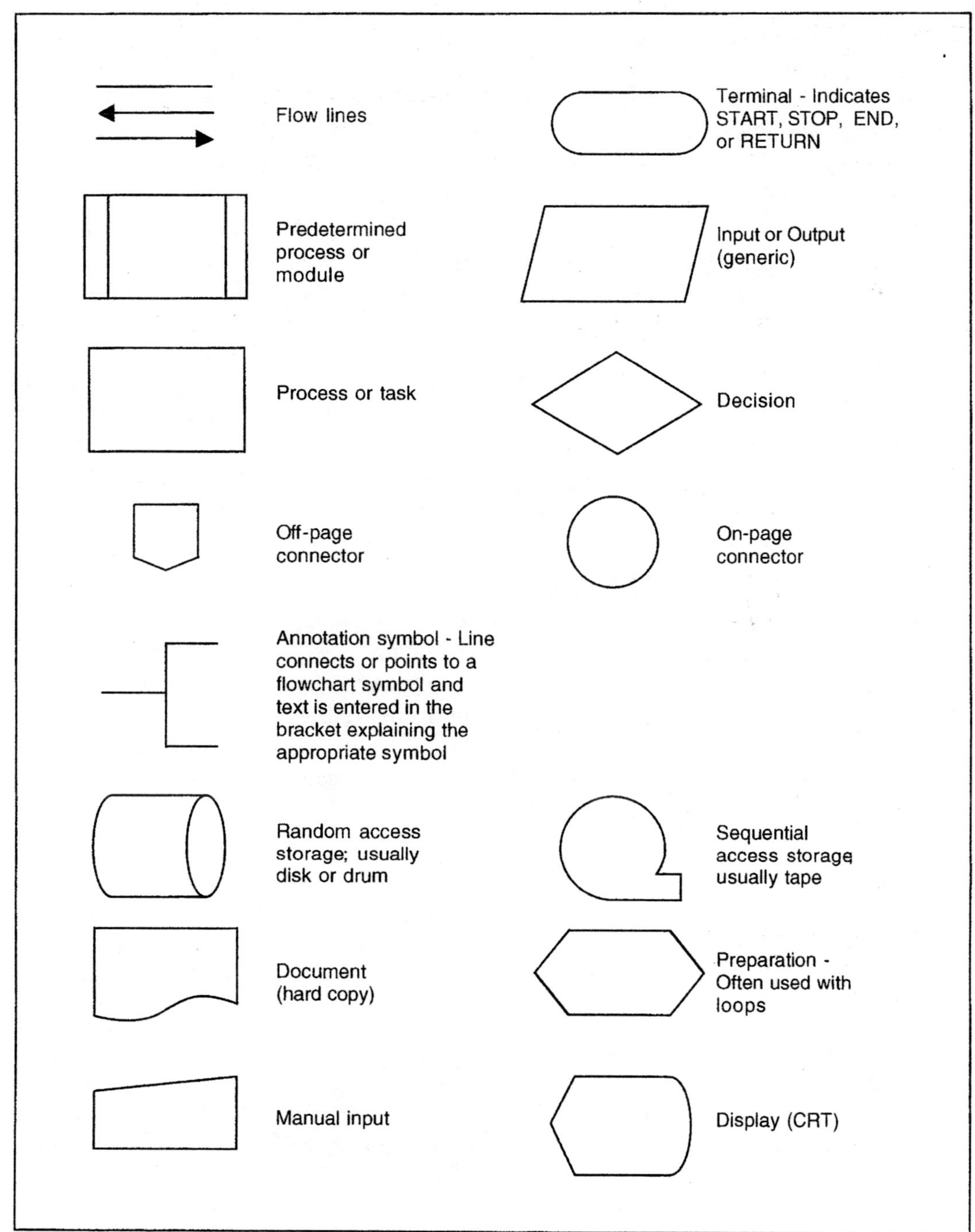

Figure 3.1 Flowchart symbols

Predetermined Process

The predetermined process symbol represents a module. Every module in the hierarchy chart can be shown on a flowchart using this symbol. The first flowchart displays the first two levels of the hierarchy chart as a sequence of predetermined processes. Each predetermined process is then described by a separate flowchart. The predetermined process is extremely useful, because we can avoid detailed explanations at any point in a flowchart by its use. If the flowchart is too large for the page, we could apply a predetermined process and describe that process on a different page.

An example of the first flowchart for the miles per gallon hierarchy chart from the previous chapter is shown in Figure 3.2.

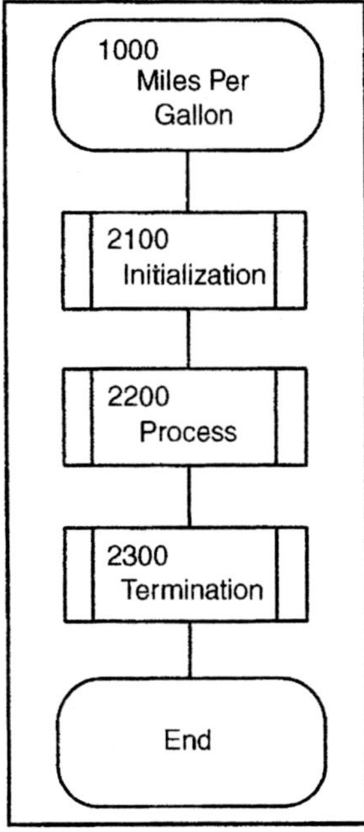

Figure 3.2 MPG flowchart

Input/Output[2]

This symbol contains words to describe data or information and whether it is input or output. For example, *display customer name* indicates output. *Read sales data* indicates input. Both statements use the input/output symbol.

Process

The process symbol is used to describe a computer processing step and typically contains an equation or formula. This is a simple processing step, and its explanation should fit inside the symbol. At most this symbol will contain one sentence. The words *if, and,* and *or* will never be used inside this symbol. Wherever possible, use mathematical symbols to shorten the sentence.

Decision

The decision symbol will contain a question. It is used when the computer is asked to evaluate an expression such as Balance > 2000? Sentences inside this symbol will end with a question mark[3].

Annotation

This symbol is used to add comments or remarks to a particular flowchart symbol. This helps the reader understand the phrases or symbols contained inside a flowchart symbol. This symbol is used only when the designer feels a part of the flowchart needs clarification.

2 This symbol is shown as a terminal interrupt symbol in some publications but can be employed as a generic interrupt that loosely translates to a start/stop function.

3 We will focus on this in Chapter 4.

On-page Connector

This symbol is used to connect two parts of a flowchart when a connecting line cannot be efficiently drawn. The two parts of the flowchart are on the same page. Inside the circle a capital letter is written that matches the same letter at the point to be entered in the other flowchart. This symbol is also used to connect flow lines when two or more flow lines follow the same logic path.

Off-page Connector

This symbol is used to connect two parts of a flowchart when the two parts of the flowchart are not on the same page. To leave a page, ensure that the pointed end of the symbol points off the page. Put the page number of the page where the flow continues inside the symbol. To enter the page that continues the flowchart, ensure that the pointed end of the symbol points on the page. Use the page number of the page where the flowchart is continued from. Figure 3.3 shows an example.

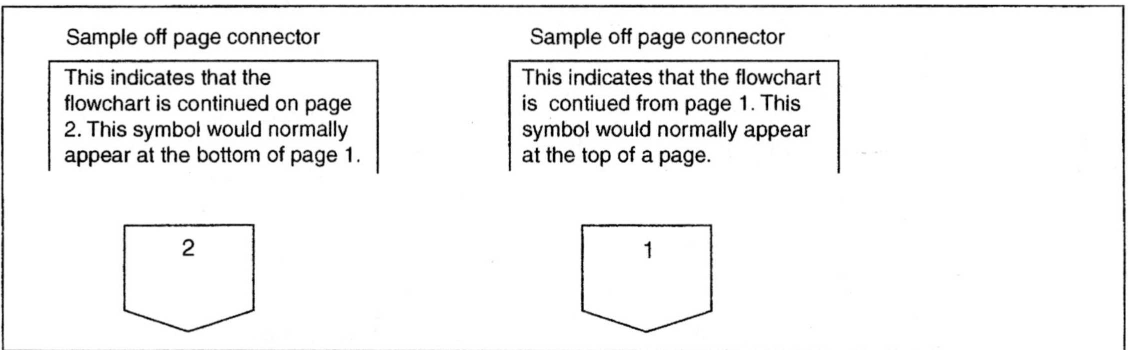

Figure 3.3 Sample Off Page Connectors

Drawing Flowcharts[4]

Figure 3.4 contains a flowcharting form. You are not required to use this form, but it is very useful if you are hand drawing the flowchart as it keeps the shapes consistent and keeps the symbols aligned. This form is useful in providing proper spacing between symbols and aids in allowing the proper amount of space between rows and columns of symbols (if you are using computer software to draw flowcharts, you shouldn't need this form). It makes a very useful item for planning your flowchart and sketching out ideas. Create this form on 8 1/2 inch paper and make the dotted line boxes large enough to enclose a standard flowchart template symbol. Draw flow lines between your symbols so that the flow lines go past the dotted lines. DO NOT simply shade in the dotted lines in an attempt to create a flowchart symbol. DRAW the real symbol inside the box.

4 Drawing software—Today flowcharts are still drawn by hand, sometimes using a programming template; however, many programs are available to draw the flowchart using the computer. Visio™ and Smart Draw™ are two well-known flowcharting programs. Even Microsoft Word™ includes flowcharting shapes as part of its drawing tool bar. You will no doubt find many more programs available that will assist you with the mechanical aspects of drawing the flowchart.

Figure 3.4 Flowcharting form

The flowcharting symbols alone can be used to provide some information about information flow. Look at the simple flowchart shown in Figure 3.5.

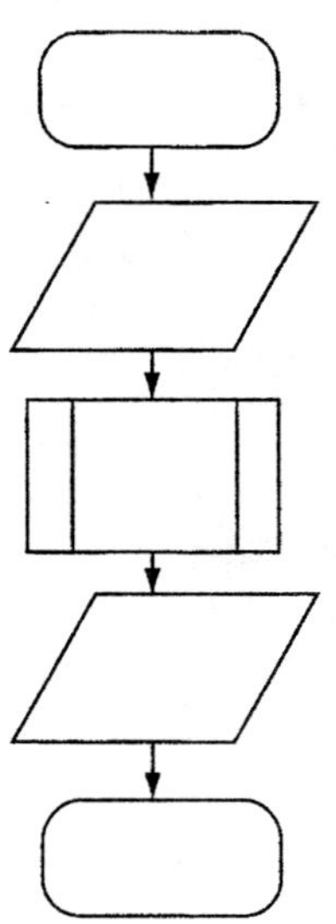

Figure 3.5
Blank flowchart

Even though there are no words on the flowchart, the symbols and flowchart rules tell us something about the flowchart. We know that flowcharts start at the top of the page and proceed down the page unless directional arrows change the flow. The top terminal symbol would be the start, and the bottom terminal symbol would be the end. The second symbol from the top is an input/output symbol; we expect the program to receive input, process the data, and produce output. This leads us to assume that the top input/output symbol is input, and the later input/output symbol is output. A predetermined process is included, and we would expect to find another flowchart explaining this predetermined process.

Now that we have the tools we need for flowcharting, let's begin drawing some flowcharts. First we'll look at the flowchart (Figure 3.6) comparable to the generic hierarchy chart shown in Chapter 2, Figure 2.3.

Flowchart Rules

The flowchart in Figure 3.6 illustrates some basic principles of flowcharts. Every flowchart must:

1. Start somewhere.
2. End somewhere.
3. Unfailingly proceed from the start to the end.

Some additional rules of flowcharting that will also be strictly enforced are the following:

4. Flow lines never cross each other.
5. Flow lines require arrowheads anytime that the flow does not move down the page.[5]
6. Flowchart symbols can only have one entry point except for on-page connectors.

1000 Start
Miles Per Gallon

2100
Intialization

2200
Process

2300
Termination

End

Figure 3.6
MPG flowchart

5 By convention, flowcharts normally flow from left to right, and some organizations do not use arrowheads for left-to-right movement. For this course, we will use arrowheads for any sideward movements for clarity.

7. Only the decision symbol can have more than one exit.
8. On-page connectors always use capital letters.
9. Off-page connectors always use page numbers.
10. All predetermined process symbols (modules) can be represented by a detailed flowchart.

As an example, let's draw the flowchart for the miles per gallon problem of Chapter 2. We'll use the flowcharting form from Figure 3.4. We begin by looking at the hierarchy chart in Chapter 2, Figure 2.4. We draw level 1 and level 2 from the hierarchy chart into the flowchart as shown in Figure 3.7 on the left side of the page.

The next flowchart drawn should be the flowchart representing the predetermined process module 2100 *Initialization.* In simple problems, you will find that the Initialization Module will fit in column two, the Process Module in column three, and the Termination Module in column four of the flowcharting form. Draw flowcharts on only one side of the paper. Modules may occur in each column. When you are flowcharting modules, it is best to include the module number and title in the start symbol. The first page of the complete hierarchy chart for the miles per gallon hierarchy chart is flowcharted in Figure 3.8. Successive pages of the flowchart will explain the other modules contained on this first page. You will find the entire flowchart of the miles per gallon program in Appendix A.

The flowchart logic that we have studied up to this point is an example of the *sequence structure.* Three types of logic structures are used in structured programming and structured design. They are *sequence*, *selection*, and *iteration* structures. A sequence logic structure simply means that instructions are processed in sequence, one right after the other. Since the logic flow in flowcharts proceeds from the top of the page to the bottom, we need to ensure that the instructions to be accomplished first occur closer to the top of the page than the instructions that occur last. Our miles per gallon program illustrates this.

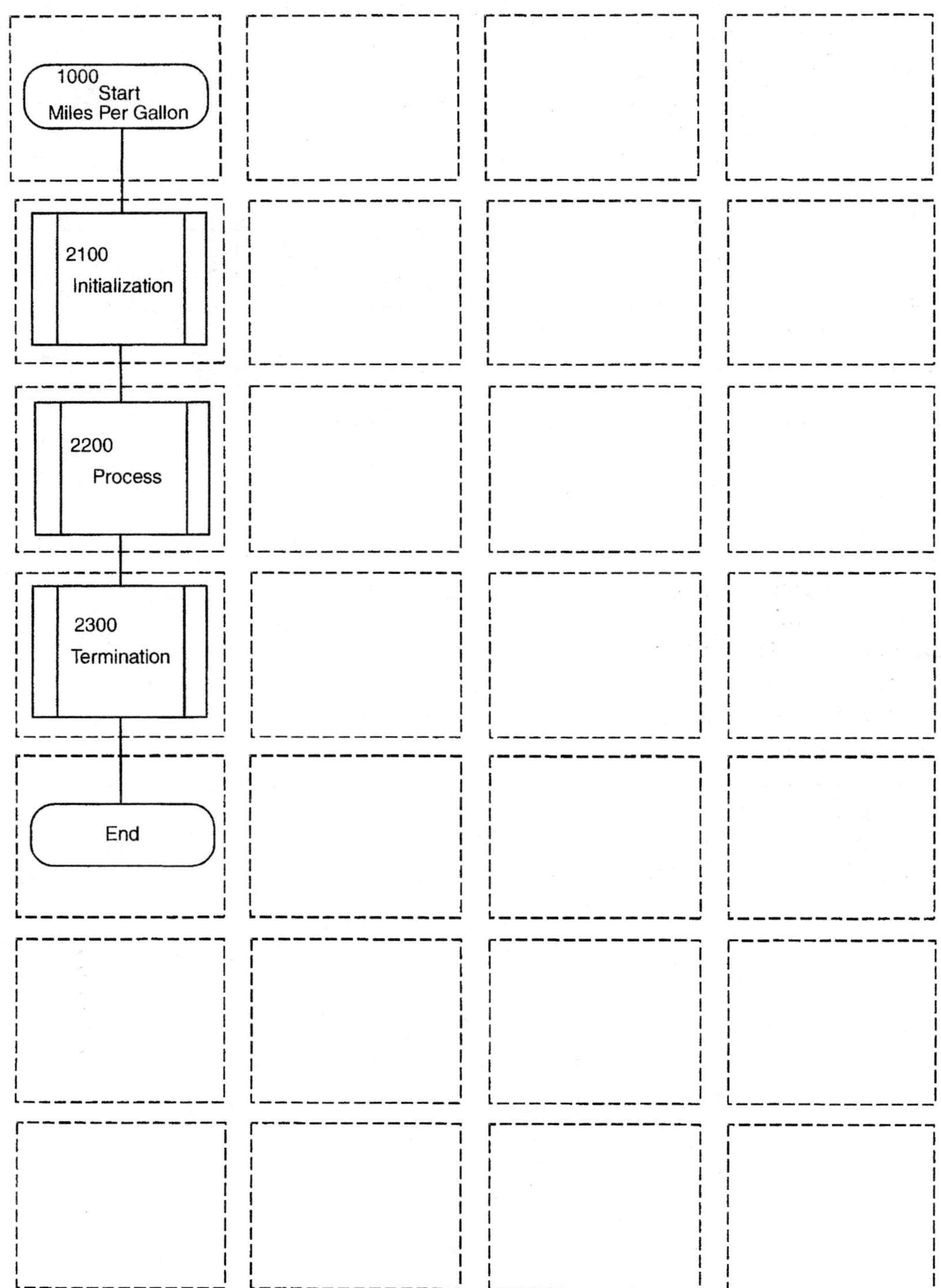

Figure 3.7 MPG major modules

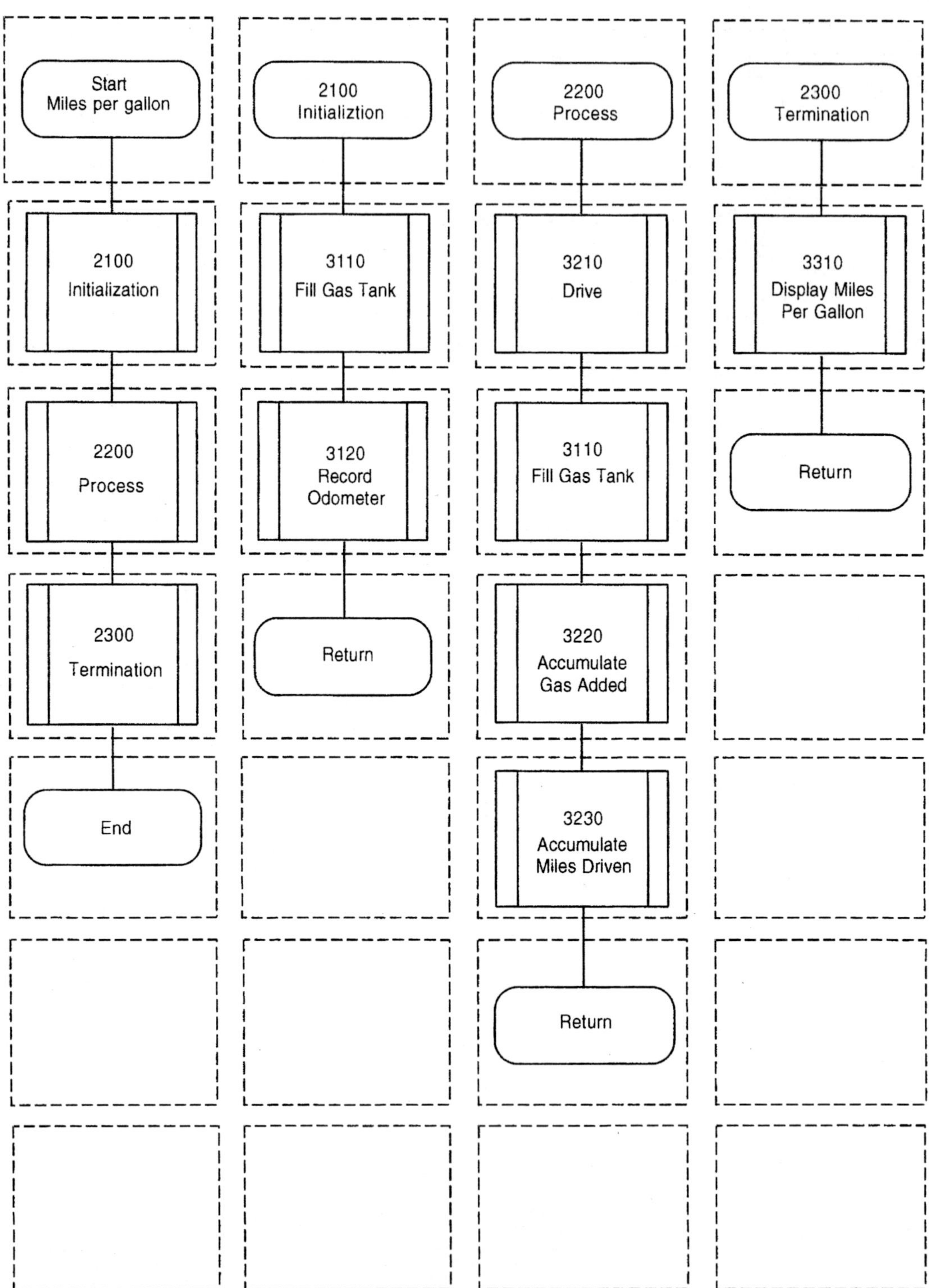

Figure 3.8 MPG *(continued)*

Look carefully at Figures 3.9a and 3.9b and observe their difference(s). Flowchart 3.9a fills the gas tank before it calculates the gas added. Flowchart 3.9b accumulates the gas added before the gas tank is filled. Which process will give us the correct answer at the end of the trip? Obviously, flowchart 3.9a will. The only difference between these two flowcharts is the sequence of instructions. On the left we execute modules 3110, then 3220, and then 3230. On the right we execute modules 3220, then 3110, and then 3230. This seemingly minor difference changes our results significantly.

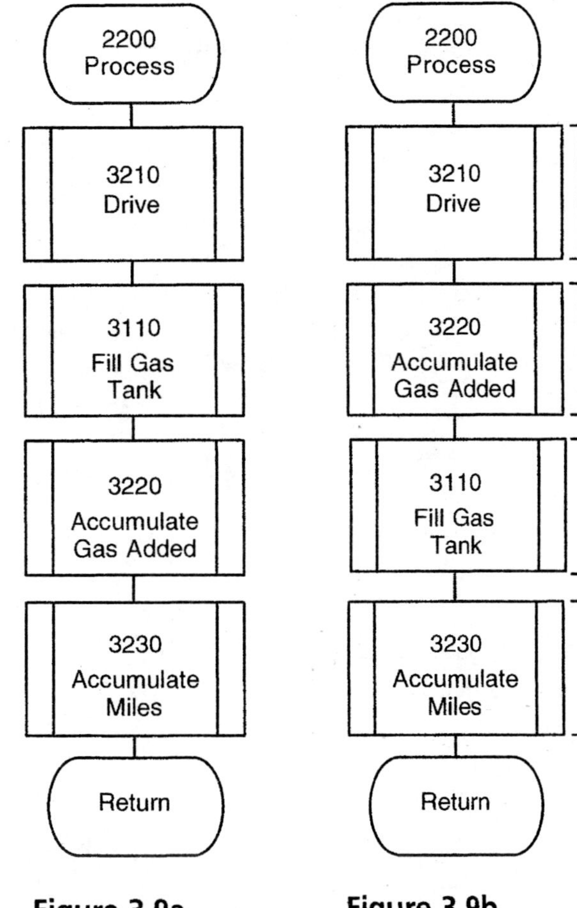

Figure 3.9a
Sequence 1

Figure 3.9b
Sequence 2

Let's examine another problem. Suppose you want to calculate the area of a rectangle (you have to pretend that you would do this using a computer). What are the steps? To see what problems we can cause, we'll skip the task list and hierarchy chart and move straight to the flowchart. We multiply the *length* times the *width* to get the area, so we draw Figure 3.10.

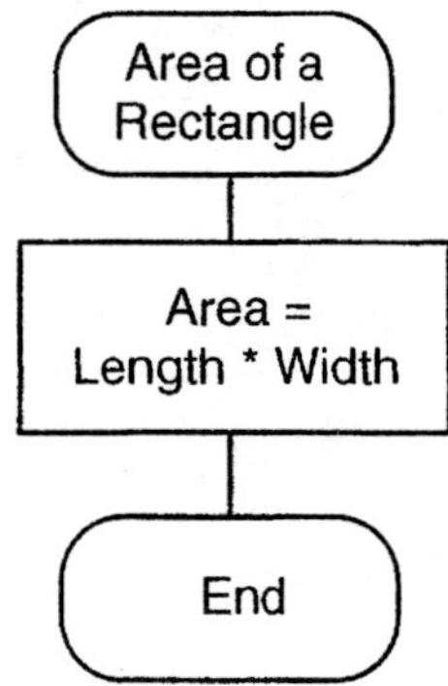

Figure 3.10
Rectangle Area

Let's assume that this is the whole flowchart. What's wrong with this flowchart? The sequence can't be wrong since there is only one step; but what area would the computer calculate? We either need to input the length and the width or initialize their values so that the computer can compute a value for the area. In our next attempt, we might draw Figure 3.11.

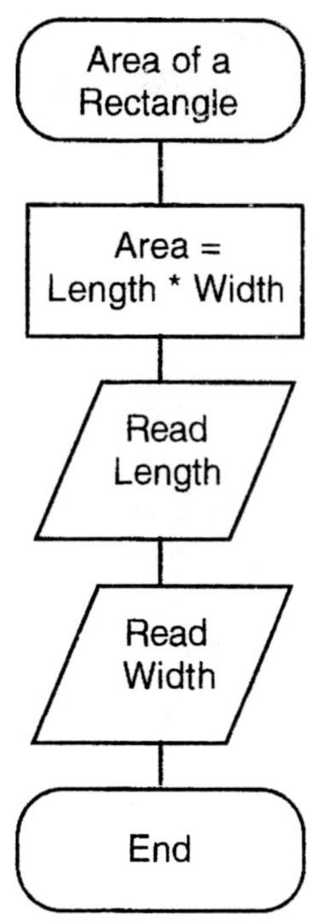

Figure 3.11
Rectangle Continued

This, too, is incorrect. The length and the width must be input before we attempt a calculation; this flowchart is out of sequence. Before you ignore this trivial example, let me advise you that most computer programming errors are this simple. The programs are much more complex, but the "bug" is usually quite simple once it is found. One other problem exists with this flowchart. When the program ends, do we know what the area is? The computer knows, but since we didn't tell the computer to share it with us, we will never know the answer to our problem.

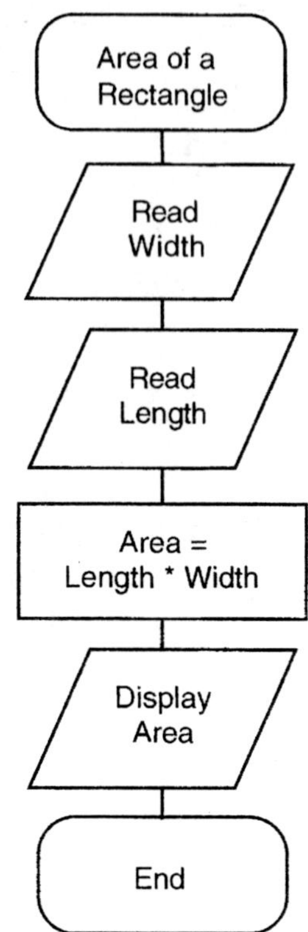

Figure 3.12
Rectangle Final

So let's modify the flowchart to look like Figure 3.12.

Could we reverse the inputs of the *length* and *width*? Yes, with no errors. We could even input the *length* and *width* simultaneously; but in this course, we will limit input to one value per input symbol. This can cause the flowcharts to be longer, but it allows you to adjust the sequence of statements easily.

Notice that we took several attempts at drawing even this simple flowchart. Some work could have been saved by first writing down the list of tasks that we needed to solve the problem. The hierarchy chart would have been very simple, and the flowchart would probably have been developed in one attempt. This is an attempt to illustrate the potential time savings of using the task list.

As the final example of a flowchart, let's produce the flowchart for the bowler's average problem begun in Chapter 1. The task list and hierarchy chart are reproduced here for ease of reference.

Bowler's Average

Produce a flowchart that describes the solution to the problem of calculating an average for a bowler. First, the task list is shown.

1. Set Counter to zero.
2. Set accumulator to zero.
3. Print message: "Input score for game 1".
4. Get bowler's first game score.
5. Accumulate total score.
6. Print message: "Total for 1 game is".
7. Print total score.
8. Print message: "Input score for game 2".
9. Get bowler's second game score.
10. Accumulate total score.
11. Print message: "Total for 2 games is:".
12. Print total score.
13. Print message: "Input score for game 3".
14. Get bowler's third game score.
15. Accumulate total score.
16. Print message: "Total for 3 games is:".
17. Print total score.
18. Average = total score/3.
19. Display average.

Next, the hierarchy chart is drawn in Figure 3.13.

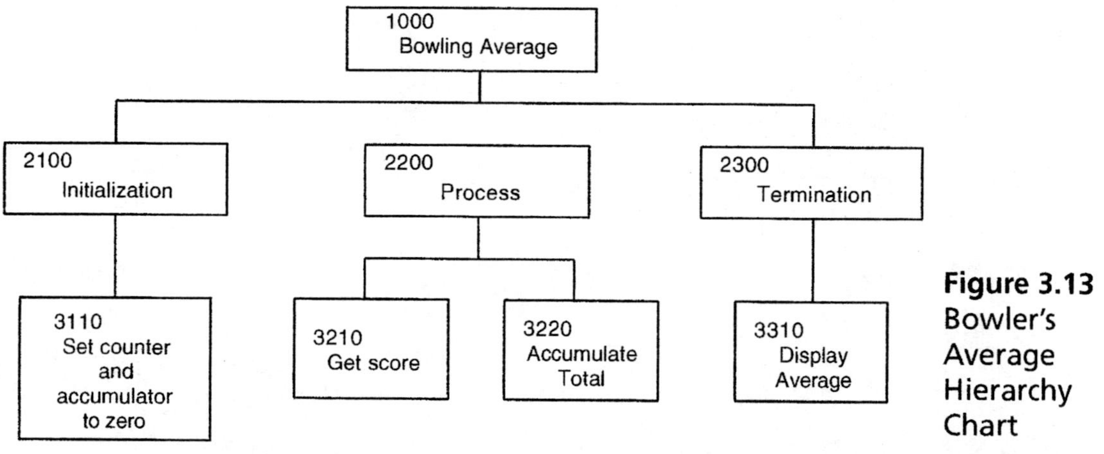

Figure 3.13 Bowler's Average Hierarchy Chart

Now draw the flowchart by decomposing each of the modules into their individual tasks. We use the hierarchy chart to identify the sequence and the task list to identify each of the tasks. The completed flowchart is shown in Figure 3.14.

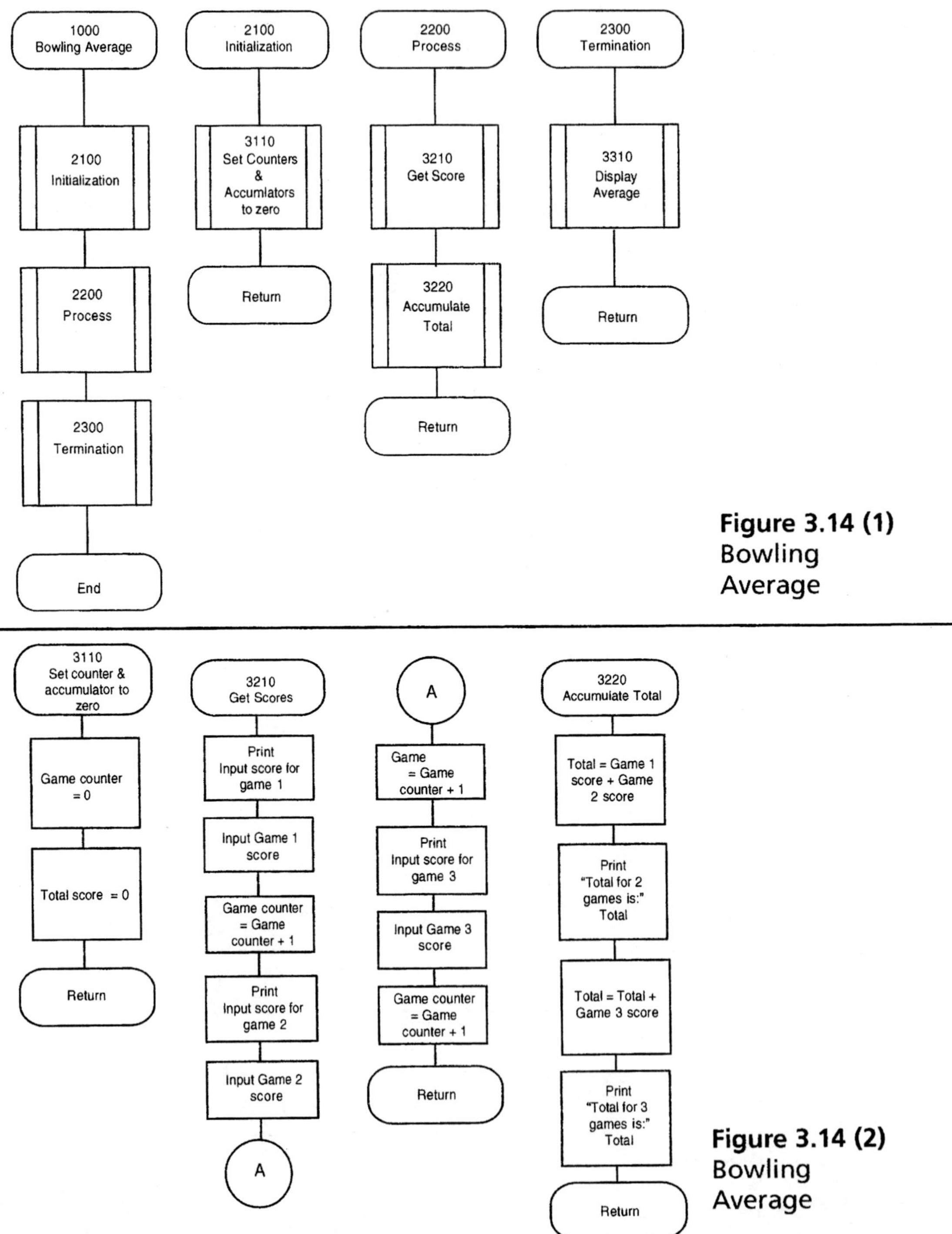

Figure 3.14 (1) Bowling Average

Figure 3.14 (2) Bowling Average

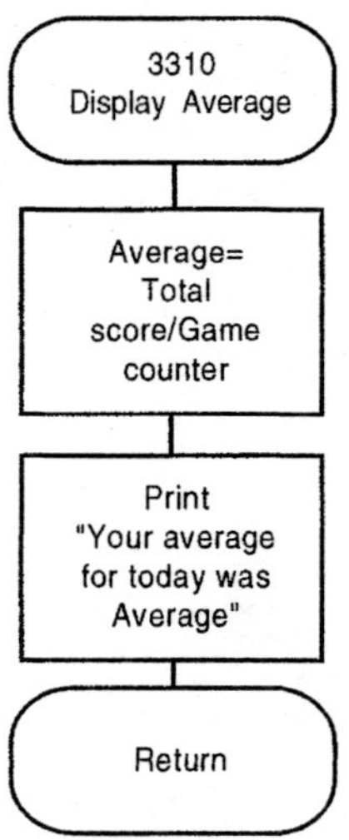

Figure 3.14 (3)
Bowling Average

Flowchart Language

Let's examine what is written inside the flowchart symbols. If you know for what computer language you're designing, you might want to use as much of that computer language as possible in the flowchart. That makes the programming task simpler. For instance, in some languages the word *print* means to output text to a printer. In other languages it means to display text on the monitor. It would be an impossible task to prepare in advance for all the multiple meanings of words in all the programming languages, so we will attempt to use enough English to clearly identify the results. Because we want our statements to remain inside the flowchart symbol, brevity is important. However, don't abbreviate to the point of losing clarity. In our *Area of a Rectangle* flowchart, for instance, we could say that A = L * W. Most mathematicians would recognize that sentence as the formula for area of a rectangle. Would everyone recognize it? What about x = y * z? Is "area = length x width" more clear?

How about: "The area of a rectangle is equal to the length times the width." The last statement is the most clear of all, but will it fit inside the process symbol? This part of flowcharting is more art than science, and no "rules" can solve the dilemma. We do have the annotation symbol that can be used in those cases where further explanation is desired. Including the annotation symbol in this case would yield Figure 3.15.
This annotation addition should leave no doubt about what the process concerns. It is probably redundant because this is a very short and simple program, but it illustrates the point.

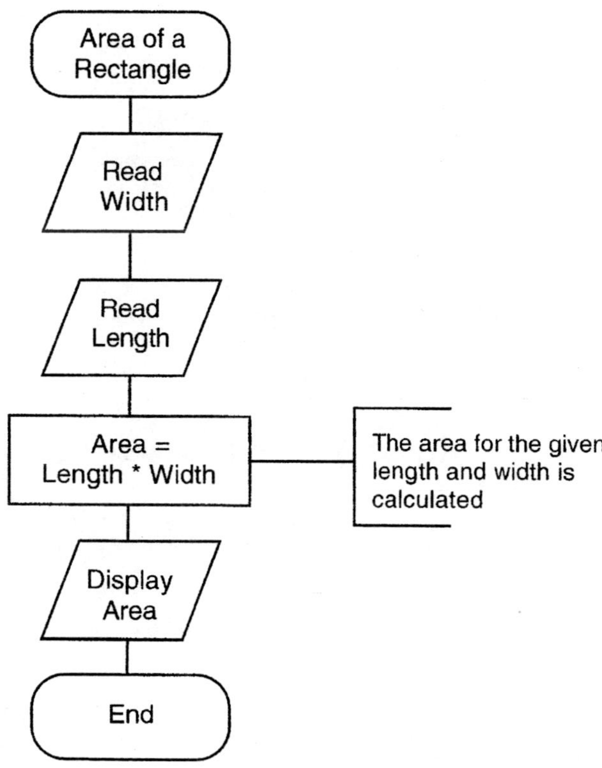

Figure 3.15 Annotation Symbol

Enrichment – Doing it with Pseudocode

Two popular formal logic plans are in use today: the flowchart and pseudocode. The flowchart provides the reader with a visual depiction of the solution to the problem and has been presented. Pseudocode is a text-based logic plan, and its primary advantage is that it can be translated to a programming language more directly than a flowchart. The pseudocode used here will have a precise syntax. We'll begin with the pseudocode necessary for sequence structures.

Table 3.1 provides a list of the basic pseudocode commands that will be used in this course. Additional commands will be added in later chapters.

Table 3.1 Pseudocode Commands

Commands that provide for input to the computer	Explanation	Commands that provide for output from the computer	Explanation
Get	Instructs the computer to get data from some input device (disk, tape, and so on) that does not involve interaction with the user.	Print	Instructs the computer to produce output to printer, disk, tape, or other hard copy device.
Input	Instructs the computer to receive some data from a user. This is normally an interactive application. The computer must wait for the user to enter the data.	Display	Instructs the computer to provide output to the monitor or other soft copy device that provides a visual display for the user.

Rules of Pseudocode[6]

1. When writing pseudocode, we will also use the assignment statement described in Chapter 1.
2. Pseudocode commands are capitalized.
3. Variable names will not have blank spaces embedded in them. When variable names consist of two or more words, use the underscore between the words. The first word of the variable name is capitalized.

6 When writing pseudocode solutions to problems, students often lapse into broken English instead of logical processes. The key to good pseudocode is not so much in the syntax as in the logic.

Example: Customer_number is a variable name that contains the value of the customer's number.

4. Control is transferred to a sub-module when the sub-module name is encountered in the logic flow of the pseudocode.
5. Pseudocode main programs end with the statement End.
6. Pseudocode sub-modules end with the statement Return
7. Mathematical symbols that will be used are shown in Table 3.2 with their definitions:

Table 3.2 Arithmetic Symbols

Symbol	Definition
=	Equal
<	Less than
>	Greater than
≤	Less than or equal to
≥	Greater than or equal to
≠	Not equal

Let's work through the previous examples, replacing the flowcharts with pseudocode.

1. Miles Per Gallon Program[7]

```
Miles Per Gallon Program
    Initialization
    Process
    Termination
    End
```

The pseudocode shown to the left illustrates the main program module. At each statement, control is transferred to the appropriate sub-module.

```
Initialization
    Fill_gas_tank
    Record_odometer
    Return
Process
    Drive
    Accumulate_gas_added
    Calculate_gas_used
    Calculate_miles_driven
    Return
```

The remainder of the pseudocode statements for this program can be found in Appendix A after the flowchart of the same problem

7 Some sub-modules of the miles per gallon program are not described completely because they require loops, which are introduced in Chapter 5. This solution shows the sequence structure only.

```
Termination
    Miles_per_gallon = Miles_driven/Gas_used
    Display Miles_per_gallon
    Return
```

2. Area of a Rectangle Program

```
Area of a Rectangle Program
 Get Width
 Get Length
    Area = Length * Width
 Display Area
 End
```

The pseudocode to the left illustrates the program module for the Area of a Rectangle Program. This program contains no sub-modules.

3. Bowler's Average program

```
Bowler's Average Program
    Initialization
    Process
    Termination
    End
```

The pseudocode shown to the left illustrates the main program module. At each statement, control is transferred to the appropriate sub-module.

```
Initialization
    Set_counters
    Return
Process
    Get_Scores
    Accumulate_totals
    Return
Termination
    Display_average
    Return
Set_counters
    Game_counter = 0
    Total_score = 0
    Return
Get_scores
    Print " Input score for game 1."
    Input Game_1_score
    Game_counter = Game_counter + 1
    Print " Input score for game 2."
```

```
        Input Game_2_score
        Game_counter = Game_counter + 1
        Print " Input score for game 3."
        Input Game_2_score
        Game_counter = Game_counter + 1
        Return
    Accumulate_total
        Total = Game_1_score + Game_2_score
        Print " Total for 2 games is " Total
        Total_score = Total_score + Game_3_score
        Print "Total for 3 games is " Total_score
        Return
    Display_average
        Average = Total_score/3
        Print " Your average for today was: " Average
        Return
```

Summary

In this chapter you were shown the basic flowcharting symbols and how to arrange them into a flowchart. You saw that you can read a flowchart to some extent even when there are no words attached. A hierarchy chart should be drawn before you proceed to flowchart a problem. The first section of the flowchart represents the first two levels of the hierarchy chart. A separate flowchart is drawn for each of the remaining levels of the hierarchy chart.

You were also introduced to the basic syntax and commands of pseudocode. A hierarchy chart should be drawn before you proceed to flowchart a problem. Pseudocode is a substitute for a flowchart.

Key Terms

Each number in parentheses indicates the page where the term first occurs in the chapter.

annotation (48)
decision (48)
flow line (46)
input/output (48)
off-page connector (49)
on-page connector (49)
predetermined process (48)
process (48)
pseudocode (60)
sequence structure (52)
terminal (46)

Chapter 3
Exercises

Objective 1 Read a flowchart containing sequence logic structures.

1. Examine the flowchart in Figure 3.16 and deter mine what problem it was designed to solve. Does it work properly? If not, why not? Draw a corrected version if it's incorrect.

   The flowchart on the right represents the detailed flowchart of the "Calculate Bonus Amount" module shown in the main flowchart on the left.

Note! The flowchart on the right represents the detailed flowchart of the "Calculate Bonus Amount" module shown in the main flowchart on the left.

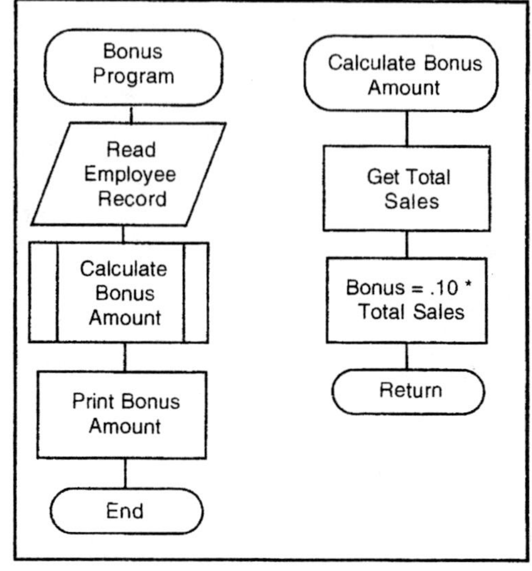

Figure 3.16 Objective 1, Exercise 1

2. Examine the flowchart in Figure 3.17 and determine what problem it was to designed to solve. Does it work properly? If not, why not? Draw a corrected version if it's incorrect.
3. Examine the flowchart in Figure 3.18 and determine what problem it was designed to solve. Does it work properly? If not, why not? Draw a corrected version if it's incorrect.
4. Examine the flowchart in Figure 3.19 and determine what problem it was designed to solve.

   Does it work properly? If not, why not? Draw a corrected version if it's incorrect.

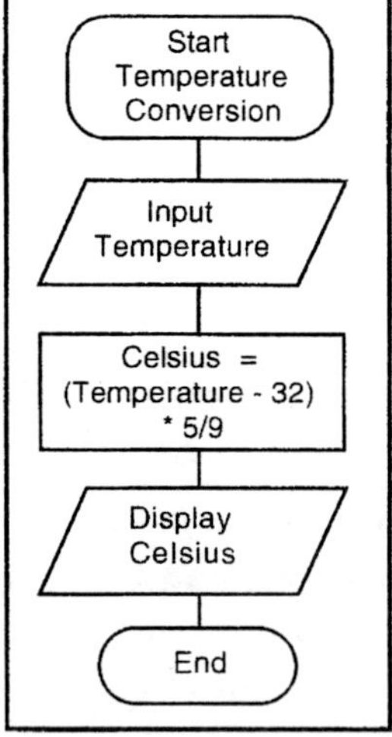

Figure 3.17 Objective 1, Exercise 2

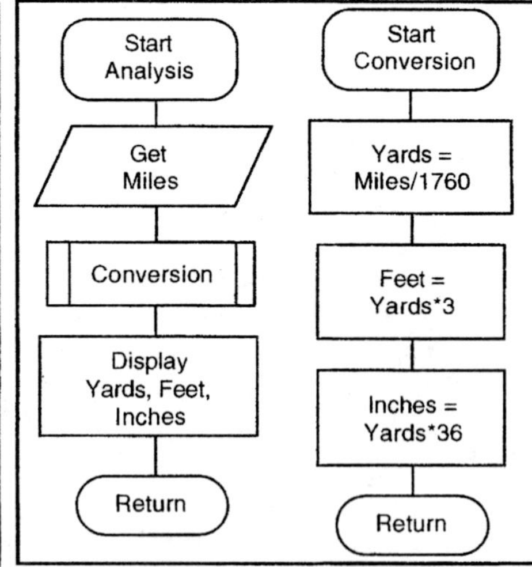

Figure 3.18 Objective 1, Exercise 4

5. Examine the flowchart in Figure 3.20 and determine what problem it was designed to solve. Does it work properly? If not, why not? Draw a corrected version if it's incorrect.

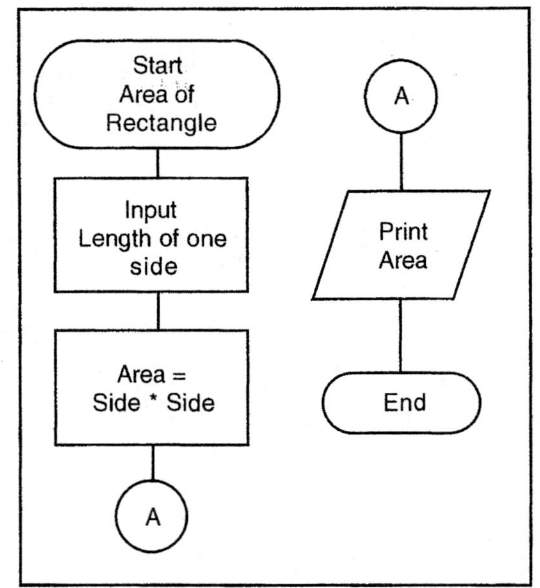

Figure 3.19 Objective 1, Exercise 4

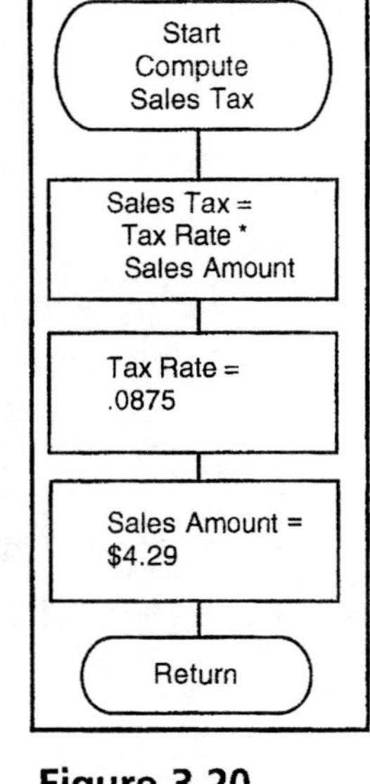

Figure 3.20 Objective 1, Exercise 5

6. Examine the flowchart in Figure 3.21 and determine what problem it was designed to solve. Does it work properly? If not, why not? Draw a corrected version if it's incorrect.

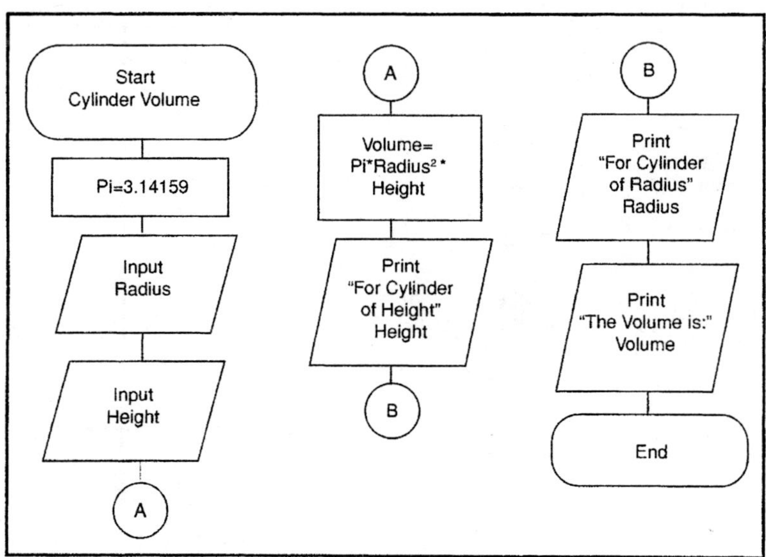

Figure 3.21 Objective 1, Exercise 6

7. Examine the flowchart in Figure 3.22 and determine what problem it was designed to solve. Does it work properly? If not, why not? Draw a corrected version if it's incorrect.

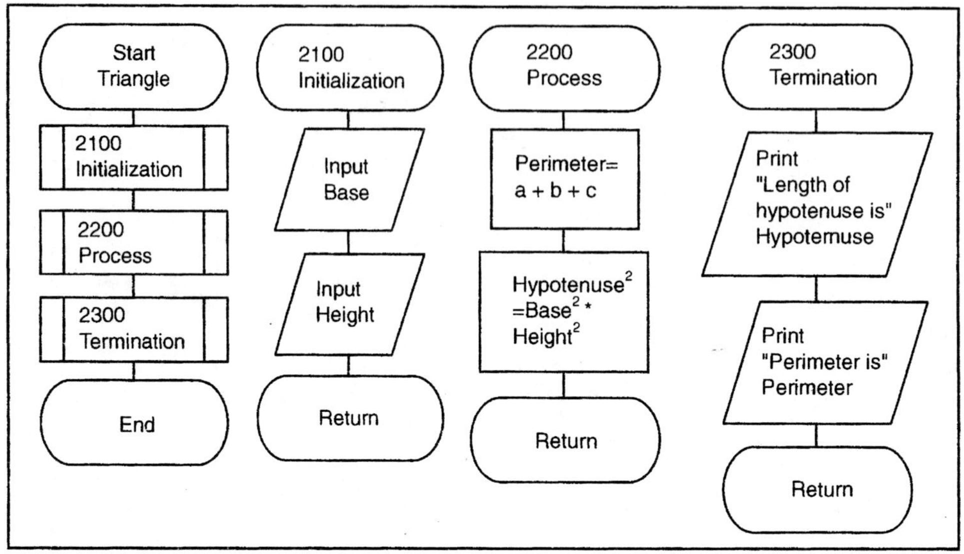

Figure 3.22 Objective 1, Exercise 7

8. Examine the flowchart in Figure 3.23 and determine what problem it was designed to solve. Does it work properly? If not, why not? Draw a corrected version if it's incorrect.

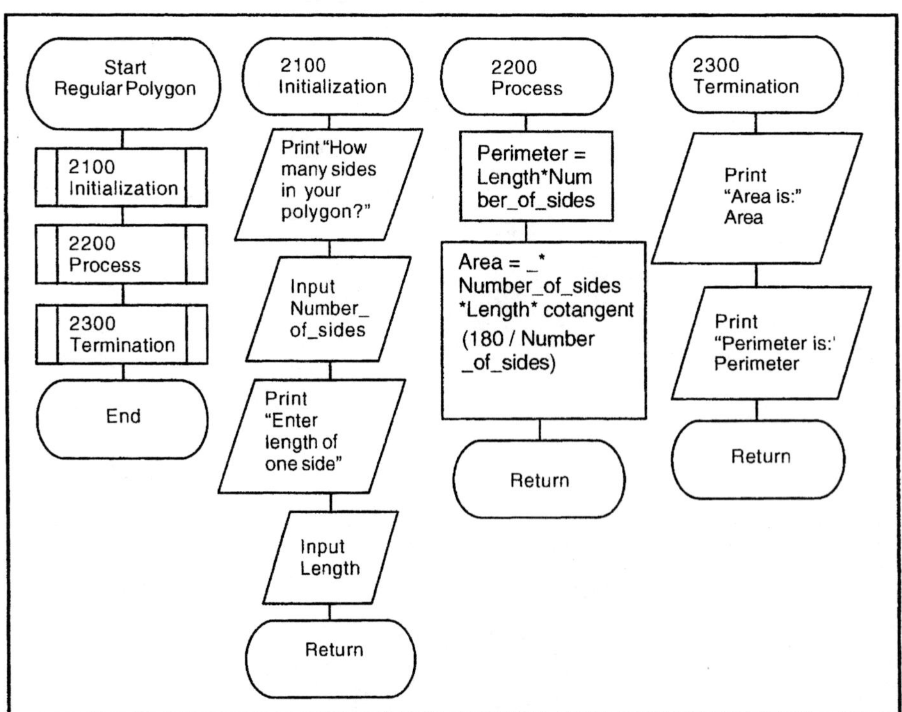

Figure 3.23 Objective 1, Exercise 8

Objective 2 Draw and revise a flowchart using sequence logic structures for a given problem.

1. Develop a task list, a hierarchy chart, and draw a flowchart to show the sequential logic involved in converting feet to meters. The formula for this conversion is 1 meter = 3.2808 feet.
2. Develop a task list, a hierarchy chart, and draw a flowchart to show the sequential logic involved in calculating an hourly employee's net pay (one employee). Assume overtime is paid for all hours over forty. Formulas you will need:

   Gross Pay = Hours Worked * Hourly Pay Rate

   Overtime Pay = Overtime Hours * Overtime Pay Rate

3. Develop a task list, a hierarchy chart, and draw a flowchart to show the sequential logic involved in the following problem:

   The program will read an item's price and description, calculate the sales tax on the item, calculate the total price for the item, display the total price, read the amount of money collected, and calculate the change due the customer. Display the change due. Assume a sales tax rate of 8.25%. Assume that there is only one item purchased.

4. Develop a task list, a hierarchy chart, and draw a flowchart to show the sequential logic involved in calculating the area of a triangle, given the base and height of the triangle. The formula for the area of a triangle is: Area = $^1/_2$ * Base * Height.
5. Develop a task list, a hierarchy chart, and draw a flowchart to show the sequential logic involved in the following problem:

   You have been asked to design a program that will calculate the averages for your bowling team. There are four players on the team, two women and two men. Input the name of the team and the names of the players, and print out the averages with each person's name.

6. Develop a task list, a hierarchy chart, and draw a flowchart to show the sequential logic involved in the following problem:

   Design a program that reads the number of students taking an exam and the number of students that have passed the exam and that displays the percentage of students that have passed the exam. The number of students taking the exam and passing the exam should also be displayed.

7. Develop a task list, a hierarchy chart, and draw a flowchart to show the sequential logic involved in the following problem:

   A program is needed that computes traffic fines. The fines are based on the speed that the driver exceeded the speed limit. For every 1 mile per hour over the speed limit, the driver is fined $7.00. The program should allow for a speed limit, as well as the driver's speed, to be input. The speed limit, amount over the limit, and the total fine should be displayed.

8: Develop a task list, a hierarchy chart, and draw a flowchart to show the sequential logic involved in the following problem:

Calculate and display the grade point average for a student who took three courses: a three-hour course with a grade of A, a two-hour course with a grade of B, and a four-hour course with a grade of C. Assume the four-point grading system (A is 4, B is 3, and so on). The formulas you will need are:

A. Grade Point Average = Total Honor Points/ Total Credit Hours

B. Honor Points = Numeric Grade * Credit Hours

Note! Do not use looping or any technique beyond this chapter to solve this problem.

Use only the sequential logic described in this chapter. Assume that there is only one student and the program is designed to work for that one student with the data above.

Objective 3 Enrichment – Doing it with Pseudocode

Read pseudocode containing sequence logic structures.

1. Read the following pseudocode program fragments and determine what problem is being solved. Does it work properly? If not, why not? Write a corrected version if it's incorrect.

```
Bonus Calculation Program
        Read Employee_Record
        Bonus_amount
        Print Bonus
        End

Bonus_amount
        Bonus = .10 * Total_Sales
        Return
```

2. Read the following pseudocode program fragments and determine what problem is being solved. Does it work properly? If not, why not? Write a corrected version if it's incorrect.

```
Temperature_conversion
        Input Temperature
        Celsius = (Temperature-32)* 5/9
        Display Celsius
        End
```

3. Read the following pseudocode program fragments and determine what problem is being solved. Does it work properly? If not, why not? Write a corrected version if it's incorrect.

```
Analysis Program
        Get Miles
        Conversion
        Display Yards, Feet, Inches
        Return

Conversion
        Yards = Miles/1760
        Feet = Yards * 3
        Inches = Yards * 36
```

4. Read the following pseudocode program fragments, and determine what problem is being solved. Does it work properly? If not, why not? Write a corrected version if it's incorrect.

```
Area_of_a_rectangle
        Get Side_Length
        Area = Side_Length * Side_length
        Print Area
        End
```

5. Read the following pseudocode program fragments and determine what problem is being solved. Does it work properly? If not, why not? Write a corrected version if it's incorrect.

```
Comput_Sales_Tax
        Sales_tax = Tax_rate * Sales_amount
        Tax_rate = .0875
        Sales_amount = $4.79
        Return
```

6. Read the following pseudocode program fragments and determine what problem is being solved. Does it work properly? If not, why not? Write a corrected version if it's incorrect.

```
Cylinder Volume Calculation
        Pi = 3.14159
        Input Radius
        Input Height
        Volume = Pi*Radius^2*Height
        Print "For cylinder height of: "; Height
        Print "For radius of:  "; Radius
        Print "The volume is:  " Volume
        End
```

7. Read the following pseudocode program fragments and determine what problem is being solved. Does it work properly? If not, why not? Write a corrected version if it's incorrect.

```
Triangle Program
        Initialization
        Process
        Termination
        End
Initialization
        Input Base
        Input Height
        Return
Process
        Perimeter = a + b + c
        Hypotenuse^2 = Base^2 + Height^2
        Return
Termination
        Print "Length of hypotenuse is: "; Hypotenuse
        Print "Perimeter is: "; Perimeter
        Return
```

8. Read the following pseudocode program fragments and determine what problem is being solved. Does it work properly? If not, why not? Write a corrected version if it's incorrect.

```
Regular Polygon Program
          Initialization
          Process
          Termination
          End
Initialization
          Print "How many sides in your polygon?"
          Input Number_of_sides
          Print "Enter length of one side."
          Input Length
          Return
Process
          Perimeter = Length * Number_of_sides
          Area = 1/4 * Number_of_sides * Length *
                    cotangent(180/Number_of_sides)
          Return
Termination
          Print "Area is: "; Area
          Print "Perimeter is: "; Perimeter
          Return
```

Objective 3 Enrichment – Doing it with Pseudocode

Write the pseudocode using sequence logic structures for a given problem.

1. Develop a task list, a hierarchy chart, and write the pseudocode to show the sequential logic involved in converting feet to meters. The formula for this conversion is 1 meter = 3.2808 feet.

2. Develop a task list, a hierarchy chart, and write the pseudocode to show the sequential logic involved in calculating an hourly employee's net pay. Assume overtime is paid for all hours over forty. Formulas you will need:

   A. Gross Pay = Hours_Worked * Hourly_Pay_Rate
   B. Overtime Pay = Overtime_Hours * Overtime_Pay_Rate

3. Develop a task list, a hierarchy chart, and write the pseudocode to show the sequential logic involved in the following problem:

   The program will read an item's price and description, calculate the sales tax on the item, calculate the total price for the item, display the total price, read the amount of money collected, and calculate the change due the customer. Display the change due. Assume a sales tax rate of 8.25%.

4. Develop a task list, a hierarchy chart, and write the pseudocode to show the sequential logic involved in the following problem:

   You have been asked to design a program that will calculate the averages for your bowling team. There are four players on the team, two women and two men. Input the name of the team, the names of the players, and print out the averages with the person's name.

5. Develop a task list. a hierarchy chart, and write the pseudocode to show the sequential logic involved in the following problem:

   Design a program that reads the number of students taking an exam, as well as the number of students that have passed the exam, and displays the percentage of students that have passed the exam. The number of students taking the exam and passing the exam should also be displayed.

6. Develop a task list and a hierarchy chart, and write the pseudocode to show the sequential logic involved in the following problem:

   A program is needed that computes traffic fines. The fines are based on the speed by which the driver exceeded the speed limit. For every 1 mile per hour over the speed limit, the driver is fined $7.00. The program should allow for a speed limit and the driver's speed to be input. The speed limit, amount over the limit, and the total fine should be displayed.

7. Develop a task list and a hierarchy chart, and write the pseudocode to show the sequential logic involved in calculating the area of a triangle, given the base and height of the triangle. The formula for the area of a triangle is:

   Area = $^1/_2$ * Base * Height.

8. Develop a task list, a hierarchy chart, and write the pseudocode to show the sequential logic involved in the following problem:

   Calculate the grade point average for a student who took three courses: a three-hour course with a grade of A, a two-hour course with a grade of B, and a four-hour course with a grade of C. Assume the four-point grading system (A is 4, B is 3, and so on). The formulas you will need are:

   A. Grade Point Average = Total Honor Points/ Total Credit Hours

   B. Honor Points = Numeric Grade * Credit Hours

   Do not use looping to solve this problem. Use only the sequential logic described in this chapter. Assume that there is only one student, and the program is designed to work for that one student with the data above. Show the grade point average that you calculated while desk checking this program.

Other Assignments

SoftSkills

Select one problem from Objective 2 or 4 or from the Internet/library research projects below; prepare and give an oral report to the class on your solution.

Internet/library research projects

A. Research the history of flowchart and write a short report describing the development of the flowchart.

B. Research the history of pseudocode and write a short report describing the development of the pseudocode.

C. Find a flowchart that describes a solution not presented in the textbook, and write a report on it.

D. Find a pseudocode solution to some problem not presented in the textbook, and write a report on it.

SELECTION LOGIC

When it is not necessary to make a decision, it is necessary not to make a decision.

(Lord Falkland)

OBJECTIVES

After completing this chapter, you will be able to:

1. Read flowcharts containing nested or sequential decision statements, or case statements.
2. Draw and revise flowcharts that require nested or sequential decision statements, or case statements.
3. Read pseudocode with nested or sequential decision statements, or case statements.
4. Write and revise pseudocode with nested or sequential decision statements, or case statements.
5. Understand how decisions add flexibility to processing.

Introduction

Until now we have only been concerned with sequential logic flow. Sequential logic flow represents one of the three control structures used in the structured design and structured programming process. The other two structures are iteration and selection. This chapter will introduce the selection structure. The *selection structure* is used in problem solving when there is a decision to be made.

For example, in the problem from Chapter 3 where we calculate the miles per gallon of gas used on a trip, we need a statement that says: "Are we at the end of the trip?" If we are at the end of the trip, then we are done with the accumulations; and we can calculate the final miles per gallon. If we're not at the end of the trip, then we will need to get gas again and accumulate the gas and miles.

The process of selection allows for options. A program can take two different paths depending on the results of a decision. In programmer jargon, the selection statement is called an if statement because most programming languages use the word "if" to begin the coding for the selection process (i.e., IF...then...else). The selection process is not depicted in a hierarchy chart, so we will use flowcharts or pseudocode for explanations of the selection structure.

Flowchart

The flowchart symbol for selection is a diamond or square that is turned on a vertex (turned "sideways"), shown here in Figure 4.1.

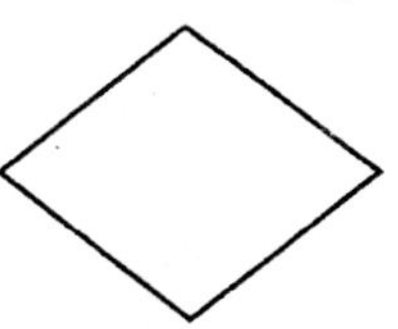

Figure 4.1 Selection Symbol

However, the symbol by itself does not describe the logic of what is being accomplished. To understand the selection process, you need to see the decision symbol in its expanded form shown in Figure 4.2. The decision symbol always contains a statement that can be answered true or false (yes or no, and so on). In many cases that statement starts with the word "if." In programming languages, the decision statement begins with the word "if"; hence the reason it is called an "if" statement. Because the decision symbol is somewhat small and an unusual shape, it is convenient to use mathematical symbols inside the decision symbol. Try to phrase the statements so that they are not compound statements. For example, assume you want to determine a letter grade for a given test score. You know that scores of 90, 91, ... 100 receive a grade of A. You could use the statement: "If test_score ≥ 90", which is a compound statement (greater than or equal to), or you could state the simple condition: "If test_score > 89." A later chapter will discuss the compound conditions and problems related to those types of statements. When talking about the selection process in this book, we will always mean the symbol as shown in Figure 4.2[1]. Perhaps the most striking aspect of this structure is that it has two exit points. Having two exit points gives the selection structure its power. From this point in the program, we can decide to move in one of two directions (hence the name "decision").

Selection Structure

The *selection structure* is the structure in programming that allows for decisions to be made. It has only one entry point, as do all the other structures in computer programming; but after the decision, we can proceed in one of two independent directions. Since two possible directions to proceed are available, we must label each branch so that the reader can determine when to follow each path. As shown in Figure 4.2, one path is labeled "true" and the other one "false." If the condition is true, then we proceed to the left-hand branch. If the condition is false, then we must take the right-hand branch. Another significant point to be made is that once we have chosen a direction, we will never be able to perform the tasks in the other branch until we somehow manage to return to the decision again. After exiting the decision symbol, Figure 4.2 depicts predetermined processes to emphasize the point that anything can occur after the decision. Remember that a predetermined process symbol implies that another flowchart exists describing that process.

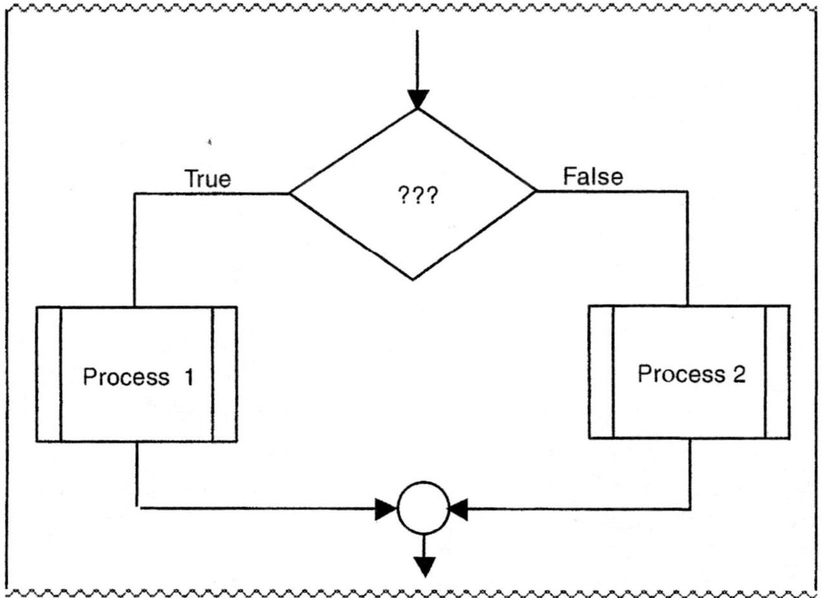

Figure 4.2
Generic Selection Structure

1 Figure 4.2 is not a complete flowchart but rather a fragment of a flowchart that depicts only the logic that we are interested in currently. You should recall from Chapter 3 that complete flowcharts have a start and an end. Figure 4.2 has neither start nor end and is an example extracted from a flowchart that depicts the selection process. We don't know what happens in the flowchart before the decision, nor do we know what happens after Process 1 or Process 2, but the flow lines with arrowheads show us that the flowchart continues.

Figure 4.3 depicts a decision where no action is taken on the false side, but there is a predetermined process on the true side. The true and false branches can be just as easily reversed. Some authors suggest that the true branch should always be on the right-hand side for standardization purposes, but the decision is arbitrary.

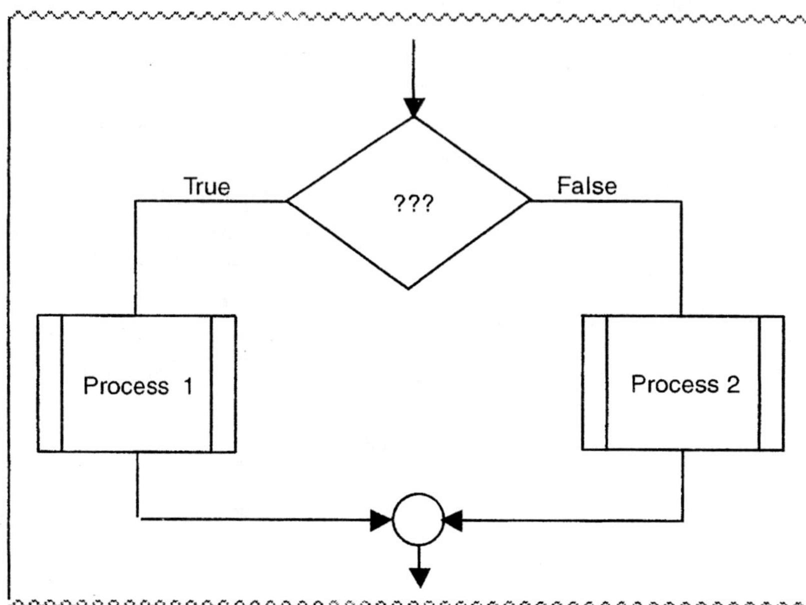

Figure 4.3 One-sided. Decision

The logical flow of the program could proceed through a great many steps on either side or both sides of the decision symbol; but at some point, these two flows should rejoin. The on-page connector can be used at the point where the two flows connect. This is shown in Figures 4.2 and 4.3. The connector does not contain a letter because no other corresponding circle is referenced. The ??? inside the decision symbol can be replaced with any condition that can be resolved into a true or false result.

There are three common, simple conditions that can be used and a great many compound conditions that can be used. The compound conditions are discussed in Chapter 5. The simple conditions that are normally used; equality (=), less than (<), and greater than (>). Figures 4.4 A, B, and C show examples of each of those conditions. The logic in Figure 4.4B assumes that grades are all integers.

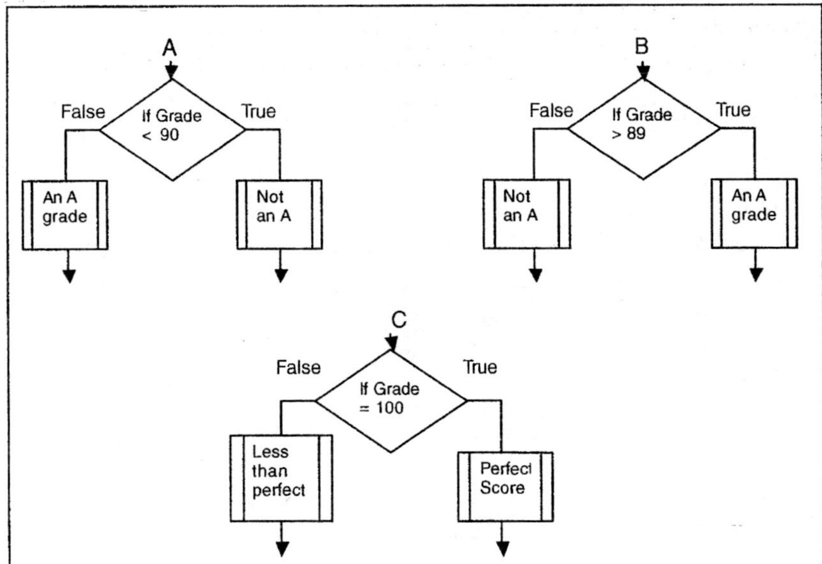

Figures 4.4 A, B, and C
Decision Conditions

Sequential Decisions

The combined structures in Figure 4.5 are called a *sequential if* or *sequential decision*, because two decisions are connected together in sequence.

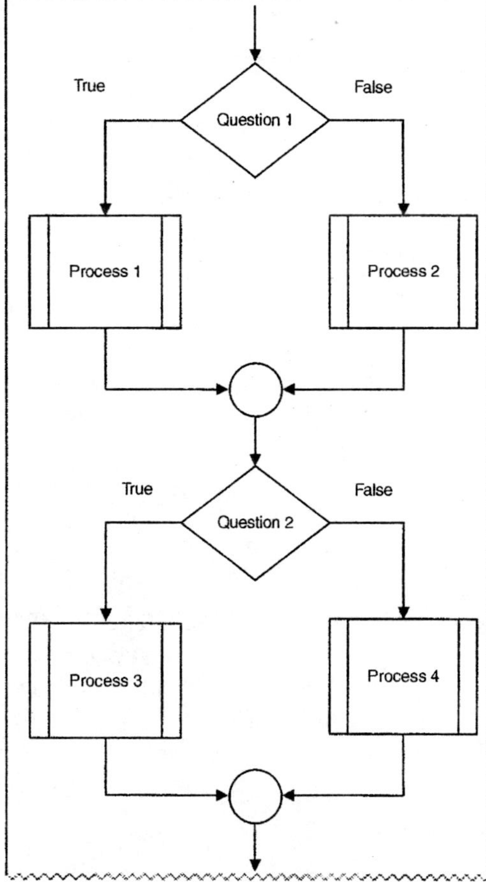

Figure 4.5
Sequential Decisions

Let's look at a sample problem to help analyze this logic. Suppose that you were performing a survey of voters, and the questionnaire used for the survey contained two questions:

1. What is your gender? (circle one) Male Female
2. What is your political party preference? (circle one) Republican Democrat

Now imagine that these responses were going to be input into a computer, and the computer was capable of recognizing which word was circled. What we want our program to do is count the number of males, females, Republicans, and Democrats. This program would use counters as defined in Chapter 1. Figure 4.6 shows the decision structure for this program.

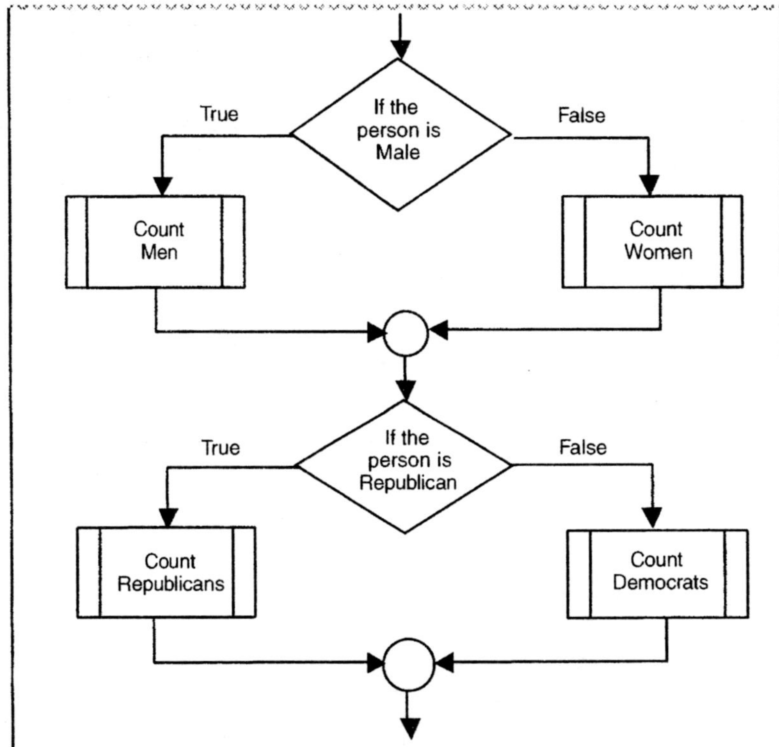

Figure 4.6
Sequential Counting

The flowchart in Figure 4.6 shows that we are counting the number of males, the number of females, the number of Republicans, and the number of Democrats. After processing is complete, we know how many men, how many women, how many Republicans, and how many Democrats took the survey. This is an example of a sequential decision. Regardless of the results of the first decision, we always check the second condition.

What might be more interesting to know would be the number of male Democrats, male Republicans, female Democrats, and female Republicans that took the survey; but the logic of Figure 4.6 cannot produce those statistics.

Nested Decisions

The next technique used to combine decision statements is called nesting. The generic form of a nested decision is shown in Figure 4.7. Notice in the nested configuration that there are still two decisions to be made just as there were in the sequential process of Figure 4.5. However, in the nested case, processes 2 or 3 can only be completed when the first decision is false. If condition 1 is true, then condition 2 is never tested and processes 2 and 3 can never occur during the remainder of the flow.

Nested decisions or *nested ifs* are always two decisions that are combined in a way that prevents one condition from being tested depending on the first condition. Notice in the sequential decisions in Figure 4.5 that the second decision will always be made, regardless of whether or not the first decision is true or false.

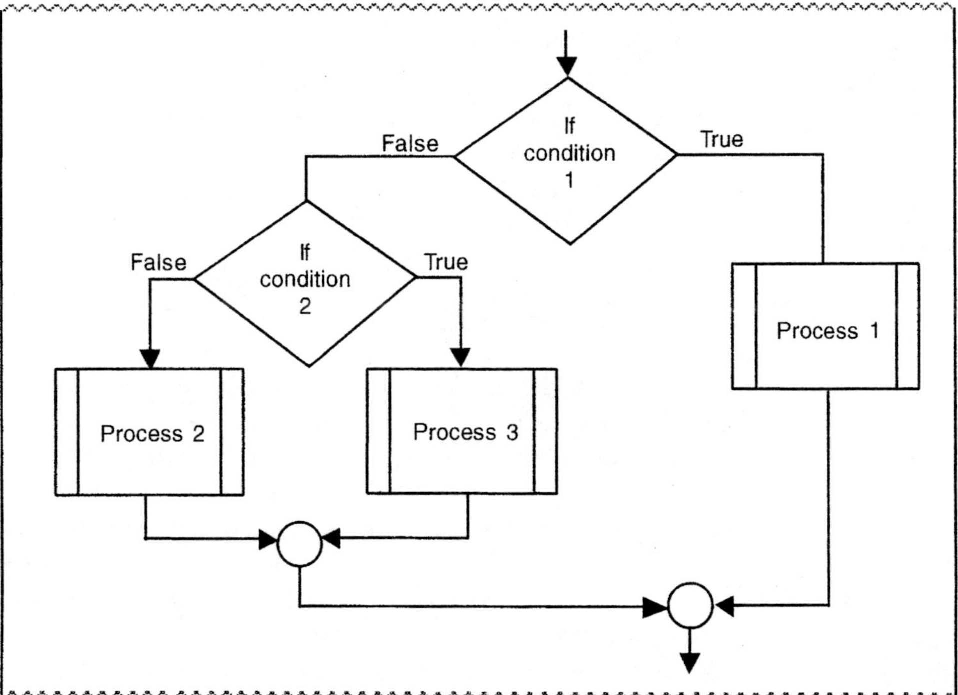

Figure 4.7 Nested Decision

As an example of a nested if statement application, let's re-examine the process of counting voters (male, female, Republican, Democrat) shown previously. Figure 4.8 shows a second method of processing the data using nested decisions. Notice that this flowchart is able to count the male Republicans and the female Republicans and still can produce the total male and female statistics shown in Figure 4.6. We need merely to add the female Republicans to the female Democrats, and we would know the total number of females.

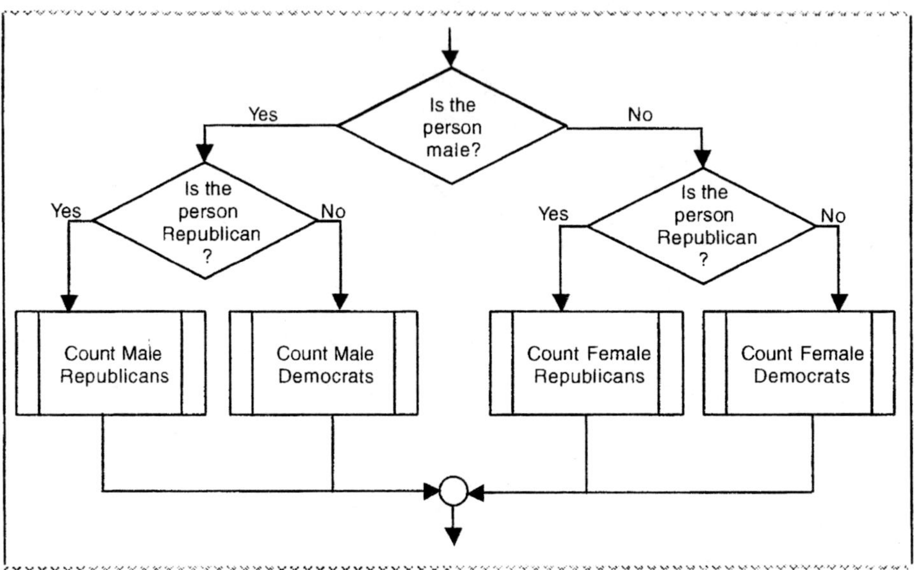

Figure 4.8 Nested Counting

Here we see that after the first condition is evaluated, we evaluate a second condition before counting. The result is that we have counted combined categories of survey respondents; and we have a total count of male Republicans, female Republicans, male Democrats, and female Democrats who took the survey. Even better, we can calculate the total number of Republicans who took the survey by adding female Republicans and male Republicans.

This nested selection structure is a very powerful tool for making decisions inside a computer program. Repeated application of this structure allows simple true/false decisions to be used to solve fairly complex decision problems. Here's another example.

Suppose you are writing a program that will determine the correct oil filter for a car, given the year, make, model, and engine size. Is this a yes/no kind of condition? Look at Figure 4.9 for the answer.

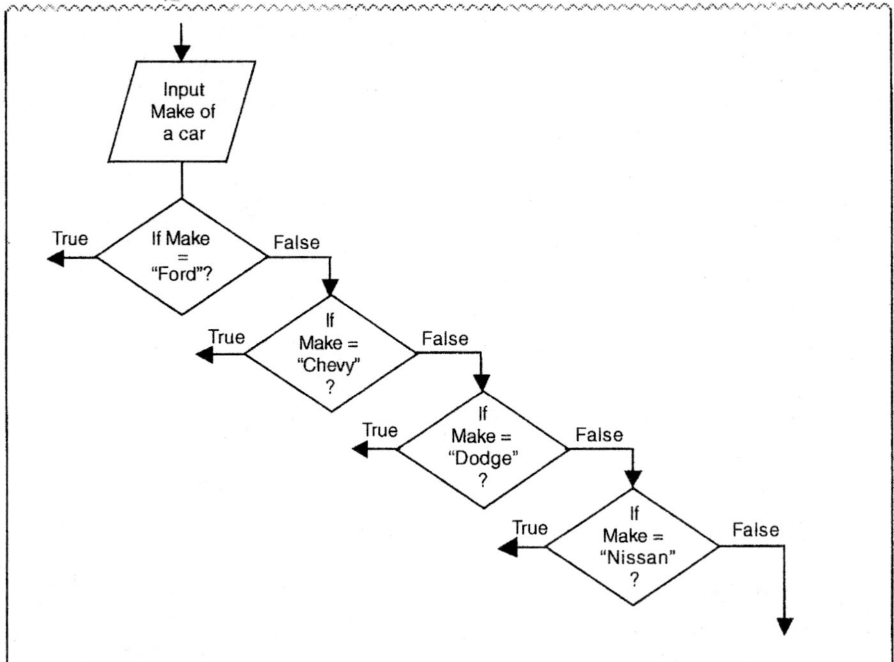

Figure 4.9 Compound Nesting

Figure 4.9 is an extract of the flowchart that might be used to begin solving the problem of finding the correct oil filter for your car. By nesting simple true/false conditions, we can focus a large amount of data into a pinpoint decision. Drawing the nested decision statements on a diagonal line is optional. The same logic can be depicted in a straight line drawing as shown in Figure 4.10.

Logically there is no difference between Figures 4.9 and 4.10. Figure 4.9 shows the "nesting" aspect in a clearer fashion; but in practice Figure 4.10 is often easier to use. The flowchart fragments shown in Figures 4.9 and 4.10 are obviously far from complete.

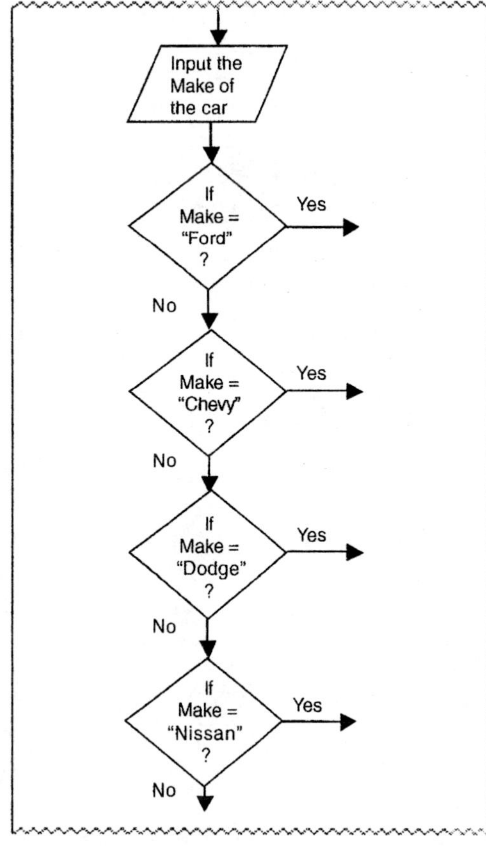

Figure 4.10 Straight-line Nesting

Compare the flowchart fragment in Figure 4.10 with the sequential flowchart fragment in Figure 4.11 to see the differences.

Notice that in the sequential decision flowchart of Figure 4.11, every decision gets evaluated regardless of the previous answer. After answering true to the first condition, the second decision makes no sense; but the logic shows it being completed anyway. The flowchart appears to accomplish the same thing as Figures 4.9 and 4.10 but much less efficiently. In general, sequential decisions will not accomplish the same tasks as nested decisions, and vice versa. There are needs for both nested and sequential decisions.

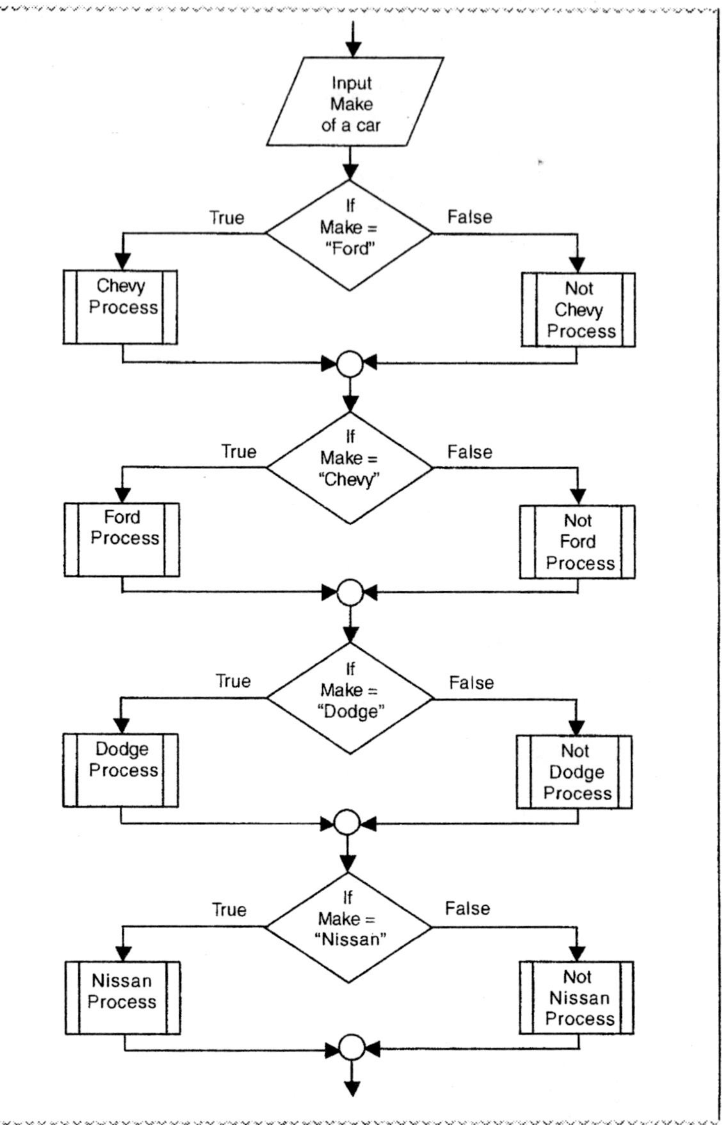

Figure 4.11 Sequential Selection

Here is one more example before we move on. Suppose that we wish to design a flowchart that will convert letter grades to numeric grades. This is important if we wish to calculate a grade point average (GPA), because we can't calculate with a letter grade. Figure 4.12 depicts the flowchart.

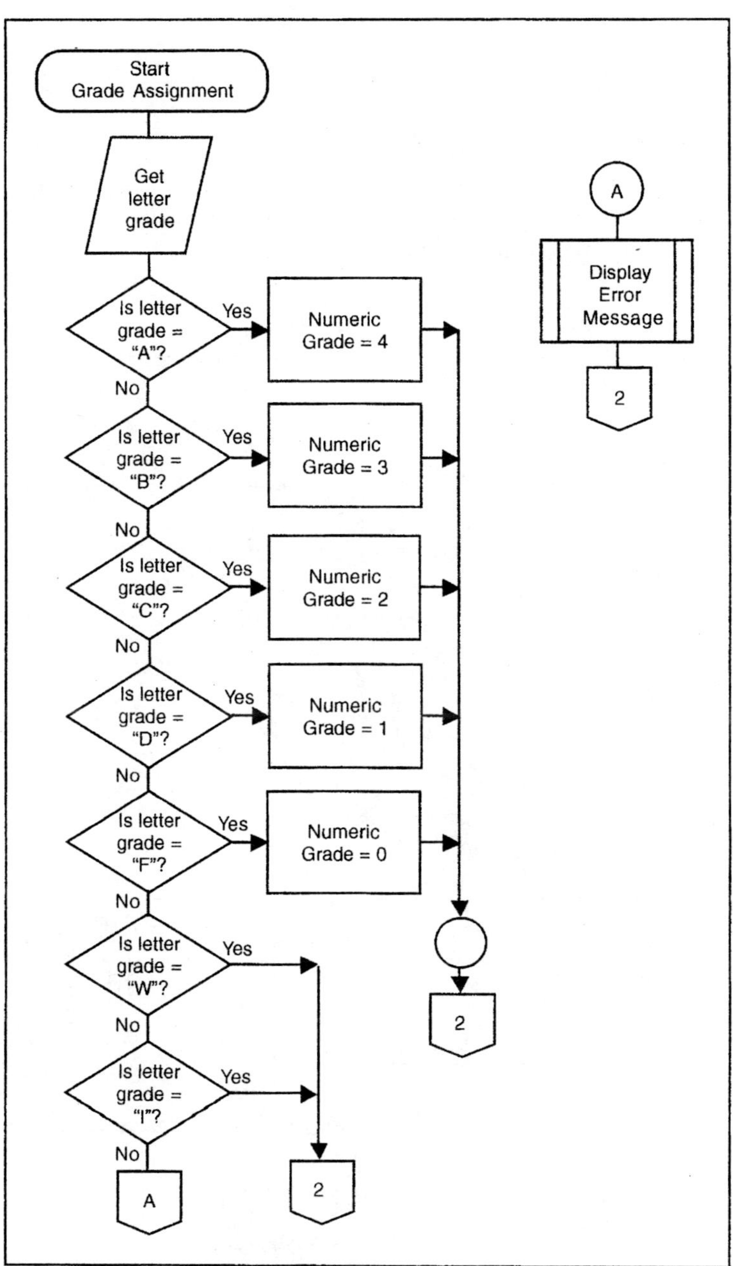

Figure 4.12 Grade Conversion

In Figure 4.12, we enter the flowchart and input a letter grade. If the grade is an A, then the variable *Numeric grade* receives the value 4 and the program continues on page 2.

If the grade is not an A, then the program checks to see if it is a B, and so on. At the bottom of the flowchart, we could still have a letter grade that has not been converted to a numeric equivalent. That would occur if the grade input were not an A, B, C, D, F, W, or I.

Case Statement

The nested decision structure is extremely powerful for making decisions. Its main shortcoming is that it takes up a lot of space. In the previous example, all we're trying to accomplish is to assign a number corresponding to a particular letter. A more straightforward picture can be developed using the case statement. The case statement is supported in many programming languages and doesn't have its own flowcharting symbol. It uses a combination of flowchart symbols and replaces the logic of some nested decisions. An example is drawn in Figure 4.13.

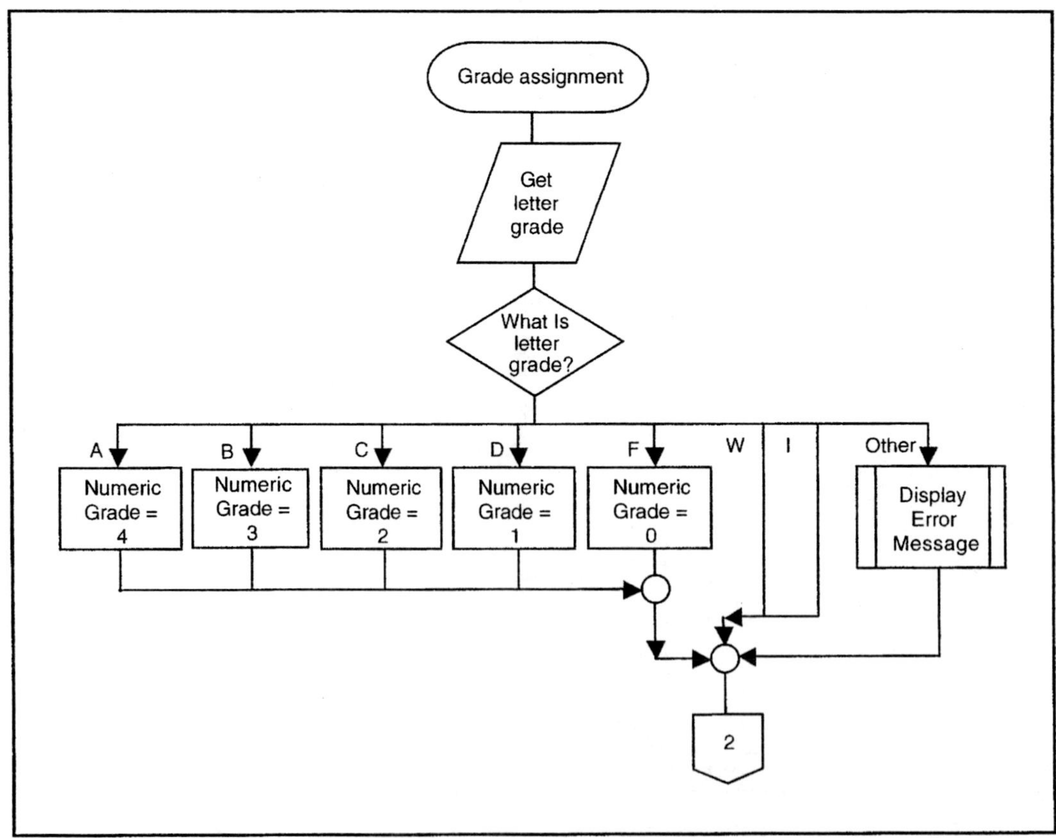

Figure 4.13 Case Statement

Figure 4.13 is a drawing of a case statement that solves the grade assignment problem from Figure 4.12. The case statement begins with a decision symbol at the top. Under the decision symbol, we find flow lines connecting to processes for each possible case. No difference in logic exists between Figures 4.12 and 4.13. In Figure 4.13, we have saved drawing the six decision symbols that were drawn in Figure 4.12. Other advantages of using the case statement include using less space and displaying a clearer picture of the logic.

Notice that Figure 4.13 contains a category identified as "other". A good case statement will have a category like "other" to handle any data that was unplanned. Grades should be limited to A, B, C, D, F, W, and I but could be others in various situations. Our case statement in Figure 4.13 handles the previous grades. If the program encounters a grade that is different, then the error module is invoked.

Bowling Problem

In earlier chapters we began solving a problem using a bowler's scores. Without the capability to make decisions, that problem was restricted to sequential tasks. Now that we have the selection structure and the capability to make decisions, the bowling analysis can be expanded. As an illustration of the decision statements, we will determine which of a bowler's games had the highest score. Let's begin by establishing a task list for finding the highest score.

- Get bowler's first game score.
- Get bowler's second game score.
- If first game score is > second game score, then the high game is the first game, else the second game is the high game.
- Save the game number for the high game (1 or 2).
- Get bowler's third score.
- If the third score is > the high game, then the third game is the high game, else the high game was previously determined.
- Replace the high game number if necessary.
- Display the high game.

We can add a module to our hierarchy chart (Figure 3.13) for finding the highest game, and we can add a task to the Display Average module that displays the high game. Let's identify the high game module as module number 3230. The flowchart for module 3230 is shown in Figure 4.14.

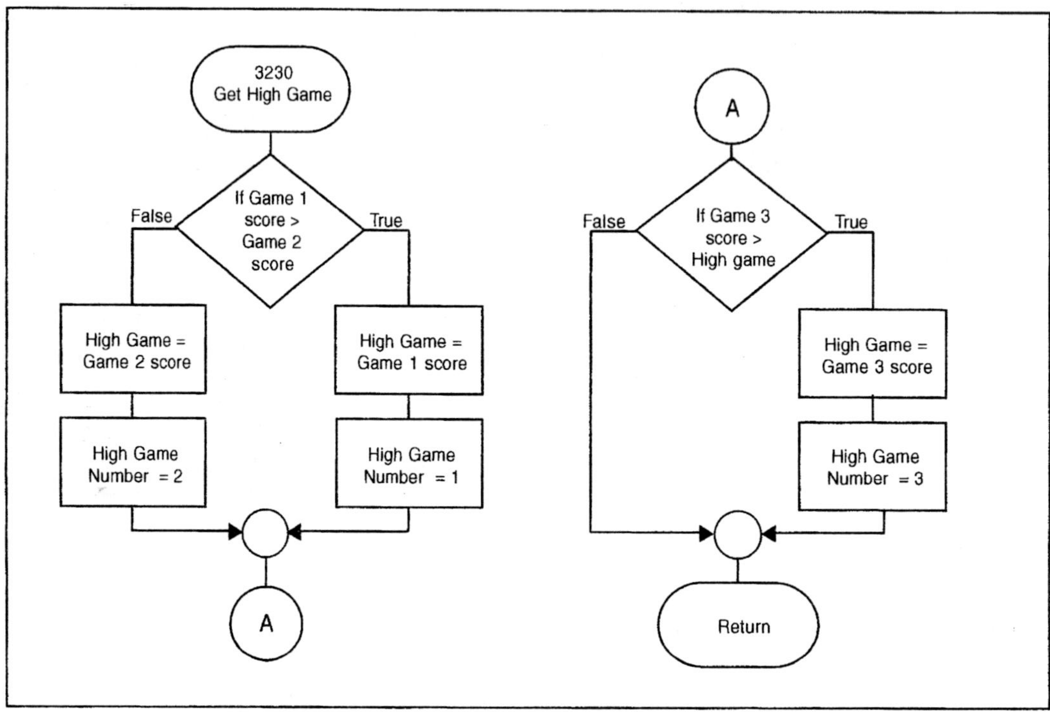

Figure 4.14 Bowling Decisions

Enrichment – Doing it with Pseudocode

Writing pseudocode for selection statements requires some new terms and rules. The selection structure will be identified in pseudocode using the statement *If Then Else Endif* (referred to as If). The If statement is an opportunity for a program to proceed on alternate paths. Its syntax is: *If* (condition) *Then* (process) *Else* (process) *Endif*. Its meaning is as follows:

The condition is a statement comparing two items. The comparison can only result in a true or false situation. If the statement is true, we continue to the Then portion of the pseudocode. After completing the tasks in the Then section, we skip to the Endif. If the statement is false, we proceed directly to the Else section, process those tasks, and continue to the Endif.

Example: suppose we are processing market surveys that have identified the respondents as either male or female. We want to count the number of male respondents and the number of female respondents. Our pseudocode would look like this:

```
Get Gender
If Gender = Male Then
   Number_of_males = Number_of_males + 1
Else
   Number_of_females = Number_of_females + 1
Endif
Return
```

Notice that the statements are indented. This improves the readability of the pseudocode and highlights the paths of each decision. The *If, Else,* and *Endif* are aligned vertically so that the reader can find the beginning and end of the statement.

Sequential if statements are created when a second If statement follows an Endif.

Example: continuing from our previous example, suppose we wanted to count the number of men, women, Republicans, and Democrats (assume the survey collected the party affiliation).

```
Get Gender

Get Party_affiliation

If Gender = Male Then

   Number_of_males = Number_of_males + 1

Else

   Number_of_females = Number_of_females + 1

Endif

If Party_affiliation = Republican Then

   Number_of_Republicans = Number_of_Republicans + 1

Else

   Number_of_Democrats = Number_of_Democrats + 1

Endif
Return
```

Nested if statements are created when an if statement is an option of a previous if statement. We see from the above example that we counted males, females, Republicans, and Democrats; but suppose we wanted to count the men Republicans, women Democrats, and so on. We would need the following logic:

```
Get Gender

Get Party_affiliation

If Gender = Male Then

   If Party_affiliation = Republican Then
         Number_of_male_Republicans =
               Number_of_male_Republicans + 1

   Else

         Number_of_male_Democrats =
               Number_of_male_Democrats + 1

   Endif

Else

   If Party_affiliation = Republican Then
         Number_of_female_Republicans =
                     Number_of_female_Republicans + 1

   Else

         Number_of_female_Democrats =
               Number_of_female_Democrats + 1

   Endif

Endif
Return
```

Notice again that each *If* is aligned with an *Endif*, and the *Then* and *Else* portions are aligned and indented appropriately. This nested if statement allows us to capture more complex data but still recover the simple data. In this example if we wanted the total males, we could simply add the male Democrats and the male Republicans.

Next we see the pseudocode for the grade conversion flowchart of Figure 4.12 depicted in Figure 4.15. Notice that the indentations continue throughout the nesting process.

```
Get Student_grade
If Student_grade = A Then
          Numeric_equivalent = 4
Else
          If Student_grade = B Then
                    Numeric_equivalent = 3
          Else
                    If Student_grade = C Then
                              Numeric_equivalent = 2
                    Else
                              If  Student_grade = D  Then
                                        Numeric_equivalent = 1
                              Else
                                        If Student_grade = F Then
                                                  Numeric_equivalent = 0
                                        Else
                                                  If  Student_grade = W Then
                                                            Numeric_equivalent = null
                                                  Else
                                                            If  Student_grade = I Then
                                                                      Numeric_equivalent = null
                                                            Else
                                                                      Print Error Message
                                                                                Numeric_equivalent = null
                                                            Endif
                                                  Endif
                                        Endif
                              Endif
                    Endif
          Endif
Endif
Return
```

Figure 4.15 Pseudocode Grade Conversion

Case Statement

While Figure 4.15 is well organized, it still appears to be quite complex; and the indenting threatens to run off the page. The case statement is intended to relieve some of this difficulty. Essentially the *case* statement allows for multiple decisions where the if statement only allows for two. We will use the following syntax: Case (variable name) to indicate that the case statement is being used, and below that we will list the various cases and the appropriate assignment statements. The case statement will end with *Endcase.*

Example: Using the grade conversion process, the grade case statement looks like this:

```
Case Student_grade
        A      :  Numeric_grade = 4
        B      :  Numeric_ grade = 3
        C      :  Numeric_ grade = 2
        D      :  Numeric_ grade = 1
        F      :  Numeric_ grade = 0
        W      :  Numeric_ grade = null
        I      :  Numeric_ grade = null
        Other  :  Numeric_ grade = null
                  Print error message
Endcase
```

The logical path followed is represented by the line that matches the grade. After processing that line, the logic continues at the Endcase instruction.

Bowler's Problem

Finally, the pseudocode for the bowler's high score is shown.

```
High game module
     If Game_1_score > Game_2_score Then
          High_game = Game_1_score
          High_game_number = 1
     Else
          High_game = Game_2_score
          High_game_number = 2
     Endif
```

```
If Game_3_score > High_game Then
     High_game = Game_3_score
     High_game_number = 3
Else
Endif
Return
```

Summary

In this chapter we have studied the selection structure, also called decision or if structure. Three varieties of the selection structure can be used: sequential, nested, and case. The sequential decision structure places decisions in sequence so that regardless of the choice on the first decision, the second decision is applied. This is in direct contrast to the nested decision, where the second decision can be ignored depending on the first decision. This is not a trivial difference, and normally the sequential will not work when the nested does work. You should use extreme care reading decision flowcharts or pseudocode to make certain that you understand the results of the decision being made. You can't assume that the logic works the way that it's supposed to. You must carefully check the logic using some real data.

Key Terms

Each number in parentheses indicates the page where the term first occurs in the chapter.

case statement (86)	If,Then,Else,Endif (88)	selection structure (77)
Endcase (92)	nested if (81)	sequential decision (79)
Endif (88)	nesting (81)	sequential if (79)
If (76)	selection (76)	

Chapter 4
Exercises

Objective 1 Read flowcharts containing nested or sequential decision statements, or case statements.

1. Given the flowchart fragment in Figure 4.16, assume that the values stored at the counters are known to you (i.e., you know how many male freshmen were counted).

   Given those values, how could you personally determine:

   A. The total number of freshmen?

   B. The total number of men?

   C. The total number of women?

   D. The total number of seniors?

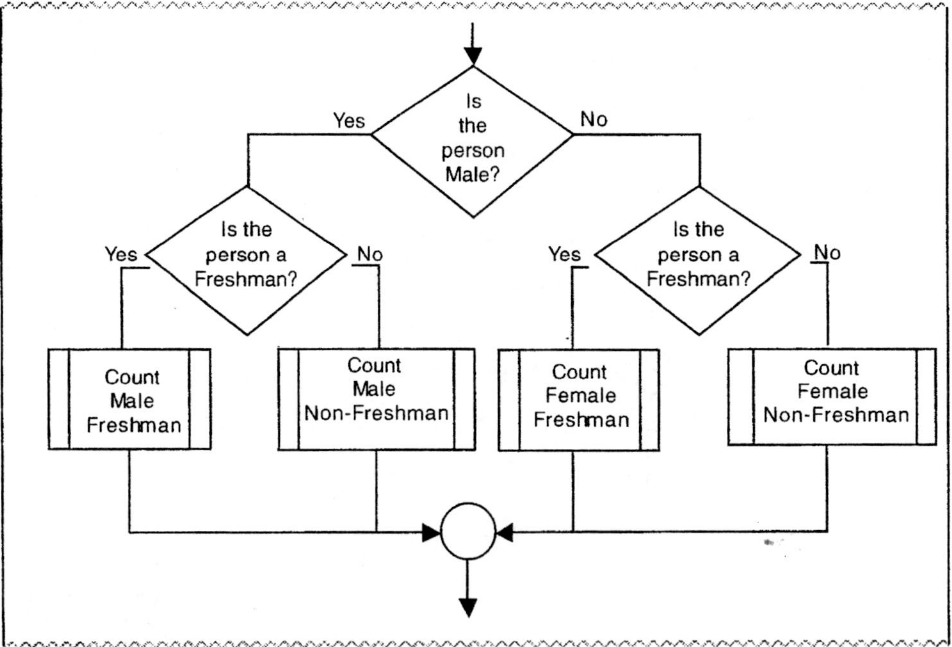

Figure 4.16 Objective 1 Exercise 1

2. Study the flowchart in Figure 4.17 and state what problem it is attempting to solve. Is it performing correctly? If not, what problems does it have?
3. Study the flowchart in Figure 4.18 and state what problem it is attempting to solve. Is it performing correctly? If not, what problems does it have?

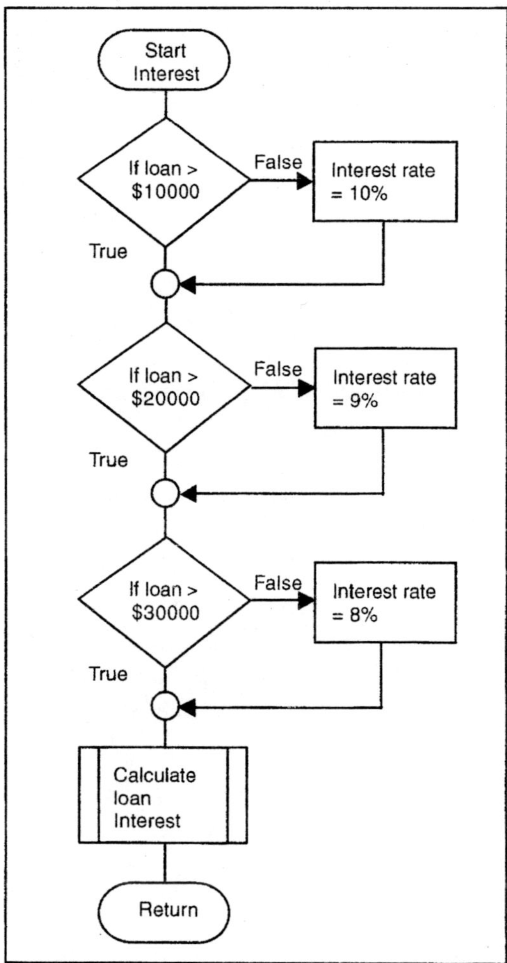

Figure 4.17 Objective 1 Exercise 2

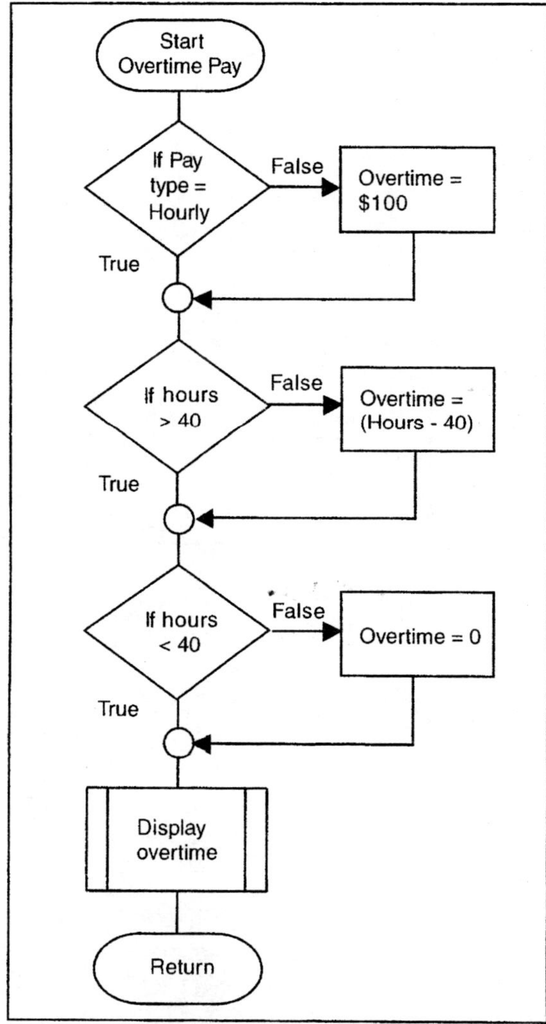

Figure 4.18 Objective 1 Exercise 3

4. Study the flowchart in Figure 4.19 and state what letter grade will be assigned to a test score of 75, based on the logic depicted.
5. Look at the flowchart in Figure 4.20 and identify the nested decisions and the sequential decisions. This requires examining decision symbols in pairs. Each decision symbol is numbered for your convenience. Examine all the pairs (1-2, 1-3, 1-4, 1-5, 1-6, 2-6, and so on). Some pairs of decisions are not related and therefore are neither nested nor sequential. Look at decisions 2 and 3, for example. Regardless of whether you answer question 2 true or false, the logic does not permit you to ask question number 3. Therefore, decisions 2 and 3 are not related.

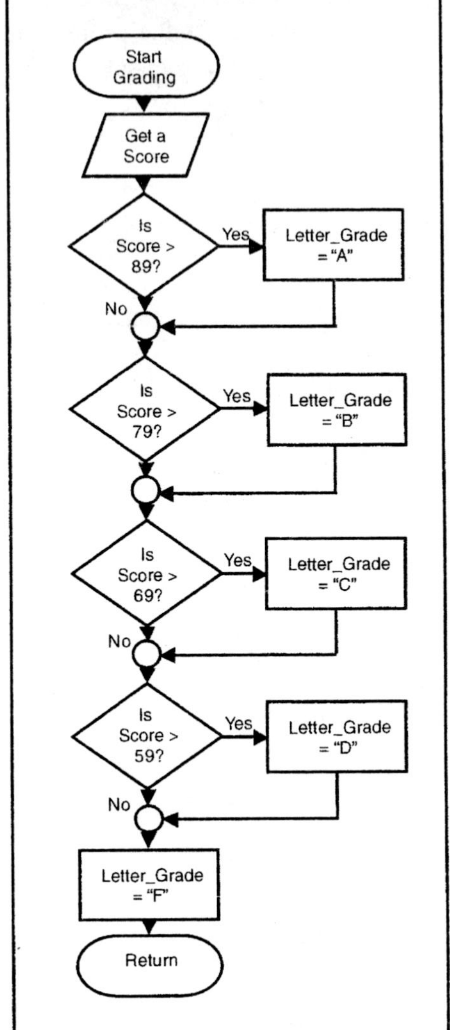

Figure 4.19
Objective 1 Exercise 4

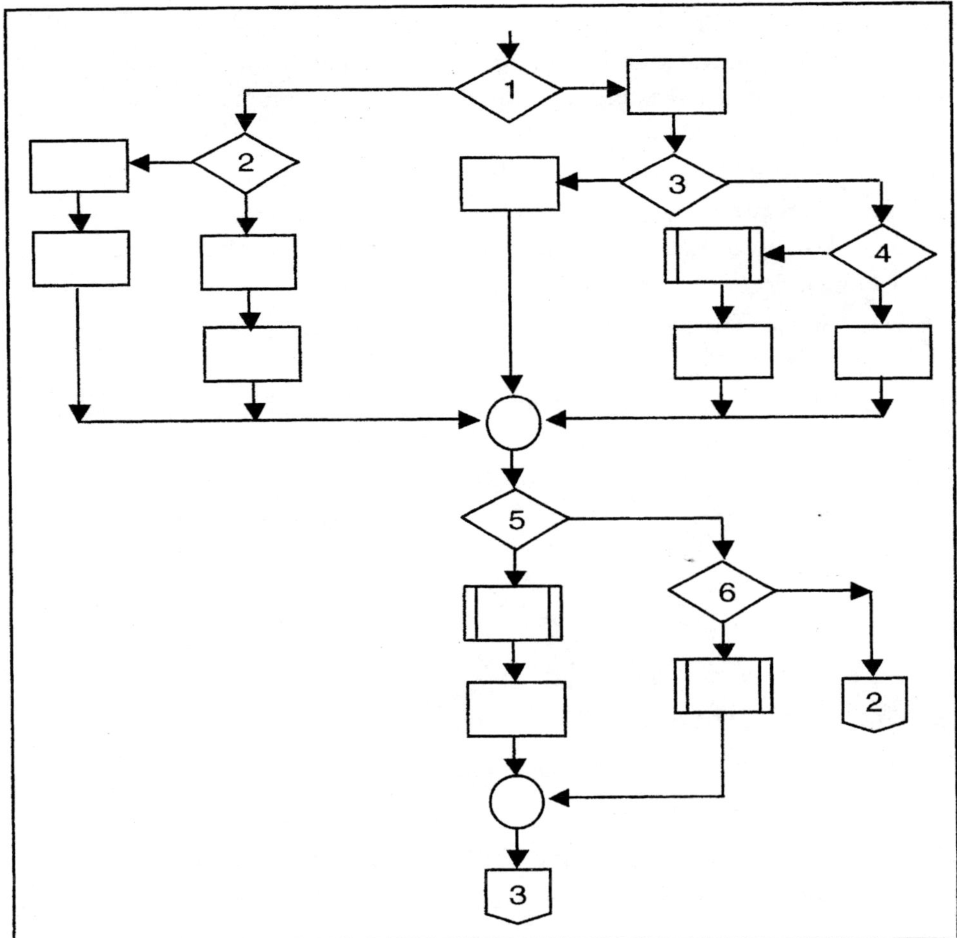

Figure 4.20 Objective 1 Exercise 5

Objective 2 Draw and revise flowcharts that require nested or sequential decision statements, or case statements.

1. Redraw the flowchart from Objective 1, Exercise 1, so that it would count the men, women, sophomores, juniors, and seniors in addition to the freshmen.

2. Redraw the flowchart in Objective 1, Exercise 2, so that it processes interest rates correctly.

3. Redraw the flowchart in Objective 1, Exercise 3, so that it processes interest rates correctly.

4. Redraw the flowchart in Objective 1, Exercise 4, so that it processes grades correctly.

5. Draw a flowchart that illustrates the logic for converting the numeric month symbols to the alphabetic month symbols. The input will be a number in the range of 1–12. The output (either printed or displayed) should be the abbreviated name of the month (Jan, Feb, and so on). So if 7 is the input, the output would be Jul. DON'T use tables or any other techniques beyond this chapter.

6. Draw a flowchart that illustrates the logic for converting the alphabetic month symbols to the numeric month symbols. The input will be the abbreviation for a month (Jan., Feb., and so on), and the output will be a number in the range of 1–12. So if Jul is the input, the output would be 7. DON'T use tables or any other techniques beyond this chapter.
7. Draw a flowchart that could be used to calculate gross pay. Allow for the possibilities of hourly, salaried, and commissioned pay rates. Allow for bonuses for all categories. Allow overtime for hourly employees only.
8. Draw a flowchart for the bowling problem that finds the lowest score and which game it occurred in.
9. Add or modify a flowchart for the bowling problem that adds three more players. Assume it's a mixed league, so there should be two men and two women on the team. The flowchart should find the highest series bowled (3 games) and which person bowled it. Provide for input of each persons name, so that the name can be displayed along with the high series. Also find the highest average and who bowled it.

Objective 3

Enrichment – Doing it with Pseudocode

Read pseudocode with nested or sequential decision statements, or case statements.

1. Given the pseudocode below, assume that the values stored at the counters are known to you (i.e., you know how many male freshmen were counted).

   Given those values, how could you determine the total number of freshmen?

   Total number of men?

   Total number of women?

   Total number of seniors?

```
Get Gender
   Get Class_status
   If Gender = Male Then
       If Class_status = Freshmen Then
            Number_of_male_Freshmen =
                  Number_of_male_Freshmen + 1
      Else Number_of_male_nonfreshmen = Number_of_male_
            nonfreshmen + 1
      Endif
```

```
Else
   If Class_status = Freshmen Then
         Number_of_female_ Freshmen = Number_of_female_
                                  Freshmen + 1
   Else Number_of_female_nonfreshmen =
                      Number_of_female_nonfreshmen + 1
   Endif
Endif
Print Number_of_male_Freshmen
Print Number_of_male_nonfreshmen
Print Number_of_female_ Freshmen
Print Number_of_female_ nonfreshmen
```

```
Return
```

2. Given the pseudocode fragment below, determine what is accomplished (be as specific as possible). What is the purpose of the program? What does it actually do? Does it do what it is supposed to? What is wrong with it, if anything?

```
Interest Rate Program
      If loan > 10000 Then
            Interest_rate = 10%
      Endif
      If loan > 20000 Then
            Interest_rate = 9%
      Endif
      If loan > 30000 Then
            Interest_rate = 8%
      Endif
      Return
```

3. Given the pseudocode fragment below, state what is accomplished (be as specific as possible).

```
Compute overtime pay
   If Pay_type = Hourly Then
```

```
   Else Overtime = $100
   Endif
   If hours_worked > 40  Then
         Else Overtime = (hours worked - 40)
   Endif
If hours_worked < 40  Then
         Else Overtime = 0
   Endif
   Ovetime_pay
   Return
```

4. Read the pseudocode fragment below, and state what grade it assigns to a score of 75.

```
Get Score
   If Score > 89 then
         Student_grade = A
   Else
   Endif
   If Score > 79 Then
         Student_grade = B
   Else
   Endif
   If Score > 69 Then
         Student_grade = C
   Else
   Endif
   If Score > 59 Then
         Student_grade = D
   Else
   Endif
   Student_grade = F
Return
```

Objective 4

Enrichment – Doing it with Pseudocode

Write and revise pseudocode with nested or sequential decision statements, or case statements.

1. Rewrite the pseudocode from Objective 3, Exercise 1, so that it would count the men, women, sophomores, juniors, and seniors in addition to the freshmen.
2. Rewrite the pseudocode in Objective 3, Exercise 2, so that it processes interest rates correctly.
3. Rewrite the pseudocode in Objective 3, Exercise 3, so that it processes overtime pay correctly.
4. Rewrite the pseudocode in Objective 3, Exercise 4, so that it processes grades correctly.
5. Write the pseudocode that illustrates the logic for converting the numeric month symbols to the alphabetic month symbols. The input will be a number in the range of 1–12. The output (either printed or displayed) should be abbreviated name of the month (Jan, Feb, and so on). So if 7 is the input, the output would be Jul. DON'T use tables or any other techniques beyond this chapter.
6. Write the pseudocode that illustrates the logic for converting the alphabetic month symbols to the numeric month symbols. The input will be the abbreviation for a month (Jan, Feb, and so on), and the output will be a number in the range of 1–12. So if Jul is the input, the output would be 7. DON'T use tables or any other techniques beyond this chapter.
7. Write the pseudocode that could be used to calculate gross pay. Allow for the possibilities of hourly, salaried, and commissioned pay rates. Allow for bonuses for all categories. Allow overtime for hourly employees only.
8. Write the pseudocode for the bowling problem that finds the lowest score and which game it occurred in.
9. Write the pseudocode for the bowling problem that adds three more players. Assume it's a mixed league, so there should be two men and two women on the team. The flowchart should find the highest series bowled (3 games) and which person bowled it. Provide for input of each person's name, so that they name can be displayed along with the high series. Also find the highest average and who bowled it.

Other Assignments

SoftSkills

Select one problem from Objective 2 or 4, or from the Internet/library research projects below, prepare and give an oral report to the class on your solution.

Internet/library research projects

A. Find a flowchart that describes a solution not presented in the textbook, and write a report on it.

B. Find a pseudocode solution to some problem not presented in the textbook, and write a report on it.

5

COMPOUND LOGIC

Somebody who thinks logically is a nice contrast to the real world

(The Law of Thumb)

OBJECTIVES

After completing this chapter, you will be able to:

1. Determine the truth of a compound logic statement.
2. Read and draw flowcharts using the compound logic of "and", "or", and "not" statements.
3. Read and write pseudocode using the compound logic of "and", "or", and "not" statements.

Introduction

Up to this point, we have focused on solving problems using simple logic statements like: "Is maximum > 10". The difference, symbolically, between this simple statement and a compound statement seems almost trivial. A compound statement would read: "Is maximum ≥ 10". However, the logic difference between these two statements is significant. In the first statement we branch when the value of the variable "maximum" becomes 11. In the second statement we branch as soon as the value of "maximum" is 10.

The symbol > means greater than, whereas the symbol ≥ means greater than *or* equal to. The word *or* creates a compound statement. Many times, confusion can be avoided by not using compound statements. Let's look at a flowchart fragment example to see how to avoid the compound logic (Figure 5.1).

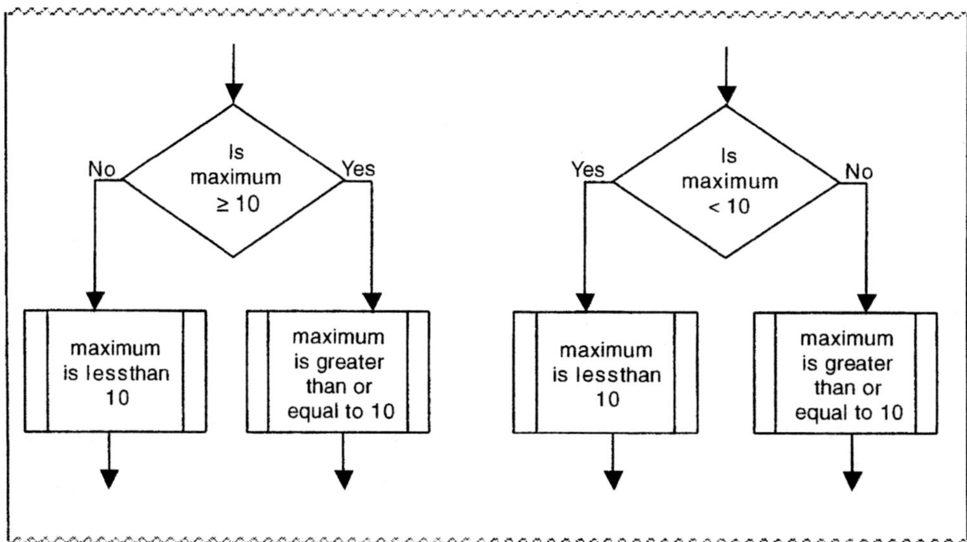

Figure 5.1 Compound Logic

Figure 5.1 depicts the flowchart for the compound statement "Is maximum ≥ 10" (read as maximum greater than *or* equal to 10) on the left side. The right-hand flowchart depicts a flowchart for a simple logic statement that accomplishes the same thing as the compound statement. On the left side of Figure 5.1, we are testing the value of the variable named "maximum" to see if it is greater than or equal to 10. If that is true, then we take the right-hand branch of the decision. If "maximum" is not greater than or equal to 10, then we take the left-hand branch of the decision.

On the right-hand side of Figure 5.1, we have reversed the "yes" and "no," and we have changed "≥" to "<". The resulting logic is identical to the left-hand side of the figure, but note that we have avoided using compound logic.

Many times we use compound logic because it accurately reflects the customer's statement and is, therefore, easier for the customer to understand. However, in general, programs are easier to write and debug if the logic is kept at the simplest possible level.

Three generic terms are used to create compound logic: *or*, *and*, and *not*. We'll look at each in some detail in the following paragraphs, but first we need to examine the order of these operations.

Order of Operations

In an earlier chapter, we examined the order of arithmetic operators. The same concern for the *order of operations* applies to logical operators. For purposes of this text, the following order of operations will apply. First, the *not* operator is evaluated; second, the *and* operator is evaluated; and third, the *or* operator is evaluated.

For example, imagine that you want to evaluate the statement: "If x is less than 7, not greater than 4, and even, or divisible by 3, then display 'Everything is OK.' Given that x = 4, we would evaluate the statement in the following order:

1. x is greater than 4 (false).
2. x is not greater than 4 (true).
3. x is less then 7 (true)
4. The resule from step 2 is true and the result from step 3 is true so the combined expression is true.
5. x is even (true).
6. The result from step 4 is true, and the result from step 5 is true, so the combined expression is true.
7. x is divisible by 3 (false).
8. The result from step 6 is true. The result from step 7 is false, but we combine them with an "or" so the result is true.
9. The compound statement is true, so we would display the message 'Everything is OK.'

The previous process is explained in greater detail in the remainder of the chapter.

And

When we use the word "and", we connect two logical statements that must both be true in order for the resulting compound decision to be true. We can see that in table form in Table 5.1.

Table 5.1 And Table

Case Number	Statement 1	Statement 2	Statement 1 and Statement 2
1	True	True	True
2	True	False	False
3	False	True	False
4	False	False	False

Notice that the compound result is only true when both Statement 1 and Statement 2 are true. Every other situation means that the result is false. Here is a real-life example:

Assume that hourly employees receive overtime pay if they work more than 40 hours.

1. Jim Smith worked 41 hours.
   Jim Smith is an hourly employee.
   Should Jim Smith get overtime pay?
2. Jim Smith worked 41 hours.
   Jim Smith is a salaried employee.
   Should Jim Smith get overtime pay?
3. Jim Smith worked 40 hours.
   Jim Smith is an hourly employee.
   Should Jim Smith get overtime pay?
4. Jim Smith worked 40 hours.
   Jim Smith is a salaried employee.
   Should Jim Smith get overtime pay?

These examples can be summarized into the truth table, Table 5.2, which is representative of our example problem.

Table 5.2 Employee Pay

Case Number	Employee is paid hourly	Employee worked more than 40 hours	Employee gets overtime pay
1	True	True	True
2	False	True	False
3	True	False	False
4	False	False	False

We can use either the written example or the truth table in Table 5.2 to draw a flowchart of the decision process. That flowchart is shown in Figure 5.2.

You might notice that the flowchart in Figure 5.2 contains a nested decision before we move on to the "or".

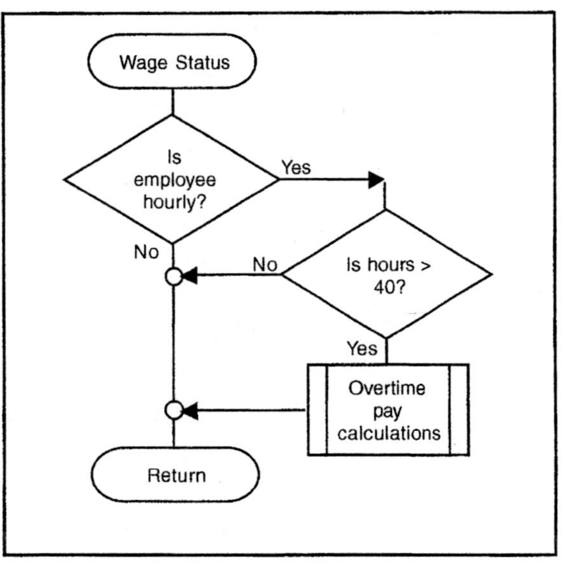

Figure 5.2 And Flowchart

Or

Using the word "or" connects two statements where the resulting compound statement is true if either one or both of the statements is true[1]. As in the "and" case, we can summarize these possibilities into a truth table, shown in Table 5.3.

Table 5.3 Or Table

Case Number	Statement 1	Statement 2	Statement 1 or Statement 2
1	True	True	True
2	True	False	True
3	False	True	True
4	False	False	False

1 Instructor note: Here we are using the inclusive form of the disjunction only. another form (exclusive is where the compound statement is not true when both statements are true, but we will leave that for another course.

Notice that the compound result is only false when both Statement 1 and Statement 2 are false. Every other situation means that the result is true. Here are some real-life examples similar to our previous examples:

Assume that hourly or salaried employees may receive overtime pay. Overtime pay is calculated based on the number of hours worked and other factors.

1. Jim Smith worked 41 hours.
   Jim Smith is an hourly employee.
   Should Jim Smith overtime pay be calculated?
2. Jim Smith worked 1 hour.
   Jim Smith is a salaried employee.
   Should Jim Smith overtime pay be calculated?
3. Jim Smith worked 40 hours.
   Jim Smith is an hourly employee.
   Should Jim Smith overtime pay be calculated?
4. Jim Smith worked 41 hours.
   Jim Smith is a commissioned employee.
   Should Jim Smith overtime pay be calculated?

And again we can summarize our example into a truth table for this specific problem as shown in Table 5.4.

Table 5.4 Employee Pay with Or

Case Number	Employee is hourly	Employee is salaried	Overtime is calculated
1	True	True	True
2	True	False	True
3	False	True	True
4	False	False	False

In this example, there is no implication that the employee will actually receive overtime pay, but the calculation will be performed. We can again display the decision process in flowchart form as shown in Figure 5.3.

You might now observe that the "or" is also flowcharted as a nested "if" statement.

The flowchart symbol in Figure 5.4 is an example of compound logic that should not be used. It can easily be interpreted incorrectly. The simple logic of Figures 5.2 or 5.3 is easier to understand.

Figure 5.5 depicts the logic that Figure 5.4 is intended to illustrate. Decide what you think Figure 5.4 says before proceeding to study Figure 5.5.

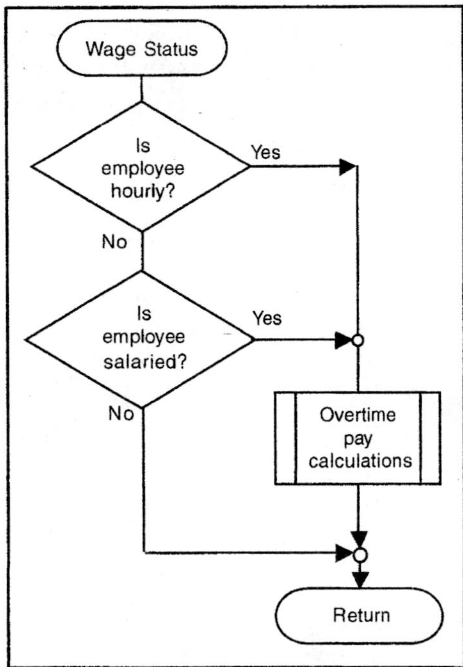

Figure 5.3 Or Flowchart

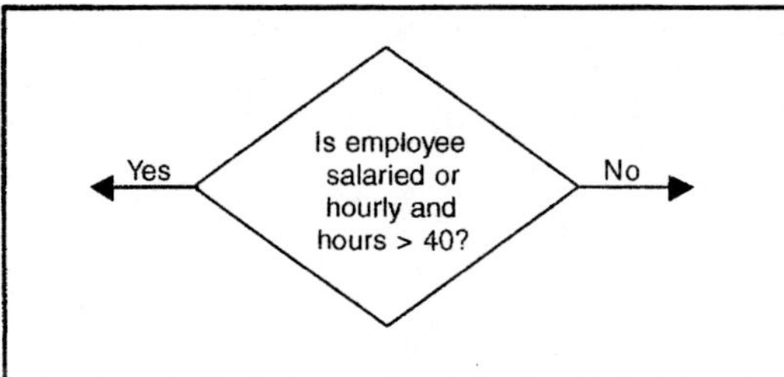

Figure 5.4 Compound Logic

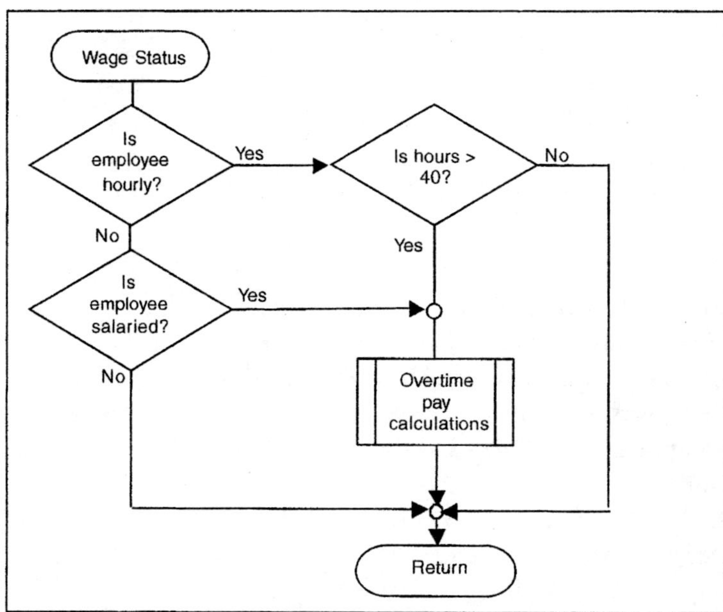

Figure 5.5 Simple Logic

Figure 5.5 shows that hourly employees only receive overtime if they work more than 40 hours, but salaried employees may receive overtime regardless of the hours worked. We have to assume that the overtime pay calculation module somehow knows how to do the calculation.

Not

Our final compound logic term is "not". In decision structures it is used to reverse the truth of a statement. So if we start with a true statement and place a "not" in front of the statement, the resulting statement is false (not true). In this simple form, "not" seems relatively harmless. We would use it easily in the sentence: "If hours worked are not greater than 40, then you don't get overtime pay." Notice that this is equivalent to saying: "If hours worked are greater than 40, you get overtime pay."

However, the "not" statement is probably the most dangerous form of compound statements because several interpretations of compound statements are available when "not" is used.

For example, what do we mean by: "Not Statement 1 and Statement 2"? Parentheses might be helpful. The previous sentence could be: "Not (Statement 1 and Statement 2)" or "(Not Statement 1) and Statement 2".

Let's see if we can produce the two generic truth tables for this example. See Tables 5.5 and 5.6.

Table 5.5 Not Both Statements

Case Number	Statement 1	Statement 2	Statement 1 and Statement 2	Not (Statement 1 and Statement 2)
1	True	True	True	False
2	True	False	False	True
3	False	True	False	True
4	False	False	False	True

Perhaps the easiest way to develop the new truth table is to take the previous truth table for the "and" statement and then reverse the truth of the fourth column to get the new result. You can compare this table with Table 5.2 to see the transformation.

Using our earlier payroll example, we might see this expression: Jim Smith does not get overtime pay if he is not salaried and did not work over 40 hours (not salaried and not over 40 hours).

Now look at Table 5.6 and compare it closely with Table 5.5. Clearly the two statements: "Not (Statement 1 and Statement 2)" or "(Not Statement 1) and Statement 2" provide dramatically different results.

Table 5.6 Not Statement One

Case Number	Statement 1	Statement 2	Not Statement 1)	(Not Statement 1 and Statement 2)
1	True	True	False	False
2	True	False	False	False
3	False	True	True	True
4	False	False	True	False

We could prepare a similar table for "(Not Statement 2) and Statement 1", but the results would be essentially the same.

For payroll, we might see this expression: Jim Smith does not get overtime pay because he is not salaried and he worked over 40 hours.

Similar problems are caused with the compound statement: "Not Statement 1 or Statement 2". Development of those tables is left for exercises.

Enrichment – Doing it with Pseudocode

Adding compound statements to pseudocode requires only the addition of the words "not", "and", and "or". These words are added to the decision statements from Chapter 4 to produce the new logic. For example, Figure 5-1 would be written in pseudocode as:

```
Get Gender
   If maximum ≥ 10 Then
         (add appropriate action)
   Else (add appropriate action
   Endif
```

For the compound condition or,

```
   If maximum < 10 Then
   Else
   Endif
```

For the simple condition.

Figure 5-2 would be written in pseudocode as:

```
Wage status program
```

```
    If Employee_code = hourly Then
          If hours > 40 Then
                Overtime pay
          Else
          Endif
    Else
    Endif
    Return
```

The Figure 5-3 pseudocode is:

```
Wage status program
    If Employee_code = hourly Then
          Overtime pay
    Else      If Employee_code = salary Then
                Overtime pay
          Endif
    Else
    Endif
    Return
```

The pseudocode for Figure 5-4 is:

```
Wage status program
    If Employee_code = hourly Then
          If hours > 40 Then
                Overtime pay
    Else      If Employee_code = salaried Then
                Overtime pay
          Endif
    Else
    Endif
    Return
```

Summary

The use of compound statements in designing, flowcharting, and programming can cause a great deal of confusion. Avoid using the compound statements when a simple statement will perform the task as well. This doesn't mean that compound logic should never be used. However, the goal of programming is to make the system work properly, and usually simple is easier to check than compound. As an example, consider the two pseudocode statements that follow:

1. If balance Not > 0 and not < 0 then print name.
2. If balance = 0 then print name.

Suppose that you have a program reading through a customer file and wish to print a list of customers' names that have a zero balance on their last invoice. Are these two statements equivalent? Why? If you said yes, what assumption did you make about the value of the balance? (Could it be less than zero?)

Truth tables can be useful in understanding the decisions that have to be made within a program. Many times the customer will be able to state the decisions in their own language. The good systems analyst will take the customer's language and translate it into a flowchart or pseudocode. Many times the truth table is used as an intermediate step between the plain language and the flowchart. In this course we have looked at very simple decisions, and the use of truth tables may seem unnecessary; but as you expand into more complex problems, you should see the value in using truth tables

One parting thought is the old business principle called the KISS principle (Keep It Simple Stupid). Computer programmers, systems analysts, and software engineers would do well to learn that business principle, especially as it applies to compound logic statements.

Key Terms

Each number in parentheses indicates the page where the term first occurs in the chapter.

and (104) or (107) order of operations (105)

not (110)

Chapter 5
Exercises

Objective 1 Determine the truth of a compound logic statement.

1. A light will come on based on the position of three switches. If one or more of the switches is off, the light will not come on. Identify all the switch positions that will result in the light being on.
2. Given the sentence: "If the value of the variable is not less than 10 and is less than 16 or is not greater than 25, then the light comes on." Determine if the light comes on for the following values of the variable:

5	10	20	25
12	100	16	

3. Develop the truth tables for the following statement:

   (not Statement 1) or Statement 2
4. Develop the truth tables for the following statement:

   not (Statement 1 or Statement 2)
5. Given the statement "Update a file if a sale or a payment was made and pay a commission to the salesperson if a sale was made, but don't pay a commission if no sale was made", explain in your own words what that statement will cause to happen in all situations that are described within the statement.
6. Given the following problem decide when to send a promotional letter, and describe the process in your own words. Send a promotional letter to a customer who owns a home and a telephone or who rents a home and has a telephone but not to anyone under 25 unless they are married.
7. At Powerhouse University (old PU), out of district students are charged a special fee if they are taking less than 12 hours for the semester, but not charged the fee if they are seniors unless they are taking less than 6 hours. Complete Table 5-7 by deciding which students pay a fee.

Table 5-7 Objective 1 Exercise 7

Name	Class	Hour load	Sex	Age	In district	Charge (y or n)
Smith	Senior	12	M	37	Yes	
Jones	Freshman	12	F	18	Yes	
Cartman	Sophomore	9	M	22	No	
Squarepants	Junior	6	F	19	Yes	
Bush	Senior	3	M	20	No	

8. Smokers and drinkers tend to have more auto accidents than non-drinkers and non-smokers. Very old and very young people also tend to have more accidents than people of ages 25-55. The insurance companies have established categories of insurance based on an individual's habits, sex, and age. Assume that a person who is not a man and is a drinker but not a smoker is under 25. Compare that person's insurance risk to a person who is a smoker or a drinker and 45 years old and is a woman. Hint: Make a table of the different categories, and assign values to each category or combination of categories and then determine where these two people fit into the table.

Objective 2 Read and draw flowcharts using the compound logic of "and", "or", and "not" statements.

1. Draw a flowchart fragment using simple logic that performs the task of the compound logic statement: "If maximum is not less than 10 or maximum is greater than 15, then display a message otherwise continue."
2. Break down the following compound statement into a combination of simple statements: "If the number of students is less than or equal to10 and the professor is a full-time employee, cancel the class, otherwise the class will make." Draw a flowchart to show how the simple logic flow would proceed.
3. Draw a flowchart fragment using simple logic that performs the task of the compound logic statement: "If maximum is not less than 10, then display a message otherwise continue."
4. Draw the flowchart for the decision process in Objective 1 Problem 2 using simple logic only.
5. Draw the flowchart for the decision process in Objective 1 Problem 5 using simple logic only.
6. Draw the flowchart for the decision process in Objective 1 Problem 6 using simple logic only.
7. Draw the flowchart for the decision process in Objective 1 Problem 7 using simple logic only.
8. Draw the flowchart for the decision process in Objective 1 Problem 8 using simple logic only.

Objective 3

Enrichment – Doing it with Pseudocod

Read and write pseudocode using the compound logic of "and", "or", and "not" statements.

1. Write a pseudocode fragment using simple logic that performs the task of the compound logic statement: "If maximum is not less than 10 or maximum is greater than 15, then display a message, otherwise continue."
2. Break down the following compound statement into a combination of simple statements. Write pseudocode to show how the simple logic flow would proceed: "If the number of students is less than or equal to10 and the professor is a full-time employee, cancel the class; otherwise the class will make."
3. Write a pseudocode fragment using simple logic that performs the task of the compound logic statement: "If maximum is not less than 10, then display a message otherwise continue."
4. Write a pseudocode fragment for the decision process in Objective 1 Problem 2 using simple logic only.
5. Write a pseudocode fragment for the decision process in Objective 1 Problem 5 using simple logic only.
6. Write a pseudocode fragment for the decision process in Objective 1 Problem 6 using simple logic only.
7. Write a pseudocode fragment for the decision process in Objective 1 Problem 7 using simple logic only.
8. Write a pseudocode fragment for the decision process in Objective 1 Problem 8 using simple logic only.

Other Assignments

SoftSkills

Select one problem from Objective 2 or 3 or from the Internet/library research projects below. Prepare and give an oral report to the class on your solution.

Internet/library research projects

Research one of the topics in compound logic below and write a paper on that subject.

Classical logic

A. Classical logic
B. Truth-functional propositional logic.
C. First-order predicate logic.
D. Symbolic logic.

THE ITERATION STRUCTURES

Iteration, like friction, is likely to generate heat instead of progress.
(George Eliot)

OBJECTIVES

After completing this chapter, you will be able to:

1. Read flowcharts containing iteration structures.
2. Draw and revise flowcharts containing iteration structures.
3. Read pseudocode containing iteration structures.
4. Write and revise pseudocode containing iteration structures.
5. Understand the iteration process and its use.

Introduction

Now that you have learned about the second structure of structured design, selection, we are ready to learn the third and final structure, *iteration*. Iteration is defined to be the repeating of a set of tasks. The three structures—sequence, iteration, and decision—are the only three structures that you need in order to design or write a computer program. The iteration structure is also referred to as *repetition* and *loop*. Here the words loop and iteration are used interchangeably.

The iteration structure was developed so that a programmer or designer could avoid some repetitious coding. Without the loop, programmers were forced to rewrite the same set of instructions repeatedly. Also, without the loop, we are forced to repeat entire programs when we only need to repeat a portion of the program. Take the flowchart fragment in Chapter 4, Figure 4.12 as an example. This flowchart assigns a numeric value for a letter grade. It allows for the input of one grade. If we want to input a second grade, based on what we see, we would have to start the program from the beginning. But if we could loop from the bottom of the flowchart back to the input symbol, we could continue to enter grades without restarting the program.

Two variations of loops are used. If the number of repetitions is known in advance and we use that number to count through the loop, we call the loop a *counter loop*. If the process is set to continue until some event (condition) has occurred, then we use the term *conditional loop*.

Flowcharting the Loop

There is no flowchart symbol for a loop. The loop is flowcharted by combining the decision symbol with a process (or predetermined process) symbol and a flow line that returns (loops) back to the decision symbol. Figure 6.1 shows one example of a generic loop flowchart.

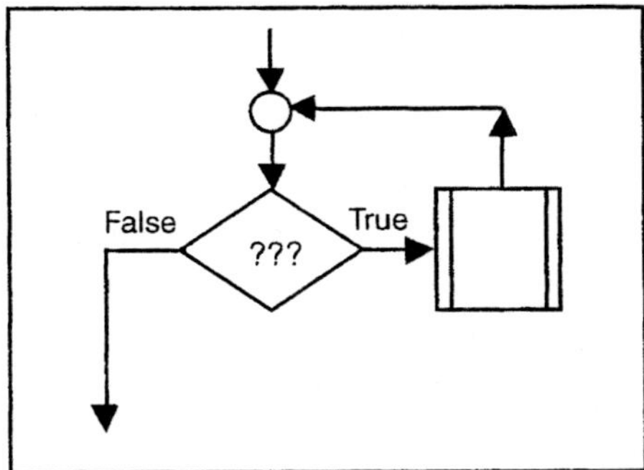

Figure 6.1 Generic loop

Counter Loop

The first type of loop mentioned in the introduction is the *counter loop*. Counter loops are loops that are controlled by a counter. This type of loop is very useful when you know that you want to accomplish a task a specific number of times. An example might be calculating the grades for a class of 20 students. Here we know that we must repeat a process 20 times. The flowchart for this problem would look like Figure 6.2. A counter loop consists of four elements. First, a counter is initialized, normally to zero, then the counter is incremented, normally by one, and then the process is accomplished. Finally, the counter is tested to determine if the loop needs to be terminated. The initialization of the counter must occur outside of the loop or the loop will continue indefinitely (infinite loop). However, the other elements of the loop can be arranged in several different ways, which may cause different results. Figure 6.2 illustrates a basic counter loop.

Figure 6.3 depicts a different arrangement of the loop elements. Study Figure 6.3 carefully and see if the loop process produces the same results as Figure 6.2.

Planning loops requires some thought. Look at the loop in Figure 6.4 and see if you can discover a problem with it.

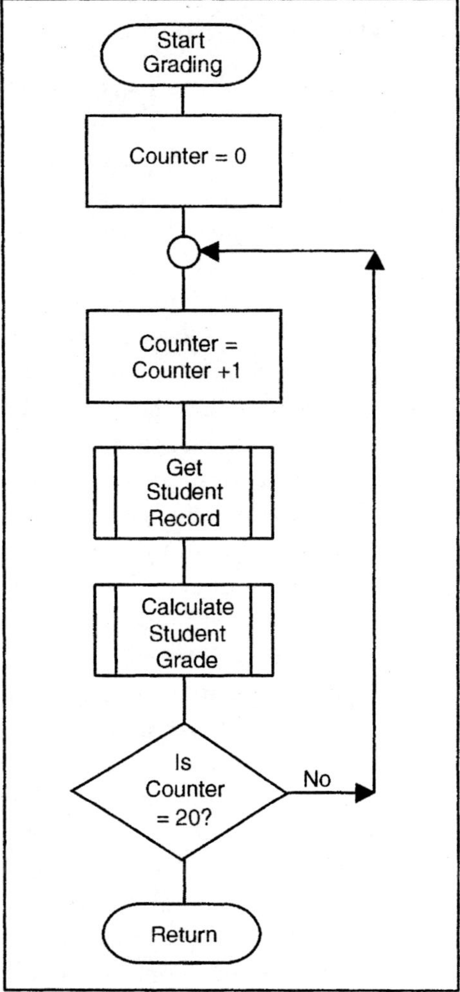

Figure 6.2 Counter loop

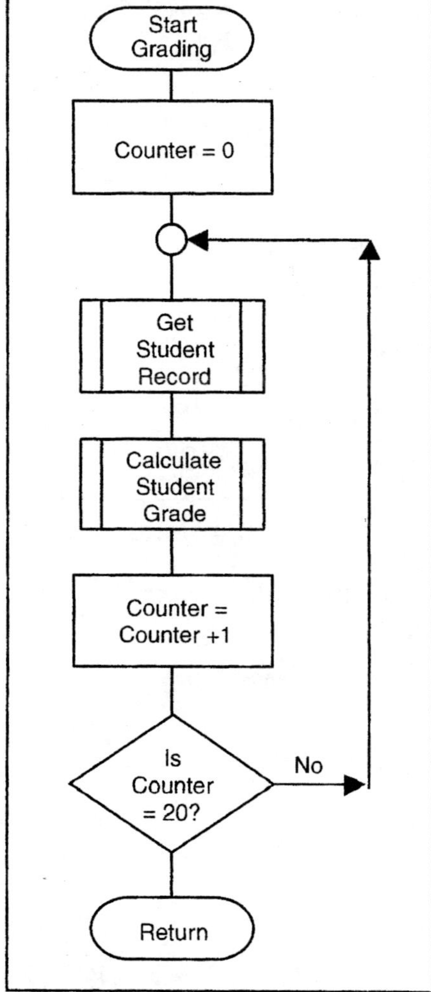

Figure 6.3
Counter loop variation

Infinite Loop

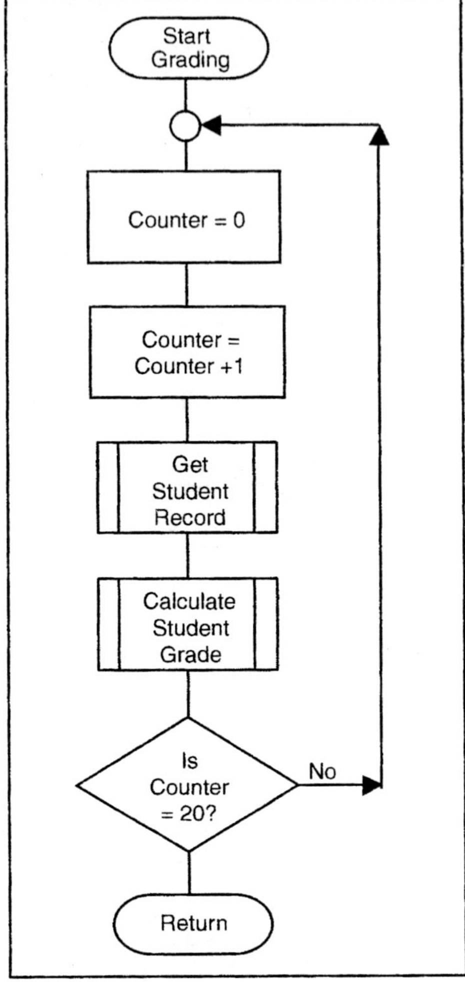

Figure 6.4 Infinite loop

Figure 6.4 depicts an *infinite loop*. The first step of the flowchart sets Counter to zero. Next Counter gets incremented to 1. Then the student record and grade processes are complete and checked against the limit of 20. Since 1 is not equal to 20, the loop repeats and Counter is set to zero. So each time through the loop Counter is reset to zero and can never reach 20. It's very important that the counter be initialized outside the loop and not inside the loop. In this example, everyone may think that an infinite loop is a trivial problem. However, in real programs, infinite loops pop up routinely, even though we do our best to avoid them. Infinite loops are seldom intentional and normally are a result of a programmer error.

A good programmer will recognize an infinite loop in a program very quickly but may spend hours trying to find where the infinite loop is created in the program. Has your computer ever "locked up" and you pressed Ctrl + Alt + Del to get it moving again? Most likely the computer was stuck in an infinite loop. The problem of the infinite loop is an excellent example of the need to desk check your programs before getting to the computer. Desk checking was introduced in an earlier chapter, but the need to check increases as the complexity of the problem increases.

Figure 6.5 illustrates another arrangement of the elements in a counter loop. Here there is a very different result in the processing when compared to Figure 6.2 or Figure 6.3. Desk check this loop carefully, and you will see that it only processes 19 students instead of the required 20.

Figure 6.5 illustrates another difficulty with planning loops. You have to make certain that the loop is incremented and exited properly, or the loop won't perform the expected calculations.

There are several other arrangements of the loop elements that produce a variety of results. The complete display of the counter loop varieties is shown in Appendix B.

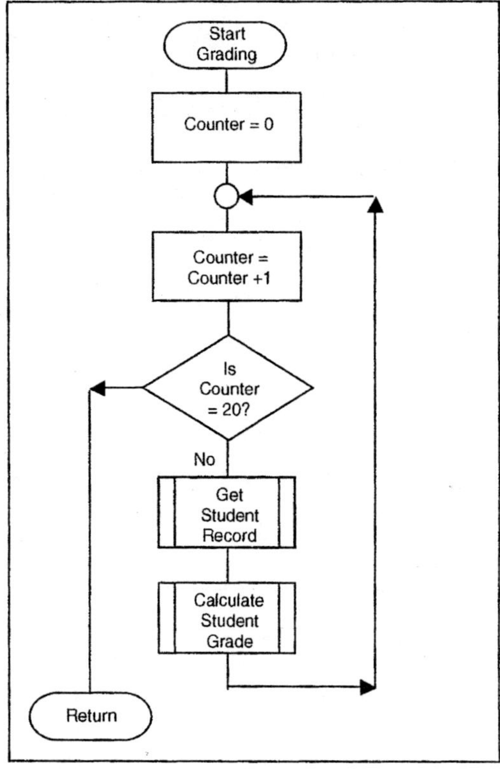

Figure 6.5
Counter loop second variation

Conditional Loops

Conditional loops can be classified in two different ways: pre-condition and post-condition. In the *pre-condition loop*, we ask a question: "Should we perform a process?" If the answer is yes, we perform the process and then ask the question again. In the *post-condition loop*, we perform a process and then ask if the process should be repeated.

Figure 6.6 shows the generic pre-condition loop. The True/False branches of the decision symbol have not been labeled because they could be assigned to either position.

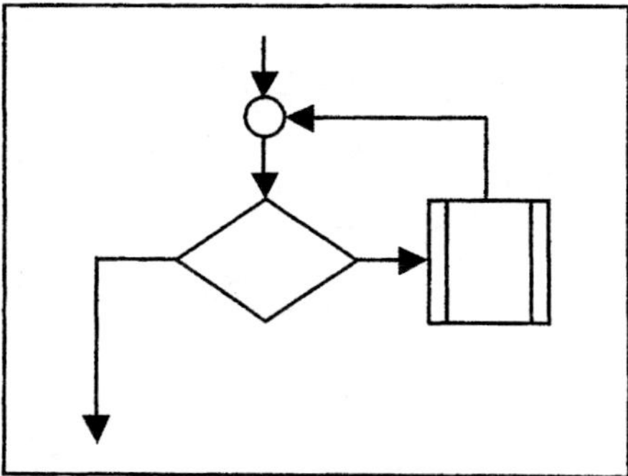

Figure 6.6 Conditional loop

Figure 6.7 shows the post-condition loop. Notice the difference between Figures 6.6 and 6.7. In the pre-condition loop, the decision is made before the process; while in the post-condition loop, the decision is made after the process.

Let's see an example. Suppose we are asked to flowchart the loop related to this statement: If an employee worked overtime, pay overtime pay. Figure 6.8 depicts a flowchart for this statement.

Now examine this statement: Calculate the pay of each employee. Figure 6.9 depicts a flowchart for this statement.

You should see from the previous two examples that the problem helps to determine the type of loop used.

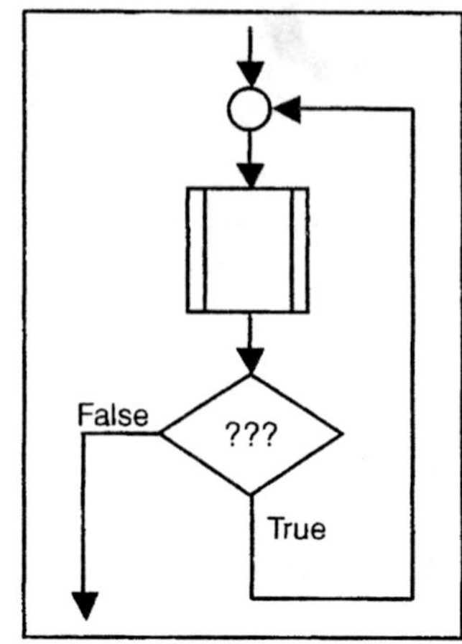

Figure 6.7
Post-condition loop

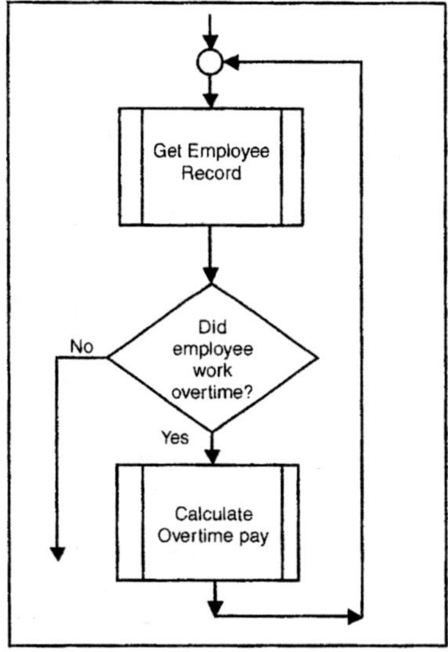

Figure 6.8 Employee pay

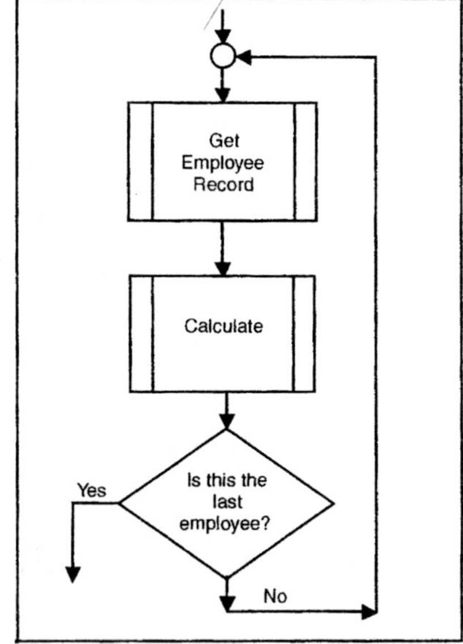

Figure 6.9
Each employee pay

Sequential Loops

The loop structure is powerful and subtle. Small changes in the structure can produce many different results. We can add another layer of complexity by adding a second loop in sequence with the first. That results in a structure called *sequential loops*, and it is analogous to the sequential decisions in Chapter 4. In sequential loops, the first loop is completed, then the next loop is started, and so on. This process is illustrated in Figure 6.10.

Notice in Figure 6.10 that the first process is completed 10 times, and the second process is completed 10 times. The loops are in sequence with the first loop completing before the second loop starts.

Since there are sequential decisions and sequential loops, you might wonder if there are nested loops to correspond with nested decisions, and the answer is "yes".

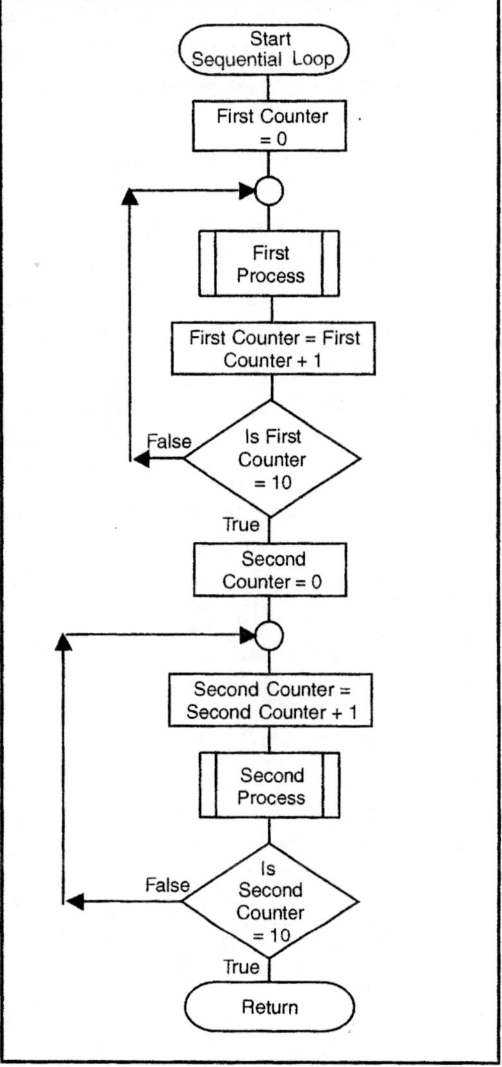

Figure 6.10 Sequential loop

Nested Loops

Nested loops are extremely useful when working with multidimensional tables, the subject of our next chapter. Before proceeding to that chapter, we'll look at the structure of a generic nested loop. Nested loops will have more than one counter. Specifically, there is one counter per loop. Sequential loops can be formed with one counter, but nested loops cannot. See Figure 6.11.

In Figure 6.11, you can see that there is a loop for process one completely contained inside the process two loop. This is a double-nested loop. Triple-nested loops would have another loop inside the innermost loop, and so on. In Figure 6.11, how many total times does process one get performed?

A note on accumulators: accumulators, like counters, require some form of loop to work properly. Remember from Chapter 1 that an accumulator begins at zero (normally) and can be incremented by variable amounts to produce a total. An accumulator flowchart is shown in Figure 6.12.

Notice in Figure 6.12 that the accumulator "Total Income" has been initialized to a value of zero. That is a necessary step to ensure that the total income is the correct total after the program has run.

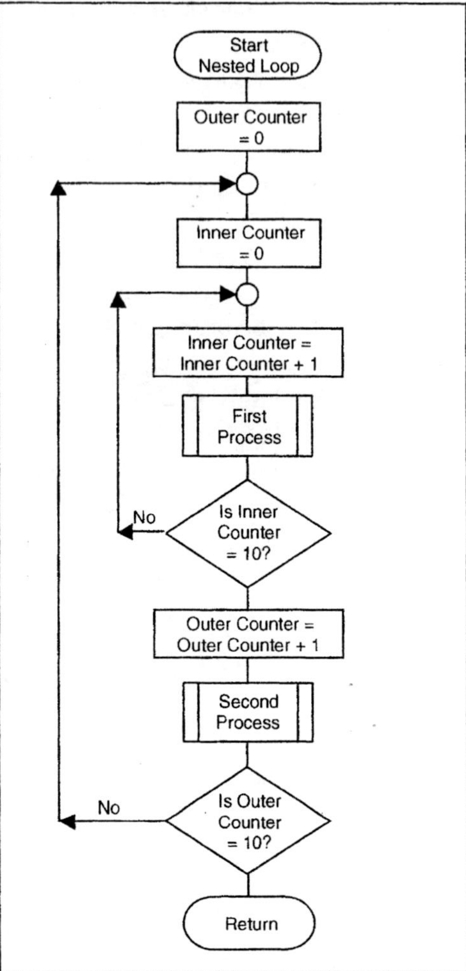

Figure 6.11 Nested Loops

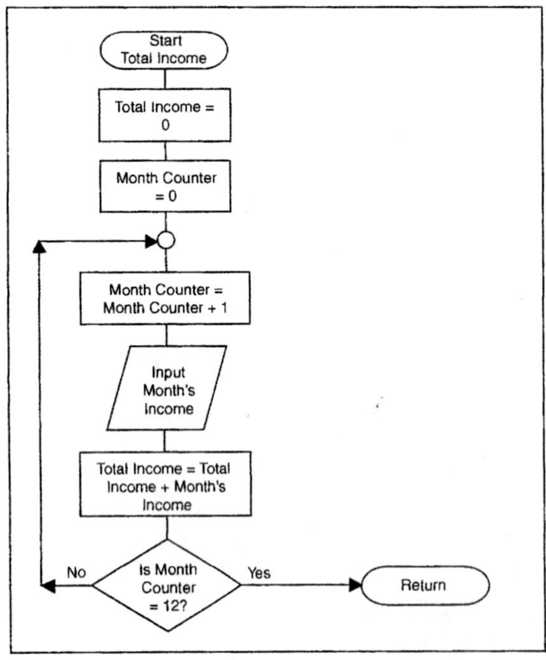

Figure 6.12 Accumulator

Bowling Problem

You have seen several general styles of loops that can be used to control the flow of a program; now let's examine how these loops can help us in the bowling program that we're developing. In previous chapters, we had to enter a bowler's score for each game and then do the calculations with all of the scores. The loop allows us to simplify the logic used to accumulate totals. Compare the flowchart in Figure 6.13 with Figure 3.14(2).

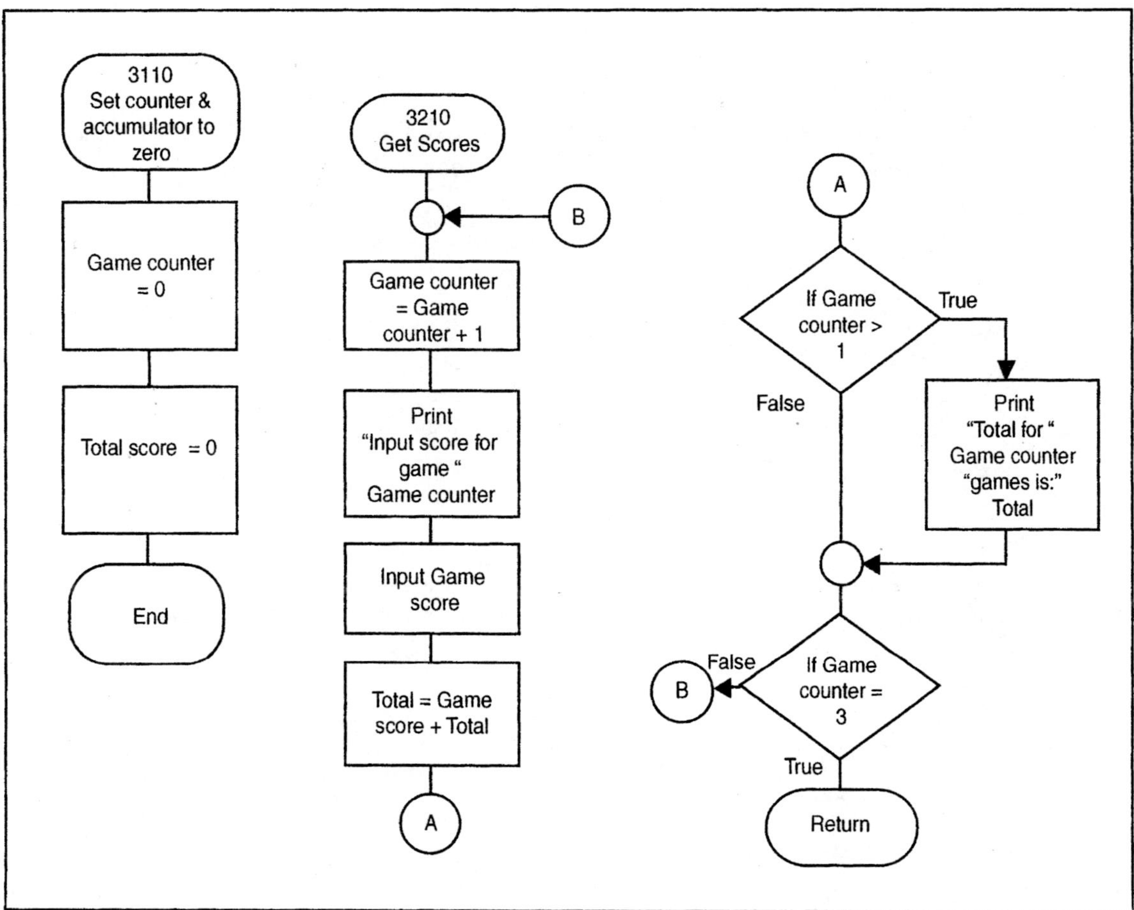

Figure 6.13 Bowling scores

The flowchart in Figure 6.13 makes full use of the decision structure and iteration structure to condense the flowchart of Figure 3.14 to the flowchart shown in Figure 6.13. One module has been eliminated, and 13 processes have been reduced to 7. Reducing the number of modules is not necessarily a goal in programming, but reducing the number of instructions is often a goal. Here we have also reduced the number of variable names, which results in saving memory, another goal in programming.

Enrichment – Doing it with Pseudocode

Pre-condition loops will be represented by the command ***While … End while***. The command for post-condition loops will be ***Repeat … Until***.

The While … Endwhile loop looks like this:

```
While condition A is True
      (tasks to be performed)
Endwhile
```

This loop tests a condition; and if the condition is true, then some task or group of tasks is completed. After the task(s) are completed, the condition is checked again. Notice that the statements inside the loop are indented. This improves readability.

Here's an example:

```
Input Investment
Interest_rate = .05
While Interest_rate is < .08
      Interest_earned = Interest_rate * Investment
      Print  Interest earned
      Interest_rate = Interest_rate + .0025
Endwhile
End
```

In this example we are printing a table of interest earned at various interest rates beginning at 5% and increasing by $^1/_2$ % until reaching 7.75%. Notice that the interest is not displayed for 8%. The user is allowed to input any investment amount, and the program prints the table.

Assuming an investment of $1,000 and the proper formatting, the program would produce the output in Table 6.1.

Table 6.1 Interest earned

Interest Rate	Interest Earned
0.0500	$50.00
0.0525	$52.50
0.0550	$55.00
0.0575	$57.50
0.0600	$60.00
...	
0.0775	$77.50

Notice that the interest rate is changed inside the loop. This is necessary to prevent the loop from continuing indefinitely. Condition loops must change the terminating variable inside the loop, or the loop will not terminate. Also notice that the interest rate was initialized prior to entering the loop. This is a critical feature. If the condition variable is not initialized, the results of the loop are unpredictable. In addition, you want to ensure that the initialization does not occur inside the loop because that would cause an infinite loop and the program would not stop.

The *Repeat* ... *Until* loop looks like this:

```
Repeat
        (tasks to be completed)
Until condition is satisfied
```

This loop performs some tasks and then checks to see if they need to be performed again. Let's examine the interest table from above using this type of loop.

```
Input Investment
Interest_rate = .05
Repeat
        Interest_earned = Interest_rate * Investment
        Print  Interest_earned
        Interest_rate = Interest_rate + .0025
Until Interest_rate is = .08
End
```

This program is very similar to the previous one. But here we will get the 8% Interest_rate printed because this is a post-condition loop, where the previous one was a pre-condition loop. Table 6.2 shows the output from this post-condition loop. Compare it with Table 6.1 to see the difference.

Table 6.2 Post-condition interest

Interest Rate	Interest Earned
0.0500	$50.00
0.0525	$52.50
0.0550	$55.00
0.0575	$57.50
0.0600	$60.00
...	
0.0775	$77.50
0.0800	$80.00

Bowling Problem

The pseudocode for the bowlers' average in Chapter 3 can be simplified using the looping techniques of this chapter and the decision structure.

```
Bowlers Average Program
Initialization
Process
Termination
End
Initialization
   Set_counters
   Return
Process
      Get_Scores
      Return
Termination
   Display_average
   Return
Set_counters
      Game_counter = 0
      Total_score = 0
      Return
   Get_scores
      Repeat
            Game_counter = Game_counter + 1
            Print " Input score for" Game_counter
            Input Game_score
            Total = Game_score + Total
            If Game_counter > 1 Then
                 Print "Total for " Game_counter "games
is:                          "Total
            Else
            Endif
      Until Game_counter = 3
      Return
   Display_average
      Average = Total_score/3
      Print " Your average for today was: " Average
      Return
```

Summary

In this chapter, we have studied the iteration/repetition/loop structure, which is used when it's necessary to repeat a group of instructions. This completes the introduction to the three structures necessary to design/write computer programs, which are sequential, selection, and iteration. In the remaining chapters, we will see applications of the loop and nested loop structures.

Key Terms

Each number in parentheses indicates the page where the term first occurs in the chapter.

- accumulator (124)
- conditional loop (118)
- counter loop (118)
- infinite loop (119)
- iteration (118)
- loop (118)
- nested loop (123)
- pre-condition (121)
- post-condition (121)
- repetition (118)
- sequential loop (122)
- Repeat ... Until (126)
- While ... End while (126)

Chapter 6
Exercises

Objective 1 Read flowcharts containing iteration structures.

1. Examine the flowchart in Figure 6.14, identify the loop as pre-condition or post-condition, tell how many records are processed, and describe the output.
2. Examine the flowchart in Figure 6.15, identify the loop as pre-condition or post-condition, tell how many records are processed, and describe the output.

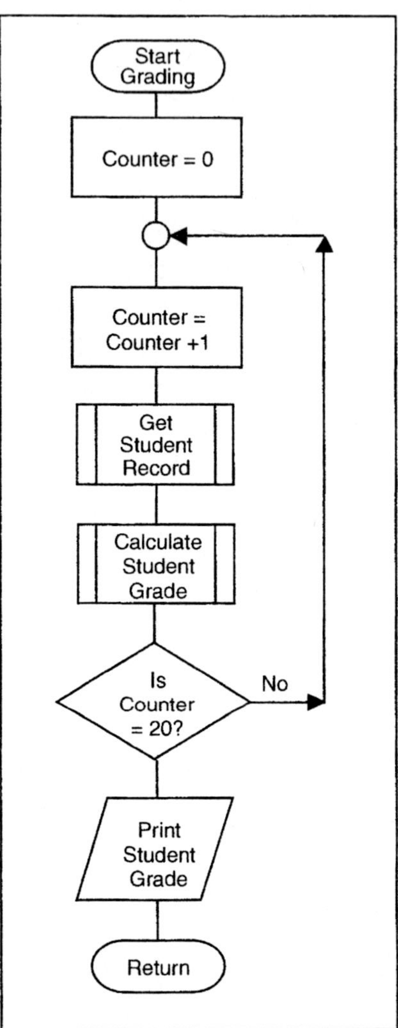

Figure 6.14 Objective 1 Exercise 1

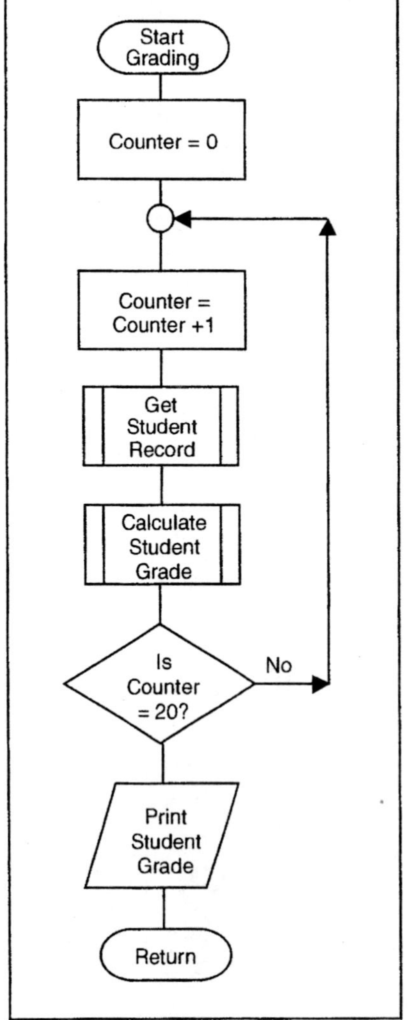

Figure 6.15 Objective 1 Exercise 2

3. Examine the flowchart in Figure 6.16, identify the loop as pre-condition or post-condition, tell how many records are processed, and describe the output.
4. Examine the flowchart in Figure 6.17, identify the loop as pre-condition or post-condition, tell how many records are processed, and describe the output.

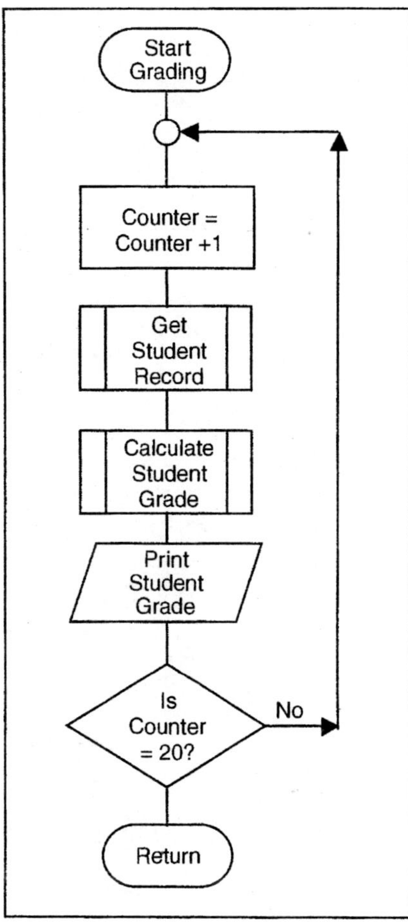

Figure 6.16 Objective 1 Exercise 3

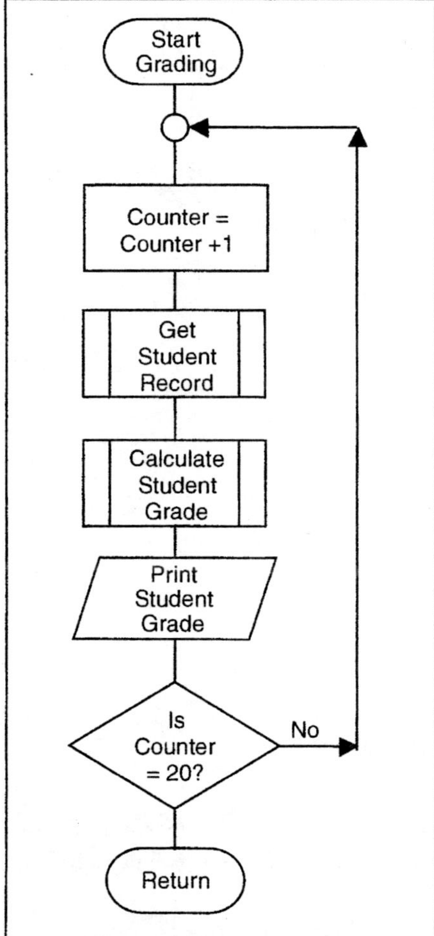

Figure 6.17 Objective 1 Exercise 4

5. Examine the flowchart in Figure 6.18 and determine:

   A. Are there any loops in this flowchart?

   B. Identify the loop(s) start and end.

   C. State whether each loop is pre-condition or post-condition.

   D. State how many iterations are performed by the loop.

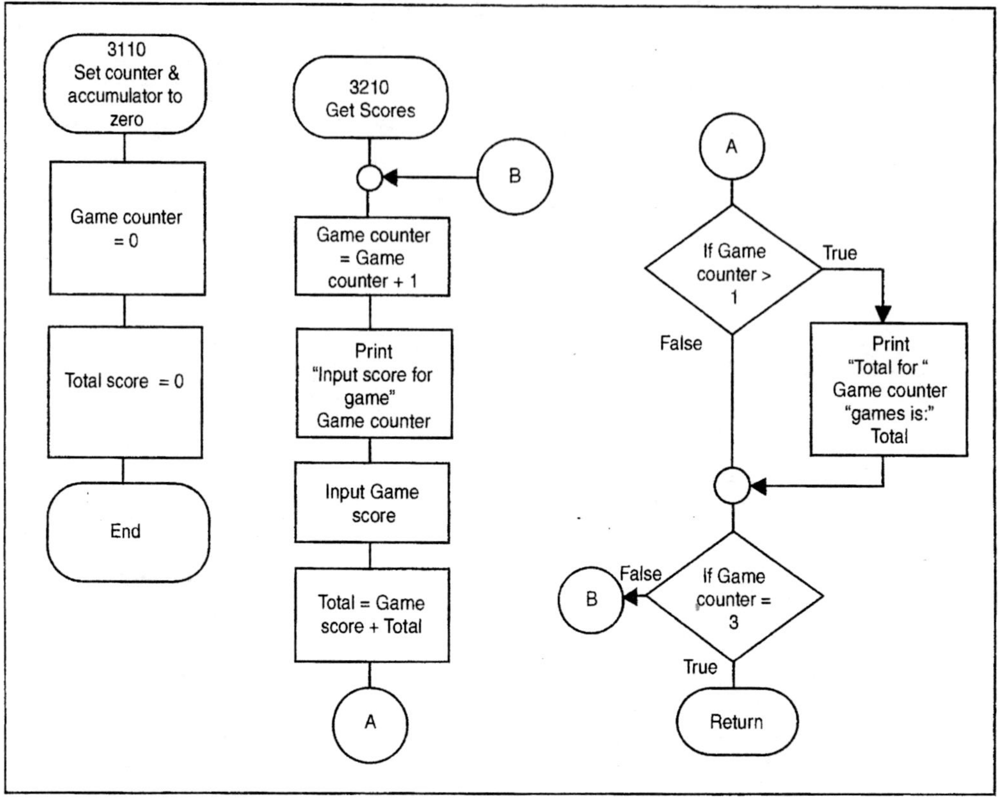

Figure 6.18 Objective 1 Exercise 5

6. Examine the flowchart in Figure 6.19 and determine:

   Are there any loops in this flowchart?

   Identify the loop(s) start and end.

   State whether each loop is pre-condition or post-condition.

   State how many iterations are performed by the loop.

   This flowchart fragment locates the largest score among a group of scores input that do not have any negative values. Given the groups of scores below, what value would Max score have at the end of the fragment?

   A. -3

   B. 3, -3

   C. 3,4,6,2,-3

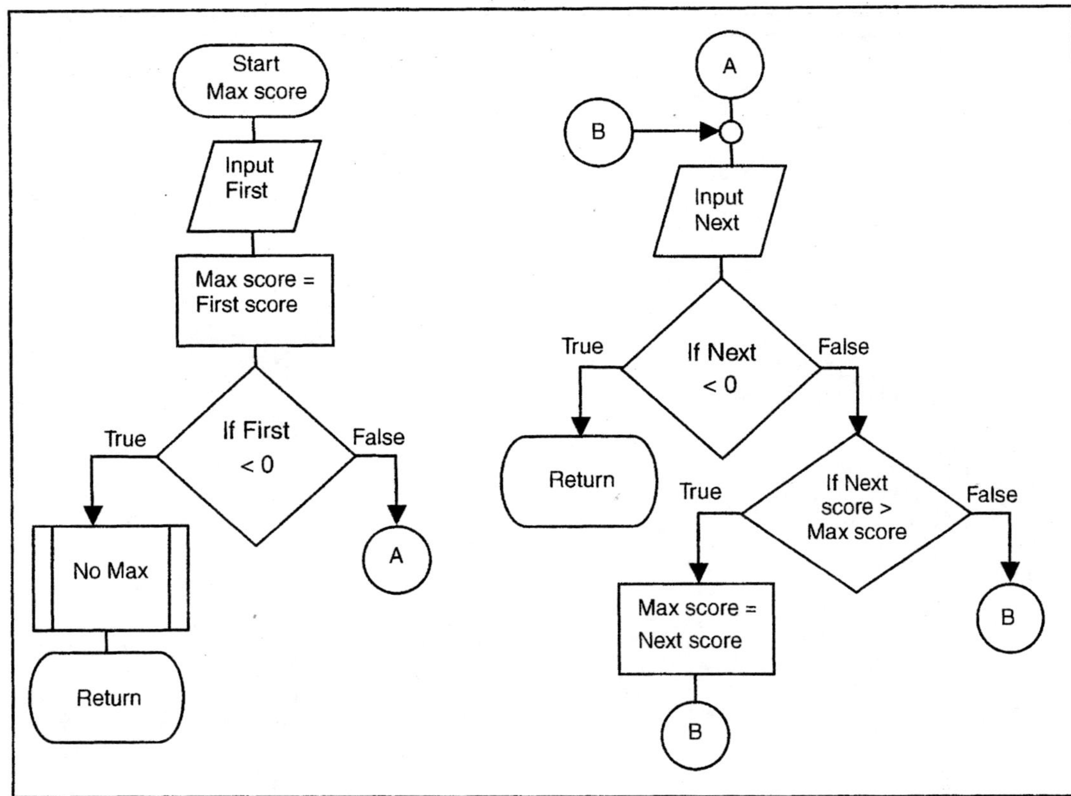

Figure 6.19 Objective 1 Exercise 6

7. Examine the flowchart in Figure 6.20 and determine:
   A. Are there any loops in this flowchart?
   B. Identify the loop(s) start and end.

      State whether each loop is pre-condition or post-condition.

      State how many iterations are performed by the loop.

      This flowchart fragment locates the smallest score among a group of scores input that do not have any negative values. Given the groups of scores below, what value would Max score have at the end of the fragment.

   A. -3
   B. 3, -3
   C. 3,4,6,2,-3

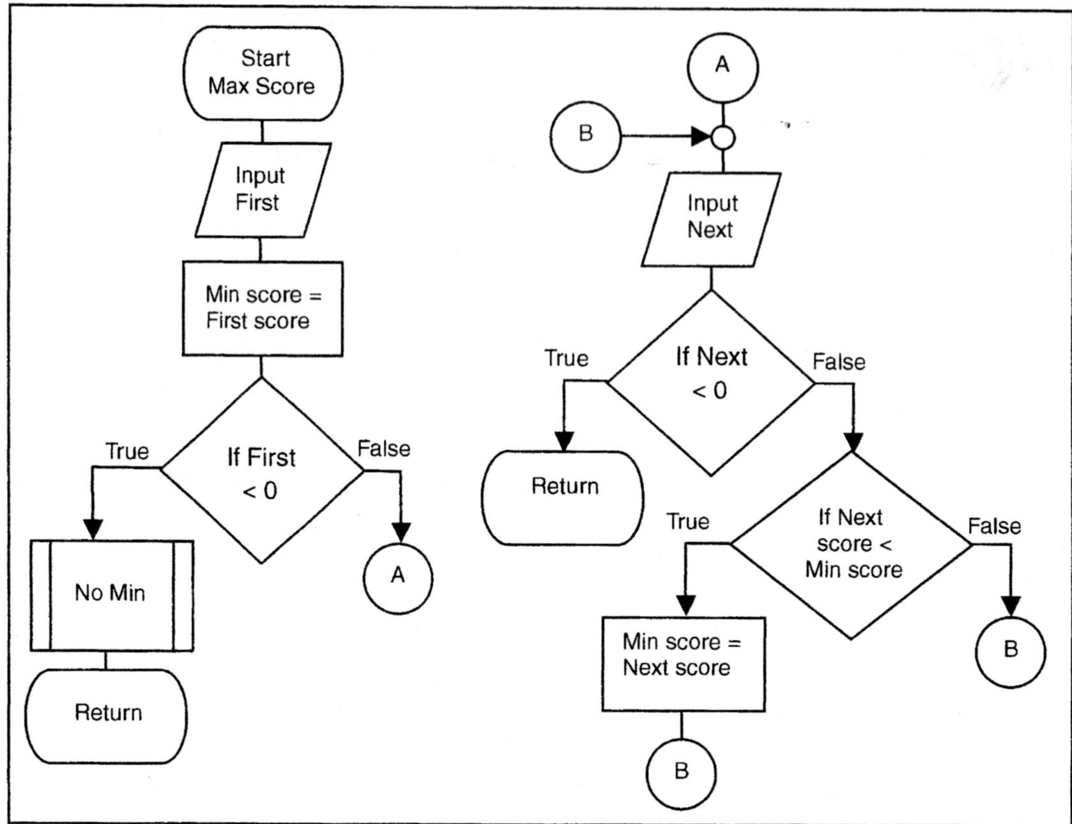

Figure 6.20 Objective 1 Exercise 7

Objective 2 Draw and revise flowcharts containing iteration structures.

1. Draw a flowchart for a counter-controlled loop that completes a process five times.
2. Draw a flowchart that reads numeric grades until it finds a grade less than zero and then computes the average of the grades input.
3. Draw a flowchart for a program that determines how many months it would take for an investment of $10,000 to accumulate to $20,000 at an annual interest rate of 6%. Assume that the interest is compounded monthly (12 months in a year).
4. Draw a flowchart that could be used to write a program for calculating a student's Grade Point Average (GPA). The program would read student records containing the course number and the letter grade, convert the letter grade to a numeric grade, and sum all of a student's honor points so that the GPA could be calculated. Honor points are equal to the numeric grade times the credit hours for the course. Assume that the hundreds digit of the course number contains the credit hours. Example: Course number 1304 identifies a course that is 3 credit hours. If the student earned a C in this course, they would have 6 honor points.

5. Draw a flowchart for a program that could be used to calculate the depreciation schedule for a business machine using the declining balance method. Data: The machine cost $10,000; has a useful life of 15 years; and a depreciation rate of .1. The declining balance method of depreciation deducts the annual depreciation from the adjusted cost. This adjusted cost is used to calculate the next year's depreciation. For example: Using the data in this problem, our first year's depreciation is $1,000 (.1 * 10,000). The second year's cost is $9,000 ($10,000 - $1,000), and the second year's depreciation is $900 (.1 * 9,000). The third year's cost and depreciation are $8,100 and $810, respectively. This process continues for 15 years or until the cost of the item is zero.
6. Draw a flowchart that accumulates Annual Income for an employee who gets paid bi-weekly.
7. Our bowlers' case study uses a league composed of 32 teams, and each team is composed of four bowlers, two men and two women. Draw a flowchart that loops through all of the bowlers on a team, calculates and displays their averages, and then loops through each of the teams until the averages have been computed and printed for all bowlers. Include the team average in the results.
8. There are nine players on a baseball team. Design and draw a flowchart that will read in each player's times at bat and number of hits and calculate batting average. (Hint: Batting average is the number of hits divided by the number of times at bat times 1,000.)

Objective 3 Read pseudocode containing iteration structures.

1. Examine the pseudocode shown below, identify the loop as pre-condition or post-condition, tell how many records are processed, and describe the output.

```
Feet_to_meter_conversion
   Feet = 10
   Conversion_factor = 2.808
   Repeat
   Meter = Feet/Conversion_factor
   Print Feet, Meter
   Feet = Feet - 1
   Until Feet = 0
End
```

2. Examine the pseudocode shown below, identify the loop as pre-condition or post-condition, tell how many records are processed, and describe the output.

```
Feet_to_meter_conversion
   Feet = 10
   Conversion_factor = 2.808
   Feet = Feet - 1
   Repeat
   Meter = Feet/Conversion_factor
   Print Feet, Meter
   Until Feet = 0
End
```

3. Examine the pseudocode shown below, identify the loop as pre-condition or post-condition, tell how many records are processed, and describe the output. Assume that the data is the even numbers from 2 through 30.

```
Accumulation
   Count = 0
   Accumulation = 0
   While Count < 6
         Read Data
         Accumulation = Accumulation + Data
         Count = Count + 1
   Endwhile
   Display Accumulation
End
```

4. Examine the pseudocode shown below, identify the loop as pre-condition or post-condition, tell how many records are processed, and describe the output.

```
Find_element_average
   Sum = 0
   Input Iterations
   Count = 0
   Repeat
   Count = Count + 1
   Sum = Sum + Count
   Until Count = Iterations
   Print Sum/Iterations
   End
```

5. Examine the pseudocode shown below and determine:

   A. Are there any loops in this flowchart?

   B. Identify the loop(s) start and end.

   C. State whether each loop is pre-condition or post-condition.

   D. State how many iterations are performed by the loop.

```
Bowlers Average Program

   Initialization
      Process
      Termination
      End

Initialization
      Set_counters
      Return
```

```
Process
      Get_Scores
      Return
Termination
      Display_average
      Return
Set_counters
      Game_counter = 0
      Total_score = 0
      Return
Get_scores
            Repeat
                  Game_counter = Game_counter + 1
                  Print " Input score for" Game_counter
                  Input Game_score
                  Total = Game_score + Total
                  If Game_counter > 1 Then
                        Print "Total for " Game_counter "games
                                    is: "Total
                  Else
                  Endif
            Until Game_counter = 3
            Return
   Display_average
            Average = Total_score/3
            Print " Your average for today was: " Average
            Return
```

6. Examine the pseudocode below and determine:
   A. Are there any loops in this pseudocode?
   B. Identify the loop(s) start and end.
   C. State whether each loop is pre-condition or post-condition.
   D. State how many iterations are performed by the loop.
   E. This pseudocode fragment locates the largest score among a group of scores input that do not have any negative values. Given the groups of scores below, what value would Max score have at the end of the fragment?

```
-3
3, -3
3,4,6,2,-3
```

Max score

```
Input First_score
Max_score = First_score
```

```
    If First_score < 0 Then
          No Max Score Found
          Return
Else
          While Next_score Not < 0
          Input Next_score
          If Next_score < 0 Then
                Return
          Else
                If Next_score > Max_score Then
                      Max_score = Next_score
                Else
                Endif
                Endwhile
          Endif
Endif
Return
```

7. Examine the pseudocode shown below and determine:

   A. Are there any loops in this pseudocode?
   B. Identify the loop(s) start and end.
   C. State whether each loop is pre-condition or post-condition.
   D. State how many iterations are performed by the loop.
   E. .This pseudocode fragment locates the smallest score among a group of scores input that do not have any negative values. Given the groups of scores below, what value would Max score have at the end of the fragment?

      A. -3

      B. 3, -3

      C. 3,4,6,2,-3@LLX

   Min score

```
    Input First_score
    Min_score = First_score
    If First_score < 0 Then
          No Min Score Found
          Return
Else
          While Next_score Not < 0
          Input Next_score
          If Next_score < 0 Then
                Return
          Else
                If Next_score < Min_score Then
```

```
                                Min_score = Next_score
                            Else
                            Endif
                            Endwhile
                    Endif
        Endif
    Return
```

Objective 4 Write and revise pseudocode containing iteration structures.

1. Write the pseudocode for a counter-controlled loop that completes a process five times.
2. Write the pseudocode that reads numeric grades until it finds a grade less than zero and then computes the average of the grades input.
3. Write the pseudocode for a program that determines how many months it would take for an investment of $10,000 to accumulate to $20,000 at an annual interest rate of 6%. Assume that the interest is compounded monthly (12 months in a year).
4. Write the pseudocode that could be used to write a program for calculating a student's Grade Point Average (GPA). The program would read student records containing the course number and the letter grade, convert the letter grade to a numeric grade, and sum all of a student's honor points so that the GPA could be calculated. Assume that the hundreds digit of the course number contains the credit hours. Example: Course number 1304 identifies a course that is 3 credit hours. If the student earned a C in this course, they would have 6 honor points.
5. Write the pseudocode for a program that could be used to calculate the depreciation schedule for a business machine using the declining balance method. Data: The machine cost $10,000; has a useful life of 15 years; and a depreciation rate of .1. The declining balance method of depreciation deducts the annual depreciation from the adjusted cost. This adjusted cost is used to calculate the next year's depreciation. For example: Using the data in this problem, our first year's depreciation is $1,000 (.1 * 10,000). The second year's cost is $9,000 ($10,000 - $1,000), and the second year's depreciation is $900 (.1 * 9,000). The third year's cost and depreciation are $8,100 and $810, respectively. This process continues for 15 years or until the cost of the item is zero.
6. Write the pseudocode that accumulates Annual Income for an employee who gets paid every two weeks.
7. Our bowlers' case study uses a league composed of 32 teams; and each team is composed of four bowlers, two men and two women. Write pseudocode modules that loop through all of the bowlers on a team, calculate and display their averages, and then loop through each of the teams until the averages have been computed and printed for all bowlers. Include the team average in the results.
8. There are nine players on a baseball team. Write pseudocode that will read in each player's times at bat and number of hits and calculate batting average. (Hint: Batting average is the number of hits divided by the number of times at bat times 1,000.)

Other Assignments

SoftSkills

Select one problem from Objective 2 or 4 or from the Internet/library research projects below, and prepare and give an oral report to the class on your solution.

Internet/library research projects

A. Research loop syntax in three different programming languages. Write a paper explaining how the loops work and what variations you found. Include either a flowchart or pseudocode instructions for each variation of loop syntax you discover. Compare and contrast the various techniques that the languages use for looping.

B. Explore a local manufacturing company to determine how they use iterative processes in their manufacturing systems. Write a paper describing the iterative processes that they use, and draw a flowchart that models one of their processes.

TABLES

Yea, from the table of my memory I'll wipe away all trivial fond records.

(Hamler (Act 1, Scene 5, Line 98)

OBJECTIVES

After completing this chapter, you will be able to:

1. State the characteristics of tables.
2. Read flowcharts containing tables.
3. Draw and revise flowcharts to solve problems using tables.
4. Read, write, and revise pseudocode using tables.
5. Given a problem, identify and describe the type of table to be used in the solution.

Introduction

To efficiently program a computer, programmers need to be familiar with a variety of methods for storing data in a computer. The method of data storage can affect the speed of a program and the memory requirements of a program. These methods of storing data are called *data structures*. In this chapter we look at a basic form of data structures called tables[1]. Some authors refer to tables as matrices, vectors, arrays, or lists. These various terms are generally associated with specific programming languages. Visual Basic and C++, for example, use the term "array," while COBOL uses the term "tables." We will use the term "table" throughout this textbook because it seems to be comfortable to more students than does the word "array."

Tables

Tables are contiguous memory locations in RAM that have a common name and can be referenced by means of that name and a *subscript* (or set of subscripts). Tables have *dimensions* and contain elements or cells. For our purposes, each element of a table can contain several bytes of memory. Therefore, when we discuss memory locations in a table, we will be talking about elements and not bytes. Subscript values (sometimes called index numbers) are values used to identify the elements in a table. In this book, the minimum value for a subscript is 1. Subscript value 1 refers to the first element in a table. Subscript value 2 refers to the second element of a table, and so on. The number of *dimensions* is equal to the number of subscripts (i.e., 3 subscripts, 3 dimensions). The total number of elements in a table (size) is computed by multiplying the values of all the subscripts together. As the various tables are described, pay close attention to the difference between the number of subscripts and the values of the subscripts. The number of subscripts relates to the number of dimensions of a table. Each subscript can have many different values representing the various elements in the table.

We will focus our work on three different types of tables: one-dimension tables, two-dimension tables, and three-dimension tables.

One-Dimension Tables

The *one-dimension* (or one-dimensional) *table* can be thought of as a list of contiguous memory locations in one row or one column. If you think of a one-dimension table as a row, then normally the left element is the first, and they proceed left to right. This is illustrated in Figure 7.1.

1 Tables are data structures used by humans. Most programming languages store tables in main memory as "arrays." Four-dimension tables are found in everyday life (two workbooks, each composed of 3 spreadsheets as an example), but most computer languages support only three dimensions. The author considers the concept of four and more dimension tables to be helpful in understanding tables and arrays.

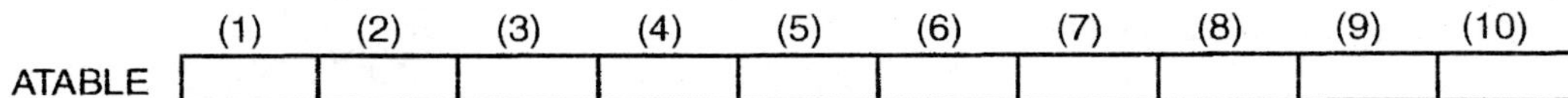

Figure 7.1 Horizontal Table Display

Figure 7.1 is a visual representation of the ATABLE table with ten elements. The ten elements are shown to be blank or empty. The numbers in parentheses are subscript values and indicate the position of each element. ATABLE(1) is the first element in the table. A one-dimension table has only one subscript; but in this table, that subscript can have ten values, because the table has ten elements. We need one value of the subscript for each of the ten elements.

ATABLE (1)
(2)
(3)
(4)
(5)
(6)
(7)
(8)
(9)
(10)

Figure 7.2 Vertical Table Display

Thinking of one-dimension tables as a row of elements is an arbitrary concept. It's just as easy to think in terms of a column of data, as is shown in Figure 7.2. Notice that the subscript values relate to a specific memory location, but the subscript values are not stored in the memory location.

In summary, a one-dimension table has one subscript; and we can visualize the table as having length.

Here's an example of how a one-dimension table can be used to help solve problems. Suppose that we want to keep a list of ten numbers and find the sum of those ten numbers. Without using a table, we would have a variable FIRST NUMBER for the first number, SECOND NUMBER for the second, THIRD NUMBER for the third, and so on. This would require ten different variable names. Adding the numbers would require this statement: SUM = FIRST NUMBER + SECOND NUMBER … + TENTH NUMBER. The flowchart to input the ten numbers and add them together would look like Figure 7.3. Imagine if we had to do this with one hundred numbers. What about ten thousand numbers? You should see that the flowchart and corresponding program would become excessively long. We need a way to use a loop to help us. The table will allow us to use a loop to simplify this flowchart.

To use a table in a flowchart, we must first *declare the table.* To declare a table, we must give it a name and specify its size. Table names are created the same way as variable names. They should be meaningful.

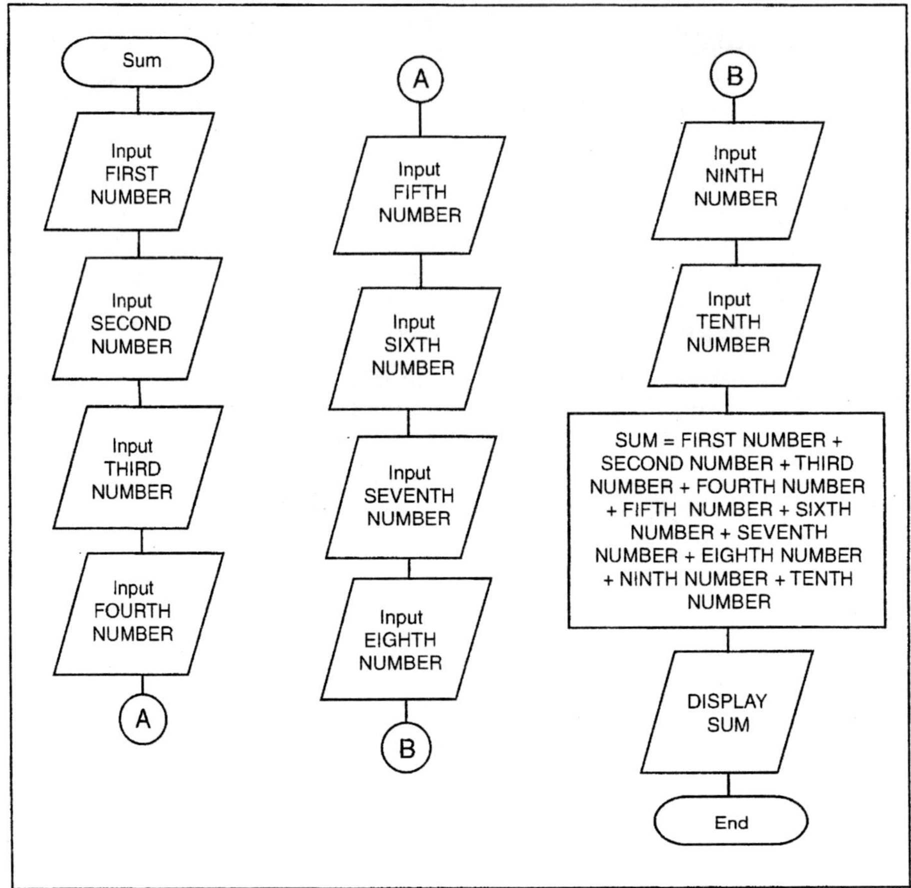

Figure 7.3 Accumulation

As an example, we will name a table "ATABLE." Next we tell the computer how big the table is so that the computer will reserve enough memory for it. We specify the size of a table by using subscripts enclosed in parentheses, like this: ATABLE (10)[2]. This statement tells the computer that we want to use a table that has one dimension and ten elements. This statement would be included in the Initialization portion of the flowchart.

Now, let's solve our sample problem. We want to input ten numbers and find their sum. The first number will be stored at ATABLE (1), the second at ATABLE (2), the third at ATABLE (3), and so on. The statement ATABLE (1)[3] is equivalent to FIRST NUMBER in the previous solution. We can use a variable name for the subscript; and if we put our addition statement inside a loop, we have something like Figure 7.4:

2 This syntax is quite common in a variety of programming languages and is the format used in this book. It is not meant to imply that this is a universal standard.

3 This statement is spoken as: "The first element of ATABLE" or "ATABLE sub one."

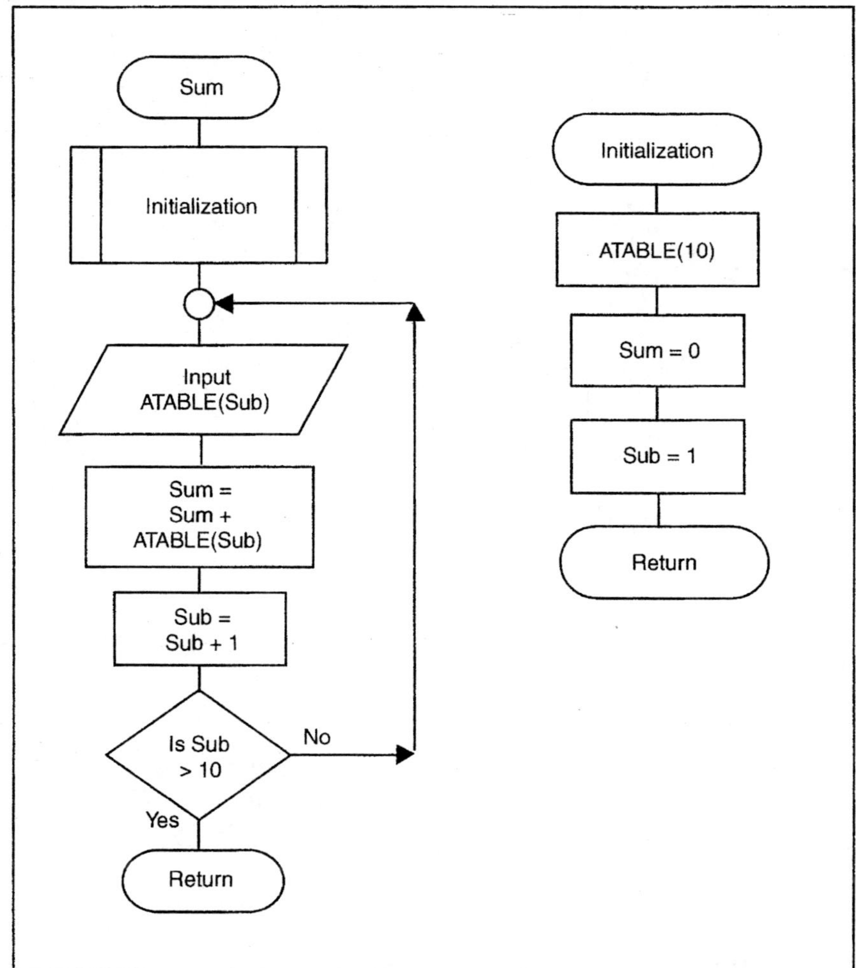

Figure 7.4 Accumulation with Table

As you can see, this flowchart requires fewer lines than Figure 7.3 and accomplishes the same task. The power of the table is shown by now imagining that we have to input 10,000 numbers and find their sum. Figure 7.3 would require 10,000 input symbols, but Figure 7.4 would contain the same symbols as it does now. Figure 7.5 shows Figure 7.4 modified to sum 10,000 numbers.

Notice that the only differences between Figures 7.5 and 7.4 are that the number 10 changes to the number 10,000.

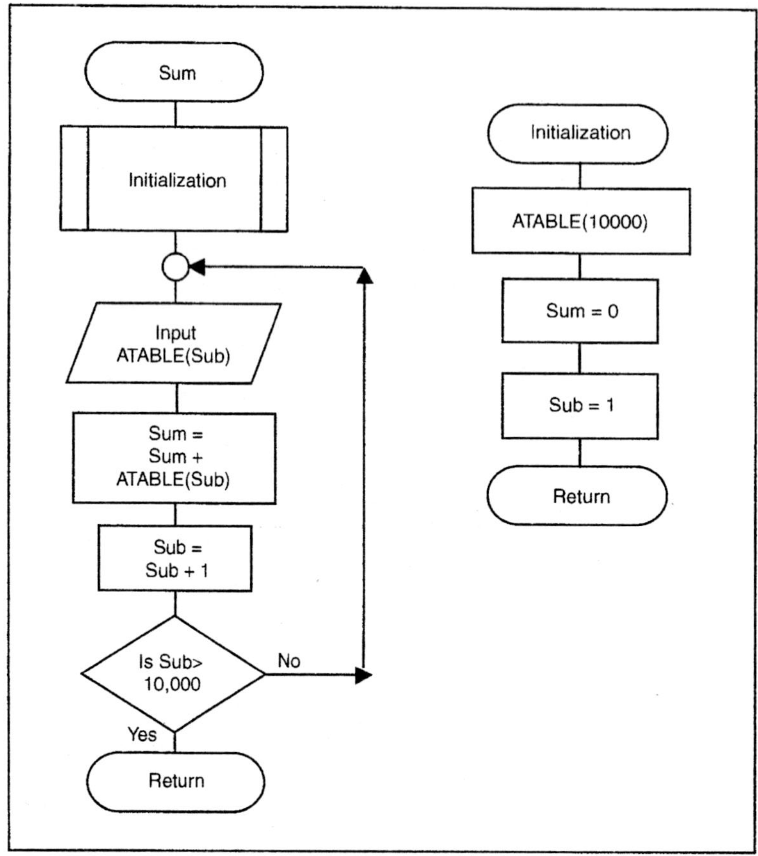

Figure 7.5
Accumulation Modified

Two-Dimension Tables

This brings us to the concept of a two-dimension table. Two-dimension tables have two subscripts. Two-dimension tables are declared by specifying their name and size in the initialization module just as we did the one-dimension table. The two-dimension table can also be thought of as two or more one-dimension tables known as parallel tables (parallel arrays). Two-dimension tables can be thought of as having rows and columns. Parallel tables treat each column as a separate one-dimension table. The data in each row can be related from one table to the next by the position in each column.

Let's imagine that we have surveyed a group of people, and we want to tabulate the results. Ten questions were on the survey, and each question had four answers. We wish to create a table that will contain a count of how many people gave each answer to each question. We can create a two-dimension table to do this. We'll call the table "SURVEY." Since we have 10 questions and each question has four answers, we might establish the size of the table as follows: SURVEY (10,4). This table has 40 elements (recall that elements could be more than one byte). The number of elements in a table

(1,1)	(1,2)	(1,3)	(1,4)
(2,1)	(2,2)	(2,3)	(2,4)
(3,1)	(3,2)	(3,3)	(3,4)
(4,1)	(4,2)	(4,3)	(4,4)
(5,1)	(5,2)	(5,3)	(5,4)
(6,1)	(6,2)	(6,3)	(6,4)
(7,1)	(7,2)	(7,3)	(7,4)
(8,1)	(8,2)	(8,3)	(8,4)
(9,1)	(9,2)	(9,3)	(9,4)
(10,1)	(10,2)	(10,3)	(10,4)

On the left, we have shown the subscript that relates to a specific element inside the element itself, but in reality the subscripts are not in the location.

A second method of showing the subscripts, on the right, is to show the first subscript as a row number and the second as a column number. Here we can clearly see the subscripts outside of the memory location. We locate a particular element by going to the intersection of the appropriate row and column. This system is very close to the system in use today by spreadsheet software.

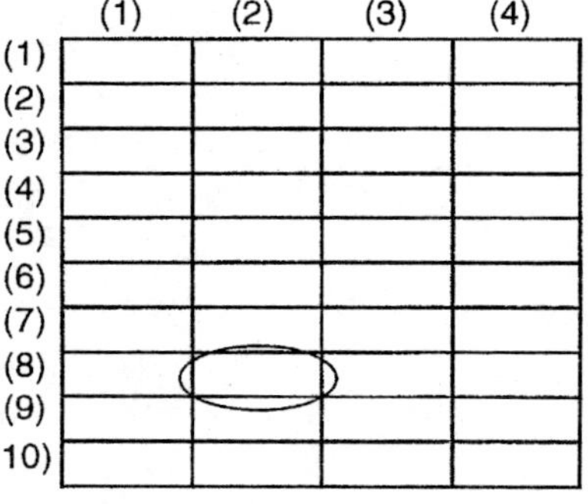

Figure 7.6 Two Dimension Table

can always be computed by multiplying the maximum value of all subscripts. So, a two-dimension table "Two_Table (5,6) " would have 30 elements.

Normally we think of two-dimension tables as having rows and columns; so SURVEY would look like Figure 7.6 (if we could see it):

On the left, we have shown the subscript that relates to a specific element inside the element itself, but in reality the subscripts are not in the memory location. A second method of showing the subscripts, on the right, is to show the first subscript as a row number and the second as a column number. Here we can clearly see the subscripts outside of the memory location. We locate a particular element by going to the intersection of the appropriate row and column. This system is very close to the system in use today by spreadsheet software.

The element with the oval around it is the element SURVEY(8,2)

Alternatively, we could have defined SURVEY to be SURVEY (4,10); and it would have had 4 rows and 10 columns. The choice between the two formats is left to the system designer/programmer. Either method will work. You only have to be certain that you refer to SURVEY the same way each time that it's referenced.

Next, we show the SURVEY table filled with data in Table 7.1.

What data is found in SURVEY (2,3)?

What data is in SURVEY (3,2)?

As you can see, two-dimension tables have rows and columns; or if you prefer a geometric interpretation, they have length and width.

5	5	5	5
7	3	4	6
8	8	3	1
3	7	4	6
4	6	3	7
3	1	11	5
3	4	3	10
14	0	4	2
8	7	5	0
16	4	0	0

Table 7.1 Survey with Data

Question 1 of the survey corresponds to row 1 of the table; question 2 is row 2, and so on. All of the respondents who picked answer 1 to question 1 are counted in the first row, first column of the table. So we see that 5 people chose answer 1 to question 1. Survey (6,3) shows us that 11 people selected the third answer to question six.

One-dimension and two-dimension tables are very common and used by nearly every application on a computer. *Three-dimension tables* are an extension of the previous concepts to a third dimension.

Notice that we cannot tell which element is the fourth element of a two-dimension table. We would probably agree that the element with subscript values (1,1) is the first element, but the second element might have subscript values (1,2) or (2,1), depending on your frame of reference. Subscript values in one-dimension tables are well correlated with the elements position in the table, but this is not the case in two-dimension tables and higher.

Three-Dimension Tables

A three-dimension table would have three subscripts and be declared by specifying its name and size. Three_Dimension_Table (3,2,4) describes a three-dimension table whose name is Three_Dimension_Table. The table's first subscript has a maximum value of three, and the second subscript has a maximum value of two, and the third subscript has a maximum value of four.

Rows and columns make little sense in this context. However, if we borrow the term *worksheet* from the spreadsheet world, we could think of the above table as having three worksheets, where each worksheet is composed of a two-dimension table containing two rows and four columns. We could also think in terms of books and page numbers, so this example shows a book of three pages, and each page contains a table of two rows and four columns. We compute the size of the table in exactly the same manner as we did for the two-dimension case. This table has 24 elements. The geometric interpretation of a three-dimension table would be a rectangular parallelpiped. Figure 7.7 is a drawing of Three_Dimension_Table (3,2,4).

Here we can see a solid object that has length, width, and height. We can assign length, width, and height to the subscripts and have an object three units tall, two units wide, and four units long.

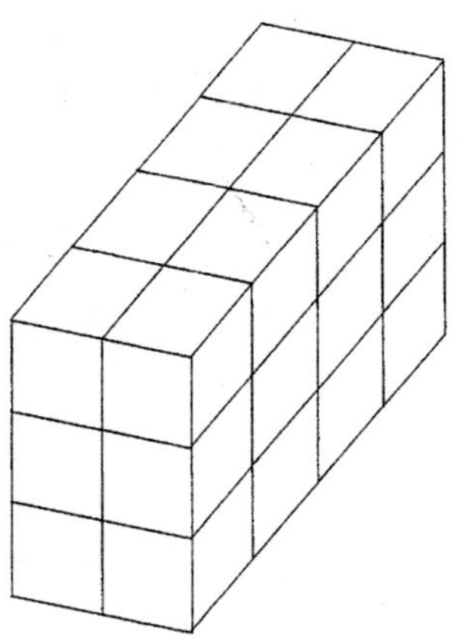

Figure 7.7 Three Dimension Table

Alternatively, we might think of this object as having three layers (from top to bottom), and each layer is a two-dimension table of two rows and four columns.

With a little work, you should be able to get several different interpretations of this object.

How could we use a three-dimension table? Refer back to the two-dimension example and imagine that our survey included a response for gender. Question 1 asked if the respondent was male or female and then the other 10 questions had four choices. Assuming we wanted to tabulate the data by gender, we could use a table that had subscript options for 10 questions, each question having 4 responses and a third subscript for gender (2 choices). These subscripts specify a three-dimension table like this: Survey_By_Sex (10,4,2). We have reorganized the subscripts to show 10 questions, 4 answers to each, and 2 genders. We could have declared the table to be Survey_ By_Sex (2, 10, 4) just as easily. Regardless of what shape you see in the table, you should see the format in which the data is stored. What is critical about table declaration and usage is that you use the same process when putting data in as you use when taking data out. If you put data into Survey_By_Sex (2, 10, 4), then you must take it out of Survey_By_Sex (2, 10, 4) to get the correct information.

Higher-Dimension Tables

Once you have learned the subscript method of storing and retrieving data, you can imagine 4-, 5-, 6-, or more dimension tables. No one will draw you a picture of six-dimension tables, but they exist in everyday life. Can you declare a four-dimension table using the methods shown for one, two, and three dimensions? Four dimension tables are common in the business world, where spreadsheets are combined into workbooks and workbooks are consolidated to make a report. The dimensions of a four-dimension table using workbooks might look like this: Report(workbook,worksheet,row,column). Each workbook consists of several worksheets. Each worksheet consists of several rows and columns. Our report is then a combination of two or more workbooks.

A simple example of a four-dimension table is this book. Each character in this book can be referenced using the four dimensions of chapter, page, line, and column. Naming this table as "Book", we could then reference items using the table. Book(2,3,1,7) would refer to the 7th character in chapter 2, on page 3, line 1.

A common application of multi-dimension tables is the market survey. Suppose you gave the same survey as our earlier example but wanted to tabulate the answers by income level and age groups. Let's say there were five income levels and six age groups. You would ask two more questions to get the respondents' income and age. The five-dimension table to tabulate this information would be defined as Survey Table (2,5,6,10,4), where the following subscripts represent the corresponding data. (see Table 7.2).

Table 7.2 Survey Table

Subscript Position	Maximum Value	Subscript Meaning
1	2	Gender of respondent
2	5	Income level of respondent
3	6	Age group of respondent
4	10	Question number
5	4	Answer number

How many elements are in this table?

In the remainder of this course, we will limit our discussions to one, two, and three dimensions; but the procedures apply to all tables. You will need to learn three basic procedures for processing tables:

1. Declare a table.
2. Load a table.
3. Extract (look at) data/information from a table.

Declare a Table

The first part of working with tables, declaring, you have seen in the previous discussion. To declare a table, we must give it a name and specify its size. The name is arbitrary but should be meaningful. The number of subscripts determines the number of dimensions, while the size of the numbers used as subscripts specifies the number of elements in each dimension. Tables are declared in the initialization module. The product of all of the subscripts gives the total number of elements in the table.

Example of declaring a table: TABLE (3,2,4). This example says that TABLE is a three-dimension table with 24 elements (3*2*4).

Load Data

Next, we want to learn how to load data into the table. To load the number 7 into the first element of ATABLE (10), we would use the following assignment statement:

ATABLE (1) = 7

In general, to load data into an element of a table, we write the table name followed by the subscript(s) identifying the table element on the left side of the equal sign. On the right side of the equal sign, we specify the data to be loaded into the table element.

Examples:

Atable (27) = 59: Loads the number 59 into element 27 of Atable.
Btable (3,4) = 23: Loads the number 23 into the twelfth element of Btable
Ctable (15) = data: Loads some value that was stored at location data into the 15th element of Ctable

Dtable (Row, Column) = data: Loads some value that was stored at location data into an element of Dtable. The specific element of Dtable can vary as Row and Column change.

We could also load data into a table through input. Input DataTable(1), for example.

Extract Data

Now that you see how to put data into a table, let's look at the procedure to get data out of a table (extract or look at data). Suppose we wish to print the data contained in the second element of the one-dimension table ATABLE(10). Inside an output symbol of our flowchart, we would say "Print ATABLE (2)".

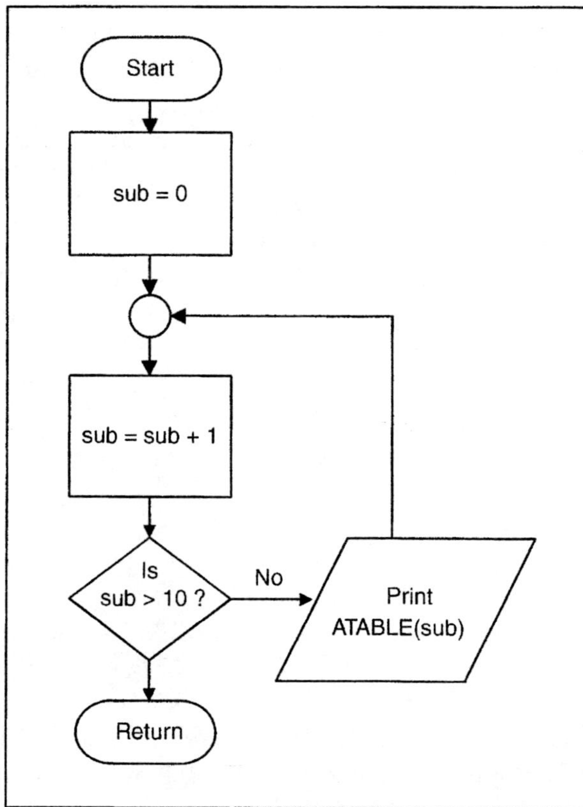

Figure 7.8 Printing a Table

Figure 7.8 depicts a flowchart for printing the contents of a one-dimension table with the first element printed first, second element printed second, and so on.

What if we want to just examine some data that are in the table and terminate the program if the table element is blank? That statement would look like: "Is ATABLE (sub)= blank?" and on a flowchart would be contained inside a decision (selection) symbol.

When Are Tables Used

If your data have a table structure, you would certainly want to use a table. Sometimes this is obvious, as in the case of a tax table. Sometimes recognizing data with a table structure requires some experience as well as some insight into the problem that you are trying to solve. Remember, we are flowcharting the solution to a problem. No one will tap you on the shoulder and tell you that you have to use a table. In many cases, tables are not appropriate. The same goes for when to use a three-, two-, or one-dimension table. In the computer, all tables are stored in one dimension. In fact, you can always design a one-dimension table that will work in place of a two-, three-, or more dimension table. We normally use a table of the appropriate dimensions for the problem being solved. Here are some examples.

Let's take the survey problem with 10 questions and four answers each. We already know how to put that problem into a two-dimension table. Let's, for fun, make it work with a one-dimension table. Define ATABLE (40). Now elements 1 through 4 contain the answers for question 1, elements 5 through 8 contain the answers to question two, and so on. This method works, but it's a little awkward; you should be able to see the advantages of using a two-dimensional table.

In the previous example, we might avoid using a table altogether and just create a variable for each answer. That's a tedious process, but it can be made to work. Additional problems are available at the end of this chapter where you can choose the type of table to fit the problem.

A couple of rules of thumb can be used to help deal with the above table dilemmas. First, tables are stored in RAM. Since tables are in RAM, they would allow for faster program running than if they were stored in auxiliary storage. Tables in auxiliary storage are called files. An advantage of using a table over a file would be an increase in speed of the program.

Our second rule of thumb is that tables are relatively small. To understand relatively small, we can compare an average computer disk storage space with its RAM size. Today, hard drives can store about 1000 times more than RAM (terabyte disk storage is popular today and RAM has just reached the gigabyte level). So disk files could be about one thousand times bigger than tables.

An example will help. Suppose you have an address book on computer. You keep the person's full name, street address, city, state and zip code. How many people's records could you keep in RAM? How many on disk? How could you use a table to make things better?

ANSWER: Assume that a person's name has at most 25 characters (do you know exceptions?), which is 25 bytes of memory. Street address should be allowed 50 bytes, city about 20 bytes, and state (remember two-letter state codes?) 2 bytes. If we use the Zip +4, we need 9 bytes for the zip code (yes, there are better ways). That's 106 bytes per person; let's round it to 100 bytes to simplify the math. If we have 100 MB RAM, can we put one million names in RAM? Trick question. We can but there won't be room for the operating system or the program; so the program won't run. We need a bunch of RAM for the software to make everything work; so to be generous, we'll assume the software uses only 90 percent of memory which leaves us room for 100,000 names, which isn't bad since most of us don't have 100,000 friends. But will this system work for the New York City phone book? So we put the names on disk, and the address book program runs very slow.

A final example of table use is found in our annual quest for filing of income tax returns. Take a look at the IRS Form 1040 instructions and find the tax table. How many dimensions does it have? What is its size? What are the dimensions? (Answer: IRS income tax tables are printed in row and column format, so they look like two-dimension tables. Their dimensions are income level and marital status. The Y2K tax table contains 2,062 rows and 6 columns.)

Bowling Problem

At this point in our studies, we have been required to enter each game into the computer and calculate an average, but we have been unable (or unwilling) to keep all of the scores for each week for every bowler. The concept of tables will allow us to save each bowlers' scores for each week of the season and retrieve or calculate with any of the scores that might be of interest, without having to re-enter the scores. This would be convenient when we want to know who scored the highest game during the entire season among all of the bowlers. A variety of possible arrangements exists for the bowling data, so the one described here is not the only solution.

The bowling league is composed of teams. Each team is composed of four bowlers. The season consists of thirty-five weeks. For this example we will assume that there are thirty-two teams. We must keep every game bowled, separated by bowler, by week, and by team. To simplify record keeping, we will identify each team by a number (1, 2, 3, ..., 32) and each player by a number (1, 2, 3, or 4). So the first bowler on team one could be identified as bowler 1,1. Our table structure would look like this:

A. League(Week,Team,Bowler,Game) declares a table where each week was composed of thirty-two teams, each with four bowlers, and each bowler with three games. This is a four-dimension table and is declared like this: League(35,32,4,3). Every game bowled could be stored in this one table and be retrieved as needed. The average for the season for bowler number one on team one could be represented by the flowchart in Figure 7.9. This scenario does not allow for the use of substitutes, which makes the problem slightly more complex.

B. Team Names(32) declares a table called Team Names, one dimension, that contains a list of the team names. The position in the table will be the teams' number. For example, the first entry in the Team Names table is the "Midnight Rollers." They would be team one.

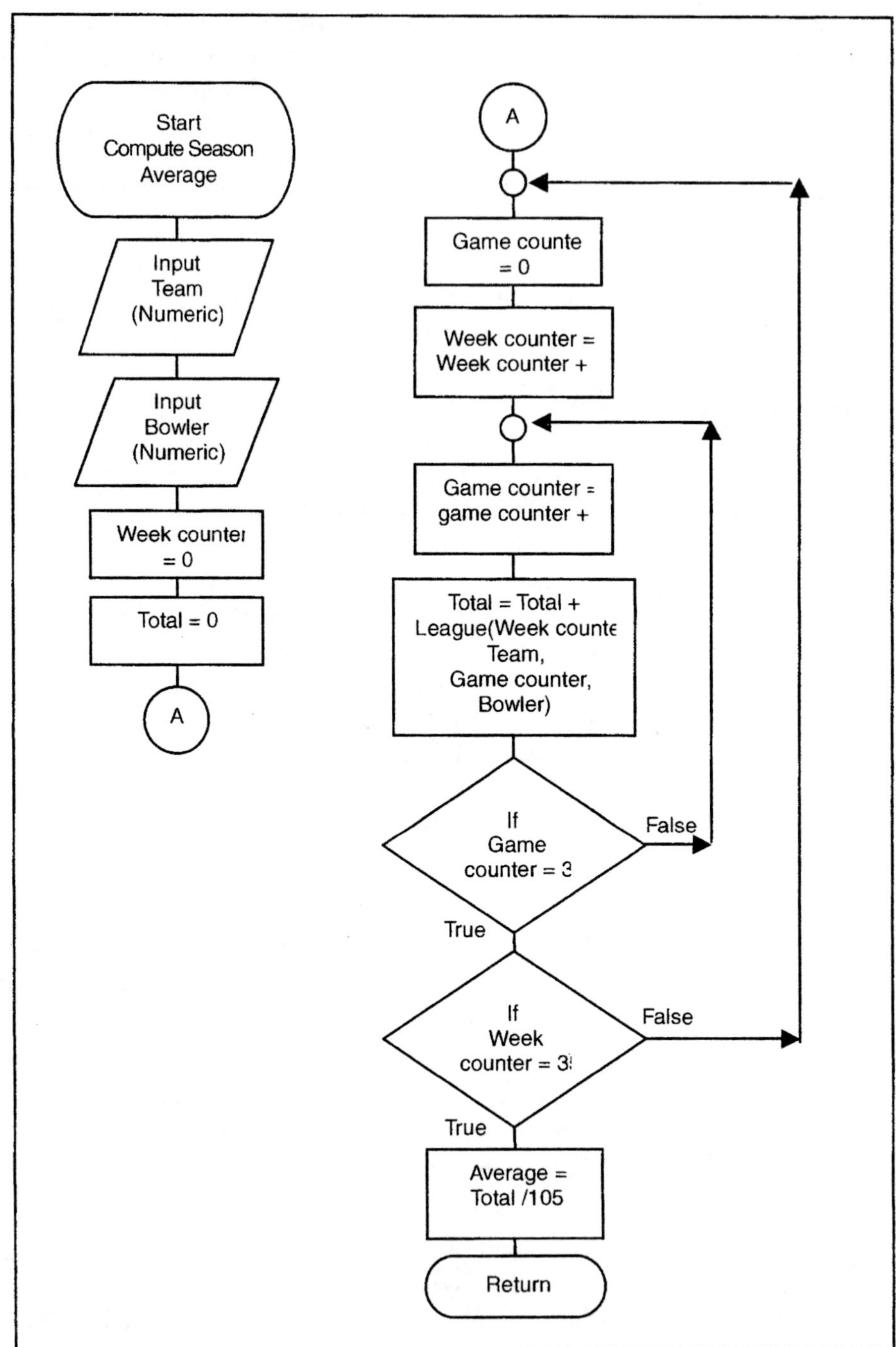

Figure 7.9 Bowling Scores

C. Bowlers(32,4) declares a table called Bowlers, two dimensions, that contains the names of the bowlers in the league. Bowlers(1,1) contains the name of bowler one on team one. Bowlers(6,4) contains the name of the fourth bowler on team 6.

Enrichment – Doing it with Pseudocode

Table handling with pseudocode is identical to table handling with flowcharts. The declaration statement for tables will always occur at the beginning of the pseudocode, immediately after the program name.

As an example, we'll write the program to add 100 numbers using a one-dimension table to store each of the numbers to be added.

```
Adding Numbers

Table_of_numbers (100)

        Sum = 0

        Sub = 1

        Repeat

              Input Table_of_numbers(Sub)

              Sum = Sum + Table_of_numbers(Sub)

              Sub = Sub + 1

        Until Sub > 100

        End
```

Using pseudocode to load data into a table is exactly the same as the examples on page 7.10. and extracting data from tables would look like the examples below.

Print Table_of_numbers(10) - would print the 10th element of the table Table_of_numbers

Save = Table_of_numbers(99) - would copy the quantity stored in the 99th element of Table_of_numbers into the storage location called Save.

Bowling Problem

The bowling scenario described previously is handled here in pseudocode.

```
Bowlers average

   Input Team_number

   Input Bowler_number
```

```
    Week_counter = 0
    Game_counter = 0
    Total = 0
    Repeat
    Week_counter = Week_counter + 1
    Repeat
    Game_counter = Game_counter + 1
    Total = Total +

    League(Week_counter,Team_number,Game_counter,Bowler_
          number)
    Until Game_counter = 3
    Until Week_counter = 35
    Average = Total/ 105
Return
```

Summary

Tables are data structures that provide a common variable name to a contiguous block of memory. Elements in the table are accessed using subscripts. The number of subscripts determines the dimensions of a table (one dimension, one subscript; two dimensions, two subscripts; etc.). The number of elements in a table is computed by multiplying the values of all of the subscripts together. The three-dimensional table 3Dsample(3,4,5) contains 60 elements (3 * 4 * 5).

Tables are relatively small in terms of storage space required and are contained in RAM. Because tables are in RAM, their use can speed up the processing of data.

Here are the three activities that we will perform when flowcharting with tables:

1. Declare the table (In the initialization module).
2. Load data into the table.
3. Extract data or look at data from the table.

Key Terms

Each number in parentheses indicates the page where the term first occurs in the chapter.

data structure (142)
declare a table (150)
dimension (142)
extract data from a table (151)
load data into a table (150)
one-dimension table (142)
subscript (142)
table (142)
three-dimension table (148)
two-dimension table (146)

Chapter 7
Exercises

Objective 1 State the characteristics of tables.

1. Write a statement to declare a one-dimension table. A two-dimension table. A three-dimension table. After declaring the table, explain what each part of the declaration statement means.
2. Explain the meaning of the following declaration statements in terms of tables. (Table name, size, and dimensions)

   George (2,3)
   Ann (4,5,6)
   Bill (8)
   Matrix (3,2,4,5,2)
3. Explain the meaning of the following statements in terms of tables. (Table name, size, and dimensions if possible.)

   Atable(row,column)
   Btable(subscript)
   Survey(age,sex,income,marital_status)
4. Explain the meaning of the following statements in terms of tables. (Table name, size, dimensions and what is happening to the element of the table)

   Atable (4) = 78
   Atable(3,5) = Q
   Atable (7,3) = Atable (7,3) + 1
   Matrix (1,1,2,1,1) = data
5. Explain the meaning of the following statements in terms of tables. (Table name, size, dimensions and what is happening to the element of the table)

```
Print Btable (3,2)
If Atable (5,6) = 7
        Then x = 5
        Else x = 6
    Endif
Display Ctable(4,6,3)
Total = Matrix (3,2) + 17
```

6. Declare a table that represents the following problem. You want to index each piece of gum in a shipment. The gum is contained in packages of five sticks. The packages are consolidated into boxes of 20 packages, and the boxes are placed on pallets with 50 boxes on each pallet. Explain your declaration statement.

7. Declare a table that represents the following problem. Imagine that you are in charge of transporting cargo aboard ocean going freighters (cargo ships). You want to establish a numeric system for tracking where a specific item is stored on the ship. Items are shipped as containers, pallets, or boxes. The items can be stored on seven different decks aboard the ship, and the decks are divided into four different holds. Think of a hold as a compartment. Part of each of the seven decks is in each compartment. Explain your declaration statement in terms of this problem.

8. Declare a table that represents the following problem. You are in charge of shipping merchandise by rail, and you want to keep track of where each shipment is located on the rail system. Each shipment is on one of twenty different trains and is either in a tank car, a freight car, or on a flat car. All of the trains have forty cars. Explain your declaration statement in terms of this problem.

Objective 2 Read flowcharts containing tables.

1. Examine the flowchart in Figure 7.10 and explain what is happening to the table and its elements.

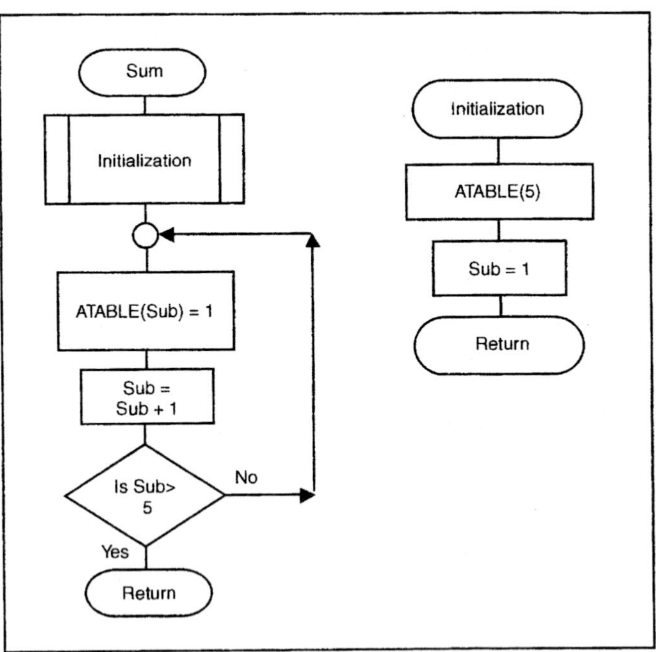

Figure 7.10 Objective 2 Exercise 1

2. Examine the flowchart in Figure 7.11 and explain what is happening to the table and its elements.

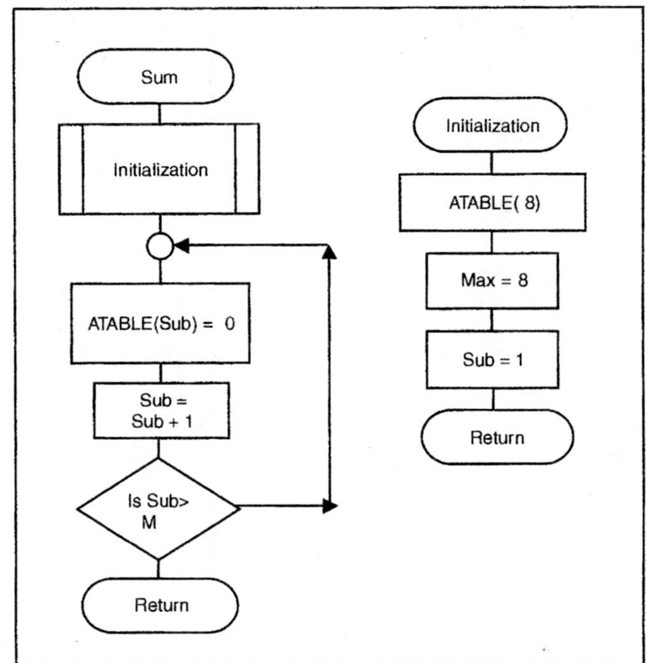

Figure 7.11 Objective 2 Exercise 2

3. Examine the flowchart in Figure 7.12 and explain what is happening to the table and its elements.

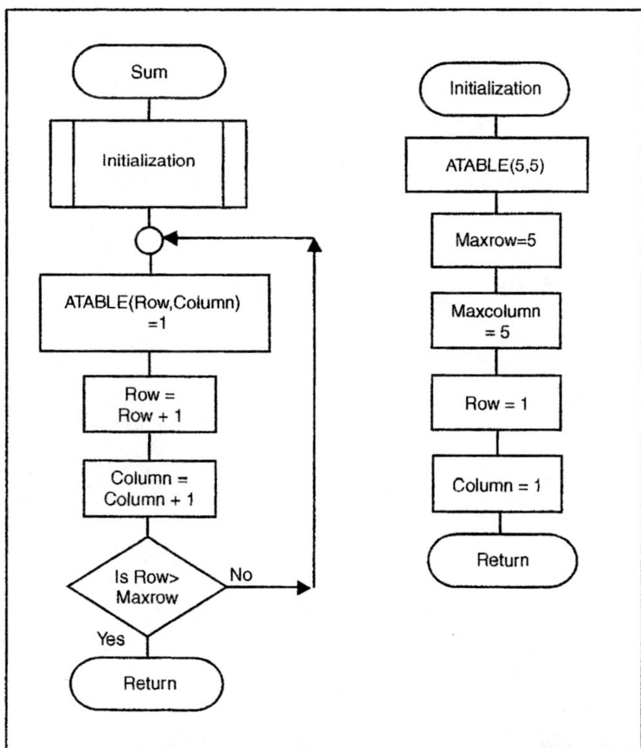

Figure 7.12 Objective 2 Exercise 3

4. Examine the flowchart in Figure 7.13 and explain what is happening to the table and its elements.

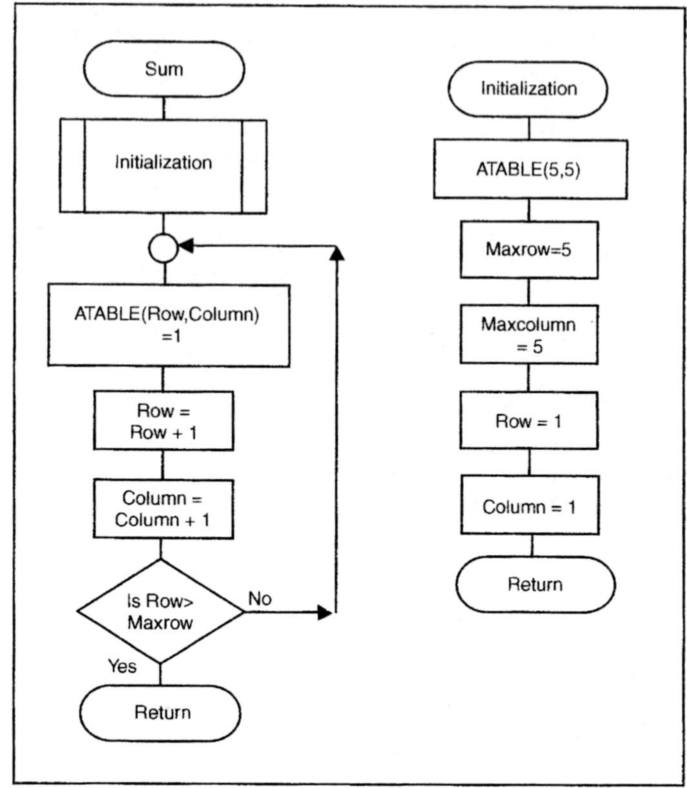

Figure 7.13 Objective 2 Exercise 4

5. Examine the flowchart in Figure 7.14 and explain what is happening to the table and its elements.

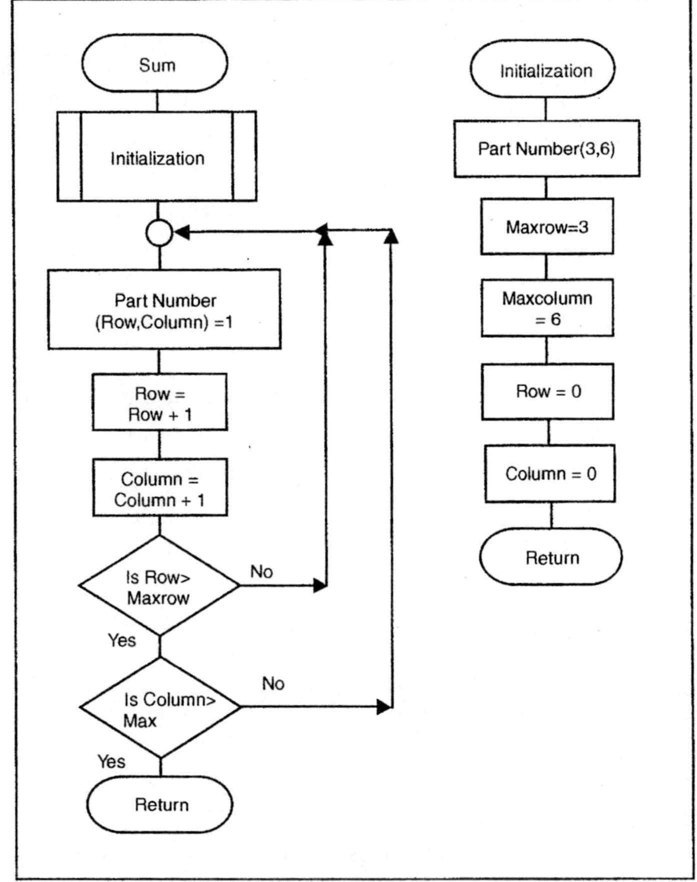

Figure 7.14 Objective 2 Exercise 5

Objective 3 Draw and revise flowcharts to solve problems using tables.

1. Draw a flowchart that prints all ten elements of a one-dimension table, using a loop structure, in reverse order (print 10th element first, then 9th, then 8th and so on, until the first element is printed). Show the statement declaring the table in the initialization module.
2. Draw a flowchart that prints all twenty elements of a two-dimension table that has four rows and five columns, using a loop structure. Show the statement declaring the table in the initialization module.
3. Draw a flowchart that determines how much income tax is owed given a particular income and number of dependents. Use current IRS Form 1040 instructions for the tax data. Determine the size of the tax table needed for this exercise. Show the statement declaring the table in the initialization module.

4. Draw a flowchart that prints all twenty-four elements of a three-dimension table that has the declaration Three_D(3,2,4), using a loop structure.
5. Draw a flowchart that loads a two-dimension table with data. The user will input the maximum values of the subscripts. The program will assume that the subscript values are less than or equal 100. The data should only be loaded into the table elements whose subscript values are less than that input by the user.
6. Redraw the flowchart in Figure 7.14 so that it works correctly and places a zero in each element of the table.
7. Redraw the flowchart in Figure 7.13 so that it works correctly and places a zero in each element of the table.
8. Draw a flowchart for a program that reverses the order of a one-dimension table. The last item goes in the first position and the first item goes into the last position, the next to last item goes into the second position and so on. Use a table of at least 7 items to do the desk check. The logic is different for even and odd length tables.

Objective 4

Enrichment – Doing it with Pseudocode

Read, write, and revise pseudocode using tables.

1. Read the pseudocode below and explain what is happening to the table and its elements.

```
Sum module
        ATABLE(5)
        Sub = 1
        Repeat
        ATABLE(Sub) = 1
        Sub = Sub + 1
        Until Sub > 5
Return
```

2. Read the pseudocode below and explain what is happening to the table and its elements.

```
Sum module
        ATABLE(8)
        Max = 8
        Sub = 1
        Repeat
```

```
        ATABLE(Sub) = 0
        Sub = sub + 1
        Until Sub > Max
Return
```

3. Read the pseudocode below and explain what is happening to the table and its elements.

```
Sum module
        ATABLE(5,5)
        Maxrow = 5
        Maxcolumn = 5
        Row = 1
        Column = 1
        Repeat
        ATABLE(Row,Column) = 1
        Row = Row + 1
        Column = column + 1
        Until Row > Maxrow
Return
```

4. Write pseudocode that prints all ten elements of a one-dimension table, using a loop structure, in reverse order (print 10th element first, then 9th, then 8th and so on, until the first element is printed). Show the statement declaring the table in the initialization module.
5. Write pseudocode that prints all twenty elements of a two-dimension table that has four rows and five columns, using a loop structure. Show the statement declaring the table in the initialization module.
6. Write pseudocode that determines how much income tax is owed given a particular income and number of dependents. Use current IRS Form 1040 instructions for the tax data. Determine the size of the tax table needed for this exercise. Show the statement declaring the table in the initialization module.
7. Write pseudocode that prints all twenty-four elements of a three-dimension table that has the declaration Three_D(3,2,4), using a loop structure.
8. Write pseudocode that loads a two-dimension table with data. The user will input the maximum values of the subscripts. The program will assume that the subscript values are less than or equal 100. The data should only be loaded into the table elements whose subscript values are less than that input by the user.
9. Write pseudocode for a program that reverses the order of a one-dimension table. The last item goes in the first position and the first item goes into the last position, the next to last item goes into the second position and so on. Use a table of at least 7 items to do the desk check. The logic is different for even and odd length tables.

Objective 5 Given a problem, identify, and describe the type of table to be used in the solution.

For each problem given below, determine what type of table you would use to help store the data (one-dimension, two-dimensions, three-dimensions, or no table). Show what the table definition statement would look like and explain what each dimension of the table would be in terms of the problem. Justify your table selection (why did you pick a one-, two-, three-, or no-dimension table). If you decided that a table should not be used, justify that decision. After selecting the table type, declare the table, load some sample data (you invent the data) into the table, and then print the data. Use either flowcharts, pseudocode, or both as directed by the instructor.

1. The results of a survey with 10 questions and 5 answers to each question is to be analyzed. The survey asks for the respondent's gender and some other demographics. The answers are to be analyzed by gender.
2. A company has 100,000 parts to use in their manufacturing process. Each part has a description, which requires up to 30 characters, and a corresponding part number of 10 characters. You want to be able to find and print the part description, given a part number.
3. A doctor with a small practice needs to keep an address listing for his patients. He needs to be able to print out a patient's name and address.
4. The university maintains a master file of all students who have ever attended the school. The file contains names, addresses, courses taken (by course number), SSN, and letter grades earned in each course. Design a program that will print a list of all students whose GPA is greater than 3.5.
5. A hotel has 750 rooms. The desk clerk needs to be able to retrieve a person's name that is staying in a particular room.
6. A hotel has 750 rooms. The desk clerk needs know if a room is occupied; and if so, what is the name of the occupant.
7. A hotel has 700 rooms. 300 rooms have one bed and 400 rooms have 2 beds. The desk clerk needs know how many rooms are available.
8. A company has four regions and each region contains several stores. The CEO wants to have a combined total of all sales in every department of every store within each region.
9. You want to design a program that will play a card game. The maximum number of players is six and each player will be able to hold five cards. The player will be able to discard one, two, or three cards and draw replacement cards.

Other Assignments

SoftSkills

Select one problem from Objective 3, 4, 5, or from the Internet/library research projects; prepare, and give an oral report to the class on your solution.

Internet/library research projects

A. Research table syntax in three different programming languages. Write a paper explaining what dimensions are supported in each language and how tables are declared. Compare and contrast the various techniques that the languages use for table implementation.

B. Find a real life application of tables and explain how tables could be used to computerize the application.

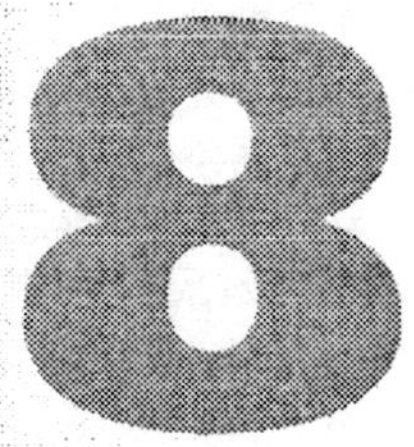

DATA VALIDATION

Too often we forget that genius. . . depends upon the data within its reach, that Archimedes could not have devised Edison's inventions.

(Ernest Dimnet)

OBJECTIVES

After completing this chapter, you will be able to:

1. Evaluate data to determine if they are correct or valid.
2. Identify the type of validity check that can be used on a given set of data.
3. Read, draw, and revise flowcharts that validate data.
4. Read, write, and revise pseudocode that validates data.
5. Understand key problems in establishing valid and correct data.

Introduction

Data managers command high salaries in today's market to accompany the high stress associated with their jobs. A data manager is responsible for the data associated with his/her company's primary business. In a credit card company, the data manager could bankrupt the business by poor management of the database. Data managers are primarily concerned with ensuring that their data are correct. Incorrect data can cause a manager to make a wrong decision, and the decision could lead to failure of the business (For want of a nail, a shoe was lost ...). The next section deals with how program designers can help ensure that data are valid if not correct.

Numeric Data and Character Data

For this text, *numeric data* is any string of elements that is composed entirely of the digits 0, 1, 2, 3, 4, 5, 6, 7, 8, or 9. The string 965 is composed of the digits 9, 6, and 5 and is therefore numeric data. The values of each digit are the ordinary numeric values. The digit 6 has a value of six. The string 965 would have the value nine-hundred sixty-five. Character data are all other data. For example, the string 67B would be considered character data. Notice, however, that there is a two-digit string 67 that would be numeric if we looked only at that portion of the data.

Correct Data

Correct data are data that can be verified through some form of calculation or comparison. For instance, 2 + 2 is 4 and 4 is the correct answer (assuming that we are working in base ten number system). If John Smith is paid at the rate of $10 per hour and he works 40 hours, his gross pay is $400. What if he tells us that he worked 40 hours, but he only worked 30 hours? Our computer database will show that he worked 40 hours, so he still receives $400 on payday, but $400 is not his correct pay. Given the limited information that he claimed to work 40 hours, a computer can't determine if the information is correct.

Is Paul Jones a correct name? What do we mean by a correct name? Most of us would agree it's a correct name if it represents a particular person and is spelled correctly. Can you tell if it is spelled correctly? What if it should be Paula Jones? It's not possible to verify that this name is correct in a computer program. The best we could hope for is to determine if it is a *valid* name.

Valid Data

Valid data are somewhat easier to discern. Using a workday as an example, it would be impossible for an employee to work more than 24 hours. Therefore, a time sheet that claimed 25 hours in one day would be an example of invalid data. Invalid data is also *incorrect*. This type of error can be eliminated by good programming (good designing) so that the program checks the input to determine if it is valid. The computer operator inputs 25 hours for a day's work; the program returns an error message stating that there are only 24 hours in a day, and the program asks for the data to be re-entered. Similarly, we would report an error if the time worked was entered as "A". Hours worked must be a number. What about working –5 hours? So we see then that valid daily work hours are limited to values between 0 and 24. To validate an "hours worked" entry, the program would check to see if the hours entered were greater than 24 (ERROR) or less than 0 (ERROR). Some computers would notice that "A" was not a number and refuse to let the operator enter a non-number. Some computers recognize a letter as a negative number so our validation routine would work without modification. That solves the majority of problems; but if you want to be certain that a number was entered, you would first check to see if the input was numeric. If the data were not numeric, then report an error; otherwise, check to see if the hours entered are within the range 0 to 24. Checking data for validity within a range is a *range test* (as you might expect).

Now let's look at date checking. What is a valid date? Is Feb. 6, 1944, a valid date? Is 6/7/78 a valid date? How did you know? Let's look at the rules for checking dates. We will assume that we are examining dates in a 6-digit sequence where there are 2 digits each for month, day, and year. The number representing months must be in the range from 1 to 12. There's our range check again. The number representing days must be in the range 1 to 31. But wait a moment. Is 09/31/99 a valid date? Nine is between 1 and 12, and 31 is between 1 and 31; but the ninth month only has 30 days, so even though this date satisfies the separate range checks for day and month, it is still an invalid date. We know that September, April, June, and November all have 30 days; whereas January, March, May, July, August, October, and December have 31 days. How can we program a computer to recognize these differences? One method is to load a one-dimensional table with the number of days in each month and then compare the input number of days with the number of days found in the table. What about February? Sometimes February has 28 days and sometimes (leap years) 29. Our question now becomes, "When are leap years?" (No, they are not just the years divisible by 4.) Simple questions can become very complex when all the facts are known. In order for us to design a computer program, we must know "all" the details; or else, the program will provide the users with wrong output. Poor designers can produce good programs, but even good designers will produce poor programs if they don't know the subject well enough to cover all the exceptions. The date problem is a good example of the problems that can be caused by poor design.

In the early days of computers, programmers had very little main memory to use; and they were famous for finding ways to save memory. One clever space-saving technique was storing the year as a two-digit number instead of a four-digit number.

Today, most people have heard of the Y2K problem; and it has been solved for the most part (what about the 2038 problem?[1]). But we still have the problem of determining exactly what year it is if the date is 09/25/00. Could it be 1900? 2000? 2100? For that matter, what year is represented by this date: 06/07/35?

To wrap up our date validity check, we need to check for valid years. Could 0000 be valid? 99? How about –5? This convention of negative years could be used to express dates BC, but that's a trick that we weren't prepared for; so for now, we'll assume that valid four-digit years have to be in the range greater than zero to 9999.

Now let's look at some examples. Suppose that you have names and addresses being input to a database, and you want to ensure that the data are as accurate as possible. You want to make sure that you check the data as it is being input, so let's begin with names. Is "John Smith" a valid name? How do you know? How would you write the rule(s) for validating a name? Are all names composed of letters? What about "C3PO?" "R2D2?" So, you didn't think of fictional names? Do you believe that there will never be a person with a numeric name? Perhaps by the time you read this, some famous rock star will have adopted a numeric name or some Star Wars fanatic will name their child after one of the fictional characters. When this book was being written, this was a humorous example in class; but I suspect there will soon be numeric names. Can you see some of the difficulties in validating data? Is "John Smyth" a valid name? Is "John Smyth" a correct name? Are you starting to see how bad things can get? Is it important? To answer these questions, think about how you would feel if your name was spelled wrong on your college transcript. Or how would you like your name spelled wrong on your paycheck, and the bank refused to cash the check? Yes, correct spelling is important. So far, no one has figured out how to write a computer program that will prevent this type of error.

How about the address part? Pretty hopeless, isn't it? The one bright spot here is the zip code. Zip codes must be numeric and either 5 or 9 digits in length, so we could do some validity checking. If we enter the city and state into a computer and then enter the zip code, we could have the computer check the master zip code directory to see if the data we entered matched the master directory. That's a second form of validity check, and a nice example of checking for correctness. Suppose we do that check and find that our zip code, city, and state don't match the master zip code directory. Does that mean we have entered incorrect data? This is an intentional trick. The master directory could be wrong, or we could have entered incorrect data.

Before you think that the validity checking is an impossible task, let's see what can be done.

1 The 2038 problem arises from the fact that the standard time library in C establishes a 4-byte integer format for the storage of time values. This format assumes that January 1, 1970 at 12:00:00 a.m. is the beginning of time (value zero). Time date values are expressed as the number of seconds occurring since the zero value. This 4-byte integer has a maximum value of 2,147,483,647, which represents the date January 19, 2038. Without intervention, any C program using the standard time library will begin having date problems after January 19, 2038. This is only one of many future computer problems that may occur as a result of the way we currently operate our computers.

Range Test

The range test is a method of checking for valid data. The range check can be used if the data are required to be in a specific range. Our date and time examples earlier are representative of this type of check. We know that there are 24 hours in a day, 7 days in the week, and 52 weeks in a year. These numbers help establish acceptable ranges for data. Figure 8.1 shows a sample flowchart for checking to see if a day is within an acceptable range. While all valid days must be numbered 1 through 31, they are not necessarily valid dates. For example, April 31 is not a valid date, even though day 31 is a valid number for a day.

Limit Test

The *limit test* can be thought of as a special version of the range check, where we only need to ensure that the data is below (above) the limit. In the credit card business, when you make a charge, the store checks with the credit card company to determine if you have exceeded your available credit limit. Notice that each customer could have a separate limit so that there is an analogy to the days in the month validation process. Another example is a checking account. When your check clears the bank, the bank checks your balance to ensure that you have funds to cover the check written.

Reasonableness Test

A third validity check is called a *reasonableness test.* This can be thought of as a range check with a little fuzzy logic thrown in. This test is not an exact test; and if some data fail this check, it usually means that a person will become involved in resolving the error. The reasonableness check is normally used to check orders for excessive quantities. Let's say that your credit card company receives a charge for you of 100 automobiles on one transaction. That's an unreasonable charge unless you are a car dealer. This transaction would not be approved until a person could verify it. Don't get overconfident; not all programs check data for reasonableness, and what is reasonable to some is unreasonable to others. The idea here is that even though you don't know an exact range for data, you could check the data for an approximate range.

Consistency Test

Another version of the reasonableness check, sometimes called a *consistency test,* uses two different fields of a record to determine validity. Suppose the data being entered consists of a birth date and an age. The birth date is entered as 02/25/99 (assume today's date is 04/14/01), and the age is entered as 11. An error exists here somewhere. Either the age or the birth date is wrong, and we can only determine that by having both data elements

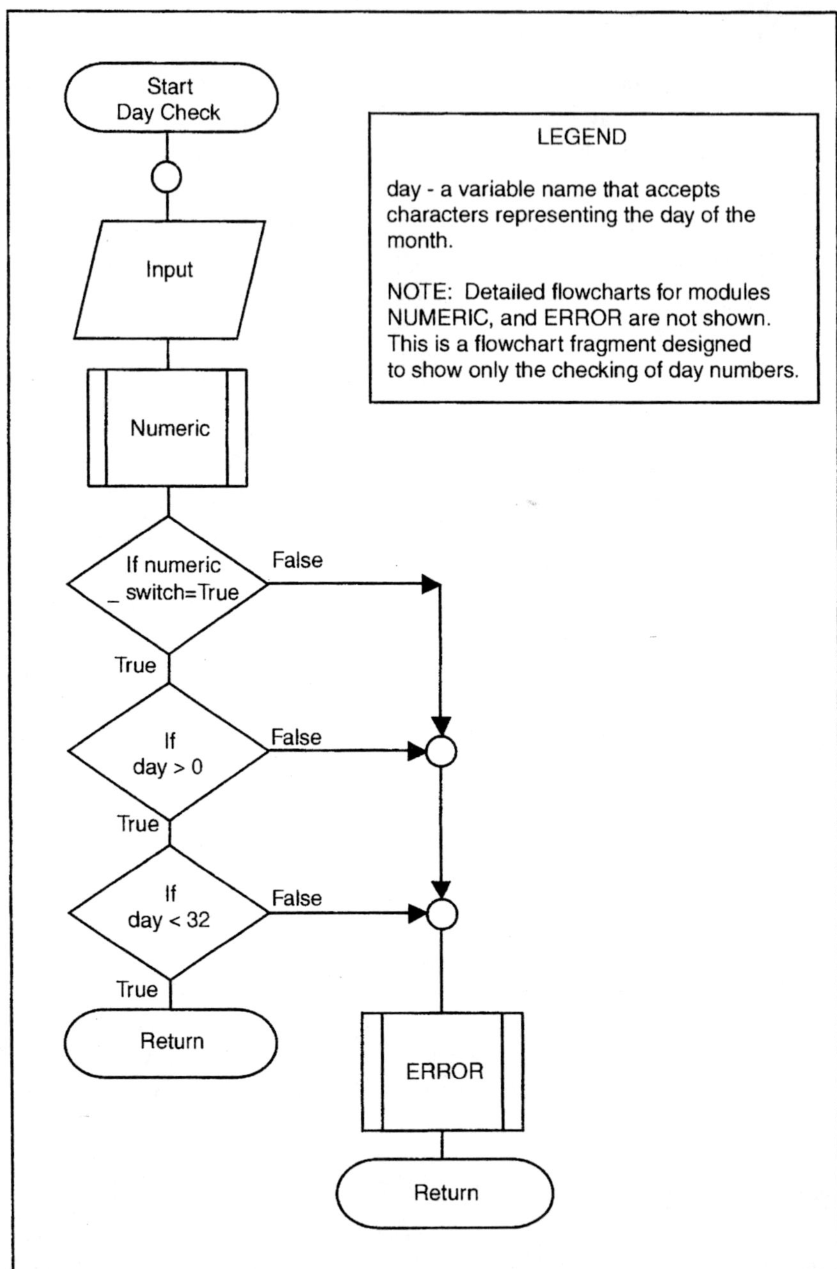

Figure 8.1 Day Range Check

available. Perhaps we have a person's birth date and wedding date: birth date 06/07/1995; wedding date 05/08/1990. While it is unusual for a person to be married before they are born, it is not impossible, so care needs to be taken when assuming data is invalid.

Completeness Test

A subtle variation of these checks is the *completeness test.* You will see this type of validation check in most of the Internet sites that ask for personal information. If you don't enter something in a required field, the program will continue requesting information until you have entered some data. In this case, valid data is any data.

Format Test

Another validity check is a *format test,* which is a variation of the completeness check. In this test, we look for a specific sequence or string of data. The standard format for a social security number is a good example. A social security number has 3 numeric digits, a dash, 2 numeric digits, another dash, and 4 numeric digits. If we are reading social security numbers into a computer, we could check to ensure that this format is followed by using a format check. Checking a social security number for the correct format does not ensure that the number is a valid number. Social security numbers also have restrictive ranges that need to be checked.

Exact Matches

The most restrictive validity check is that of *exact matches.* To see how this works, imagine that a customer purchases a widget by mail order and the computer has to determine if the widget is in stock. What range is acceptable? Well, it has to be an exact match. A gadget, in this example, is not a substitute for a widget. This type of check is often used on part number checking to ensure that a user doesn't request a part that doesn't exist. Each company that assigns part numbers keeps a record of all the part numbers assigned.

Class Test

Another type of validity check is a *class test,* which is used to determine if the data is of the proper class. Most computers support at least two classes of data: character and numeric. Numeric data are numbers, and character data are letters and other characters that are not numbers.[2]

Some computer languages support user-defined classes so that the programmer can define a specific class of data and the computer will "understand" how the class of data is manipulated. Once a class of data has been defined, the computer can usually determine whether or not a particular item is in that class. Data classes are particularly useful in object-oriented programming (OOP), as the objects are usually designated as a class. For

2 Character data is a very easy class of data to misunderstand. There is a character 7 (ASCII value 55 or binary 0011 0111) and a numeric 7 (ASCII value 7 or 0000 0111). Characters may look like numbers to people but may not really be numbers. To see the difference, write a simple program that adds characters, and compare the results of char 7 + char 7 to 7 + 7 (char stands for character). More detailed information on this subject can be found in Module 1.

example, in a college software system, it would be useful to have a class of data known as students. Students would have certain characteristics (like GPA, student number,and so on); and the software would be able to distinguish whether or not a given object was, in fact, a student. Student data would have operations defined like registering, dropping, and so on. The ability to define "classes" of data is an extremely powerful tool, and object-oriented software is becoming extremely popular at least partly as a result of this ability.

Testing to see if data is part of a particular class of data can be illustrated by showing how we test to see if data are numeric. If data are numeric, then they consist only of the digits 0, 1, 2, 3, 4, 5, 6, 7, 8, or 9. We can test data for these conditions as shown in Figure 8.2. This test assumes that data are input to the computer in strings of elements. Each element is represented in the computer with an ASCII value (see Appendix C). For simplicity we will use the decimal representation of the binary value in our flowcharts and pseudocode.

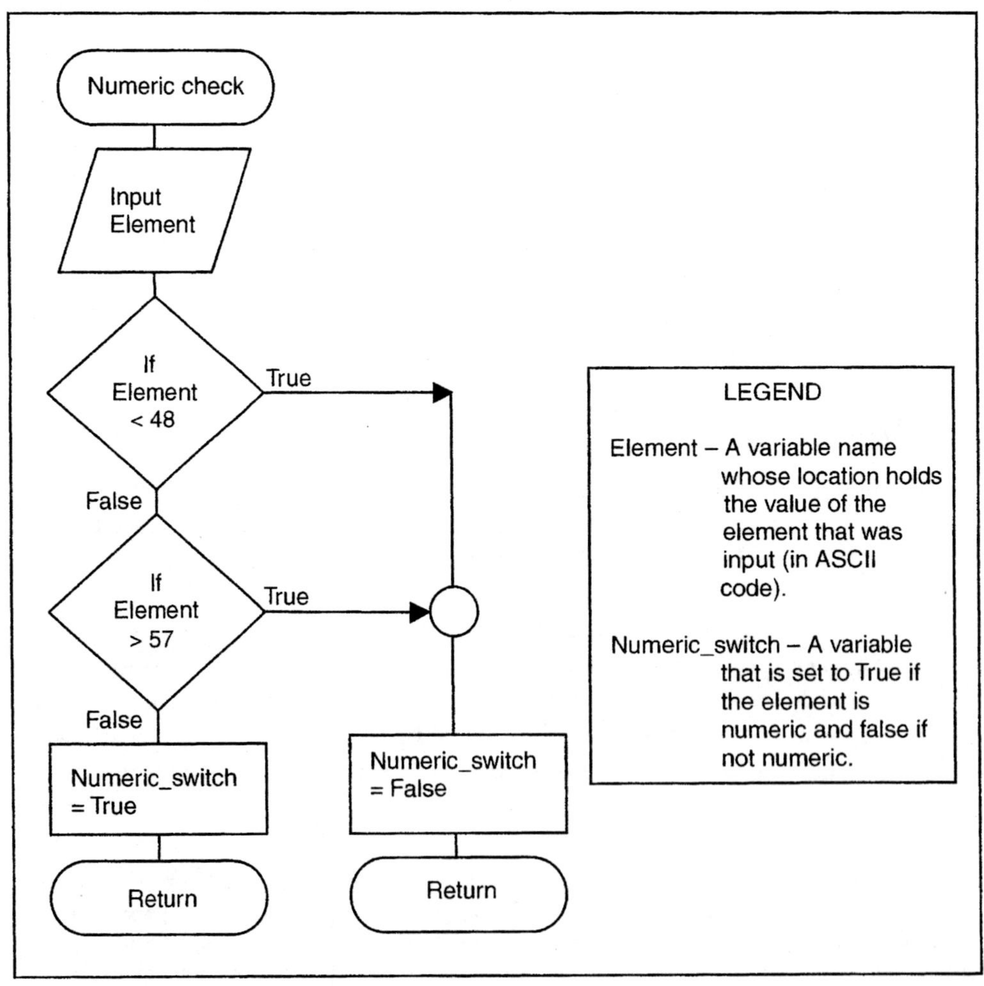

Figure 8.2 Numeric check

After studying Figure 8.2, how would you modify it so that you could test for alphabetic characters? Alphabetic characters refers to just the letters of the alphabet in this example.

If you study the ASCII code table in Appendix C, you should discover that the "numeric values" of the alphabet range from 65 to 90 for capital letters and 97 to 122 for lowercase letters. Therefore, a range check could be used to examine a character to determine if the character is a letter of the alphabet. A possible flowchart for this problem is shown in Figure 8.3.

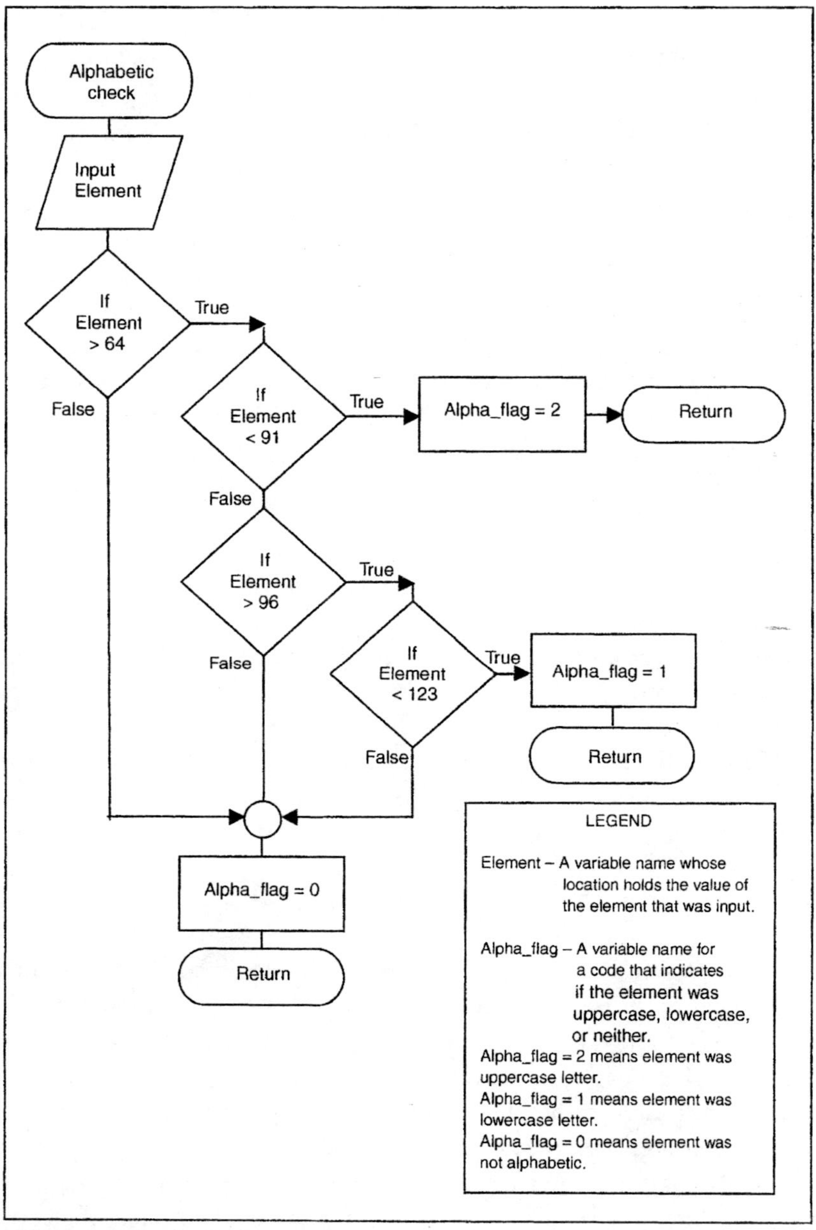

Figure 8.3 Alphabetic Check

This program examines an input element and determines if the element is an alphabetic character. If the character's value is greater than 64 and less than 91, then it is a capital letter. If the character's value is greater than 91 but less than 97, it is not a letter; and if it's greater than 96 and less than 123, it is a lowercase letter. A variable is set to the value "0" if the element is not a letter, "1" if the element is a lowercase letter, and "2" if the element is an uppercase letter.

Sequence Test

So far, we've been looking at validity checks that examine one record to find errors in that record. It's also possible to use multiple records to detect errors in data. For example, think of a bank program that processes checks and prints the check numbers of the processed checks on the checking account statement. Usually the checks are printed in numeric sequence; and if a sequence number is not present, the statement has an asterisk to indicate a missing sequence number. This validation check can be accomplished any time that data is in some form of sequence and is referred to as a *sequence test.* Suppose, for example, that your check numbers 101, 103, and 104 have cleared the bank. If you processed each check separately, you would never notice that check 102 was "missing." Thus we see that we would need to examine the check after 101, and see if it was 102 or something else. If the check number following 101 was not 102, and the checks were sorted by number, then we would know that check 102 was missing.

Validation Codes

Some programs use a table of codes or symbols called *validation codes* that help validate data on entry. For example, we could have a table of customer types that contains the description of the customer type and a simple numeric code (such as 1, 2, 3, 4, 5) that relates the description to the code that is being input. If the operator inputs a numeric code with a value not listed in the table, then we know there is an input error (unless of course the table is wrong). Over a period of time, the table can be corrected so that the table data have no errors; and therefore, any data retrieved from the table will have no errors.

Accuracy

Now that you've seen how data can be checked for validity, let's look at the more difficult test of checking for *accuracy*. We want all of our data to be accurate (correct). Unfortunately, no known computer test will guarantee accurate data. The old saying of "garbage in, garbage out" will continue to haunt us unless we can find a way to eliminate erroneous data. Here's the problem: Someone mistypes a name on entry to the computer so that the computer database has the name Messenger instead of Messinger. This is certainly valid data, but it contains a typographical error so it is wrong, and therefore not accurate. The only way it can be corrected is for someone to know the correct spelling, to recognize the error, and to have the database corrected. If you have ever tried to correct an error like this, you know that it can be impossible. In today's environment, names are re-sold on a mailing list as quickly as they are entered into someone's database. Thus the error is spread like a disease. A backup tape is made with the error on it; so if the backup is needed, the error is regenerated regardless of how it was repaired. The message here is that we will have to put up with some errors. As long as fallible humans are in the data loop, we will continue to generate errors in the data. The goal is to eliminate any errors that we can. Perhaps someday humans will be completely eliminated from the data chain and then there will be no errors?

Bowling Problem

Which of these validation tests can we apply to our bowling problem? One of the more obvious tests would be a limit test to ensure that no person bowled higher than a perfect score (300). We might also check bowlers' names against the table of names to ensure that no one bowled that was not on the official list. We would need to allow for misspellings when the names were input; so if a name did not match, we should display a message like: "Name not found, please check the spelling and re-enter."

Enrichment – Doing it with Pseudocode

The discussion of the previous algorithms doesn't differ in the pseudocode. Therefore, the pseudocode versions of the algorithms are provided here with no further discussion. We begin with Figure 8.4 and the range check algorithm as shown in Figure 8.1. We have introduced a special variable called Numeric_day that is set to "False" in the module Numeric_check if the "day" variable is not numeric. If the "day" variable is numeric, then Numeric_day is set to "True". We have also included a statement to prompt the user to input the data.

```
Day check
        Error = 0
        Print "Please enter the day that you want
             Checked."
        Input day
        Numeric_check
        If Numeric_switch = False Then
             Error
        Else
             If day > 0 Then
             If day < 32 Then
                  Valid_day
             Else
                  Error
             Endif
        Else
             Error
        Endif
         Endif
Return
```

Figure 8.4 Pseudocode Day Range Check

Next we show the numeric check algorithm in Figure 8.5 that was flowcharted in Figure 8.2.

```
Start Numeric_check
      Print "Please enter an element to
check."
      Input Element
      If Element < 48 Then
            Numeric_switch = "False"
      Else
            If Element > 57 Then
                  Numeric_switch = "False"
            Else
                  Numeric_switch = "True"
            Endif
      Endif
Return
```

Figure 8.5 Pseudocode Numeric Check

And finally, the pseudocode for alphabetic checking in Figure 8.6 as shown in the flowchart of Figure 8.3.

```
Alphabetic_check
   Print "Please enter an element to be checked."
   If Element > 64  Then
         If Element < 91 Then
               Alpha_switch = 2
         Else
               If Element > 96 Then
                     If Element < 123 Then
                           Alpha_switch = 1
                     Else
                           Alpha_switch = 0
                     Endif
               Else
                     Alpha_switch = 0
               Endif
         Endif
   Else
         Alpha_switch = 0
   Endif
Return
```

Figure 8.6 Pseudocode Alphabetic Check

Summary

In this chapter we examined methods to check data for validity and accuracy. Table 8.1 provides a summary of the major techniques for validating data in a single record and some examples of valid and invalid data.

Table 8.1 Validity Test Summary

Validity Test	Type of Data	Valid Data	Invalid Data
Range check	Days of the month	1, 2, 3, 4, 5, ... 31	0, -4, A, 45
Limit check	Credit Limit $5,000.	Any amount less than or equal to $5,000	Any amount greater than $5,000
Reasonableness check	Sales Transaction for an individual	1 stapler	1,000 staplers
Exact match	Model 123 gizmo	Model 123 gizmo	Anything other than the model 123 gizmo
Class Test	Numeric	All elements in a string are 0, 1, 2, 3, 4, 5, 6, 7, 8, or 9	Any element in a string containing other than 0, 1, 2, 3, 4, 5, 6, 7, 8, or 9

We really want accurate data, but the best we can do is to check for valid data. In many cases no validity checks can be done to establish valid data. Because of these limitations, we can always expect to have errors in our data. Since we know there are errors in the data, it makes sense to establish some procedures for correcting these errors. The next chapter addresses the topic of maintaining files, which is precisely the same as correcting errors in the data.

Key Terms

Each number in parentheses indicates the page where the term first occurs in the chapter.

accuracy (176)
class test (173)
completeness test (173)
consistency test (171)
correct data (167)
exact match (173
format test (173)
limit test (171)
range test (171)
reasonableness test (171)
sequence test (176)
valid data (167)
validation codes (176)

Chapter 8
Exercises

Objective 1 Evaluate data to determine if they are correct or valid.

1. Select the invalid dates from the list below and explain why they are invalid.

   A. 06/31/00 B. 02/30/00 C. 02/28/98
   D. 12/32/99 E. 13/01/01 F. 04/11/55
   G. 02/29/00 H. 12/25/-4 I. 02/29/1900

2. Select the invalid social security numbers from the list below and explain why they are invalid. (HINT: Check the library or Internet for validity requirements)

   A. 123-45-6789 B. 256-67-1256 C. 33A-46-3289
   D. 123-45-567A E. 312—4-6980 F. 000-00-0000
   G. 123-00-1234 H. 345-76-999 I. 369-01-0000

3. A computer prints out a grade point average for a college student as one of the values listed below. Determine if the values could be correct, or valid, or both, and explain why. Assume that the college is using the 4 point grading system.

   A. 4.9 B. 2.4 C. 4.0
   D. – 1.6 E. 0.5 F. 0.0

4. Credit card numbers are not randomly assigned. Examine the list below and determine which could not be valid VISA credit card numbers. Explain why they are not valid. (HINT: Check the library or Internet for validity requirements.)

   A. 1234 5678 1234 5432 B. 4111 1111 1111 1111
   C.4111 1111 1111 1121 D. 5121 2121 2222 3333
   E. 6011 0000 0000 0004 F. 4021 1212 3333 8016

5. Zip codes are not randomly assigned. Examine the list below and determine which could not be valid U.S. zip codes. Explain why they are not valid. (HINT: Check the library or Internet for validity requirements.) If the zip codes are valid, tell what city and state they belong to.

   A. 6247-2405 B. 76449 C. 01101-2114
   D. 98765 E. 99999-9999 F. 00001

6. The Library of Congress' Cataloging Policy and Support Office and Network Development and MARC Standards Office maintains a geographic area code list that includes separate codes for countries, first order political divisions of some countries, regions, geographic features, outer space, and celestial bodies. Select the valid geographic codes from the list below and tell what geographic area they are assigned to. (HINT: Try this web site for help http://www.loc.gov/marc/geoareas/gacshome.html)

   A. [n-us-tx] B. [zmo] C. [x]
   D. [a-xx] E. [zma] F. [zsu]

Objective 2 Identify the type of validity check that can be used on a given set of data.

1. Given the input data described, determine which validity checks should be used to validate the data. A date is in the format mm/dd/yy where mm stands for month, dd stands for day, and yy stands for year. Explain how the validity check would verify the data.
2. Given the input data described, determine which validity checks should be used to validate the data. A customer number is in the format xxxx-yy-xx-xxxxx, where the x stands for a numeric digit, and the y stands for an alphabetic character. Explain how the validity check would verify the data.
3. What validity checks would you use to verify that a social security number was valid? Explain how the validity check would verify the data. Could you determine if a social security number was correct? Explain.
4. What validity checks would you use to verify that a U.S. postal code (two-letter abbreviation for a state) was valid? Explain how the validity check would verify the data.
5. What validity checks would you use to verify that a U.S. telephone number was valid? An international telephone number? (HINT: Check the library or Internet for information pertaining to these items.) Explain how the validity check would verify the data.
6. What validity checks would you use to verify that a MasterCard credit card number was valid. Explain how the validity check would verify the data. (HINT: Check the library or Internet for information pertaining to these items.)

Objective 3 Read, draw, and revise flowcharts that validate data.

1. Draw a flowchart for a program that reads in groups of strings and determines if the string is numeric or not.
2. Draw a flowchart for a program that reads in and validates bowling scores (the maximum score in bowling is 300).
3. Draw a flowchart for a program that reads a date in an 8-digit sequence (month, day, year) and determines if the date is a valid date. IGNORE LEAP YEAR. Assume that February has 28 days, and establish a table of days in a month so that you can access the appropriate month to determine the correct number of days in a month. (EXTRA CREDIT: Add a leap year module to the flowchart, so that the flowchart determines when a leap year occurs and changes to allow February to have 29 days.)
4. Find the algorithm for leap year, and draw the flowchart that could be added to problem 3 to solve for leap years.
5. Draw a flowchart for checking the validity of a social security number. Can we draw a flowchart for checking the correctness of a social security number? Explain why or why not.

6. Draw a flowchart for a program that accepts a maximum of 10 characters of input from the keyboard and checks each character to see if it is numeric. A non-numeric character ends the computation. For the numeric characters, combine their values (0 through 9) and their place values (ten, hundred, thousand, and so on) to produce a number. Numeric characters are made into numbers using the following formula: If there's only one digit, the number is that digit. If there are two or more digits, then multiply the first digit by 10, and add the second. Multiply the combined result by ten and add the third. Continue multiplying the combination by ten before adding the next number. Do not multiply the last combination by 10.

   Example 1: The input was 1, Q. The number created is 1.

   Example 2: The input was 3, 2, 1, B. The number created is 321; (3 * 10 + 2); (32 * 10 + 1).

   Example 3: The input is 4, 6, 7, 3, A. The number created is 4673; (4 * 10 + 6); (46 * 10 + 7); (467 * 10 + 3).
7. The Luhn Mod 10 test is used as a part of the validity checking algorithm for credit card numbers. Draw a flowchart for the Luhn Mod 10 test algorithm. (Find the algorithm in the library or on the Internet.)
8. A subnet mask is a string of 32 bits. A valid subnet mask must have a "1" in the leftmost position and a "0" in the rightmost position. Draw a flowchart that will input a subnet mask, and determine if it is invalid.

Objective 4 Read, write, and revise pseudocode that validates data.

1. Write the pseudocode for a program that reads in strings and determines if the string is numeric or not.
2. Draw a flowchart for a program that reads in and validates bowling scores (the maximum score in bowling is 300).
3. Write the pseudocode for a program that reads a date in a 6-digit sequence (month, day, year) and determines if the date is a valid date. IGNORE LEAP YEAR. Assume that February has 28 days, and establish a table of days in a month so that you can access the appropriate month to determine the correct number of days in a month. (EXTRA CREDIT—add a leap year module to the pseudocode, so that the pseudocode determines when a leap year occurs and changes to allow February to have 29 days.
4. Find the algorithm for leap year, and write the pseudocode that could be added to problem 3 to solve for leap years.
5. Write the pseudocode for checking the validity of a social security number. Why can't we write pseudocode for checking the correctness of a social security number?
6. Write the pseudocode for a program that accepts a maximum of 10 characters of input from the keyboard and checks each character to see if it is numeric.

A non-numeric character ends the computation. If each character is numeric, combine the characters to produce a number. Numeric characters are made into numbers using the following formula: If there's only one digit, the number is that digit. If there are two or more digits, then multiply the first digit by 10, and add the second. Multiply the combined result by ten and add the third. Continue multiplying the combination by ten before adding the next number. Do not multiply the last combination by 10.

Example 1: The input was 1, Q. The number created is 1.

Example 2: The input was 3, 2, 1, B. The number created is 321; (3 * 10 + 2); (32 * 10 + 1).

Example 3: The input is 4, 6, 7, 3, A. The number created is 4673; (4*10+6), (46*10+7), 467*10+3).

7. The Luhn Mod 10 test is used as a part of the validity checking algorithm for credit card numbers. Write pseudocode for the Luhn Mod 10 test algorithm. (Find the algorithm in the library or on the Internet).
8. A subnet mask is a string of 32 bits. A valid subnet mask must have a "1" in the leftmost position and a "0" in the rightmost position. Write a pseudocode routine that will input a subnet mask and determine if it is invalid.

Other Assignments

SoftSkills

Select one problem from Objective 3 or 4 or from the Internet/library research projects below. Prepare and give an oral report to the class on your solution.

Internet/library research projects

A. Conduct some research to discover another date problem similar to the 2038 problem, and write a paper describing the problem that you discover.

B. Research the validity checking of e-mail addresses, and write a report on the results. Include a flowchart or pseudocode of any algorithm that you discover.

C. Research your state driver's license numbering system, and determine if there is an algorithm to check for valid driver's license numbers. Also check to see if there are invalid license plate numbers. Write a paper describing your findings.

FILE PROCESSING AND MAINTENANCE

Is not the whole world a vast house of assignation to which the filing system has been lost?

(Quentin Crisp)

OBJECTIVES

After completing this chapter, you will be able to:

1 Describe random and sequential access files and maintenance processes.

2 Read, draw, and revise flowcharts that process data files.

3 Read, write, and revise pseudocode that processes data files.

Introduction

Files were developed early in the computer game because early computers had very limited RAM. Today, even though we have millions and even billions of bytes of RAM, we still don't have anywhere near enough main memory to hold all of the data that we want to process. Therefore, data continues to be stored on auxiliary storage such as magnetic tape, magnetic disk, and optical disks (CD, DVD). The data stored on these external storage media are data files. This chapter will deal with disk files and tape files primarily, but the techniques are valid for any auxiliary storage device.

A great many file-handling procedures were established when files were stored exclusively on magnetic tape, and data stored on tape were accessed sequentially. Data stored on disk (CD or magnetic) can be accessed randomly, and this capability of random retrieval has revolutionized the data storage and retrieval processes. We need to develop an understanding of *sequential access* and *random access* before proceeding further into the chapter.

Sequential Access

Data stored in auxiliary storage are typically referred to as *files*. Files are composed of *records*. Within each record, components of the record are referred to as *fields*. As an example, consider a school with student records as shown in Table 9.1.

Table 9.1 Sample File of Student Records

Record Number	Last Name	First Name	Student Number	Street Address	Zip Code	Phone Number
1	Smith	Edward	123456	123 Mockingbird Ln	66601	817-555-1212
2	Jones	William	234561	456 Cherry St	66602	817-555-1213
(etc.)						

We have a file composed of student records (2 are shown). Each record in Table 9.1 consists of 7 fields: Record Number, Last Name, First Name, Student Number, Street Address, Zip Code, and Phone Number.

Now, imagine that 100,000 student records are stored on a magnetic tape. We want to find record number 45,678. To find that record, we process the tape using *sequential access*, which means we read the first record and see if it has record number 45,678. If not, we look at the second record; if it's not there, we look at the third and so on sequentially through the tape. We could, of course, start at the end of the tape and search backwards, provided we had tape drivers that supported backward reading of tapes. The point is, in sequential access, you must pass each record in turn before getting to the next one. Figure 9.1 is a flowchart for reading records from a tape and looking for a particular record. (See Figure 9.7 for the pseudocode example.) Many students suggest that we can fast forward through a tape, but that process is precisely the same as the flowchart in Figure 9.1. This flowchart uses the predetermined process symbol at the end to avoid describing the process that occurs after we find the given record.

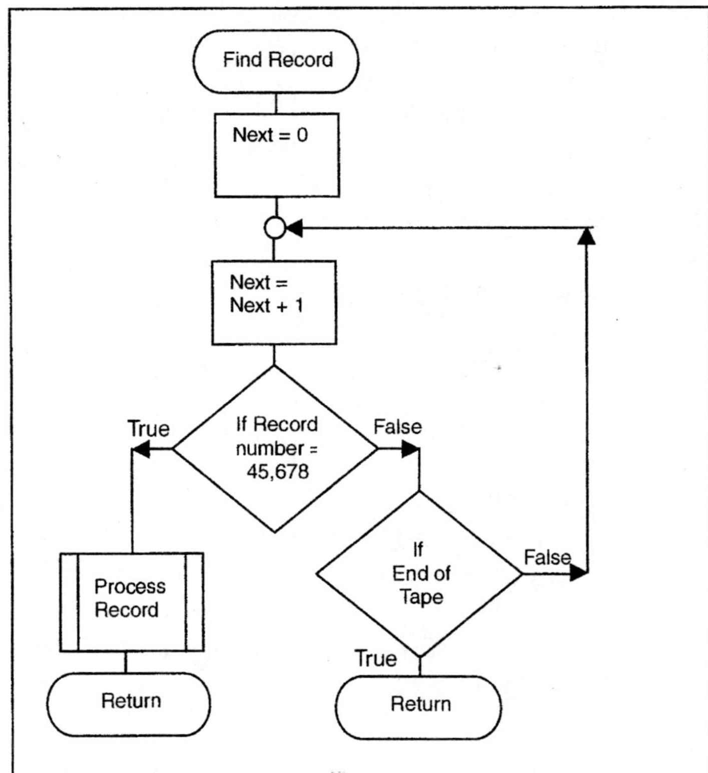

Figure 9.1 Sequential Access Flowchart

This flowchart also is only valid for finding the particular record number identified in the first decision symbol. To make this flowchart useful, we would want to put a variable name in place of the numbers; and then we could look for any number that might be input by the user. The point that this flowchart is making is that we must look at every record on the tape until we either reach the end of the tape, or we find what we are looking for. This process is identical to the sequential search of Chapter 8 except that the Chapter 8 search takes place in RAM, whereas this search is looking through a tape file. Notice that we used a decision symbol to ask the question: " Is this the end of the tape?" We'll expand on this "end-of-file" in a moment, but first let's see about the random access of records.

Random Access

In this case, each record is stored somewhere on the disk; and if we were clever enough to use the record number as our key to the storage location, we can use the *random access* method of finding the record. We simply ask for record number 45,678; and the disk operating system picks up that record without ever looking at the previous, first, or last record. This is a dramatic improvement over sequential access, and people often ask why we still bother with sequential access. It seems that magnetic tape is immune from obsolescence. Magnetic tape is still the best way to store huge amounts of data. We can store many terabytes of data on hard drives today, but businesses keep accumulating data. So, if this year's data is on disk, where do we put last year's data? We could buy another disk, but tapes are still a less expensive way to archive this data. Of course, if we have tape, we must have sequential processing. Let's revisit the flowchart of Figure 9.1 here in Figure 9.2, modified to conduct the record search using random access. (See Figure 9.8 for pseudocode.) The flowchart in Figure 9.2 was drawn with the assumption that record number 45,679 exists.

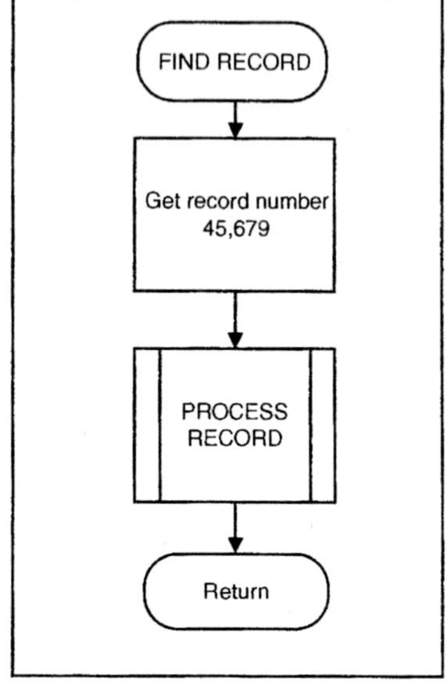

Figure 9.2 Random Access

Index (Key) Files

A popular method of referencing records in a data file is the use of an index or key field. In the indexed file, a special field is added to each record, and that field contains a key or index number. The index number is an integer assigned sequentially to each record so that the first record stored would have key number 1, the second record would have key number 2, and so on. When records are added to this file, they receive the next key number available automatically. The index can be used to generate a cross-reference table in RAM that can help us find a record quickly in a file that is not sorted. Let's look at an example where we are filing names and addresses. We will input a name to find that person's address. We could sort the file and do a binary search for the name (these techniques will be discussed in a later chapter). But if the file is very big and we are always adding and deleting names, we might find that there was insufficient computer time to keep the file sorted so we might try the index method. We would establish a two-dimensional table, where the first column contains the names in the file and the second column contains the key (index) number. So our table might look like Table 9.2.

Table 9.2 Index Table

Name	Index
Smith	1
Jones	2
Baker	3
Dragon	4
Beavis	5
Cartman	6
(etc.)	

You can see that the names are not in alphabetical sequence, but the keys are in numeric sequence. The next step is to sort the table. Notice that the table does not contain the address information. That information is stored on disk (auxiliary storage) and will be retrieved using the index number. Now we sort the table giving the results in Table 9.3.

Table 9.3 Index Table

Name	Index
Baker	3
Beavis	5
Baker	6
Dragon	4
Jones	2
Smith	1
(etc.)	

We now have a table in alphabetic order. When a name is input, we can quickly do a binary search to find the index number. The index number is the record number of the record in storage. As an example, suppose we want to find Mr. Cartman's address. We input the name Cartman; and the program determines that he has an index number of 6, which means that he is the sixth record in storage. We retrieve record number 6 and print the address from that record.

Index files allow us to store large unsorted files and retrieve the information from the file as if it was sorted. The key to success is the key field. Index files require an index table. As records are added to the file, deleted from the file, or changed, the table must be updated to match the file.

End-of-File

Most computer operating systems mark the ends of files on disk or tape with a special character. It's called an end-of-file mark on all systems, but it is not the same character on all systems. Its purpose is to let the operating system know where a file ends. Beginning programmers think that the end of a file is obvious, but it's not obvious to the computer so the ends are always marked. Some operating systems mark the beginning of a file as well.

If the programmer is familiar with the operating system's end-of-file mark, he or she can use the end-of-file mark to determine when the end of a file has been reached. Or, if the programmer knows how many records are in the file, then the end of file mark need not be accessed. Assume that you want to read a file from disk into main memory, and you know how many records the file has. You could count the number of records you read, compare that count with the known total, and then calculate when you had reached the last record of a file. Now suppose you don't know how many records are in a file. How will you know when you've reached the last one? The end-of-file mark tells us that we have reached the end of the file so we have actually passed the last record.

Now, if you don't know what the operating system's end-of-file marker looks like, what can you do? In this case, the programmer will have to invent a record to mark the end of the file so that when it is read in the future, the program can find the last record. Historically, the last record in a file was a record with the digit 9 in all field positions. The user could check for this record of nines after reading each record; and when this record was found, the program would know if it had reached the end of the file. This technique caused some businesses to be concerned during the Y2K crisis of 1999. They feared that the date 9/9/99 would trick the computer program into thinking that the end of the file had been reached, when in fact 9/9/99 was a real date[1].

An extremely important point to notice now is that the end-of-file mark is not a record in the file. It should not be processed, whereas the last record in a file should be processed. This difference requires a slight adjustment in the programming logic. Look at Figure 9.3 for the flowchart example or Figure 9.9 for the pseudocode example. On the left side of Figure 9.3, we see a flowchart for processing a file while checking for the end-of-file mark; and on the right, we have the logic for checking for the last record. You should see immediately the difference between the two flows. If the programmer/designer decides to add a dummy record to the end of the file, which logic of Figure 9.3 should we use? That's a little tricky; we don't want to use either exactly. We can modify the end-of-file logic to check for our dummy record and terminate so we want basically the logic shown on the left side of Figure 9.3.

1 The concern over the nines record was misplaced. If a programmer had used the nines technique in place of the end-of-file, then the nines record for the date field should have been 99/99/99. That date is obviously not the real date 9/9/99, so this expected problem turned out to be a false alarm.

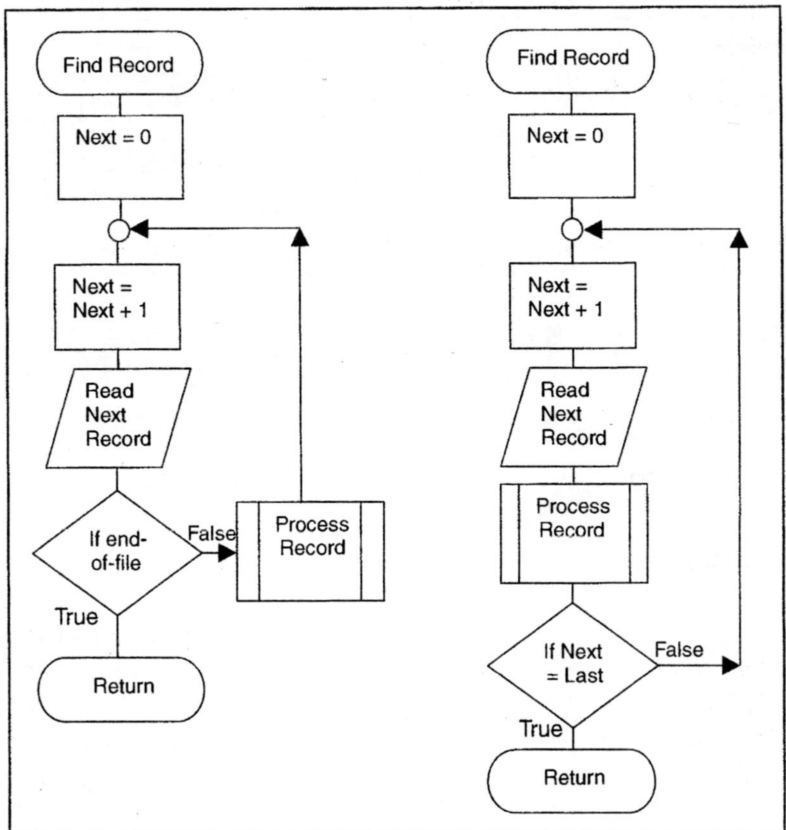

Figure 9.3 End of file/Last Record Comparison

Special Symbols

Until now, we have used the generic input/output symbol to get the data into memory. We could use the special symbols shown in Figure 9.4 to perform the same task of reading data files. Notice that in these symbols, we have indicated the name of the file that contains the data we are using. When flowcharting file operations, it is imperative that you identify the source and title of the file. Use of these special symbols is optional.

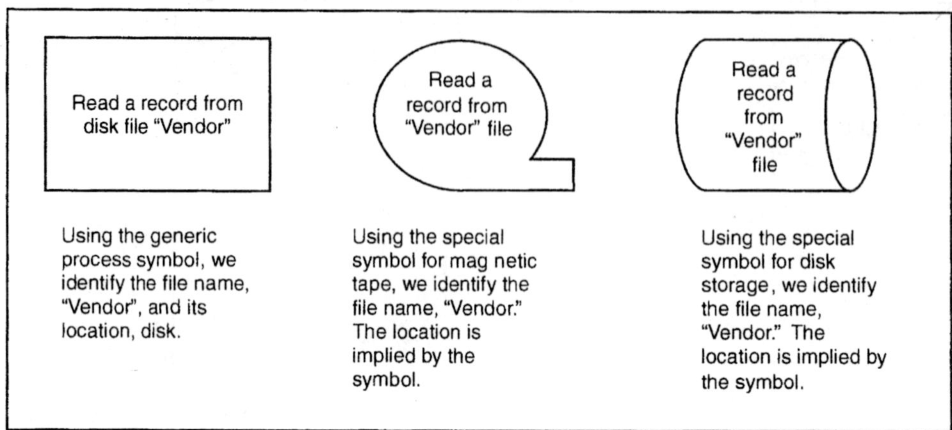

Figure 9.4 Special Symbols

File Maintenance

Why do we want to read files? Files contain data. Sometimes we want to look at the data, sometimes we want to change the data, and sometimes we want to reorganize (sort) the data. Remember from the previous chapter that our data always contain errors? File maintenance is the place that we repair those errors. Experience has shown that there are four things we can do with records in a file:

1. Create new records.
2. Delete records.
3. Read the records.
4. Change data in the records.

These four items represent **all** the actions that can be taken on data. Performing these actions is referred to as *file maintenance*, and the programs that perform these tasks are called *maintenance programs*. Various people have invented mnemonics to help them memorize the four items. One of the more popular mnemonics is:

CRUD:

C = Create

R = Read (this would include printing, sorting, and viewing)

U = Update (this is equivalent to change)

D = Delete

Other mnemonics include AUDI (Add, Update, Delete, Inquire) and ACID (Add, Change, Inquire, Delete). Whichever mnemonic you select, you will find that there are only four basic operations to perform on file data. These operations are performed regularly in all businesses on practically all files. Therefore, as a programmer or program designer, you can expect to create maintenance programs that perform these operations.

Let's examine the maintenance operations in more detail. To do that, let's take a familiar case where data is used like a college student database. Our imaginary database will contain records of students' names, addresses, courses taken, social security numbers, grades, and class standings (freshman, sophomore, and so on).

Creating Data

We begin with *creating data*. Creating data means that we are adding records to the database. This would occur when a new student enrolls in the college. Creating data is also considered to be entering data or adding data.

Reading Data

We *read data* anytime that someone wants to see some information about a student. This is equivalent to "inquire" in the AUDI and ACID mnemonics and is often referred to as querying the database because most database languages use the term query (SQL, for example, is the Structured Query Language). In our example, the advisor would want to see what courses a student had completed before advising what courses to take.

Updating Data

Updating data is equivalent to changing data and correcting data. When we say "changing," notice that this could include deleting some items, adding some items, or updating some items; so in effect, three of the four maintenance activities are all incorporated in the overriding property of change. For example, someone's name is misspelled in the database so we have to delete the wrong part and insert the correct part. You may think of this as a deletion and an addition or simply as an update. If the whole record is incorrect, you would probably choose to do a deletion and a creation, but usually small errors can be corrected more easily using the update process. A simple example of updating, which should occur automatically, is the case of a student advancing from freshman to sophomore.

Deleting Data

Finally, there is the *deleting data*. This means that the data is removed from the database and might represent a student dropping out or graduating from college. Normally, dropping data from one database requires adding it to another database. Colleges, for example, must keep student records of grades forever, but the computer space for student records is limited so we might find a separate tape file of inactive students.

This completes the study of maintaining files. You should be able to fit any data maintenance into one of the four categories discussed above. In some cases, you may be able to fit an operation into more than one category.

Using Files

Whenever you design a program that uses files, it is important that the files be identified to the programmer so that the programmer accesses the correct files at the correct time. All computer files have a name. File naming procedures are similar to the procedures used for naming variables. That is to say that filenames should be meaningful to the reader. Which name is better: VXB123, or Payroll Master File? Hopefully you picked the second name, although it's possible that VXB123 has a special meaning for some project and could someday be a meaningful filename.

When you intend for a program to use a file, the file should be opened in the hierarchy chart under the Initialization section. In addition, the file should be closed in the Termination section of the hierarchy chart. Some computer languages require that files be opened and closed within the program; some require the files to be opened before the program is run; and some languages open and close the files automatically as they are accessed in the program. You should assume that file opening and closing is required unless you are certain that it is not. In the flowchart, always show the proper name for a file so that there can be no misunderstanding as to which file is being used at a particular time.

If there are a fixed number of records in a file, you can plan to use a record counter to determine the end of the file. Applications can be designed so that the number of records in a file is always known, but that sometimes requires some programming overhead. If there is a system end-of-file marker, it is important for the programmer to be familiar with it and its use. A word of caution, however, for the programmer who is writing a program to run on a variety of machines. Since each machine could have a different end-of-file mark, the programmer would need to invent an end-of-file marker or have the program determine the system's end-of-file marker when it is run, rather than program in a specific end-of-file mark. A final caution on using files is to be certain that you check for empty files. If a file doesn't contain any records, it is critical that no records be processed. The dummy record was developed in part to be used to prevent any file from being empty. However, empty files are not a problem, as long as you are prepared for them[2].

Bowling Problem

In a previous chapter, we placed bowling scores into a table for processing. One problem with the table concept that we were using was that the table was stored in temporary storage (RAM) and could be lost if the computer's power failed. In that case, the data would have to be re-entered into the computer. That problem can be avoided by placing all of the bowling data onto a disk file (permanent storage). We can use the same structure for the disk file that we used for the table, and the processing will be very similar. Processing

2 Many people are curious as to how a file can be empty. One non-obvious way to have an empty file is to delete a record from a file that only had one record.

the disk file will take slightly longer than processing the table, but the processing time increase would be substantially less than re-entering the table. Table 9.4 depicts the file structure for the bowling scores. Ways to store this data more efficiently exist, but that discussion is beyond the scope of this text.

Table 9.4 Bowling Scores File

Record	Week	Team	Bowler	Game	Score
1	1	1	1	1	125
2	1	1	1	2	140
3	1	1	1	3	164
4	1	1	2	1	225
(etc.)					

To get the data into a disk file, we might use a flowchart like Figure 9.5.

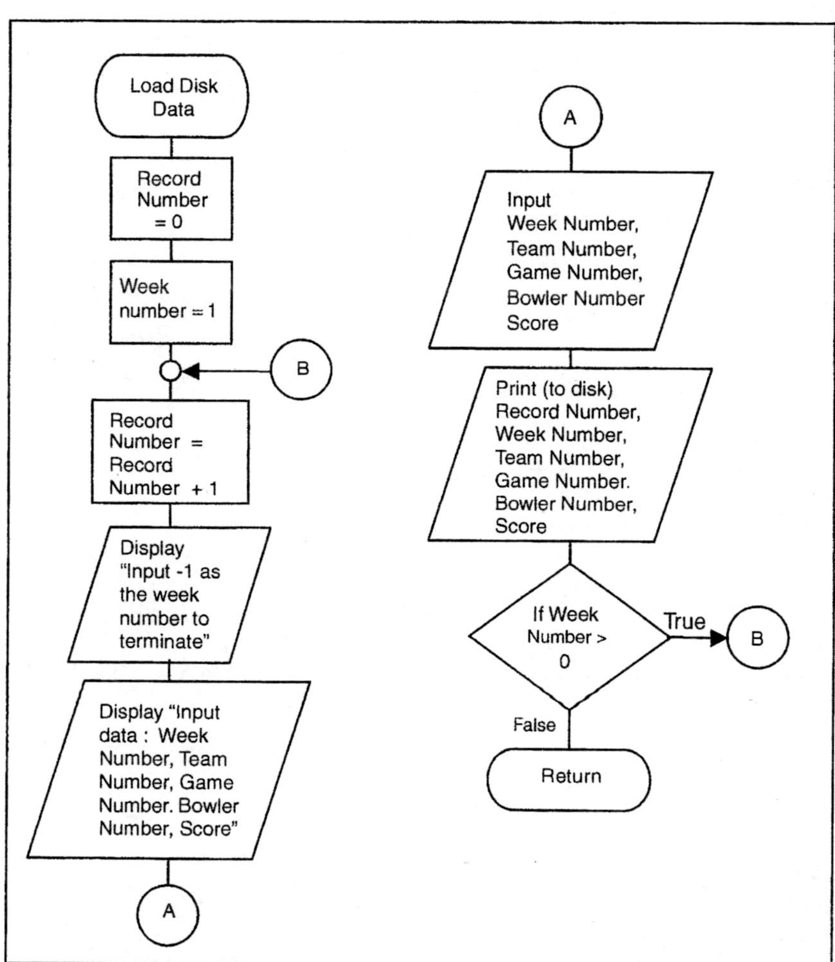

Figure 9.5 Bowling Data Input

To process the data in Table 9.4, we could use the flowchart in Figure 9.6. Notice that the flowchart of Figure 9.5 only reads the data from disk and then stores it in the table that was discussed in Chapter 7. The table can then be used to process the necessary statistics. The advantage of having the file is to maintain the data in permanent memory.

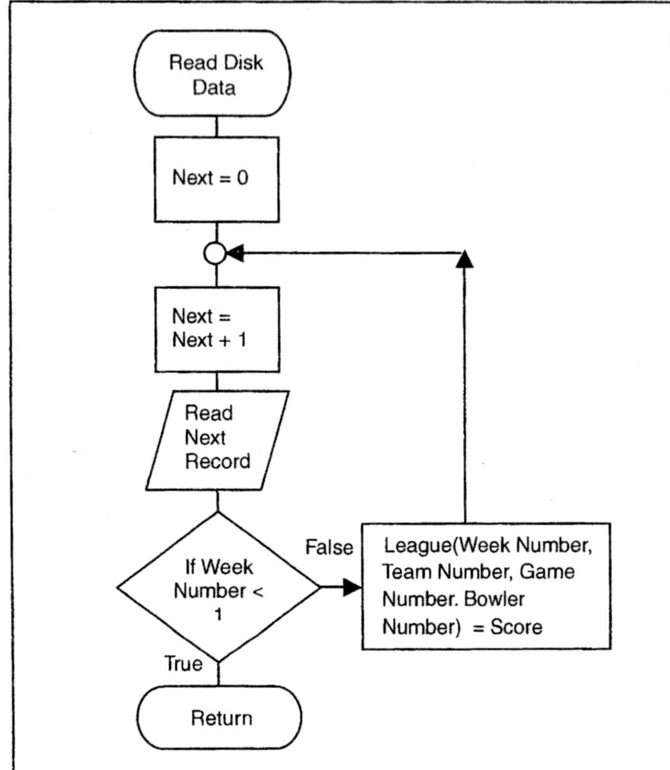

Figure 9.6 Bowling File Flowchart

Enrichment—Doing it with Pseudocode

Continuing the theme of demonstrating the solutions in pseudocode as well as flowcharts, we will next describe the file maintenance process using pseudocode.

To read through a sequential file and identify a record, we could use the module shown in Figure 9.7. You may want to refer to Figure 9.1 to compare the two methods.

```
Sequential_read
Next = 0
While Record_numbdr End_of_tape
Next = Next + 1
Read Next Record
If Record_number is 45,678 Then
        Process_record
Else
Endif
Endwhile
Return
```

Figure 9.7 Sequential Access Pseudocode

To find a record using random access files, we could use the code described in Figure 9.8. Figure 9.2 has the corresponding flowchart. Notice that this logic assumes that record number 45,679 actually exists.

```
Find_record
Get Record Number 45,679
Process_record
Return
```

Figure 9.8 Random Access Pseudocode

Our final example is shown in Figure 9.9, where we compare the two methods of processing an entire file. On the left, we have a process that continues until the end of file is located, while on the right, the logic progresses through a known number of records.

```
Read_until_end_of_file
Next = 0
While End_of__file = "False"
   Next = Next + 1
   Read Next record
   Process record
Endwhile
Return
```

```
Read_all_records
Next = 0
Repeat
        Next = Next + 1
         Read Next Record
        Process record
Until Next = Last
Return
```

Figure 9.9 End-of-file/Last Record Pseudocode

The logic in the right column can be used because we know what the last record number is, whereas the logic in the left column assumes that we don't know how many records are in the file, so we continue processing until the end of file is detected.

The bowling data input flowchart from Figure 9.5 is implemented next in pseudocode.

```
Load Disk Data
   Record_number = 0
   Week_number = 1
   Dowhile Week_number > 0
         Record_number = Record_number + 1
         Display " Input '-1' as the week number to terminate"
         Display " Input data: Week Number, Team Number, Game
                            Number, Bowler Number, Score"
         Input Week_number, Team_number, Game_number,
              Bowler_number, Score
         Print Record_number, Week_number, Team_number,
              Bowler_number, Score
   Endwhile
Return
```

And finally, we implement the flowchart from Figure 9.6 in pseudocode.

```
Read Disk Data
       Next = 0
       Dowhile End_of_file = False
            Next = Next + 1
            Read Record Next
            League(Week_number, Team_number, Game_number,
               Bowler_number) = Score
       Endwhile
Return
```

Summary

This chapter was devoted to processing data from files. Sequential access and random access are the two types of file access available. Files consist of records, and records consist of fields. The operating system marks the end of files using a special end-of-file character. File maintenance is always necessary because we expect all data to have errors. We maintain files by creating the data, reading the data, updating the data, and deleting the data.

Key Terms

Each number in parentheses indicates the page where the term first occurs in the chapter.

creating data (195)
CRUD (194)
data files (188)
deleting data (195)
end-of-file (189)
fields (188)
file (188)
file maintenance (194)
index (key) files (190)
maintenance programs (194)
random access (190)
reading data (195)
records (188)
sequential access (188)
updating data (195)

Chapter 9 Exercises

Objective 1 Describe random and sequential access files and maintenance processes.

1. When would it make sense to use sequential access to access a disk file? Explain your answer.
2. Compare and contrast random access files with sequential access files.
3. ROM (Read Only Memory) is an important memory/storage device in today's computers. Describe a ROM device that uses sequential access. Describe a ROM device that uses random access.
4. Three mnemonics, ACID, CRUD, and AUDI, were mentioned in the chapter. Explain how each letter of each mnemonic describes the actions of the others.
5. The acronym CRUD was used to describe the operations that could be performed on data. Examine the list of data maintenance terms listed here and determine where they belong in the CRUD list. Explain why you classified each item as you did.

   A. add records   B. change records   C. change fields
   D. add fields   E. delete fields   F. correct data
   G. back up data

6. Describe the process for deleting a record from a disk file. What does deleting mean? (HINT: What happens, exactly, when you delete a file from your disk?) Assume there were five records in a disk file, and you deleted the third one. Show the file contents before and after the third record was deleted. Include the record numbers in your description.
7. Do you suppose that we can create a file without errors? Defend your position in writing. You should assume that the file is very large and changes can be made to the file to repair any errors that are discovered.

Objective 2 Read, draw, and revise flowcharts that process data files.

1. Read the flowchart in Figure 9.10 and determine what task(s) is(are) being accomplished.

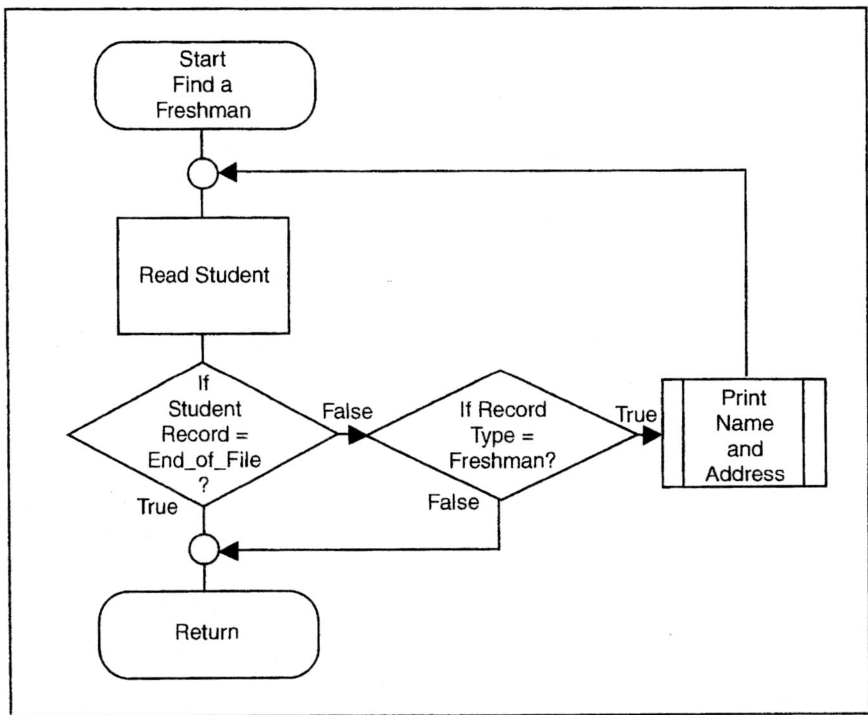

Figure 9.10 Exercise 1, Objective 1

Objective 2:

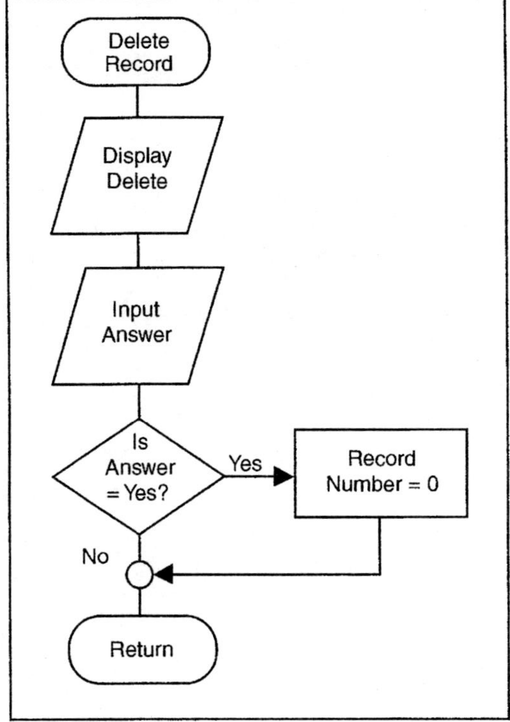

Figure 9.11 Exercise 2, Objective 1

2. Read the flowchart in Figure 9.11 and determine what task(s) is (are) being accomplished.
3. Draw a flowchart that reads a customer file from disk and allows an operator to change the spelling of the name of a customer listed in that file. The corrected name replaces the incorrect name in the file.
4. Draw a flowchart that reads through a student data file and prints out all the information on students that don't have a valid social security number.
5. Draw a flowchart that reads all of the records from a file and combines them with the records of another file. (NOTE: This is commonly called merging files.)
6. Draw a flowchart that will read the bowling league disk file and compute the average for each bowler.
7. Draw a flowchart that will read the bowling league disk file and find the highest game and highest series bowled. (HINT: You must calculate the series scores because they are not in the disk file.)
8. Create a task list, and draw a hierarchy chart for a program that performs file maintenance. You should have modules for each letter of the mnemonic CRUD. Include a detailed flowchart for each of those modules.

Enrichment – Doing it with Pseudocode

Read, write, and revise pseudocode that processes data files.

1. Read the pseudocode fragment shown below and determine what task(s) is (are) being accomplished.

```
Print_name
      Next = 1
      Read Student_record
      While Student_record ≠ End_of_file
      If Student type = F Then
           print student name and address
      Else
      Endif
      Read Student_record
      End while
Return
```

Read the pseudocode fragment shown below and determine what task(s) is (are) being accomplished.

```
Delete_record
      Display Delete_question
      Input Delete_answer
      If Delete_answer = yes Then
           Record_number = 0
      Else
      Endif
Return
```

3. Write the pseudocode that reads a customer file from disk and allows an operator to change the spelling of the name of the customer. The corrected name replaces the incorrect name in the file.
4. Write the pseudocode that reads through a student data file and prints out all the information on students that don't have a valid social security number.
5. Write the pseudocode that reads all of the records from a file and combines them with the records of another file. (NOTE: This is commonly called merging files.)
6. Write the pseudocode that will read the bowling league disk file and compute the average for each bowler.
7. Write the pseudocode that will read the bowling league disk file and find the highest game and highest series bowled. (HINT: You must calculate the series scores because they are not in the disk file.)
8. Create a task list, and draw a hierarchy chart for a program that performs file maintenance. You should have modules for each letter of the mnemonic CRUD. Include detailed pseudocode for each of those modules.

Other Assignments

SoftSkills

Select one problem from Objective 1, 2, or 3, or from the Internet/library research projects. Prepare and give an oral report to the class on your solution.

Internet/library research projects

A. Find a business that uses computer files, and determine what type of file access they use (sequential or random). Write a report describing the company, their file structure, and file access mechanism.

B. Research file handling application software, and write a report detailing your findings.

C. Research end-of-file marks, and write a report discussing the various techniques that you discover.

D. Research other mnemonics like CRUD, AUDI, and ACID, and compare their explanations with what you have learned. Describe the other mnemonic that you found in a written report.

10

BUSINESS REPORTS

This report, by its very length, defends itself against the risk of being read.
(Sir Winston Churchill))

OBJECTIVES

After completing this chapter, you will be able to:

1 Evaluate data to determine if they are correct or valid.

2 Read, draw, and revise flowcharts for business reports, including the control break report.

3 Read, write, and revise pseudocode for business reports, including the control break report.

Introduction

Business reports contain the information that keeps businesses busy. Reports are gathered from managers, provided to managers, provided to the government, and provided to the stakeholders (stockholders are one form of stakeholder). There seems to be an unlimited requirement for reports in business. Of course, every different business requires some different reports. However, from a systems analyst point of view, we can reduce the types of reports to a manageable number without much loss of detail. Many methods are available to simplify the types of reports; the author has chosen one method here.

Report Types[1]

For this course, business reports come in three basic styles: the detail report, the summary report, and the exception report. The names of the reports have a great deal of meaning, as you will see in the following paragraphs.

Detail Report

The *detail report* is a list of details. In a college environment, a complete list of all students enrolled in the college would be a detail report. In business, this might be the list of all parts stocked, the complete payroll list, or a customer list. This report contains all of the details, hence its name "detail report." This report is also sometimes called a listing. In computer jargon it can be known as a "dump."

Summary Report

A *summary report* is a summarization of the details. To see an example of a summary report, the user can print the summary section of a detail report. In a college this might be something like the total number of students registered in each semester of this school year. We don't list all the students, but we do provide a count. Notice in this example that the detail report is longer and has more details than the summary report. In the business example, we could look at total payroll by department as a summary report.

Exception Report

Finally, we have the *exception report.* The exception report is typically a list of errors (exceptions) that were found when printing some other report or when validating the data. A college example of this type of report would be a list of all students enrolled who didn't have a student number. Surely everyone in the database has a student number. How did they get in the database without a number? Well, it happens sometimes,

1 This chapter deals with business reports in their simplest form. Many details are avoided in favor of describing the logic. Modern business reports are printed in various formats and in a variety of fonts and pitches. These style changes can be added to the flowcharts shown in this chapter quite easily.

and printing an exception report provides a list of exceptions so that the data can be cleaned up. Our exception report for payroll might be a list of the non-hourly employees, or perhaps the list of employees who didn't get paid.

Report Sections

Regardless of which type of report you are printing, all reports normally have three sections: *heading*, *detail*, and *summary*. The terms are generally self-explanatory and should require little effort to remember. The three sections are aligned with the three major modules in a hierarchy chart.

Heading Section

The *heading section* of a report contains the title and column headings and is usually programmed in the initialization section of the hierarchy chart. In an English paper, the heading section would be known as the introduction. Obviously, all three types of reports would have headings.

Detail Section

The *detail section* of the report contains the details of the report (in English class, this is called the body) and is usually programmed in the process section of the hierarchy chart. The *detail lines* of a report should not be confused with a detail report. All three report types discussed above have a detail portion. The detail lines are the details of the particular report being printed. In an exception report that lists college students without a social security number, each student listed would be listed in the detail portion. In a summary report, there would also be some details.

Summary Section

Finally, the *summary section* of a report contains the summary statistics for the report. In this final section, you find the grand total and the "bottom line." This section of the report is normally printed in the termination section of the hierarchy chart. Again, all three types of reports have a summary section. In English class this is called the conclusion.

Input and Output Forms

In order to properly design programs for business reports, the designer should be familiar with various *input forms* and *output forms*. These include print layout or printer output forms, file specification forms, and screen design forms. Input and output forms come in a variety of shapes, sizes, and styles. When the normal input device was a card reader, the input form was laid out like an 80-column card[2] so that the designer could quickly see which columns contained which data. In today's computer environment, the input can come from disk, keyboard, tape, and occasionally from other devices.

2 In the early days of computers data was input and output to/from a computer on a heavy piece of paper called a card. The card was approximately 3 inches by 8 inches and had holes punched into it to record the data.

The designer needs to know where the data are coming from and in what format they will arrive in order to process them correctly. Output can be delivered to a monitor, disk, tape, and other devices; and the designer must know which output device is being used in order to properly format the output.

File Specification Form

Table 10.1 shows a sample disk input/output format for a disk file. The form is called a *file specification form* because it gives the specifications for the information in the file and its location within the file.

This form is required by the programmer/analyst so that the variable names are standardized across the system and so that data gets stored and retrieved from the proper fields. The preceding file structure is a fictitious sample and is used only to illustrate some of the information required for processing a file.

Similar forms can be used for input so that the operator knows which fields contain certain data, and other forms are used to show the output format. Today, some of the more common forms used for output are the printer form and the screen form.

Table 10.1 Sample File Specification Form

File Specification Form—Student File

Location (Starting Byte	Length (In bytes)	Type	Field Name	Contents
1	9	N	SSN	Social Security Number
10	20	A	Last	Student Last Name
30	15	A	First	Student First Name
45	10-	A	Middle	Student Middle Name
55	30	A	Street	First address line
85	10	A	Apt	Second address line
95	20	A	City	City of residence
115	2	A	State	Two letter state code
117	5	N	Zip	5-digit zip code
122	4	N	Zip4	4-digit zip extension

** Type code: A means alphabetic data and N is numeric

Printer Output Form

A sample printer output form is shown in Figure 10.1. The designer fills in the printer layout chart exactly as the user wishes to see the final report. Thus it is very simple to see if the page is wide enough to hold all of the information, and the designer can ensure that the user is satisfied with the format before the computer is programmed.

Printer Output Form

Application: ____________________ Date: ______________

Programmer: ____________________

```
 2                                              Report   Title    Centered    Here
 4                                                                Dollar        Dollar        Dollar          TOTAL
 5    Seq          Heading 1       Heading 2                      Amount 1      Amount 2      Amount 3
 7      1          AAAAAAAAAAA     AAAAAAAAAAAAAAAAAAAA            xxx.xx        xxx.xx        xxx.xx       X,XXX.XX
 9      2
11      3
13      4
15      5
17      6
19      7
21      8
23                                   Column Totals               x,xxx.xx      x,xxx.xx      x,xxx.xx     XX,XXX.XX
26                                                                                          GRAND TOTAL   XXX,XXX.XX
```

Figure 10.1 Sample Printer Output Form

Looking at our sample form, we see a generic printer output form. The Xs represent numbers, and the As represent letters. The title is normally centered, and many times a sequence number is printed on the left side of each record. This sequence number makes the report reader's task somewhat easier in many cases. The output form shows a "last" page of the report so that the grand total can be shown. In this form, we see the headings section of the report, the detail lines (prefixed by sequence numbers), and the summary section (column totals and grand total). The form is set up for a printer that can print 50 lines to a page and 120 characters across the page. If your printer could not print 120 characters across, you could use the part of the form that you need or buy a different form. The point to be made here is that you will design/draw the report before you start writing the program. Once the customer has approved the form format, the programmer can proceed.

The designer must know in advance what type of printer is being used so that the report is printed properly. Quite often, changing a printer requires changing a program so that the output is correct. You may have noticed an analogous operation on your PC if you have ever changed printers. When you change printers on a PC, you must install a new printer driver. The printer driver program is the program that translates what you see on your monitor into the proper printed format.

Screen Design Form

Another form that is commonly used is the screen output form or *screen design form*. The screen design form is similar to the printer output form, but its usage differs. The screen design form is laid out for a monitor, whereas the printer form is laid out for a printed page. The screen output form is a form that contains a number of rows and columns equal to the number of rows and columns that can be contained on the monitor screen. The systems analyst can draw the desired output on the form and provide it to the customer to verify the format before the programmer begins writing the code to produce the screen. Many business reports today are produced on monitor screens and not on paper, although there is usually an option to print the screen if the customer so desires.

The screen design form can also be used as an input form because the monitor is often used to display the data as they are input. Screen design forms look very much like printer forms. The primary difference is in the number of rows and columns available. Proper screen design is a challenging art of its own and is best addressed in a course on web-page design or desktop publishing.

Control Break

Many times, a special report format is used called a *break report, control break* report, or multi-level report. This report can be any of the three types described earlier, and its purpose is usually to provide subtotals based on a particular field changing in the data. For this report to work properly, the data must be sorted according to the levels of the report.

An example should make it clear. My Mart stores are located in various regions. Sometimes My Mart would like to know how many shoes are sold in each department, in each store, in each region, and how many are sold in the whole country. To print this report, the programmer would establish a "break" on shoe sales and print a total for each department and store. After an entire region was processed, a region total would be printed for that region, and then the next region would start. Of course, at the end of the report (in the summary section), we would see a grand total of all shoes sold. The logic for a break report is a simple decision statement that determines if the break field has changed. In our example, we're breaking on department (imagine that several departments sold shoes), store, and region so the flowchart would look like Figures 10.2 and 10.3. In this flowchart, we first check to see if the region changes. If the region has not changed, we must check to see if the store has changed. If the store has not changed, we still must check to see if the department has changed.

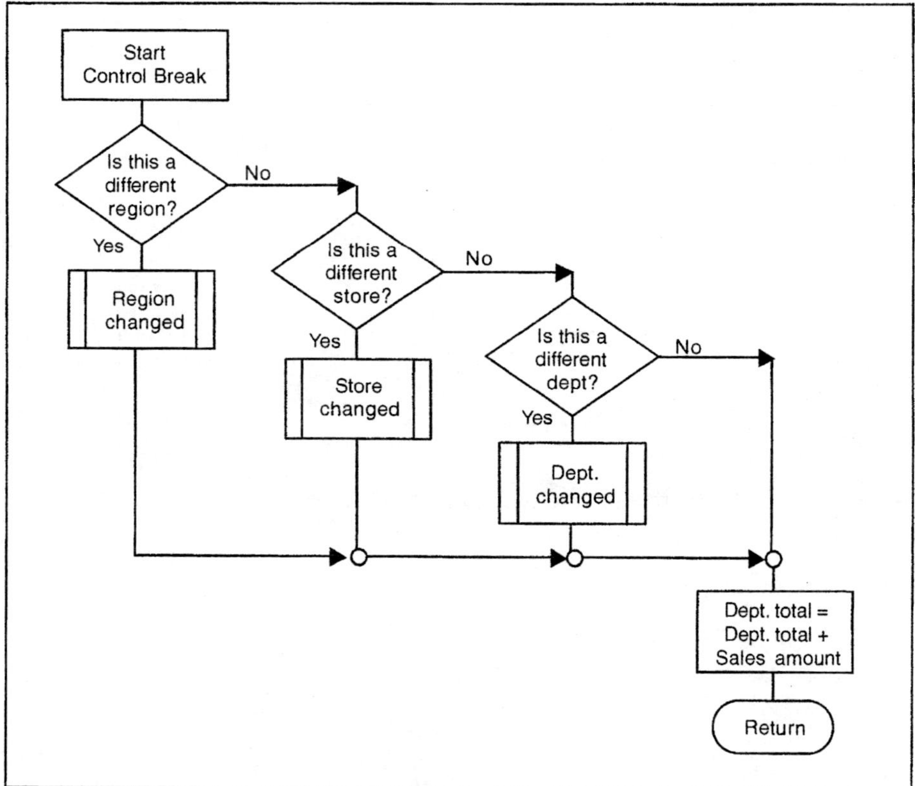

Figure 10.2 Control Break Flowchart

You should quickly recognize this as a nested decision process, and the control break is a common use of nested decisions. The details of the break are not obvious on the flowchart in Figure 10.2, so you will need to look at the next layer of flowcharts (the ones that explain the predetermined processes) shown in Figure 10.3.

We can see in Figure 10.3 that when the region has changed, we must process a store change. When we process a store change, we must also process a department change. Many beginning programmers overlook this efficiency and create redundant code for these modules. The key to success is recognizing that a high-level break forces all lower-level breaks. Here, a change in the region means that the store must have changed, which means that the department must also have changed.

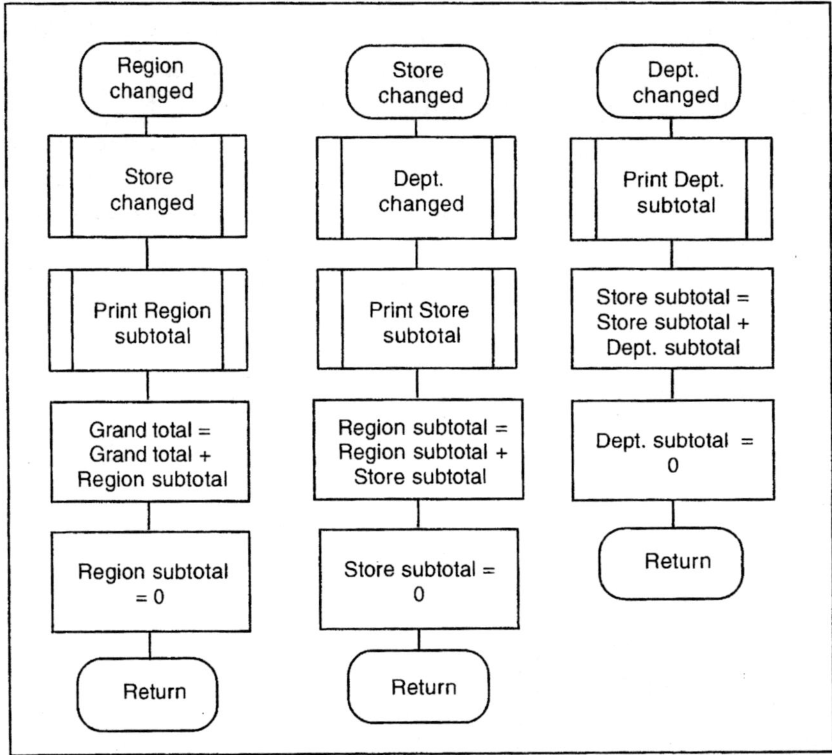

Figure 10.3 Control Break Flowchart Continued

Notice that the print symbols are predetermined process symbols, which means another flowchart would explain what's happening in that module.

This same procedure can be used for page breaks. When a page becomes full, what information do we want at the top of the next page? Normally, we need to reprint the heading section before we continue printing the details. We also need to change page numbers and zero out any page totals that have been accumulating. Changing pages in a program is a control break.

Bowling Problem

Continuing our work on the bowling league software, we will apply the control break technique to the printout of the bowling scores. Assume that we want a report of every bowler's game scores and total and the team totals for each week of the league. Sample printer output forms are shown in Figures 10.4 and Figure 10.5. Since the data will not all fit on one page, we show the two different styles of pages that would be used to print the entire report. Figure 10.4 shows the page format for pages that do not have weekly totals, and Figure 10.5 shows pages that do have weekly totals. No summary section is shown for this detail report, but a summary section could be created. The flowchart and pseudocode for this example are left to the exercises.

```
                                              Bowler, Team and Week Totals

 WEEK:   1                                                                                                      Page   1

     Team:   1

               Bowler Name                 Game 1     Game 2     Game 3     TOTAL

               AAAAAAAAAAAAAAAAAAAAAAAAA    XXX        XXX        XXX        XXX
               AAAAAAAAAAAAAAAAAAAAAAAAA    XXX        XXX        XXX        XXX
               AAAAAAAAAAAAAAAAAAAAAAAAA    XXX        XXX        XXX        XXX
               AAAAAAAAAAAAAAAAAAAAAAAAA    XXX        XXX        XXX        XXX

               TEAM TOTAL                                                   XXXX


     Team:   2

               Bowler Name                 Game 1     Game 2     Game 3     TOTAL

               AAAAAAAAAAAAAAAAAAAAAAAAA    XXX        XXX        XXX        XXX
               AAAAAAAAAAAAAAAAAAAAAAAAA    XXX        XXX        XXX        XXX
               AAAAAAAAAAAAAAAAAAAAAAAAA    XXX        XXX        XXX        XXX
               AAAAAAAAAAAAAAAAAAAAAAAAA    XXX        XXX        XXX        XXX

               TEAM TOTAL                                                   XXXX


     Team:   3

               Bowler Name                 Game 1     Game 2     Game 3     TOTAL

               AAAAAAAAAAAAAAAAAAAAAAAAA    XXX        XXX        XXX        XXX
               AAAAAAAAAAAAAAAAAAAAAAAAA    XXX        XXX        XXX        XXX
               AAAAAAAAAAAAAAAAAAAAAAAAA    XXX        XXX        XXX        XXX
               AAAAAAAAAAAAAAAAAAAAAAAAA    XXX        XXX        XXX        XXX

               TEAM TOTAL                                                   XXXX


     Team:   4

               Bowler Name                 Game 1     Game 2     Game 3     TOTAL

               AAAAAAAAAAAAAAAAAAAAAAAAA    XXX        XXX        XXX        XXX
               AAAAAAAAAAAAAAAAAAAAAAAAA    XXX        XXX        XXX        XXX
               AAAAAAAAAAAAAAAAAAAAAAAAA    XXX        XXX        XXX        XXX
               AAAAAAAAAAAAAAAAAAAAAAAAA    XXX        XXX        XXX        XXX

               TEAM TOTAL                                                   XXXX
```

Figure 10.4 Bowling Report Page 1

```
                                              Bowler, Team, and Week Totals

WEEK:  1                                                                                     Page XXX

        WEEK 1 TOTAL:  XXXXXX




WEEK:  2

        TEAM  1

                    Bowler Name                    Game 1     Game 2     Game 3     TOTAL

                    AAAAAAAAAAAAAAAAAAAA            XXX        XXX        XXX        XXX
                    AAAAAAAAAAAAAAAAAAAA            XXX        XXX        XXX        XXX
                    AAAAAAAAAAAAAAAAAAAA            XXX        XXX        XXX        XXX
        Team:  2    AAAAAAAAAAAAAAAAAAAA            XXX        XXX        XXX        XXX

                    TEAM TOTAL                                                      XXXX




                    Bowler Name                    Game 1     Game 2     Game 3     TOTAL

                    AAAAAAAAAAAAAAAAAAAA            XXX        XXX        XXX        XXX
                    AAAAAAAAAAAAAAAAAAAA            XXX        XXX        XXX        XXX
                    AAAAAAAAAAAAAAAAAAAA            XXX        XXX        XXX        XXX
        Team:  3    AAAAAAAAAAAAAAAAAAAA            XXX        XXX        XXX        XXX

                    TEAM TOTAL                                                      XXXX




                    Bowler Name                    Game 1     Game 2     Game 3     TOTAL

                    AAAAAAAAAAAAAAAAAAAA            XXX        XXX        XXX        XXX
                    AAAAAAAAAAAAAAAAAAAA            XXX        XXX        XXX        XXX
                    AAAAAAAAAAAAAAAAAAAA            XXX        XXX        XXX        XXX
        Team:  4    AAAAAAAAAAAAAAAAAAAA            XXX        XXX        XXX        XXX

                    TEAM TOTAL                                                      XXXX
```

Figure 10.5 Bowling Report Page 2

The pseudocode for the break report from Figures 10.2 and 10.3 is shown next.

```
Break_report
If Region = Old_region Then

      If Store = Old_store Then

            If Department = Old_department Then

                  Dept_subtotal = Dept_subtotal +
                  Sales_amount

            Else

            Dept_change
            Endif

      Else

      Store_change

      Endif

Else

   Region_change
Endif

Return

Region_change

   Store_change

   Print_region_subtotal

   Grand_total = Grand_total + Region_subtotal

   Region_subtotal = 0

Return

Store_change

   Dept_change

   Print_store_subtotal

   Region_subtotal = Region_subtotal + Store_subtotal

   Store_subtotal = 0
```

```
Return

Dept._change

         Print_dept_subtotal

         Store_subtotal = Store_subtotal + Dept_subtotal

         Dept_subtotal = 0

Return
```

Summary

This chapter has been an overview of business reports. The three types of reports are detail, summary, and exception. All three reports contain heading, detail, and summary sections. The sections of the reports correspond to the three sections of a hierarchy chart. Control break reports are a special report format that could be used for any of the three types of reports. Printer output forms are a special form useful in designing the printed output form of a report.

Key Terms

Each number in parentheses indicates the page where the term first occurs in the chapter.

break report (213)
control break (213)
detail lines (209)
detail report (208)
detail section (209)
exception report (208)
file specification form (210)
heading section (209)
printer output form (210)
screen design form (212)
summary report (208)
summary section (209)

Chapter 10
Exercises

Objective 1 Identify types of business reports and their parts.

1. The detail portion of a report contains (choose the best answer):

   A. The total of all the details from the report.

   B. Lines of information that are typically summarized in the summary portion.

   C. The titles for the report that indicate what details are found on the following pages.

   D. The details of the summary section.

2. Describe each of the three types of business reports in your own words. Compare and contrast their similarities and differences.
3. Describe the three major parts of a business report. Create a sample report and describe the data that you placed in each section.
4. A customer has asked for the following report to be printed. The report is for the monthly payroll and will list each employee's name, their social security number, and net pay for the month. A one-character field is needed that is a code used to identify hourly, commissioned, and salaried employees (if the code is an S, they are salaried; C is commissioned; and H is hourly). Columns are to be provided for overtime pay (if appropriate) and bonuses (if appropriate). Table 10.2 shows the length of each field and the type of data.

Table 10.2 Objective 1 Exercise 4

Variable Name	Type of data	Field Width	Description
Last Name	Alpha	20	Employee's last name
First Name	Alpha	10	Employee's first name
MI	Alpha	1	Employee's middle initial
SSN	Numeric	11	Social security number (dashes must be inserted while printing)
Pay Code	Alpha	1	Type of pay, S = Salary, H =Hourly, C = Commissioned
Regular Pay	Numeric	9	Amount of regular (straight) pay due
Bonus	Numeric	9	Bonus amount
Overtime	Numeric	9	Overtime amount
Total Pay	Numeric	11	Calculated form 3 fields above.

Design the output on a printer output form that has 120 columns. Only 20 employees should be listed on each page. The report needs title and column headings, as well as room for totals of each pay column. At the end of each page, there should be a page total for each pay column; and at the end of the report, there should be a grand total of all pay columns. Draw a sample printout of the printer output form.

5. Create your own imaginary company, and design a detail report for your company. Use the printer output form or make a screen design form to show what the report would look like.
6. Create your own imaginary company, and design a summary report for your company. Use the printer output form or make a screen design form to show what the report would look like.
7. Create your own imaginary company, and design an exception report for your company. Use the printer output form or make a screen design form to show what the report would look like.
8. This chapter described three types of business reports: detail, summary, and exception. Later in the chapter, a break report was mentioned. Decide whether a break report is one of the three types, and write a short explanation of why you chose a particular type. Defend your selection.

Objective 2 Read, draw, and revise flowcharts for business reports, including the control break report.

1. Draw a control break flowchart for the Acme Manufacturing Company. They want to see break totals for each salesman, in all departments, and a grand total.
2. Draw a control break flowchart for the Beta Credit Card Company. They need a report that shows the total charges for all the customers in each state of the United States and a grand total.
3. Draw a control break flowchart for the control break report shown in Figures 10.4 and 10.5.
4. Draw a control break flowchart that will produce a list of students by class (assume a four-year college with a 4.0 grade system). The report should be grouped by class (freshman, sophomore, junior, senior) and should show each student's name and their overall grade point average. There should be a total credit hours, total honor points, and overall grade point average for each class.
5. Modify the flowchart in Exercise 3 (this objective) to print a summary page of the teams' averages for each of the weeks of the league.
6. Draw a flowchart that will produce the report required in the following scenario.

   A gift shop sells merchandise in four different categories: books, videos, models, and bumper stickers. The owner of the shop would like a report that summarizes sales for each month by category. She currently has sales data for each individual item for each day, and that information has been saved on a disk file in the format shown in Table 10.3. Table 10.3 is not the complete file, but only a sample to show the data format.

Table 10.3 Sales Data Disk File

Record Number	Item Number (One character and 4 numeric characters	Category	Number Sold	Date Sold	Sale Price
1	V0001	Video	3	6/19/2003	$19.95
2	S0005	Bumper sticker	6	6/20/2003	$2.00
3	B0002	Book	2	6/21/2003	$25.00
4	B0007	Book	1	6/22/2003	$15.00
5	M0003	Model	1	6/22/2003	$22.50
6	V0123	Video	2	6/23/2003	$9.95

The sales price of the item is the price for one. The owner wants to see a list of sales by item number, with subtotals for each week of the month.

Objective 3

Enrichment – Doing it with Pseudocode

Read, write, and revise pseudocode for business reports, including the control break report.

1. Write a pseudocode module that creates a control break report for the Acme Manufacturing Company. They want to see break totals for each salesman, in all departments, and a grand total.
2. Write a pseudocode module that creates a control break report for the Beta Credit Card Company. They need a report that shows the total charges for all the customers in each state of the United States and a grand total.
3. Write the pseudocode for the control break report shown in Figures 10.4 and 10.5.
4. Write the pseudocode for the control break report that will produce a list of students by class (assume a four-year college with a 4.0 grade system). The report should be grouped by class (freshman, sophomore, junior, senior) and should show each student's name and their overall grade point average. There should be a total credit hours, total honor points, and overall grade point average for each class.
5. Modify the pseudocode in Exercise 3 (this objective) to print a summary page of the teams' averages for each of the weeks of the league.
6. Write the pseudocode for problem 6 of Objective 2.

Other Assignments

SoftSkills

Select one problem from Objectives 1, 2, 3, or from the Internet/library research projects. Then prepare and give an oral report to the class on your solution.

Internet/library research projects

A. Find a business that prints detail reports, summary reports, and exception reports. Write a paper describing each of their reports with respect to the material in this chapter. Identify the information in each section of the report. Describe the type of business and why they produce each report.

B. Research business reports and produce a list of different reports that are printed by businesses. Classify all of the reports into the categories used in this chapter. Example: Home Depot produces a daily store report that provides a summary of weekly data. It's a summary report. You should have at least twenty different reports in your list.

C. Research business reports and find other methods to categorize reports (static, Parameterized reports, and interactive, for example). Compare and contrast those report types and methods with the methods and report types of this chapter.

11

OTHER PROGRAMMING PARADIGMS

Your paradigm is so intrinsic to your mental process that you are hardly aware of its existence, until you try to communicate with someone with a different paradigm.

(Donella Meadows, The Global Citizen (1941–2001))

OBJECTIVES

After completing this chapter, you will be able to:

1 Design a GUI for a given problem.

2 Identify Objects, attributes, and interactions in an object-oriented design problem.

Introduction

This textbook has been oriented toward the procedural programming paradigm. Other programming paradigms exist; visual and object oriented are the two most often found. Before moving into the explanation of these two programming paradigms, it's important to note that the procedural programming techniques that have been studied so far will apply inside the other programming paradigms. Also, each of these programming paradigms represents a complete field of study, and the reader should not assume that this one chapter is a complete coverage of either paradigm. Rather, this chapter attempts to relate portions of the two paradigms that apply generally to the content of this book.[1]

The Visual Paradigm

Visual (GUI) Programming

One popular programming paradigm in common use is the paradigm of visual programming. Visual programming in this text refers to languages like Visual Basic that use a graphical GUI builder to make programming visual interfaces easier for the programmer. The discussion of true visual programming is beyond the scope of this text.[2] We will, however, use the term "visual" to describe what we're doing. In the context of this book, visual programming is concerned with the interface between the user and the computer. The specific interface used in visual programming is called a *graphic user interface* or *GUI* (pronounced gooey). A GUI uses pictures (graphics or icons) as commands for the user. This system has developed because humans appear to interact more easily with graphics than with text. Since many of our computers now operate on the "point and click" system, it is imperative that programmers be adept at programming pictures. Several computer languages have evolved to make graphic programming easier, and these languages are known as *visual languages* (Visual Basic is an example). Other languages (Java and Python, for example) have included the GUI paradigm internally.

Beginning programmers in a visual language first learn to display an object (picture) and then assign attributes and procedures to that object. Many times, the procedures applied to the object will be sophisticated enough that they will require use of the procedures developed in this textbook.

1 For the Object-oriented paradigm, the reader should begin with Ali Bahrami, Object Oriented Systems Development, Irwin McGraw-Hill 1999. For the GUI paradigm, the reader could begin with The Essential Guide to User Interface Design : An Introduction to GUI Design Principles and Techniques, by Wilbert O. Galitz, John Wiley & Sons, 1996.

2 On the Web, see sites like http://www.hypernews.org/~liberte/computing/visual.html or http://cui.unige.ch/eao/www/Visual/Visual.Programming.biblio.html or http://www.cs.berkeley.edu/~maratb/cs263/paper/node2.html for excellent discussions on the subject.

Visual programming also requires programmers to develop good visual design skills. Placing an object in the appropriate section of the screen can be as important as knowing how to program the procedure. This skill can be aided by the use of a screen design form. The *screen design form* is a simple representation of the computer monitor screen and is based on the pixels available on the monitor.

Designing a GUI

This discussion is not intended to make you a visual programmer, but should give you a basic understanding of the steps involved in the design process and acquaint you with the terminology.

A GUI consists of a picture (form) or window with controls attached to it. The controls and forms are assigned properties, and the properties are used to enter data or manipulate the window. A simple form is shown in Figure 11.1[3]

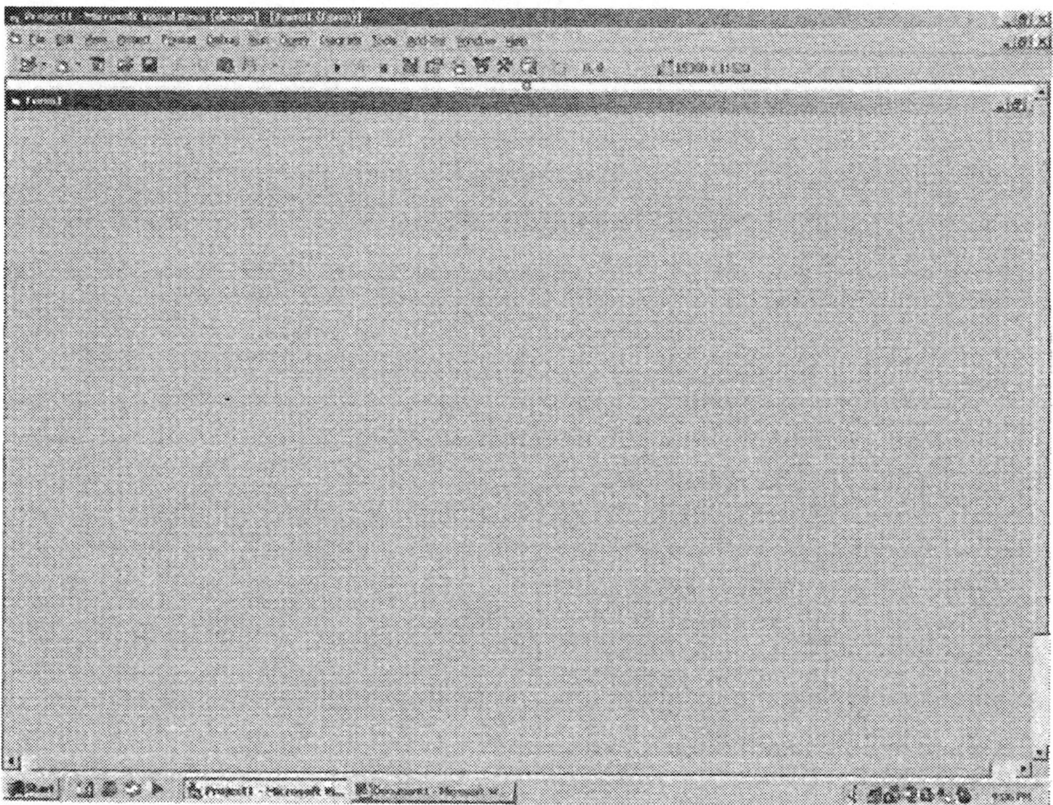

Figure 11.1 Simple Form

3 This blank form was prepared using Microsoft Visual Basic 6.0.

Figure 11.1 is a blank form. It is useless until controls and instructions are added to the form to allow the user to interact with the computer. Figure 11.2 shows the form with several representative controls added.

Controls may vary from one visual language to another; but all visual languages should contain buttons, boxes, and scroll bars. The basic concept of visual programming is to display a window that provides the users with intuitive instructions that will let them operate the program with a minimum of documentation.

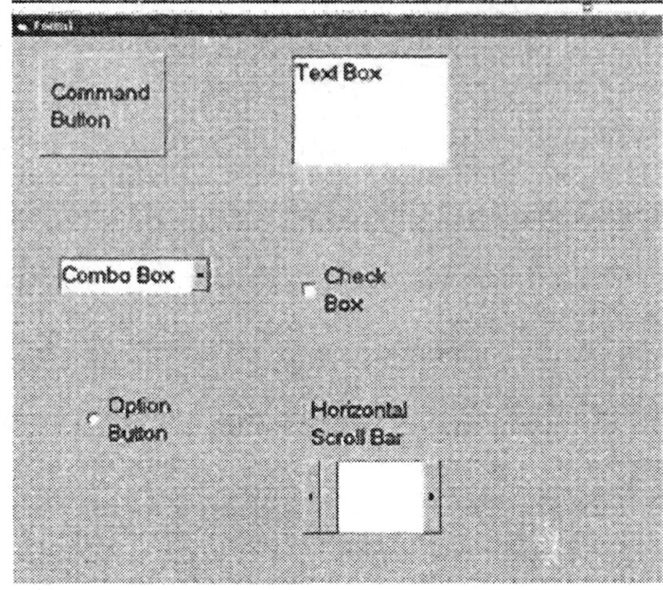

Figure 11.2 Form with Controls

Let's look at a sample problem and compare the two programs using a procedural method with the visual method. Suppose that we want to write a program that will convert miles to feet.

Problem statement: This program converts the number of miles that you enter into the corresponding number of feet.

Using a normal text-based program, we would develop a task list like this:

Get the number of miles to convert
Multiply miles times 5,280 feet
Display the number of feet.

The on-screen dialog might proceed as shown in Table 11.1.

Table 11.1 On-screen Dialog

User Input	Computer Output
Start the program	Please enter the number of miles that you wish to convert.
15	
	15 miles is equal to 79,200 feet.
	Do you wish another conversion? (yes or no)

If we wanted to design a solution to this problem using visual tools, we could develop the following event sequence:

Start program
Enter miles to convert
Display feet

The onscreen display might look like Figure 11. 3.

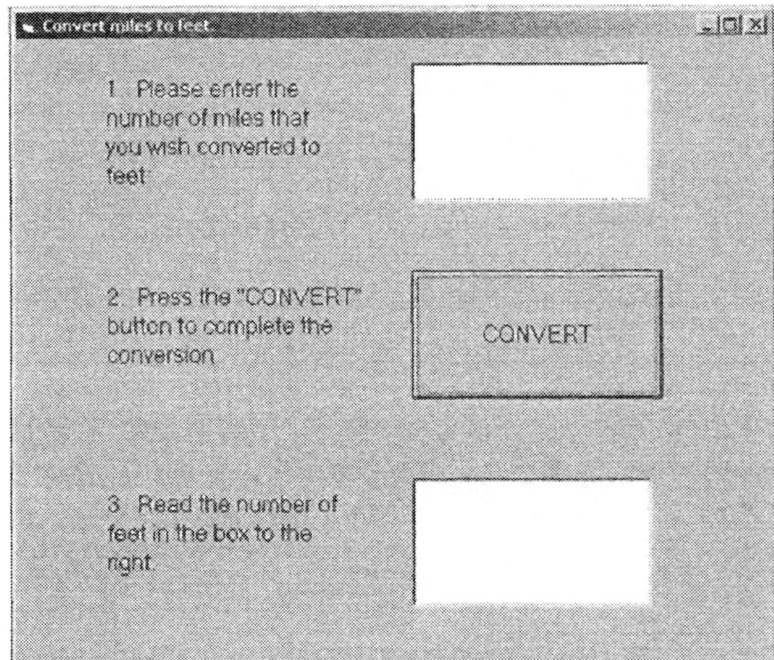

Figure 11.3
On-screen Display

Notice that the window title bar shows that this window is used to convert miles to feet. Two text boxes separated by the command "CONVERT" and the instructions make it obvious that the user should enter the number of miles in the top box and press the button to get the number of feet displayed in the bottom. This window could be used to solve any conversion problem: dollars to yen, yards to centimeters, and so on, by simply changing the labels and the internal formula. It could also be used as a simple calculator where the number entered is multiplied, divided, or added to some constant, and the result is displayed in the second box.

The visual program may be easier to use and understand, but remember that the logic that makes both programs work is exactly the same. Visual programmers must be concerned with two separate skills: designing and programming. Designing visual applications requires that the programmer think in terms of events. Input and output are defined first so that the visual portion of the program can be designed. This visual design requires knowledge of placement on the screen, the use of colors, the use of size, and the use of text to ensure that the user is successful in operating the GUI. Once the visual portion is completed, the programmer will need to return to programming the process that converts the input into the desired output.

The Object-Oriented Paradigm

Recent History

Throughout the 1980s and 1990s, object-oriented analysis, design, and programming was developing in fragments. A few excerpts from the history of this development are listed below.

1986—Grady Booch developed the object-oriented design concept, the Booch method.

1987—Sally Shlaer and Steve Mellor created the concept of the recursive design approach.

1989—Beck and Cunningham produced class-responsibility-collaboration (CRC) cards.

1990—Rebecca Wirfs-Brock, Brian Wilkerson, and Lauren Wiener came up with responsibility-driven design.

1991—Jim Rumbaugh led a team at the research labs of General Electric to develop the object modeling technique (OMT).

1991—Peter Coad and Ed Yourdon developed the Coad lightweight and prototype-oriented approach to methods.

1994—Ivar Jacobson introduced the concept of the use case and object-oriented software engineering (OOSE).

1996—Grady Booch, Ivar Jacobson, and Jim Rumbaugh established the Unified Modeling Language (UML) based on the best principles of their modeling notations.

Unified Modeling Language (UML)

UML is the most commonly used graphical language for modeling object-oriented methods. UML is not a programming language. It is intended to be a graphical language for specifying, constructing, visualizing, and documenting the software system and its components. UML uses a series of diagrams to model software solutions. These various diagrams are useful during the design stage and help bridge the communications gap between the programmers and the customers. The UML diagrams use shapes to simulate various systems models, much like flowcharts and pseudocode do in traditional software systems.

Learning the UML is not a prerequisite to programming object-oriented programs, but rather the UML is a tool for designers to use as an aid to understanding very complex systems. Computer systems continue to be developed for more complex systems, and programmers must find tools to help them understand the systems because the systems are too complex to be translated immediately into a programming language. That was precisely the point made in Chapter 1 when task lists were introduced.

Object-Oriented Programming

The object-oriented programming paradigm is most concerned with modeling the real world and establishing re-useable code. Its name comes from its fixation with objects. An object *simulates* a real-world thing that a computer program wants to operate with. In bank software, some objects are savings accounts, customers, ATMs, and checking accounts. In a boat dealership, some objects are boats, motors, trailers, and customers.

Groups of similar objects form a *class*. The various forms of savings accounts would make up a savings account class in the banking example. In the boat example, each boat might have a different manufacturer; but all boats would be part of the class called boats. An object is called an *instance* of its class.

Objects have *attributes*. Attributes are characteristics of an object. In the banking example, the attributes for a savings account might be the account number, the current balance, the minimum balance, and the authorized signers for the account. In the boat example, boats would have manufacturers, serial numbers, colors, engine types, and accessories. Attributes can be variables and are similar to fields in a traditional software system.

Objects also have procedures, (or behaviors). The *procedures* for an object determine what processes can be applied to the object. In our banking example, we would have processes for depositing money, withdrawing money, and reporting an overdraft. In the boating example, a boat could have processes for calculating price based on options selected.

To design an object-oriented program, a programmer/designer/analyst would first identify the classes of objects that identify the system. Identifying objects often leads to identifying classes of objects. Methods, attributes, and associations for the classes are also identified. Designing the program is an iterative process. More classes may be developed as the associations, attributes, and methods are defined.

Encapsulation

Each object contains all the programming instructions that are needed to process the object so that the object can interact with the system. This *encapsulation* of processes protects the object from being altered by the system. Processes are developed that mirror the reallife use of the objects so that users can understand the system better, and the system can be translated directly from real life into the computer system. Programmers are encouraged to use the real-world terminology for objects wherever possible. Thus bank account objects are called Bank_Accounts inside the program. When you want to make a withdrawal from a Bank_Account object, the programming code would look something like:
Bank_Account.withdraw.

Advantages of Object-Oriented Designs

Object-oriented programming has the primary advantage of reflecting the real system. A system can be thought of as a collection of objects and transactions between those objects. The banking example is perhaps the easiest to understand. Customers have bank accounts. The accounts can be accessed in several ways. Money can be withdrawn from the account, deposited into the account, and the account balance can be checked. The classes for this part of the problem would be customers and accounts. A savings account would be an object within the account class. By using the systems' own terminology, the program can be developed using the everyday language of the system. Thus, understanding the program is very similar to understanding the system.

A second major advantage of object-oriented designs is that the classes and/or objects have a high degree of reuse. Since an object contains all of its relevant information and processes, it could be re-used in any applications that contain the same object. Bank customer objects might be re-used as customers of retail stores, for example. Once an object has been developed and tested, it can be used in additional applications without testing, thus speeding the process of developing new applications.

Object-Oriented Example

Perhaps the classic example of an object-oriented system is the ATM (automated teller machine). Let's examine the software for an ATM using our traditional task list approach and compare it with the object-oriented approach. This is not intended to result in a working program but only to highlight the differences between the two methods. This example is overly simplified for our purposes.

Using the traditional approach, we would first identify the tasks we need to accomplish at the ATM. Our list might look like this:

Display menu of choices
- View balance
- Withdraw
- Deposit
- Transfer funds

Log off
Log on
Enter PIN number
Enter account number
Select menu item
Enter dollar amount
Display balance
Insert card
Remove card

The hierarchy chart for the ATM might look like Figure 11.4.

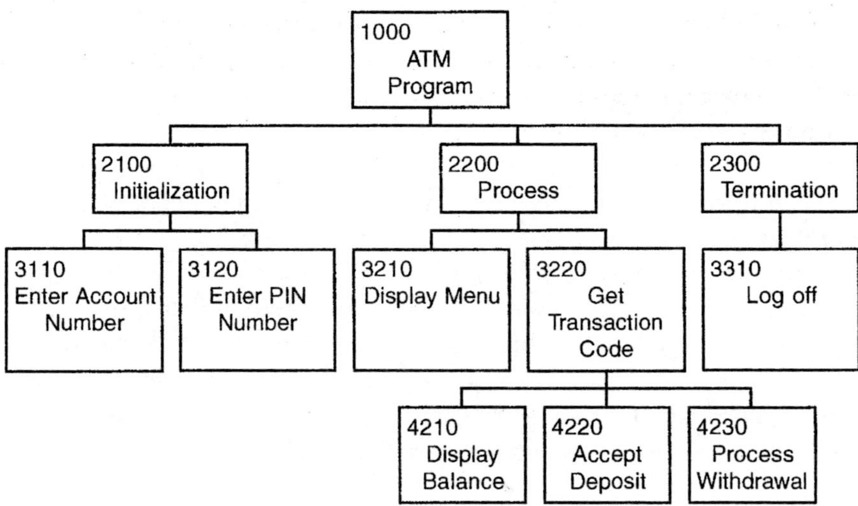

Figure 11.4 ATM Hierarchy Chart

Our next step would be to develop the flowcharts for each of the modules and finally write the programming code for each module. Notice that when we use this procedure, we identify processes that need to be performed; the resulting program does not necessarily model the real world well.

ATM
Location
Serial Number

Figure 11.5 ATM Object

Now let's look at designing this program using the object-oriented process. We'll begin by identifying the objects that are involved with an ATM machine. We can do this by examining the ATM machine operation and noting what objects appear. Perhaps the least obvious object is the ATM machine itself. If a bank had several machines, then each machine would have attributes that would identify it so that each machine's transactions could be separated for processing. Figure 11.5 depicts an ATM object with some of its attributes using a class diagram.

Certainly customers interact with the ATM so we would need a customer object. It should be obvious that the customer has a bank account that is accessed through the ATM so we would also need an account object. The customer object is depicted in Figure 11.6 with some of its attributes.

Customer
Name
Account Number
PIN Number

Figure 11.6 Customer Object

The object definitions would continue until all the objects and their attributes had been identified. Once the objects are identified, we can examine their processes and attributes and begin the programming process.

Notice the tremendous differences between the end results in the traditional process and the object-oriented process in our simplified example. Using the first method, we established processes to be programmed; whereas in the object-oriented method, we determined objects that were to be programmed. While this is very oversimplified for our purposes, it does demonstrate the techniques involved. If we were to follow through with the programming of these two examples, we would find that the object-oriented process resulted in a program that better reflected reality and was easier to modify than the program generated by the traditional method. The reader should note that the ATM is a relatively new device and results in a more complex banking process than the traditional banking process. Thus, today, the object-oriented process is probably more important than it was 50 years ago.

Unified Modeling Language™ (UML)

The Unified Modeling Language (UML) is a third-generation method for specifying, visualizing, and documenting the artifacts of an object-oriented system under development[4]. The UML is a graphical language and is the object-oriented counterpart of the procedural languages flowchart. A full description of the UML is beyond the scope of this textbook. Some of the diagrams will be described in this section; if the reader is interested in more detail, the reader should refer to the Web sites listed in the footnote. The UML is primarily concerned with graphically depicting objects, their properties, and interactions. According to Kendall Scott[5], the UML diagrams can be divided into two general categories: structural diagrams and behavioral diagrams.

Structural Diagrams

These consist of the class, package, object, component, and deployment diagrams. Package diagrams are not standard UML and will be omitted here. Component and deployment diagrams are beyond the scope of this text and will be omitted as well. The class diagram is an example of a diagram that can be used to describe an object. The class diagram consists of three parts, drawn as rectangles. Figure 11.7 is an incomplete example of a class diagram for a boat dealership. The top rectangle identifies the class name, the center rectangle describes the properties, and the lower rectangle describes the operations that are to be

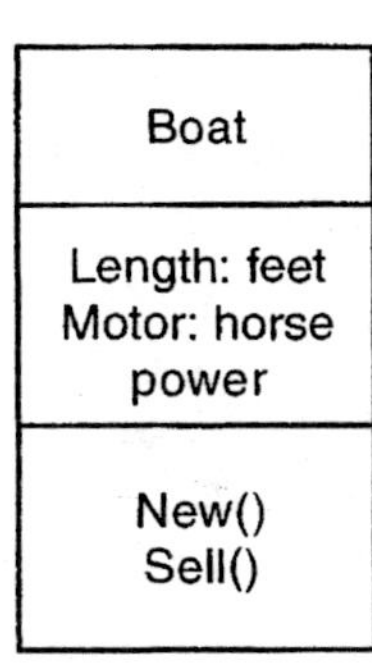

Figure 11.7 Class Diagram

4 Microgold Software Inc, http://microgold.com/Stage/UML_FAQ.html#UML1. Also available at http://www.rational.com/uml/index.jsp

5 Scott, Kendall 2000. An Introduction to the Unified Modeling Language (UML). Available online at http://www.iconixsw.com/UMLzone.html

performed on this object. A class diagram may be drawn with only the first rectangle or with any combination of the other two rectangles.

An object diagram shows a set of objects, and their relationships, at a specific point in time. Figure 11.8 illustrates the object diagram. Note that each object is connected to the related information via a line segment.

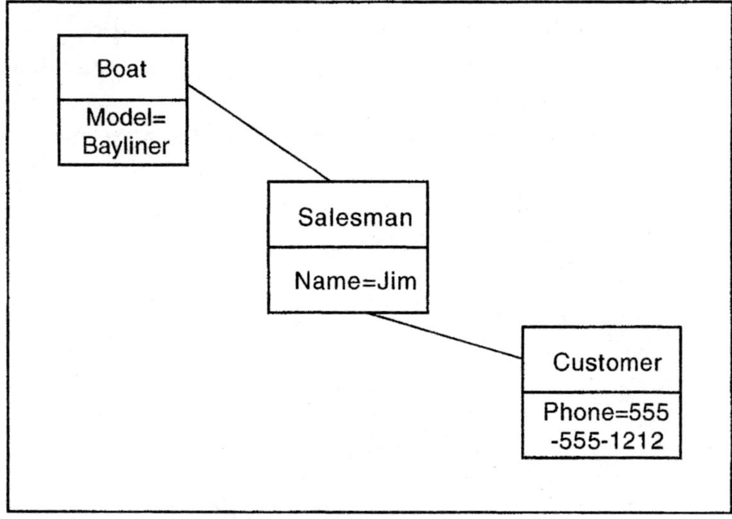

Figure 11.8 Object Diagram

Behavioral Diagrams

These consist of use-case diagrams, interaction diagrams, statechart diagrams, and activity diagrams. A use-case is a scenario that a user would perform while interacting with a system. A simple use-case diagram is depicted in Figure 11.9. This diagram shows a user using the buy a boat option of the system. Notice that the user is depicted as a stick figure in this case.

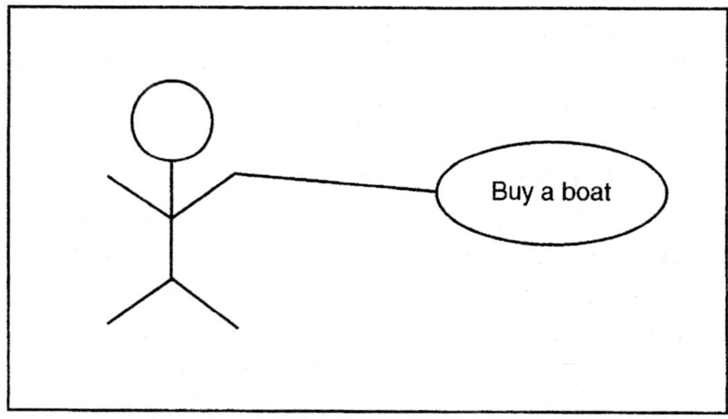

Figure 11.9 Use-case Diagram

Interaction diagrams illustrate how groups of objects interact. They come in two varieties: sequence diagrams and collaboration diagrams. Sequence diagrams depict the objects and the sequence of events that occur between the objects; whereas collaboration diagrams emphasize the organization of the objects. The events are given sequential numbers in the diagram. The sequence and collaboration diagrams are mutually exclusive. You would use one or the other.

Figure 11.10 depicts a sequence diagram for our ATM machine.

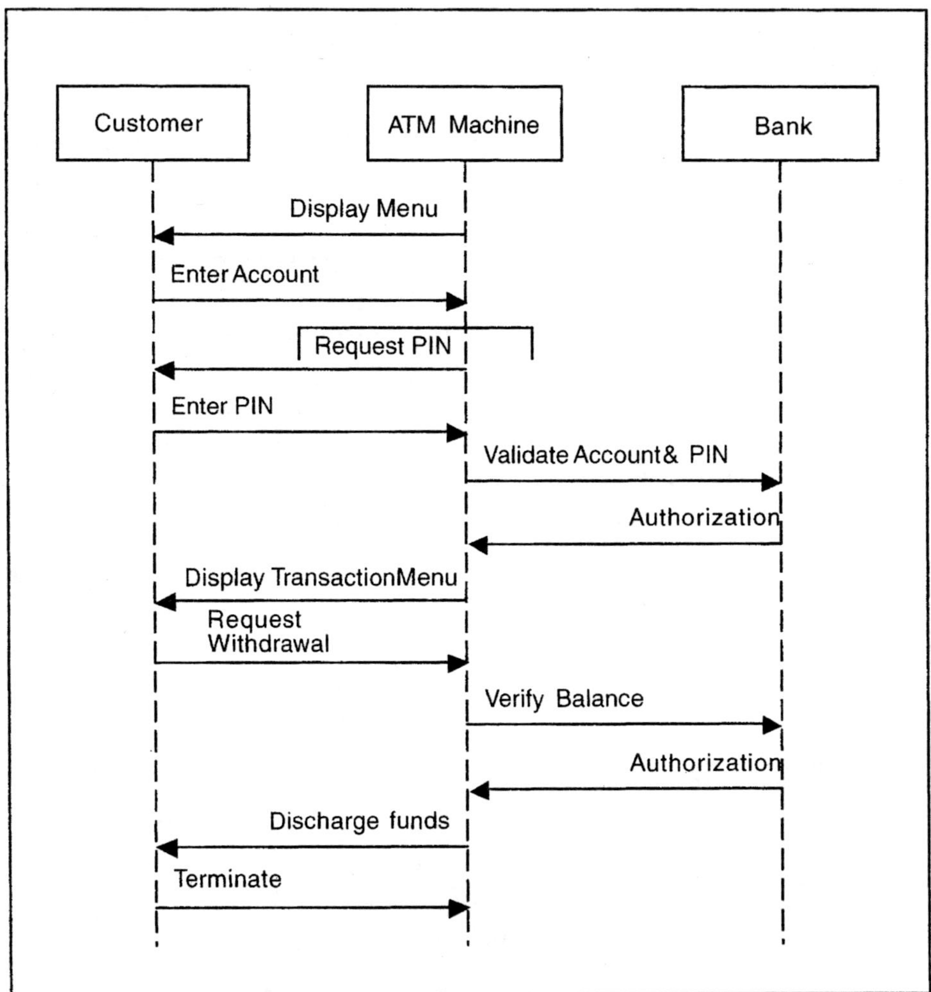

Figure 11.10 Sequence Diagram for ATM

Statechart diagrams depict the sequence of states of an object during its lifetime. A heating/air-conditioning system would have the following states: heating, cooling, fan only, idle. The statechart diagram would show how those various states interact. Figure 11.11 gives an example.

In Figure 11.11 we see new symbols. The solid circle indicates a starting point, while the half-filled circle indicates an end point. The diamond indicates a splitting or merging of flows.

Other diagrams and symbols are associated with object-oriented programming, and the task of explaining them all is beyond the scope of this book. The previous examples were intended to be a starting point in understanding how object-oriented programming differs from other paradigms.

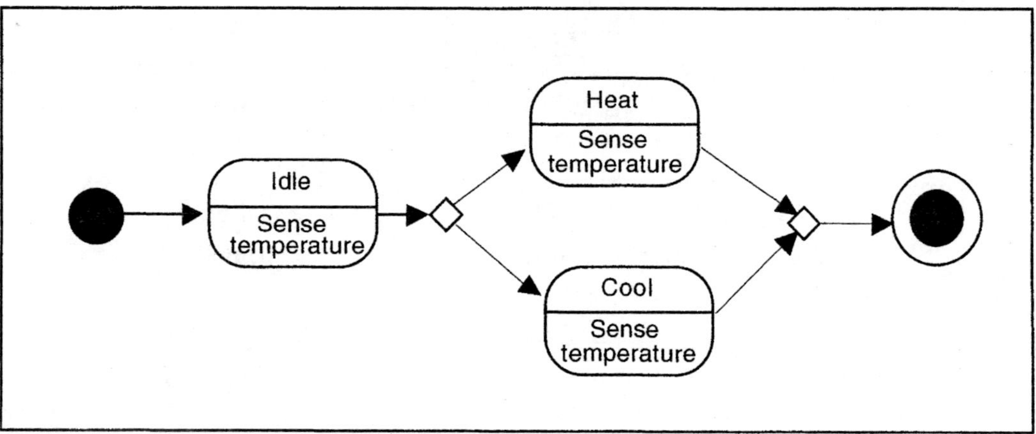

Figure 11.11 Statechart Diagram

Summary

This chapter looked at two programming paradigms—GUI and object-oriented—that are significantly different from the procedural paradigm discussed in the previous chapters of this book: Table 11.2 provides a comparative summary of the three paradigms.

Table 11.2 Paradigm Comparison

Procedural	GUI	Object Oriented
Organized by procedures	Organized by events	Organized by objects
Begin by identifying tasks to complete.	Begin by identifying output.	Begin by identifying classes.
Best for manipulating data.	Best for interaction between user and computer.	Best for large systems that operate with/on objects
Procedures are the program.	Procedures are contained in the graphics.	Procedures are con tained in the objects.

The different programming paradigms are not mutually exclusive. GUI and object-oriented programs contain procedural programming. Object-oriented and procedural programs can produce graphic interfaces. GUI and procedural programs can be modularized like object-oriented programs.

The reader should also recognize that there are other programming paradigms (Table-oriented programming, for example), and other paradigms will continue to be developed as new computer applications are developed.

Key Terms

Each number in parentheses indicates the page where the term first occurs in the chapter.

attributes (226)
class (231)
GUI (226)
instance (231)
object(229)
procedures (226)
screen design form (227)
visual languages (226)
visual programming(226)
Unified Modeling Language(234)

Chapter 11
Exercises

Objective 1 Design a GUI for a given problem.

1. Design a GUI with the logic necessary for a program that calculates the sales tax on a purchase at the Refreshall Drug Store. The customer can enter the price of the item, and the price plus tax will be displayed. (Assume that the sales tax rate is .0825 on all items.)
2. Design a GUI with the logic necessary for a car wash that provides three services:

   Full wash and wax $25.00

   Wash and dry $15.00

   Wash only $5.00
3. Design a GUI with the logic necessary for a fruit market that sells fruit by the pound. Apples cost $1.00 per pound, while all other items are $.75 a pound. If a customer buys more than 5 pounds and less than 10 pounds, they will receive a 10% discount. If the customer buys more than 10 pounds, they will receive a 15% discount. Allow for mixed purchases.
4. Design a GUI with the logic necessary for a simple calculator. The user will enter a number and select an operation from a menu containing add, subtract, multiply, divide, or clear. The calculator will provide the answer.
5. Design a GUI with the logic necessary for calculating areas of various objects. The user will select an object (circle, rectangle, right triangle, regular polygon) and enter the necessary data so that the program can calculate the result.
6. Design a GUI with the logic necessary for our bowling league problem that would allow a bowler to enter three scores and have the computer produce a total and average score.
7. Design a GUI with the logic necessary for our bowling league problem that would accept a bowler's name and calculate his or her average for the season to date. Assume that the bowler's scores are in a disk file.
8. Design a GUI with the logic necessary for our bowling league problem that would accept a bowlers' team name and produce the team statistics for the season. Minimum statistics to produce are: high game for the team, high individual game (male and female), high series for the team, and high series for the individual (male and female), and number of games won and lost. Develop a task list, hierarchy chart, and flowchart or pseudocode to describe the procedural logic.
9. Design a GUI with the logic necessary to display a menu of report options available for the bowling league problem (some reports you should have are high score, high average, relatively team places in the league). The interface would accept a selection from the user and print the desired report. Develop a task list, hierarchy chart, and flowchart or pseudocode to describe the procedural logic.

10. Design a GUI with the logic necessary to display a menu of food options available at a simulated restaurant (use at least ten items). Items should have a name and a price and an option for the user to ask for a description of the item. Allow the user to select multiple items, and calculate the total bill to include sales tax. Develop a task list, hierarchy chart, and flowchart or pseudocode to describe the procedural logic.

Objective 2 Identify Objects, attributes, and interactions in an object-oriented design problem.

1. Identify the objects that might be associated with an automobile dealership system.
2. Identify the objects that might be associated with a miniature golf course system.
3. Identify the objects that might be associated with a credit card system.
4. Identify the objects that might be associated with a library system. Draw a class diagram for the objects you identified and include their attributes.
5. Identify the objects that might be associated with a school system. Draw a class diagram for the objects you identified and include their attributes.
6. Establish the relationships among the objects you identified in problem 4 previously, and draw an object diagram for the objects in problem 4.
7. Establish the relationships among the objects you identified in problem 5 previously, and draw an object diagram for the objects in problem 5.
8. Using the relationships and objects from problem 6, develop a sequence diagram that depicts a correct sequence of events among several of the objects.
9. Using the relationships and objects from problem 7, develop a sequence diagram that depicts a correct sequence of events among several of the objects.
10. Review the bowling league problem that is threaded through this book, and establish an object-oriented version of this problem. Describe the objects using the class diagram and object diagrams shown in the chapter. Develop a use case diagram and a sequence diagram that can be applied to the bowling league problem.

Other Assignments

SoftSkills

Select one problem from Objective 1 or from the Internet/library research projects. Prepare, and give an oral report to the class on your selection.

Internet/library research projects

A. Research a programming paradigm other than the three mentioned in this chapter. Write a paper describing the paradigm that you found.

B. Write a research paper on visual programming languages.

C. Write a research paper on object-oriented languages.

12

SEARCHING

As long as one keeps searching, the answers come.
(Joan Baez (1941–)

OBJECTIVES

After completing this chapter, you will be able to:

1 Read and draw flowcharts for searching algorithms.

2 Read and write pseudocode for searching algorithms.

3 Understand the basic logic of searching for data.

Introduction

Storing data on computers would be a meaningless exercise unless we intended to use the data sometime for something. Many times we wish to use data for some purpose other than what it was intended. For example, most employees' files contain a data field indicating the gender of the employee. Initially, this data field was just a statement of gender; but after the Federal Government passed laws about sexual discrimination, a company that wished to satisfy the government needed to produce data that showed how many men and women they employed in various jobs and what their salaries were. To find all the women in a database, the database had to be searched. Today, special hardware solutions are available to aid the searching process (associative memories, for example); but here we will confine our discussion to searching lists (tables, arrays, and so on) of data in RAM. We will examine two methods of searching data tables in the next section: *sequential search* and *binary search*. Searching a database is essentially equivalent to the process of searching a table.

We will limit our discussion to searching for numbers, when in reality we usually want to search for letters or names (words). The relationship between letters and numbers will be explored in more detail in Module 1. For now, remember that all data stored in a computer is stored as a number. For instance, an uppercase A is stored in binary ASCII form, in a byte of memory, as 0100 0001. The binary 0100 0001 is equivalent to the letter A. What we are doing with our search algorithm is attempting to find a byte in a list that matches the byte that we have. It could be a letter, a number, a special character, or even a blank.

Sequential Search

The first method of searching a data table is the sequential search. The sequential search uses the following algorithm.

1. Look at the top element of a table.
2. If the top element is the data that you are looking for, then stop.
3. Otherwise, look at the next element in the list.
4. If the next element is the data you are looking for, then stop.
5. Repeat steps 3 and 4 until the last element has been checked.

A flowchart for the sequential search is shown in Figure 12.1.

We begin illustrating the sequential search by naming an item to search for (Search), and we set a pointer to the top of the list (Top = 1). If the top item is our search item, we proceed to a predetermined process that will print a message.

If our search item is not found in the table called List at the List(Current Position), we must increment the Current Position variable and ensure that we have not used up all of the items in the list (Top > Length).

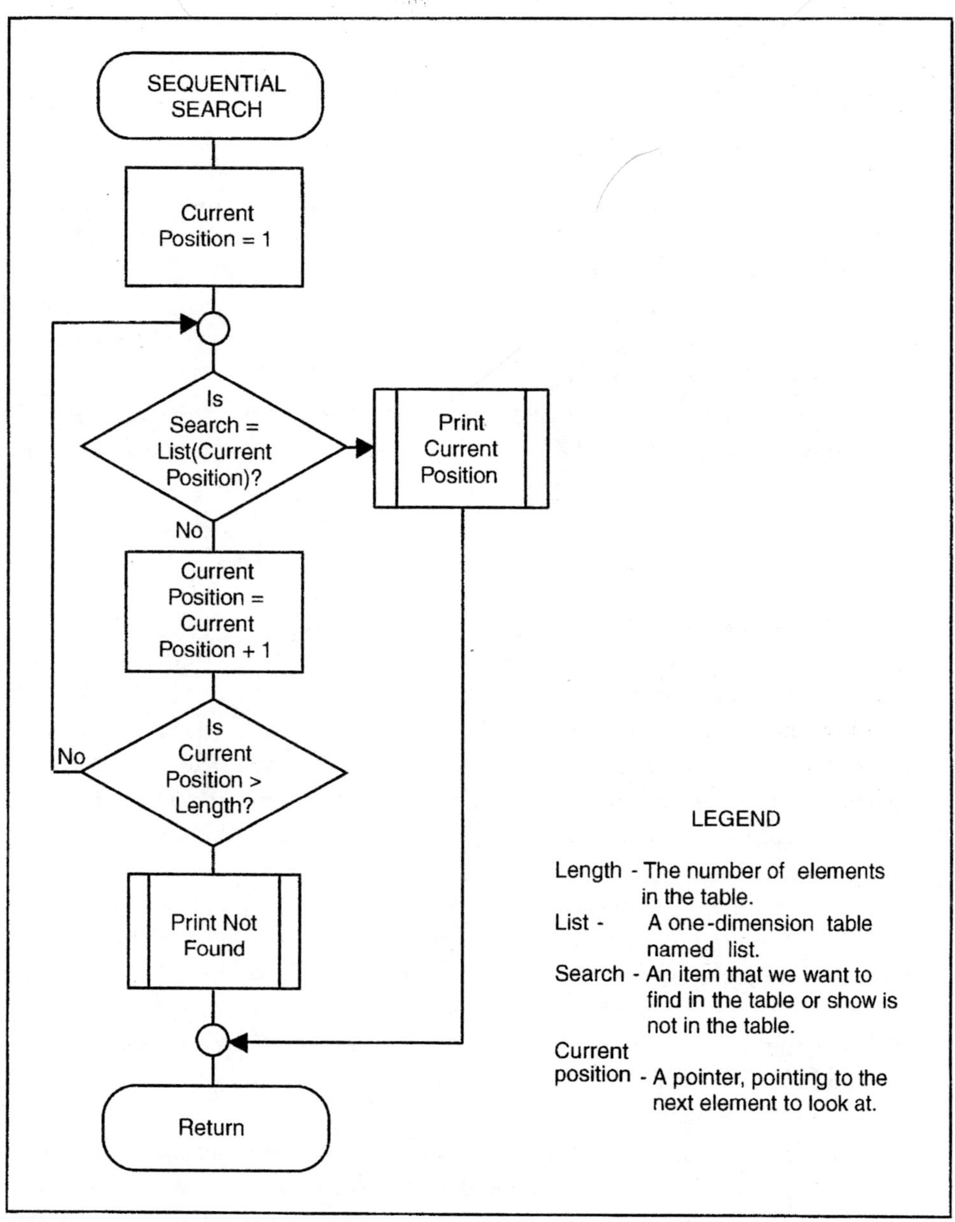

Figure 12.1 Sequential Search

We then check to see if the next item is our search item and continue the process until:

1. We find the item we wanted.
2. We look at every item in the list and our item is not found.

The second result above is a critical point to mention. In many cases, the item we are searching for is not in the list so we must ensure that we report that fact when it occurs in order to promote good error-checking skills.

As an example, assume our list (variable named List) contains the five numbers 22, 45, 17, 9, 99. Let's use the sequential search to find the number 17. We look at the first element to see if it is 17; it's not, so we continue and look at 45. The second element is not 17, so we look at the third element; we find the number 17 that we have been searching for. We then proceed to the Print Current Position sub-module and terminate the search module.

Binary Search

The sequential search is a relatively slow process because we have to continue looking at each element until we find the correct one. In the worst case (our search element is not in the list), we must look at every element in the list. The binary search is a search that can speed up the process by recognizing when an element is not in the list before reaching the end of the list. In order for the binary search to work, the list must be sorted. The list may be sorted in ascending or descending sequence as long as the binary search is modified to accept the particular case. The flowchart in Figure 12.2 assumes that the list is sorted in ascending order.

We begin the searching process by establishing the top and bottom of the list. Normally, the top is 1 and the bottom is equal to the number of data elements in the table, but we could work with a part of the table and have the top and bottom be unique values. For example, if we are working with a table of 12 elements, the top pointer would be 1 and the bottom pointer would be 12. But imagine that you want to investigate the bottom half of the table only. In this case the top pointer would be 6 and the bottom pointer would be 12.[1]

Once we have the top and bottom established, we compute the midpoint of the list. This involves a tricky bit of arithmetic. Using ordinary division, we know that 7 divided by 2 is equal to 3.5. But there is no element corresponding to subscript 3.5. Subscripts are normally integers; and in the computer, when using integers, 7 divided by 2 ends up being 3.[2]

1 The bottom half of the table consists of the sixth, seventh, eighth, ninth, tenth, eleventh, and twelfth elements. The top item in this list is the sixth element. The value of the variable named "Top" is therefore equal to 6 in this example.

2 Some computer languages have an automatic rounding feature so that 7 divided by 2 would end up being 4. The search routine can be modified to work as well in that case. The programmer must know the results on the machine in the programming language being used before implementing this algorithm.

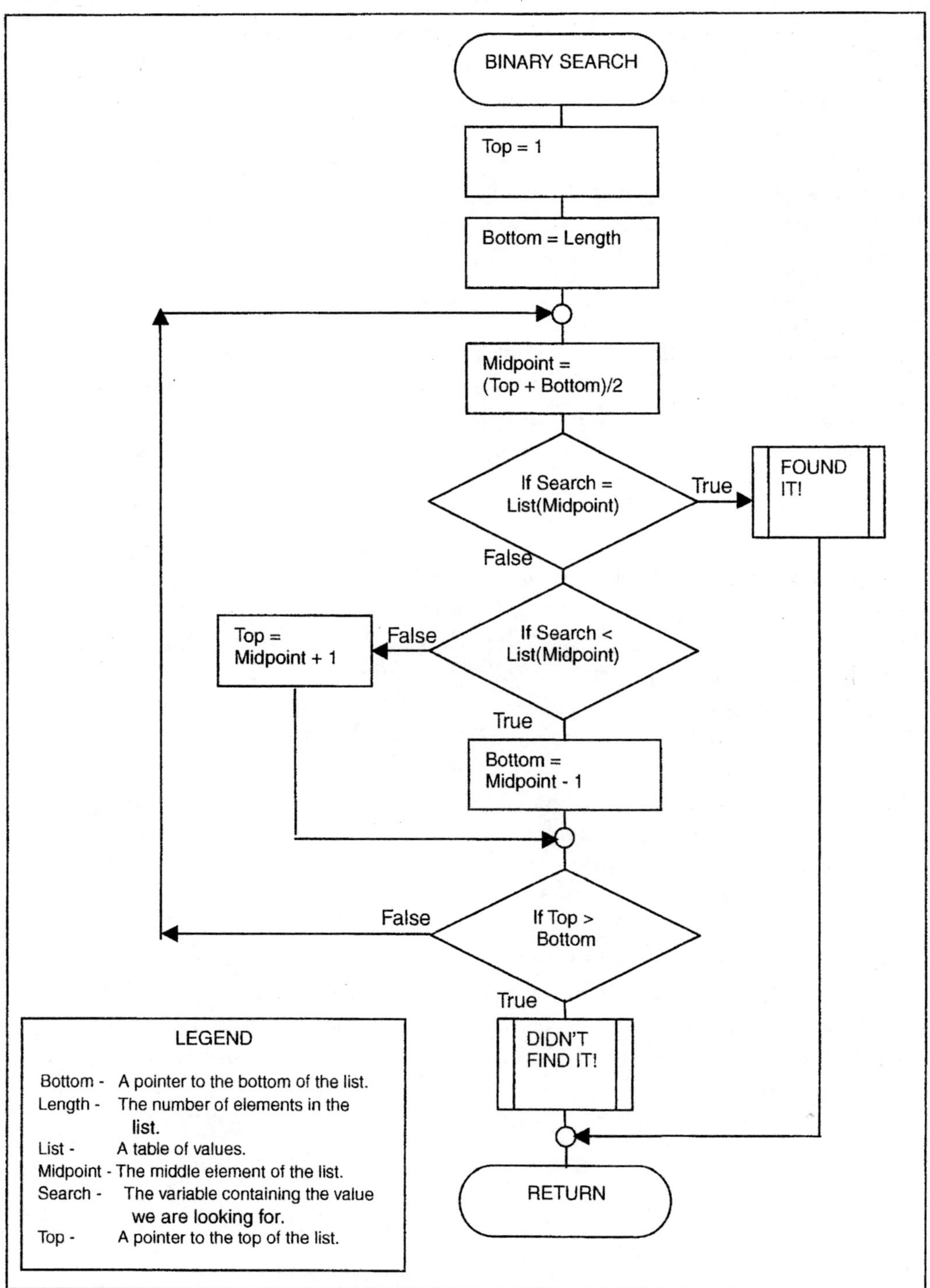

Figure 12.2 Binary Search

Now we look at the middle element of this list to see if it has the value for which we are searching. If it does, we're done. If the value we are trying to locate is not in the middle of the list, then the value must be less than or greater than the middle element's value. This leads us to two possible situations. The value we are attempting to locate could be less than the value of the middle element, or it could be greater than the middle element. Let's assume that the value is smaller than the middle element. This means that the value must be somewhere in the first half of the table, or else it's not in the table at all.

Our next step is to adjust the bottom pointer for our list so that the bottom is now one less than the midpoint.

This results in establishing a smaller list that is part of our original table. We now calculate the midpoint of this new list and check the middle element against our value. As we continue this process, we eliminate half of the list on each cycle, which results in a very fast search compared to a sequential search.

Let's work through a numeric example. Assume we have the list of elements (List (7)); 13, 17, 21, 25, 29, 33, and 37. Let's use the binary search to see if we can find the number 17 in the list. Follow along on the flowchart or the pseudocode.

Top is 1, Bottom is 7, and we calculate the Midpoint to be (1+7)/2 = 4. Now we look at the fourth element in the list and see if it is 17. It's not, so is it smaller than List (4)? Yes. Therefore, we adjust the bottom pointer (Bottom = Midpoint –1), and Bottom is now equal to 3. We have already verified that our search item (17) cannot be in List (4), List (5), List (6), or List (7). Since the list is sorted and the value we are searching for is smaller than the 4th element, it must also be smaller than the 5th, 6th, and 7th elements.

To continue, we now have Top = 1, Bottom = 3, and we calculate the Midpoint to be 2. So we compare 17 with List (2) and we're finished.

What would happen in the preceding example if we were searching for the number 20? The same thing would happen as in our previous search until we got to the midpoint equal to 2. Now we see that 20 is greater than List (2), so we would have to adjust the top pointer (Top = Midpoint +1).

At this point Top is equal to 3 and Bottom is also equal to 3. This will yield a new midpoint of 3, and we examine List (3) to see if it is the number 20. It is not 20; it is greater than 20, so we decrease our bottom pointer (Bottom = Midpoint – 1) and Bottom becomes 2. Now we see that Bottom is less than Top, so we have checked the entire list and the number 20 is not in the list. Figure 12.3 contains a picture of what's happened.

Search item	Sorted List	Second List	Third List
	13	13	21
20	17	17	
	21	21	
	25		
	29		
	33		
	37		
NOTE - Number shown in bold is the middle number in each list			

Figure 12.3
List Reduction

Each time that we didn't find the item, we reduced the length of the list by half and began searching in the reduced list. Remember that the list had to be in sequence, or this search would not always work.

Search Efficiency

To emphasize the differences between a sequential search and a binary search, we need to analyze the results of searches using the same data with both methods. We have already seen that the binary search must have sorted data in order to work properly, and we have said that it is much faster than the sequential search that was demonstrated on unsorted data. To some extent we've been comparing apples to oranges. To level the playing field, let's examine a sequential search on sorted data. We'll use the List provided in the binary search example (List (7)).

Modified Sequential Search

Suppose that we wish to look for the number 20 in that list using a sequential search. We would look at the first element and not find the number 20. Then we would look at the second element and not find the number 20 again. Then we would look at the third element and not find the number 20. Do we need to keep looking? Since we know the list is sorted, we should stop looking for the number 20 after we examine the third element in the list. The 20 is obviously not in the list if we have not found it before looking at the third element (in this case). Figure 12.4 shows the sequential search flowchart modified to take advantage of the sorted data.

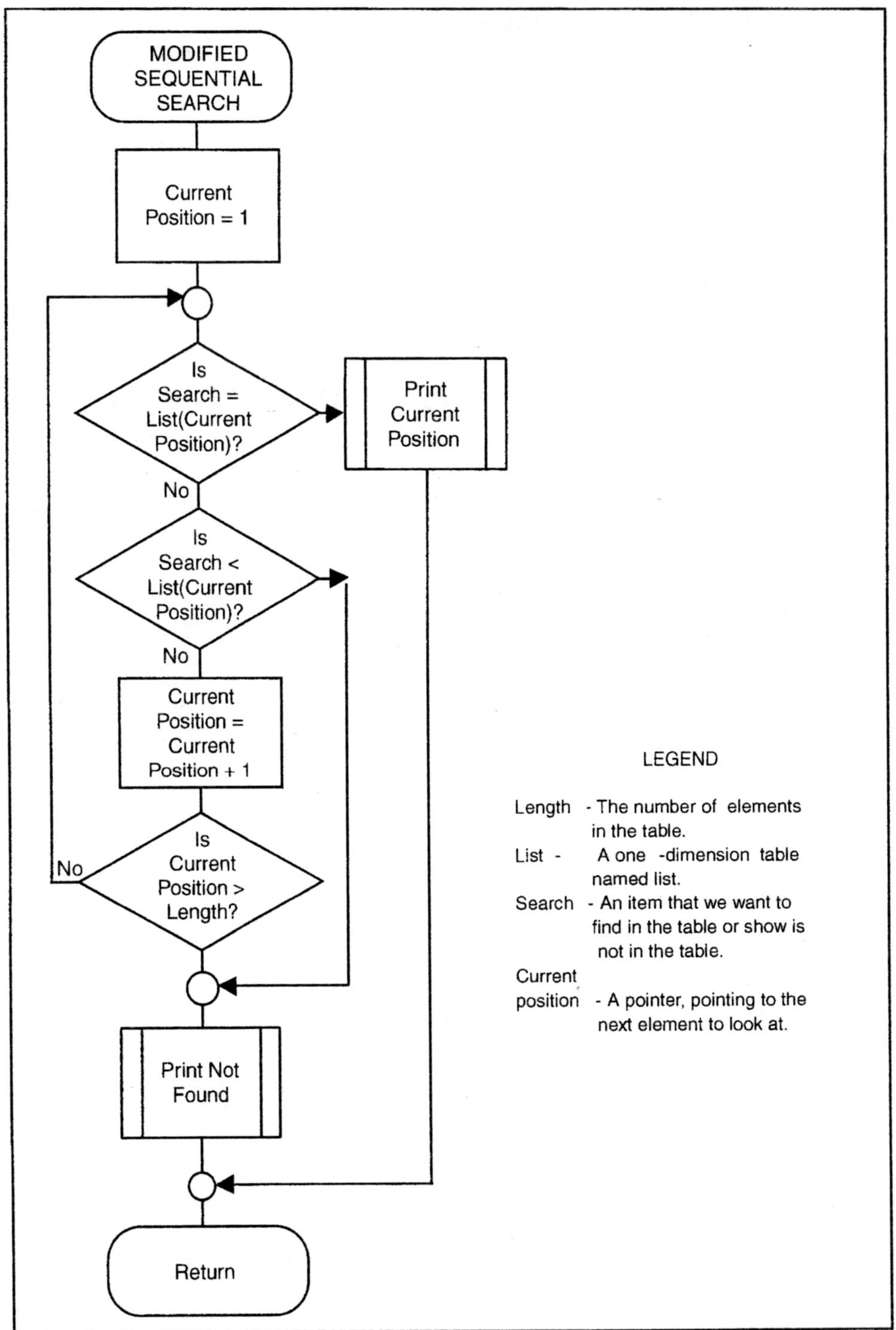

Figure 12.4 Modified Sequential Search

Search Comparisons

In our binary search, we had to look at three positions in the table in order to determine that the number 20 was not in the list. In the sequential unsorted search, we looked at 7 positions to determine the same thing, but in the sequential sorted search, we only looked at three positions again as in the binary search. So you can see that sorting makes a difference. Let's look at three statistics to compare the sequential and binary searches. We'll look at the best possible case, the worst possible case, and the average number of looks that we must perform to find (or not find) an element. For our example, we'll assume a list of length 4.

First the sequential; the best case would be to find the element on the first attempt (this does happen when you are looking for the first number in the list). Worst case would be that we have to look at all the numbers in the list. For a list of 4 numbers we would look 4 times; for 7 numbers, 7 times; and so on. What does the average look like? If we assume that we are going to look for all the numbers eventually and we are equally likely to look for any particular number, then our average number of attempts becomes the sum of 1+2+3+4 divided by 4. For a list of 4 elements, our average would be 2.5. These data are summarized in Table 12.1, columns 2, 3, and 4 of the second row.

Now for the binary. In the best case, we find the number on the first try (this happens when the number we are looking for is in the middle of the list). Worst case: for a list of 4 elements we have to make three attempts. This is an improvement over the sequential search. What about the average number of attempts? Here, we need to do some more detailed analysis. We could find the middle number in one attempt. We could find the second or third number on two attempts, and it would take three attempts to find the fourth number. So we would average all of the attempts using this formula:

(1*1 + 2*2 + 3)/4

giving an average of 2. These data are summarized in Table 12.1, columns 5, 6, and 7 of the second row.

Let's consider lists of other lengths using the formulas discovered previously. Suppose you only have two elements to search. The sequential is: best case = 1, worst case = 2, average = 1.5; and the binary is: best case = 1, worst case = 2, and average = 1.5. For two elements, there is no difference between the sequential and the binary.

Next let's look at 7 elements. To simplify the reading and writing, Table 12.1 contains a summary of the statistics for a variety of table sizes. You may wish to verify the data for some of the smaller numbers before moving on.

Table 12.1 Efficiency Table

	Sequential Search			Binary Search		
Table Size	Best Case	Worst Case	Average	Best Case	Worse Case	Average
2	1	2	1.5	1	2	1.5
4	1	4	2.5	1	3	2.0
8	1	8	4.5	1	4	2.6
16	1	16	8.5	1	5	3.4
32	1	32	16.5	1	6	4.2
64	1	64	32.5	1	7	5.1
128	1	128	64.5	1	8	6.1

Obviously, the search techniques are equivalent in the best case. Looking at the worst case, however, we see that the binary search is far superior to the sequential search; and even on average, the binary search is substantially better than the sequential. The binary search is a very powerful tool for searching data IF the data is sorted. If the data are not sorted, the binary search should not be used.

Sorting the data brings us to another evaluation point. The binary search is very fast compared to the sequential search if we only look at the search time. However, since the binary search requires sorted data, what happens to the "total" time if the data are not sorted? This question can have a significant impact on the programming solution used. It's possible that the sequential search would be preferred over the binary search in certain circumstances. If the data are not sorted, and the amount of time to sort the data is large, and we very seldom have to search the data, then the sequential search might be preferred. Even if the data are partially sorted, we still can't use the binary search. So to be fair, we have to consider the sort time somehow in our analysis.

Other Special Considerations

Some other significant considerations have not been mentioned. Our data in the previous example assumed that there were no duplicate items in the list. Suppose our data looked like this List (7): 45, 45, 51, 67, 79, 97, 106. Where in the list would we find the number 45? What would the binary search find? The binary search would look at the 67 first and determine that the number 45 was before that and search the sublist: 45, 45, and 51. This search would discover the number 45 in the second position. Notice that the sequential search would discover the number 45 in the first position. Is this a problem? Maybe! If our task was to find an occurrence of the number 45, there's no problem. If we were looking for all occurrences of the number 45, or the first occurrence, then our algorithm would require some modification.

Other Searches

After learning the sequential and binary searches, you might well ask, "Are there other searches?" The answer, of course, is yes. Fibonacci search, tree search, and hashing search are three major areas of searching algorithms. A rather interesting search method is the random search, where the list is searched in a random order. A record is kept of each location searched so that a location is not checked twice. Using this method is equivalent to the sequential search when an element is not in the list. It can be faster than the sequential method when the item is in the list. Searching is still an active area of computer science research, and many varieties of searching exist. Students interested in more varieties of searching should begin with Knuth Volume 3.[3]

Searching Applied to the Bowling League

Imagine that a two-dimension table was established for each bowler. The first dimension contained a number that was assigned to each bowler in order to establish index numbers for the bowling data file. The second dimension contained the name of the bowler. In order to access the bowler's data in the file, we need only to ask the bowler (user) to input the bowler's name. The program would search the table until finding the name and then locate the bowler's number to access the file data. A similar process could be used for team names and team numbers.

The various algorithms for searching are shown here as pseudocode modules.

In the sequential search (Figure 12.5), a special purpose variable has been added (variable name "Found") that determines if the item is found or not. This special variable is a switch, as discussed in Chapter 1. The variable named Found is tested at the end of the loop to determine if the item was found. Found = "Yes" indicates that the item was found. Found = "No" indicates that the item was not found.

```
Sequential_Search
        List (5)
        Current_position =1
        Found = "No"
        Repeat
                If Search = List (Current_position) Then
                       Print_ Current_position
                       Found = "Yes"
                          Current_position = Length + 1
                Else Current_position = Current_position + 1
                Endif
        Until Current_position > Length
        If Found = "No" Then
            Print_not_found
        Endif
Return
```

Figure 12.5
Pseudocode Sequential Search

3 Knuth, Donald E. 1997. The *Art of Computer Programming.* Addison-Wesley.

The pseudocode for the binary search is shown in Figure 12.6. Again the switch "Found" is used to signal when an item has been found. The variable named Found is tested at the end of the search process to print the message that the item was not found.

```
Binary_search
        Top = 1
        Bottom = Length
        Found = 0
                Repeat
                Midpoint = (Top + Bottom)/2
                        If Search = List (Midpoint) Then
                            Print Found_it
                            Top = Bottom + 1
                            Found = 1
                        Else    If Search > List (Midpoint) Then
                                    Top = Midpoint + 1
                                Else Bottom = Midpoint -1
                        Endif
                Until Top > Bottom
        If Found = 0  Then
            Print Didn't_find_it
        Else
        Endif
Return
```

Figure 12.6 Pseudocode Binary Search

Figure 12.7 shows the pseudocode for the modified sequential search. Again we see the "Found" variable employed.

```
Sequential_Search_Modified
        List (5)
        Current_Position =1
        Found = "No"
        Repeat
                If Search < List (Current_Position) Then
                    Current_Position = Length + 1
                Else
                    If Search = List (Current_Position) Then
                        Found = "Yes"
                       Current_Position = Length + 1
                     Else
                       Current_Position = Current_Position + 1
                     Endif
                Endif
        Until Current_Position > Length
        If Found = "No"
                Then Print_not_found
                Else
        Endif
Return
```

Figure 12.7 Pseudocode Modified Sequential Search

Summary

This chapter provided an introduction to algorithms for searching data. The three algorithms studied were the sequential search, the modified sequential search, and the binary search. The sequential search starts with the first element in the list and looks at every element in sequence until the element is found or the list is exhausted. The modified sequential search assumes that the list is sorted and terminates when the element is smaller than the search item. The binary search begins at the center of the list and reduces the size of the list by half until the element is found or the list length is reduced to zero.

Table 12.2 provides a summary of the important characteristics of the sequential and binary searches.

Table 12.2 Search Comparison

Sequential Search	Binary Search
Data are not required to be in a particular order. known.	Data must be sorted either ascending or descending, and the order must be
Algorithm must inspect every item in the list when the item is not in the list.	Algorithm will inspect at most N + 1 items where the list constains 2^N items. Search time is much less than sequential search.

Key Terms

Each number in parentheses indicates the page where the term first occurs in the chapter.

binary search (242) search (242) sequential search (242)

Chapter 12 Exercises

Objective 1 Read and draw flowcharts for searching algorithms.

1. Desk check the binary search flowchart shown in this chapter using the following data: 23, 56, 7, 4, 99. Don't sort the data, but perform the binary search routine, and describe what happens when you search for the number 4.
2. Desk check the binary search flowchart shown in this chapter using the following data: 4, 33, 18, 12, 99. Don't sort the data, but perform the binary search routine, and describe what happens when you search for the number 4.
3. Explain what causes the difference in problems 1 and 2.
4. Modify the binary search flowchart in this chapter so that it works with a list (table) of data in descending sequence. You should be able to keep most of the flowchart and change one or two small portions to make this work. Be sure to desk check your solution using a list of numbers sorted in descending sequence.
5. Modify the modified sequential search flowchart so that it will display a message if the table contains a value greater than the value of the search item. Example: Assume a table of five items (1, 3, 4, 5, 8). If we had "3" as the search item, the routine would report that the numbers 4, 5, and 8 were in the table.
6. Modify the binary search flowchart so that it will display a message if the table contains a value greater than the value of the search item. Example: Assume a table of five items (1, 3, 4, 5, 8). If we had "3" as the search item, the routine would report that the numbers 4, 5, and 8 were in the table.

7. Compare the flowcharts in problems 4 and 5 to determine which is the most efficient.
8. Modify the modified sequential search flowchart so that it will display a message if the table contains a value less than the value of the search item. Example: Assume a table of five items (1, 3, 4, 5, 8). If we had "3" as the search item, the routine would report that the numbers 4, 5, and 8 were in the table.
9. Modify the binary search flowchart so that it will display a message if the table contains a value less than the value of the search item. Example: Assume a table of five items (1, 3, 4, 5, 8). If we had "3" as the search item, the routine would report that the numbers 4, 5, and 8 were in the table.
10. Modify the binary search flowchart so that it will find all the occurrences of a data element. In other words, it will find duplicates if they exist. Have the flowchart display the data element that was repeated and count how many times the data element was repeated.

Objective 2

Enrichment – Doing it with Pseudocode

Read and write pseudocode for searching algorithms.

1. Desk check the binary search pseudocode shown in this chapter using the following data: 23, 56, 7, 4, 99. Don't sort the data, but perform the binary search routine, and describe what happens when you search for the number 4.
2. Desk check the binary search pseudocode shown in this chapter using the following data: 33, 4, 18, 12, 99. Don't sort the data, but perform the binary search routine, and describe what happens when you search for the number 4.
3. Explain what causes the difference in problems 1 and 2.
4. Modify the binary search pseudocode in this chapter so that it works with a list (table) of data in descending sequence.
5. Modify the modified sequential search pseudocode so that it will display a message if the table contains a value greater than the value of the search item. Example: Assume a table of five items (1, 3, 4, 5, 8). If we had "3" as the search item, the routine would report that the numbers 4, 5, and 8 were in the table.
6. Modify the binary search pseudocode so that it will display a message if the table contains a value greater than the value of the search item. Example: Assume a table of five items (1, 3, 4, 5, 8). If we had "3" as the search item, the routine would report that the numbers 4, 5, and 8 were in the table.
7. Compare the pseudocode in problems 4 and 5 to determine which is the most efficient.

8. Modify the modified sequential search pseudocode so that it will display a message if the table contains a value less than the value of the search item. Example: Assume a table of five items (1, 3, 4, 5, 8). If we had "3" as the search item, the routine would report that the numbers 4, 5, and 8 were in the table.
9. Modify the binary search pseudocode so that it will display a message if the table contains a value less than the value of the search item. Example: Assume a table of five items (1, 3, 4, 5, 8). If we had "3" as the search item, the routine would report that the numbers 4, 5, and 8 were in the table.
10. Modify the binary search pseudocode so that it will find all the occurrences of a data element. In other words, it will find duplicates if they exist. Have the pseudocode display the data element that was repeated and count how many times the data element was repeated.

Other Assignments

SoftSkills

Select one problem from the Internet/library research projects. Prepare and give an oral report to the class on your selection.

Internet/Library Research

A. Research various searching algorithms and write a paper describing some of the other searching algorithms available. Include a flowchart description of a search algorithm that you found that was different from any in the text.

B. Research various searching techniques and write a paper describing some of the other searching algorithms available. Include a pseudocode description of a search algorithm that you found that was different from any in the text.

13

SWAPPING AND SORTING

People who like this sort of thing will find this the sort of thing they like.
(Abraham Lincoln (1809–1865)

OBJECTIVES

After completing this chapter, you will be able to:

1 Understand the basic sorting processes.

2 Read, modify, and analyze flowcharts for sorting algorithms.

3 Read, modify, and analyze pseudocode for sorting algorithms.

Introduction

In this chapter we will study one of the most common algorithms in use in computer programs: sorting algorithms. Sorting data occurs very frequently in computer programming. Even in the non-computer world, we find ourselves putting data on 3x5 cards and then sorting them to find information. In some cases we found we could sort the cards and find information much faster than when the cards were unsorted. That analogy still holds in the computer world.

Tables and files are two of the most common objects sorted by computers. Tables are sorted in RAM by *internal* sorting algorithms, and files are normally sorted using *external* sort algorithms. There may be as many sorting algorithms as there are people, since no two people are exactly alike. However, there are relatively few "good" sort routines. This text will look exclusively at internal sorting. For the reader interested in external sorting, please see Knuth[1] volume 3 for a beginning point. We will examine three types of internal sort routines: exchange sort, selection sort, and insertion sort. These three sort routines offer three unique approaches to the sorting of data. Sorting is still a dynamic field of study, and new algorithms are developed continually.

A preliminary note is in order as well. We have two styles in which data can be sorted. They can be sorted in either *ascending* or *descending sequence*. If data are sorted in ascending sequence, the smallest one occurs first in the list, and the bigger one second, and so on. In descending sequence, the biggest occurs first, followed by the next biggest, and so on. If we have a list sorted in ascending sequence and we need it in descending sequence, do we need to sort it again? If we simply process the list in reverse order, we can produce the list in the opposite sequence of the one that existed.

Suppose there is a table of numbers 2,6,8. This table is sorted in ascending sequence. If we print the 3rd element, then the second element, and finally the first element, we would see the list 8,6,2, which is the list in descending sequence. Techniques like that are often used to save programming time and to speed up a program. Recall from Chapter 7 that the data could just as easily be names (characters, letters, and so on) as they could be numbers. The algorithms would work as well, and we use numbers here to simplify the explanations.

Swapping

For most sorting algorithms to work properly, we find an even simpler algorithm, *swapping*, is required. Swapping means that we exchange data between two locations. As you know from previous work, a computer can only store one value in a storage location. At the bit level that could be a 1 or a zero. At the byte level that can be any character or a variety of numbers. The point is that if you store an 8 in location MEMORY and later put a 9 in location MEMORY, the 8 is gone from location MEMORY. This is known as overwriting. In our sorting discussions below, we're going to swap positions of data (swap data), which means that we're going to move data from one memory location to

1 Knuth, Donald E. 1998. The Art of Programming, Volume 3. Addison-Wesley.

another without losing the data in the other location. This sounds complicated, and it causes some trouble with beginning programmers but is easily overcome.

Suppose that we have the number 15 stored in location FIRST and 8 stored in location SECOND. What we want to do is put the contents of FIRST into SECOND and the contents of SECOND into FIRST. If we say FIRST = SECOND, we lose the data in FIRST. If we say SECOND = FIRST, we lose the data in SECOND. We need an extra memory location to be used as a temporary holding area in order to make the trade. In a task list it looks like this:

Put the contents of FIRST into a temporary storage location.
Put the contents of SECOND into location FIRST.
Put the contents of the temporary storage location into SECOND.
OR:
Put the contents of SECOND into a temporary storage location.
Put the contents of FIRST into location SECOND.
Put the contents of the temporary storage location into FIRST.

Either of the above methods works as well. The flowchart is shown in Figure 13.1.

This is probably the simplest algorithm in computer programming and is necessary anytime you need to rearrange data.

Swap
Temp = First
First = Second
Second = Temp
Return

Figure 13.1 Swap flowchart

Sorting

For all of the sort algorithms in this chapter, we will use a one-dimensional table of numbers with 6 elements. The values in the 6 elements will start in the following sequence: 47, 59, 7, 999, 14, 300. We will sort the above data into ascending sequence so that the final table becomes: 7, 14, 47, 59, 300, 999[2].

By using the same data repeatedly, we will be able to easily compare the differences in the methods that each sort algorithm uses. The flowcharts (and later pseudocode) were drawn to be generic in nature, so variables are used for length.

Selection Sort

First, we will look at the *selection sort*. The selection sort looks at the list of numbers and finds the smallest number. The smallest number in the list is then swapped with the number at the top of the list (or, if the smallest number started at the top, it is left there). Then we ignore the first element in the

2 The algorithms can be easily modified to allow for multidimensional tables and/or to be sorted in descending sequence. Those processes are left to the exercises.

table, and we look for the smallest number remaining in the list. That number is swapped with the top of this shortened list, and then the process is repeated. Our task list (algorithm) then looks like this:

Find the smallest number in the list.

Swap the smallest number with the number at the top position of the list.

Reduce the size of the list (move the top down one position), and repeat steps 1 through 3 until there is only one element (the last element) that has not been examined.

The flowchart for this algorithm is shown in Figure 13.2. In order to "read" this algorithm, you will find it necessary to use paper and pencil to keep track of the steps as they occur. The narrative is provided here for the sort routine, but it will make little sense without following the steps in the flowchart. Keep in mind our table of numbers as we proceed.

We begin by setting the top of the table pointer to 1 (Top = 1)[3]. Next, we determine if we are finished by comparing the top pointer with the length of the table. If Top is less than Length, we have not finished processing the table. So our decision answers "Yes", which moves us to the PASSES module (note that module names are in capitals for clarity).

In the PASSES module, we temporarily save the value of Top (Hold = Top); and we establish a subscript, which is one greater than the top (Subscript = Top + 1). Now we enter the COMPARE module.

In the COMPARE module, we will check to see if the first element in the table is the smallest element. If it is not the smallest element, we will hold on to the subscript of the smaller element and continue searching the table until we have found the smallest element; and we will have its subscript retained in the variable Hold. Once we know the subscript of the smallest number, we know its position in ATABLE.

We return to the PASSES module at the bottom of the COMPARE module and test the value of the Hold variable with the value of the Top. If the Hold value has changed, we know that we need to swap the two numbers in the table. This swapping is done in the SWAP module, and you should be familiar with that process. Table 13.1 shows the values in ATABLE when the program started in the second column. The third column contains the values in ATABLE after the first swap.

3 In the flowchart, Top = 1 is the first statement on the left side of the page. In the pseudocode the sub-modules are listed in the beginning of the program, but the program actually begins at the statement Top = 1 about halfway down the page.

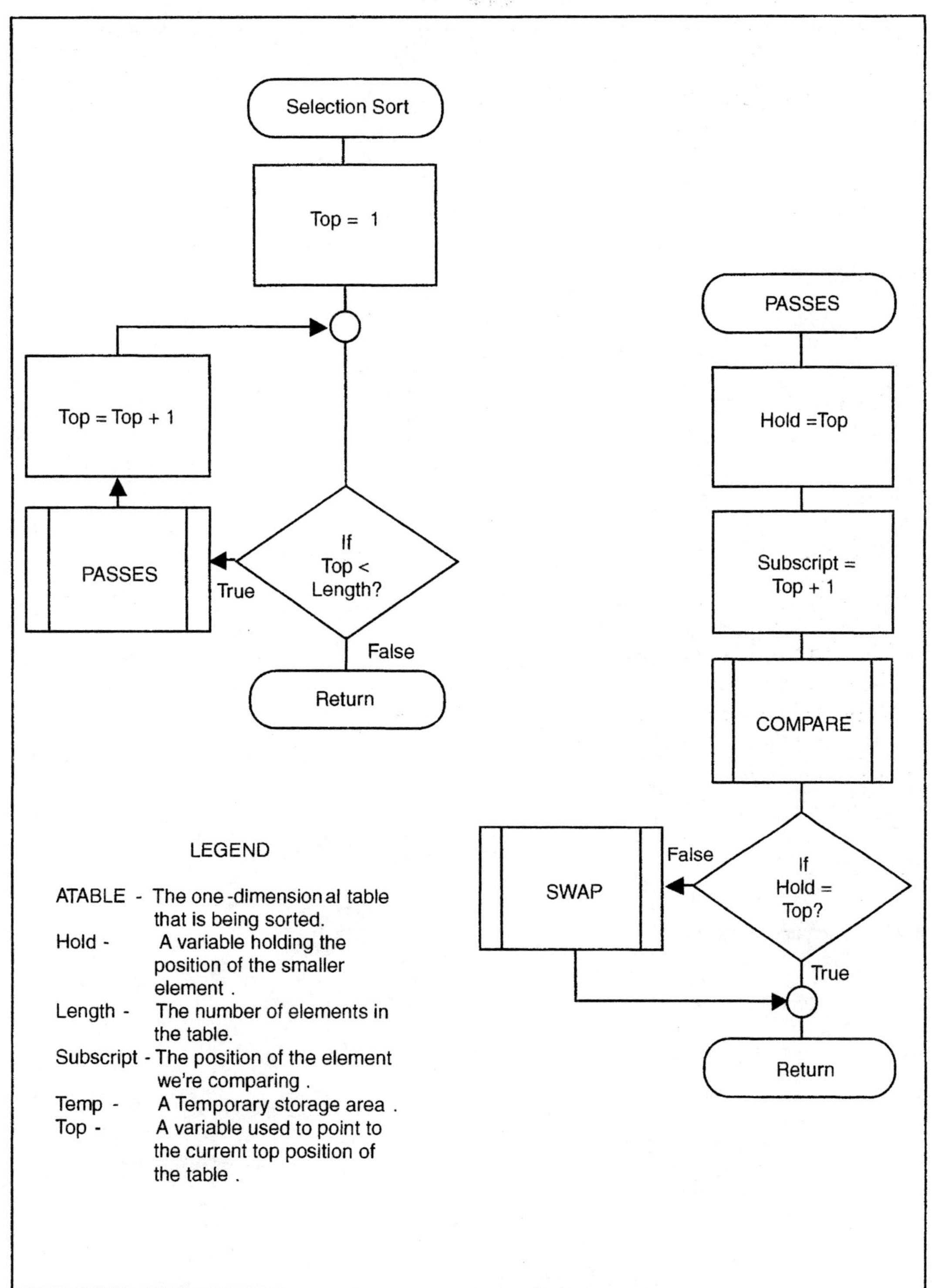

Figure 13.2 Part I–Selection sort flowchart

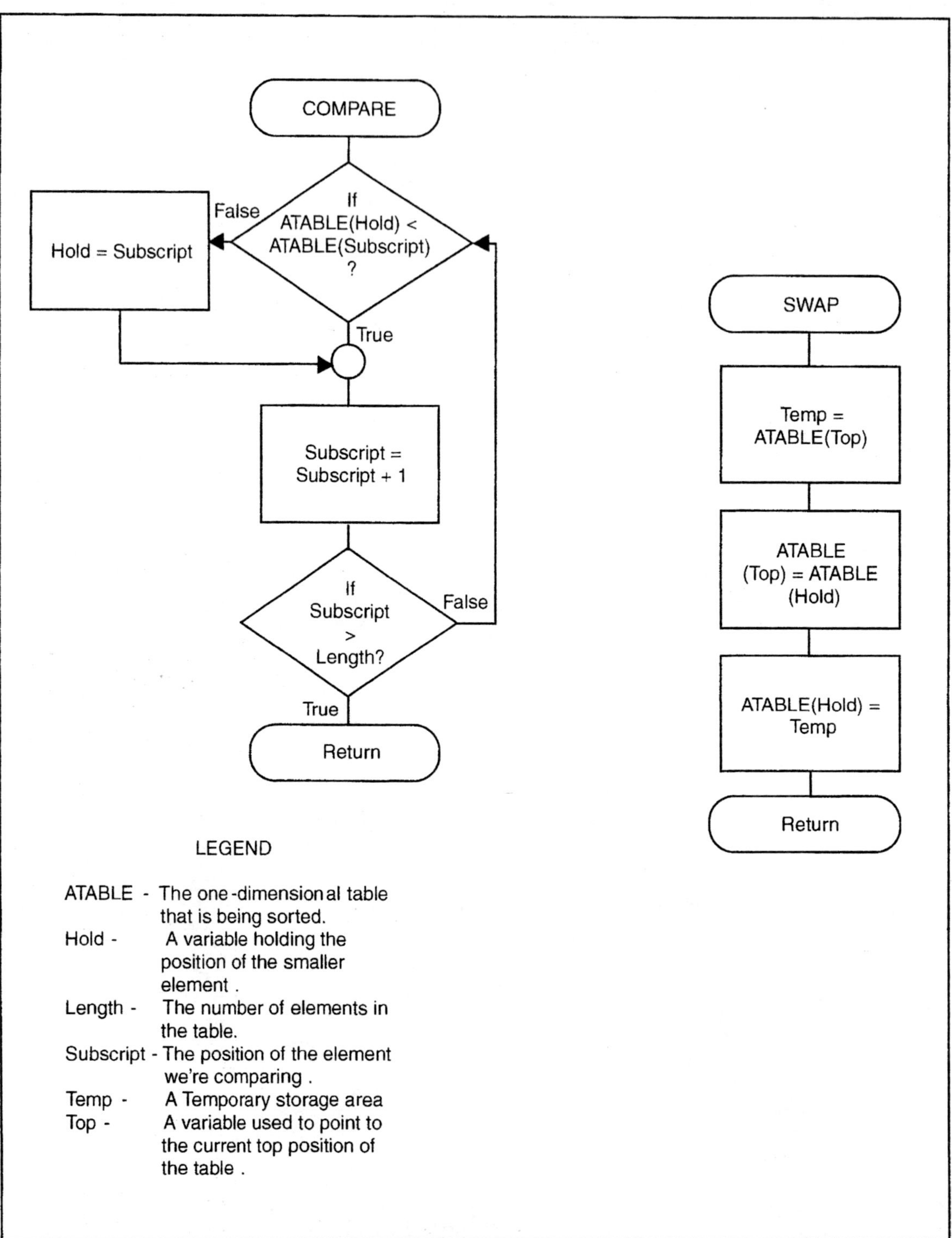

Figure 13.2 Part 2–Compare and swap modules

After swapping we will return to the PASSES module and then return to the starting (Selection sort) module at the top of the PASSES symbol.

Now we increment the top of our list. This is the key step. We have moved the smallest item in the table to the top of the list (position 1). We no longer wish to include the first item in our search, so we change our top pointer to indicate that the top of ATABLE is position 2. We are now searching through the second through sixth elements of the table looking for the smallest of these.

ATABLE

Subscript	Starting Values	After first Swap
1	47	7
2	59	59
3	7	47
4	999	999
5	14	14
6	300	300

Table 13.1 Element positions

We will next repeat the decision "Is Top < Length?" Since we are working with a table of length 6, we can see that we are not finished with our example. From here we repeat the earlier processes.

We move to the PASSES module, set Hold = Top (now 2), Subscript = Top + 1 (now 3), and move into the COMPARE module. We're comparing the second element in the new list to see if it's the smallest in the list. What do we find? The fifth element is the smallest in the list.

We return to the PASSES module and then proceed to SWAP. After this swap, the new list is shown in Table 13.2.

You should be able to work through the rest of the steps, sorting the table into its final order. Table 13.3 shows all of the intermediate results.

If you work through the algorithm carefully, you will notice that there is a pass through the table after the second swap, where the number 47 is found to be in the correct position. Working through the list is generally referred to as a *pass*, so we see that there were five passes through the list but only four swaps.

ATABLE

Subscript	Starting Values	After first Swap	After 2nd Swap
1	47	7	7
2	59	59	14
3	7	47	47
4	999	999	999
5	14	14	59
6	300	300	300

Table 13.2 Second swap positions

ATABLE

Subscript	Starting Values	After first Swap	After 2nd Swap	After 3rd Swap	After 4th Swap
1	47	7	7	7	7
2	59	59	14	14	14
3	7	47	47	47	47
4	999	999	999	59	59
5	14	14	59	999	300
6	300	300	300	300	999

Table 13.3 Fourth swap positions

Exchange sort

Next we look at the simple *exchange* sort using the "bubble" sort as our example.

The bubble sort is a very simple sort that effectively demonstrates the basic tasks required to sort a list of numbers or characters. This sort compares two elements in the list and rearranges them (swap) if they are not in the proper sequence. The flowchart is Figure 13.3. Our task list for the bubble sort looks like this:

1. Compare top element with the next element.
2. If they are out of sequence, swap them.
3. Increment the top.
4. Repeat steps 1, 2, and 3 until a pass has been completed.
5. If no swaps were made, terminate the algorithm.
6. If swap(s) were made, reset the top and reduce the length of the list by one.
7. Repeat 1 through 6.

The sort gets its name from the process of the smallest item "bubbling" to the top. It might be more appropriately named the "sinker" sort as the largest element sinks to the bottom at each pass.

In the bubble sort we will compare the first two elements. If the first is smaller than the second, we leave things alone and move on to compare the second and third elements and so on. When we find two elements out of sequence, we swap them and then return to comparing elements. In our example we eventually compare the fifth and sixth elements and swap them if they are out of sequence. This completes our first pass through the data. If we haven't swapped any numbers, we are finished sorting. But if some elements were out of sequence, then we may still need to compare further elements. Let's look at our example in detail.

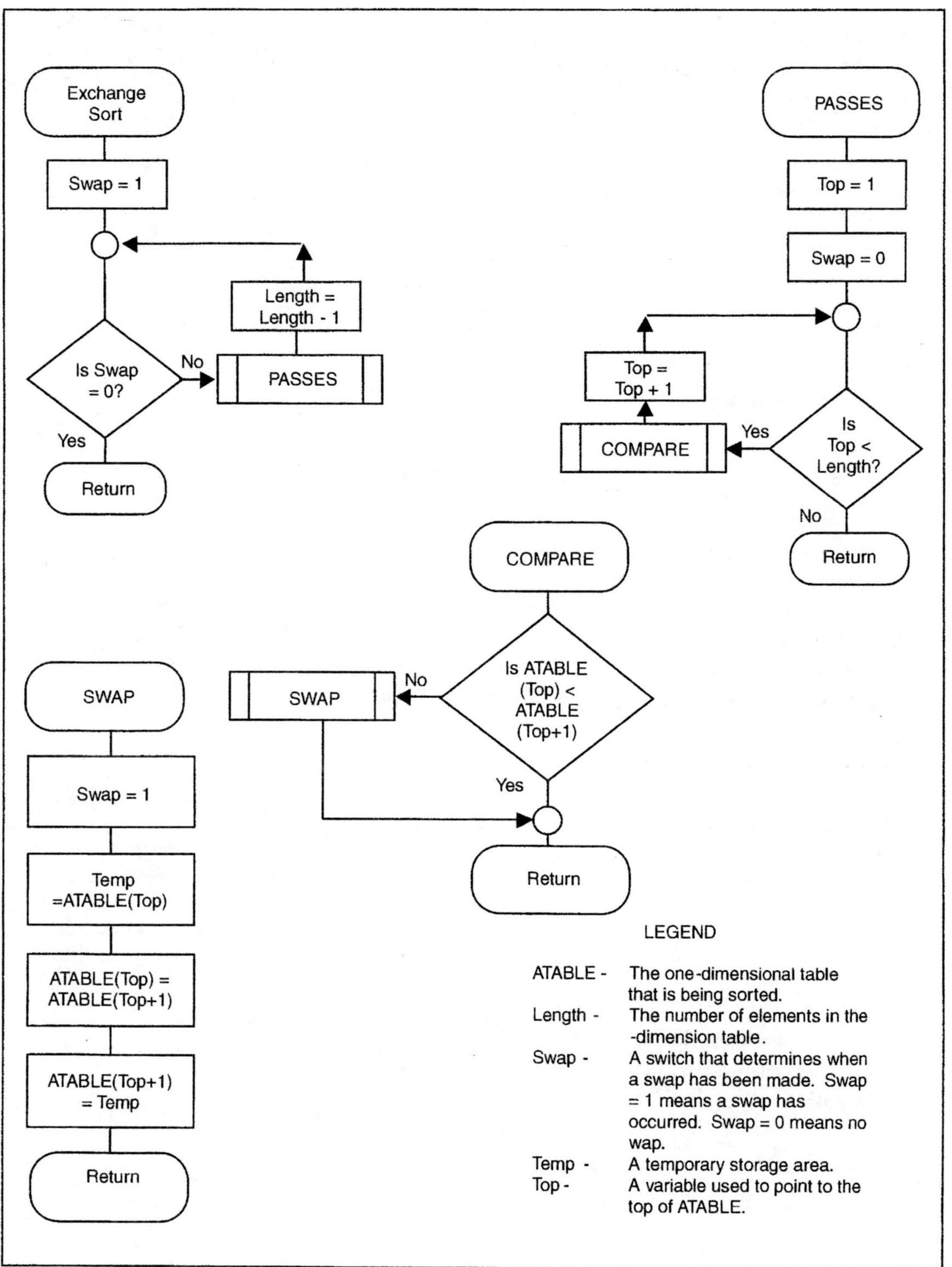

Figure 13.3 Exchange sort flowchart

During our first pass, we compared the contents of ATABLE (1) with ATABLE (2). Their values are in sequence so we don't swap them. Now we compare the contents of ATABLE (2) with ATABLE (3) [59 with 7]. They're out of sequence so we swap them, and we have the status of Table 13.4.

ATABLE		
Subscript	Starting Values	After first Swap
1	47	47
2	59	7
3	7	59
4	999	999
5	14	14
6	300	300

Table 13.4 First swap positions

Continuing this process, we arrive at the position shown in Table 13.5.

We've completed one pass through the data, made three swaps, and as you can plainly see, the list is not in sequence. This means we must make another pass through the list. Before we proceed, notice that the largest number in the list is in the last position. This is a feature of the Bubble Sort. After the first pass, we are guaranteed that the largest number will be at the bottom. This means that we will not have to compare this last element again. So the length of our list has effectively been reduced to five elements.

ATABLE				
Subscript	Starting Values	After first Swap	After 2nd Swap	After 3rd Swap
1	47	47	47	47
2	59	7	7	7
3	7	59	59	59
4	999	999	14	14
5	14	14	999	300
6	300	300	300	999

Table 13.5 Third swap positions

Making our second pass, we first compare the contents of ATABLE (1) with ATABLE (2) and swap the values. Continuing exactly as we did previously, we arrive at the position shown in Table 13.6.

ATABLE 2nd pass			
Subscript	Starting Value	After first Swap	After 2nd Swap
1	47	7	7
2	7	47	47
3	59	59	14
4	14	14	59
5	300	300	300
6	999	999	999

Table 13.6 Second pass positions

This time we only made two swaps; and, again, the list is not in sequence. In this case, a third pass through the list will result in a completely sorted list.

Insertion sort

Finally, we complete our study of sorting by looking at the simple *insertion* sort. This algorithm is similar to the way card players sort their cards when picking them up. Typically a card player will sort the first two cards; and when picking up the next card, the player "inserts" it into the proper position. As each card is picked up, the player inserts the card into the proper location. As a card is added to the hand, typically other cards have to be moved. The insertion sort algorithm replicates that process. Remember our sample list of numbers from previous exercises and begin the process:

1. If the first two numbers are out of sequence, swap them.
2. Find the correct position for the next number.
3. Move all elements so that the next number can be inserted into its proper position.
4. Insert the next number into position.
5. Increment next.
6. Repeat 1 through 5 until all elements have been processed.

The flowchart is shown in Figure 13.4 Part 1 and 2. For this sort to work properly, the table must contain at least three elements. If we have zero elements or one element, the table is already sorted. If we only have two elements, we need only check the first two and swap them appropriately. If we have three or more elements, we then proceed to the FIND POSITION module to determine in what position in the table the next element belongs. This sorting algorithm makes use of pointers to point to the top (Top) of the table, the bottom of the table (Bottom), and to point at the next item in the table (Next) to be considered.

Let's begin the algorithm with our sample table of numbers. We must first check the first two elements, and we are then prepared to enter the FIND POSITION module.

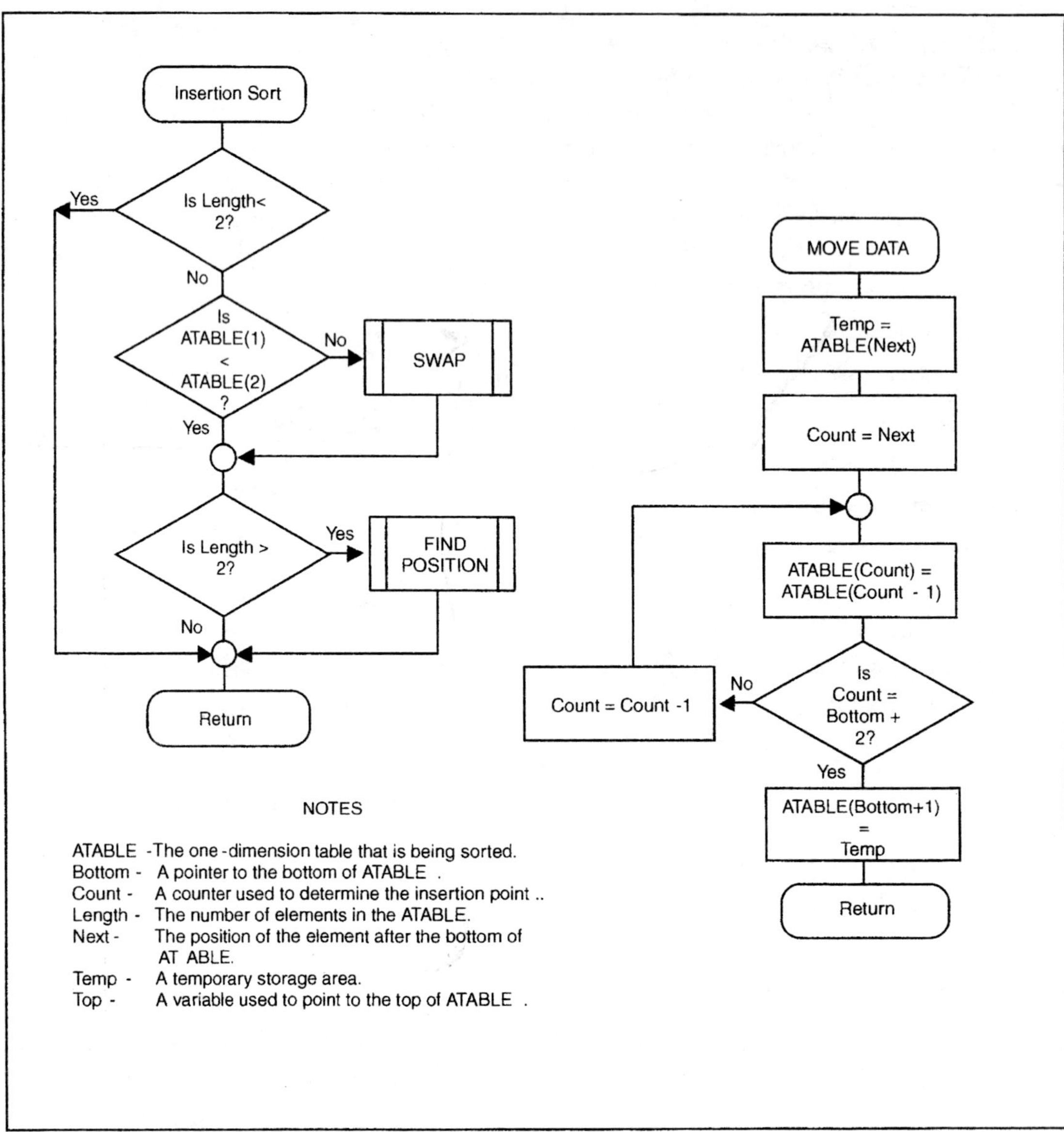

Figure 13.4 Part 1–Insertion sort flowchart

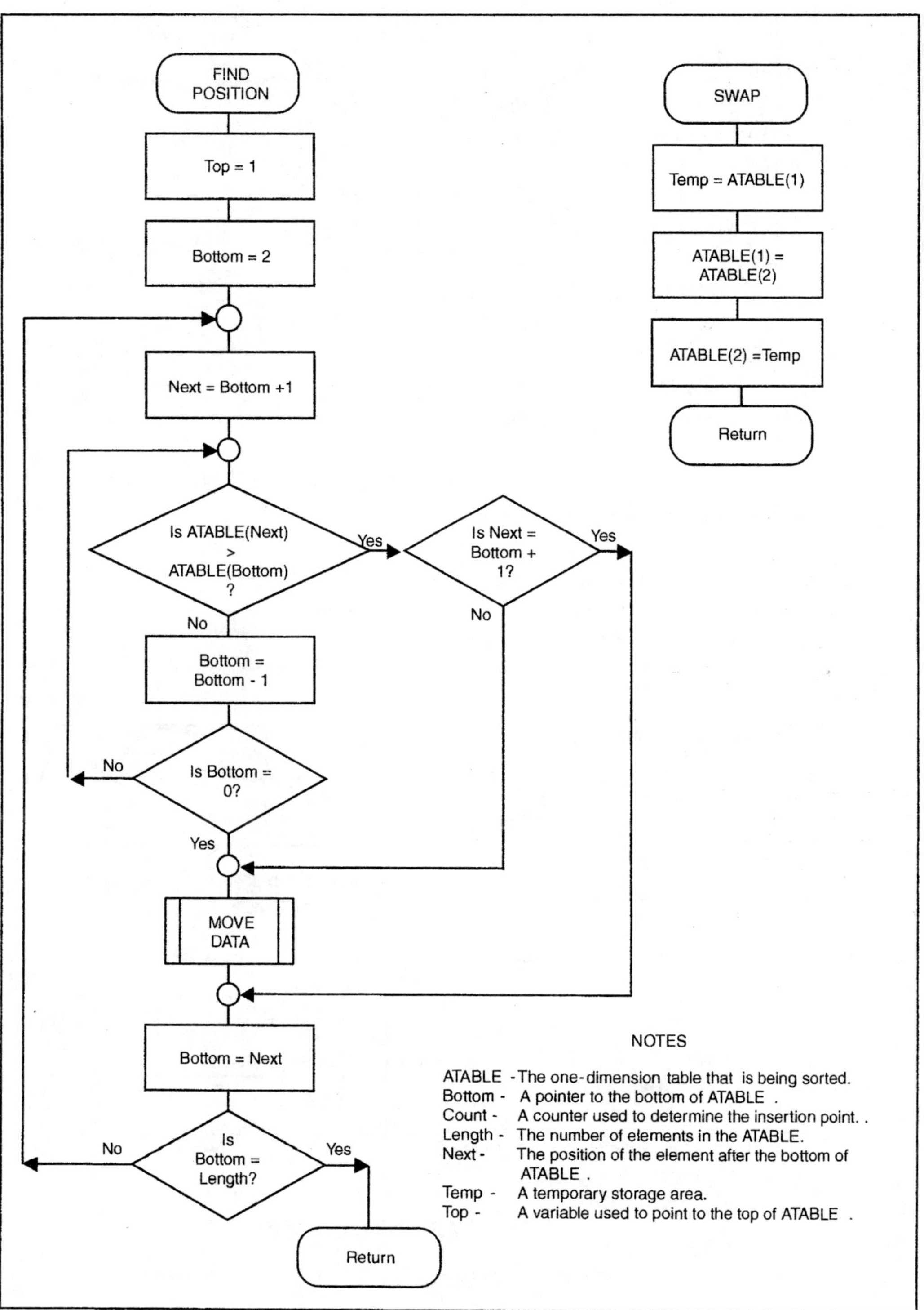

Figure 13.4 Part 2–Find position and swap modules

Table 13.7 shows the status of the elements in the table before entering the FIND POSITION module.

Top (the top pointer) is set to one, Bottom (the bottom pointer) is set to two, and Next (the next pointer) is set to three. Now we will find where the third element in the table belongs by comparing it to the second and first elements. We see that the number three should be in the first position; so we move into the MOVE DATA module to rearrange the table. The Count variable is used to move data down in the table until the correct position has been reached to insert the next element. The status of the table is shown in Table 13.8.

ATABLE entering FIND POSITION module

Subscript	Starting Values
1	47
2	59
3	7
4	999
5	14
6	300

Table 13.7 Entering find position

We now have four elements in position. We move the bottom and next pointers again and determine where in the list the number 14 belongs.

Now you can see that one more iteration of the FIND POSITION module will complete the sorting of the table of numbers. Table 13.9 shows the final positions.

This completes our demonstration of the three sorting techniques. Hopefully, this short demonstration was sufficient to show that sorting can take on a variety of forms.

ATABLE after moving the third element

Subscript	Starting Value	After first Swap
1	47	7
2	59	47
3	7	59
4	999	999
5	14	14
6	300	300

Table 13.8 Status after first move

Other Sorting Techniques

Other techniques for internal sorting include: Shell, Quick Sort, enumeration (counting), bucket, radix, heap, merge, Fibonacci, and distributive (to name a few). The interested reader will find a wealth of sort demonstrations available on the Internet (try a search on bubble sort, for instance). The literature is extremely rich in this category, and I would encourage the reader to begin with Knuth Volume 3 (Knuth, Donald E. 1998. *The Art of Programming.* Addison-Wesley) for a starting bibliography.

At this point, the reader should be asking: "Which sort is best?" The short answer is that the answer is still being researched. Another answer is that the best sort is the sort that orders the data in the least amount of time.

ATABLE after moving the fifth element

Subscript	Starting Values	After first Swap	After 2nd Swap
1	47	7	7
2	59	47	14
3	7	59	47
4	999	999	59
5	14	14	999
6	300	300	300

Table 13.9 Status after second move

Sorting Analysis

At this stage, you should know that speed of processing is a key reason for using computers. Many problems that computers solve in minutes could take weeks, years, or even lifetimes if done by hand. So our measure of "best" sorting would be time dependent. Generally, data movement requires the most time of a sorting algorithm so the fastest sort would be the one that moves data the least. Of the three sort algorithms presented, is there a method that moves the data less than the others?

Looking at the sort routines in reverse order of their presentation we see: The numbers 7, 47, and 59 are moved (this requires a move into temp and out of temp) for 4 moves. Nothing moves until we sort the 14 and then we move 14, 47, 59, and 999 (5 moves). Finally, we move the numbers 999 and 300. This is a total of 12 data movements.

In the bubble sort we swap the 7 and 59. Then we swap the 14 and 999 and the 300 and 999. In the second pass we make two swaps; and in the third pass, we swap once. So the bubble sort yields 18 data movements.

In the selection sort, we swap once for each element that is out of position. We can see from Figure 13.4 that this requires only 4 swaps or 12 data movements. Based on data movement alone, we would expect the selection sort or insertion sort to be fastest and the bubble sort to be slowest *on this set of data.*

Would a different set of data result in a different "fastest" sort algorithm? Try sorting the data 4, 3, 2, 1 using the three algorithms. You should find that the selection has the least moves, with the bubble sort next, and the insertion sort the most.

The message here is that the data is a determining factor in which sort to choose. If we know something about the data, we can choose a better sort algorithm than if we don't know anything about the data. Additionally, the programming language can affect the speed of sorting and the type of hardware can affect the sorting speed. So to fully answer the question of which sort is best, we must know three things:

1. What does the data look like?
2. What hardware are we using?
3. What programming language are we using?

For general purpose sorting of small data sets that are generally in some random order, we would likely use the quicksort or perhaps the Shell sort. The analysis of "best" sort is left for future study of algorithm analysis in later courses.

The pseudocode sort routines are displayed in the same sequence as the flowchart sort routines. You should find that the descriptions from the flowchart portion of the chapter work as well with the pseudocode as they do with the flowchart.

The same variable names have been used in the pseudocode as were used in the flowcharts.

Swapping

We begin with the swapping algorithm. Typically we call the temporary storage location TEMP so that in pseudocode the process is:

```
TEMP = SECOND
SECOND = FIRST
FIRST = TEMP
```

Selection Sort

The selection sort pseudocode is presented in Figure 13.5. The beginning of the pseudocode is slightly below the middle of the page, as the modules are placed before the main program. The table is declared first and then the main program begins with the statement Top = 1. The Dowhile Top < Length, transfers control to the PASSES module, which transfers control to the COMPARE module. When the smallest element is found, it is moved by the SWAP module; and the process continues until the elements are in order.

```
Selection_sort_program
ATABLE (6)
Top = 1
        Dowhile Top < Length
                PASSES
                Top = Top + 1
        Endwhile
Return
End Selection-sort_program
        PASSES
                Hold = Top
                Subscript = Top + 1
                COMPARE
                If Hold = Top Then
                    SWAP
                Else
                Endif
                Return
        COMPARE
                Repeat
                If ATABLE (Hold)  !  ATABLE (Subscript) Then
                    Hold = Subscript
                Else
                Endif
                Subscript = Subscript + 1
                Until Subscript > Length
                Return
        SWAP
                Temp = ATABLE (Top)
                ATABLE (Top) = ATABLE (Hold)
                ATABLE (Hold) = Temp
                Return
```

LEGEND

ATABLE –	The one-dimensional table being sorted.
Hold -	Holding the position of the smaller element.
Length -	The number of elements in the one-dimensional table.
Subscript -	The position of the element being compared.
Temp -	A temporary storage area.
Top -	A variable used to address the top position of the table.

Figure 13.5 Selection sort pseudocode

Exchange Sort

Next we show the exchange sort pseudocode in Figure 13.6.

```
Exchange_sort_program
ATABLE (6)
Swap =1
        Dowhile Swap = 1
                PASSES
                Length  = Length + 1
        Endwhile
Return
End Exchange-sort_program
        PASSES
                Top = 1
                Swap = 0
                Dowhile Top < Length
                COMPARE
                Top = top + 1
        Endwhile
        Return
COMPARE
        Repeat
        If ATABLE (Top)  !  ATABLE (Top + 1) Then
            SWAP
        Else
        Endif
        Return
SWAP
        Temp = ATABLE (Top)
        ATABLE (Top) = ATABLE (Top + 1)
        ATABLE (Top + 1) = Temp
        Swap = 1
        Return
```

NOTES

ATABLE –	The one-dimension tableal being sorted.
Length -	The number of elements in the one-dimensional table.
Swap -	A switch that tells us if a swap has been made.
Temp -	A temporary storage area.
Top -	A variable used to address the top position of the table.

Figure 13.6 Exchange sort pseudocode

Insertion Sort

And finally, we show the insertion sort in Figure 13.7.

```
Insertion_sort_program
ATABLE (6)
If Length > 1 Then
   If ATABLE (1) > ATABLE (2) Then
      SWAP
   Endif
If Length > 2 Then
   FIND POSITION
Endif
Endif
Return
End Insertion_sort_program
       FIND_POSITION
              Top = 1
              Bottom = 2
              Repeat
                     Next = Bottom + 1
                     Repeat
                     If ATABLE (Next) > ATABLE (Bottom) Then
                        If Next = Bottom +1 Then
                            Bottom = 0
                         Else
                            MOVE DATA
                            Bottom = 0
                        Endif
                     Else
                         Bottom = Bottom –1
                     If Bottom = 0 Then
                        MOVE DATA
                     Endif
                     Endif
                     Until Bottom = 0
              Bottom = Next
              Until Bottom = Length
       Return
```

LEGEND

ATABLE -	The one-dimensional table being sorted.
Bottom -	A pointer to the bottom of ATABLE.

Count - A counter used to determine the insertion point of the element being considered.

Length -	The number of elements in the one-dimensional table.
Next -	The position of the element after the bottom of ATABLE.
Temp -	A temporary storage area.
Top -	A variable used to address the top position of the table.

Figure 13.7 Part 1–Insertion sort pseudocode

```
SWAP
        Temp = ATABLE (Top)
        ATABLE (Top) = ATABLE (Top + 1)
        ATABLE (Top + 1) = Temp
        Swap = 1
        Return
MOVE DATA
        Temp = ATABLE (Next)
        Count = Next
                Dowhile Count > Bottom + 2
                ATABLE (Count) = ATABLE (Count-1)
                Count = Count –1
                Endwhile
        ATABLE (Bottom + 1) = Temp
        Return
```

NOTES

ATABLE -	The one-dimensional table being sorted.
Bottom -	A pointer to the bottom of ATABLE.
Count -	A counter used to determine the insertion point of the element being considered.
Length -	The number of elements in the one-dimensional table.
Next -	The position of the element after the bottom of ATABLE.
Temp -	A temporary storage area.
Top -	A variable used to address the top position of the table.

Figure 13.7 Part 2 Insertion sort pseudocode

Summary

In this chapter, we examined the three basic types of sorting: selection, exchange, and insertion. The selection sort finds the smallest element in a list and places it first. It then continues through the remainder of the list, placing the smallest element next until the list is in order. The selection sort will make n passes through the list where n is equal to the length of the list. The exchange sort examines two elements and swaps them if they are not correctly sorted. This process will make a maximum of (n-1)![4] passes through the list and a minimum of one pass. The insertion sort places the first two elements in sequence and then adds each additional element in the proper position. This sort requires only one pass to sort a list.

4 The exclamation point signifies factorial.

Key Terms

Each number in parentheses indicates the page where the term first occurs in the chapter.

ascending sequence (258)
descending sequence (258)
exchange sort (264)
external sort (258)
insertion sort (267)
internal sort (258)
pass (263)
election sort (259)
swapping (258)

Chapter 13 Exercises

Objective 1 Understand the basic sorting processes.

1. Group/Team Exercise—Form a group of three or more and invent a sorting algorithm. Working together, develop an informal logic plan that will sort a list of numbers (one-dimensional table), then construct a hierarchy chart for this task list, and finally prepare a flowchart or pseudocode explanation.
2. The sorting routines discussed in this chapter are designed to sort numbers into an ascending sequence. Describe how each of the three sort routines might be modified in order to produce a table of numbers sorted in descending sequence.
3. The tables of numbers used for examples in this chapter never contained duplicate values. For each of the three sort routines described in this chapter, explain what will happen when a table containing duplicate values is sorted. Use the table "Duplicate(7)" whose values are: 2, 3, 5, 3, 7, 1, 4.
4. Examine the selection sort flowchart (and/or pseudocode) in the chapter and identify all of the loops in the routine. Tell what type of loop you find (pre-condition or post-condition) and how many times the loop is executed. Organize your answer by modules.
5. Examine the exchange sort flowchart (and/or pseudocode) in the chapter and identify all of the loops in the routine. Tell what type of loop you find (pre-condition or post-condition) and how many times the loop is executed. Organize your answer by modules.
6. Examine the insertion sort flowchart (and/or pseudocode) in the chapter and identify all of the loops in the routine. Tell what type of loop you find (pre-condition or post condition) and how many times the loop is executed. Organize your answer by modules.
7. A common method of sorting elements of a table is to place the smallest element of the first table into the first position of a second table. Then the process continues by finding the next smallest element of the first table and moving it to the second position of the second table. This process continued until the second table was a sorted version of the first table. Examine this process and determine advantages and disadvantages of this method. Prepare a written report of your findings.

Objective 2 Read, modify, and analyze flowcharts for sorting algorithms.

1. Examine the flowchart shown in Figure 13.8. Explain what the sort routine does using a narrative explanation (what things get compared and in what order, how/when do things get into sequence, and so on). Using the following six numbers, show how the numbers move during the sorting process of Figure 13.8. 326, 14, 79, 86, 400, 8. Compare these results with the three sort routines in the chapter.
   Figure 13.8 Part 1–Objective 1 Exercise 1
2. The flowchart in Figure 13.9 represents a variation on the exchange sort shown in this chapter. Examine the flowchart shown. Explain what the sort routine does using a narrative explanation (what things get compared and in what order, how/when do things get into sequence, and so on). Using the following six numbers, show how the numbers move during the sorting process of Figure 13.9: 326, 14, 79, 86, 400, 8.

   Compare this process with the exchange sort shown in the chapter and explain how they differ. Compare these results with the three sort routines in the chapter.

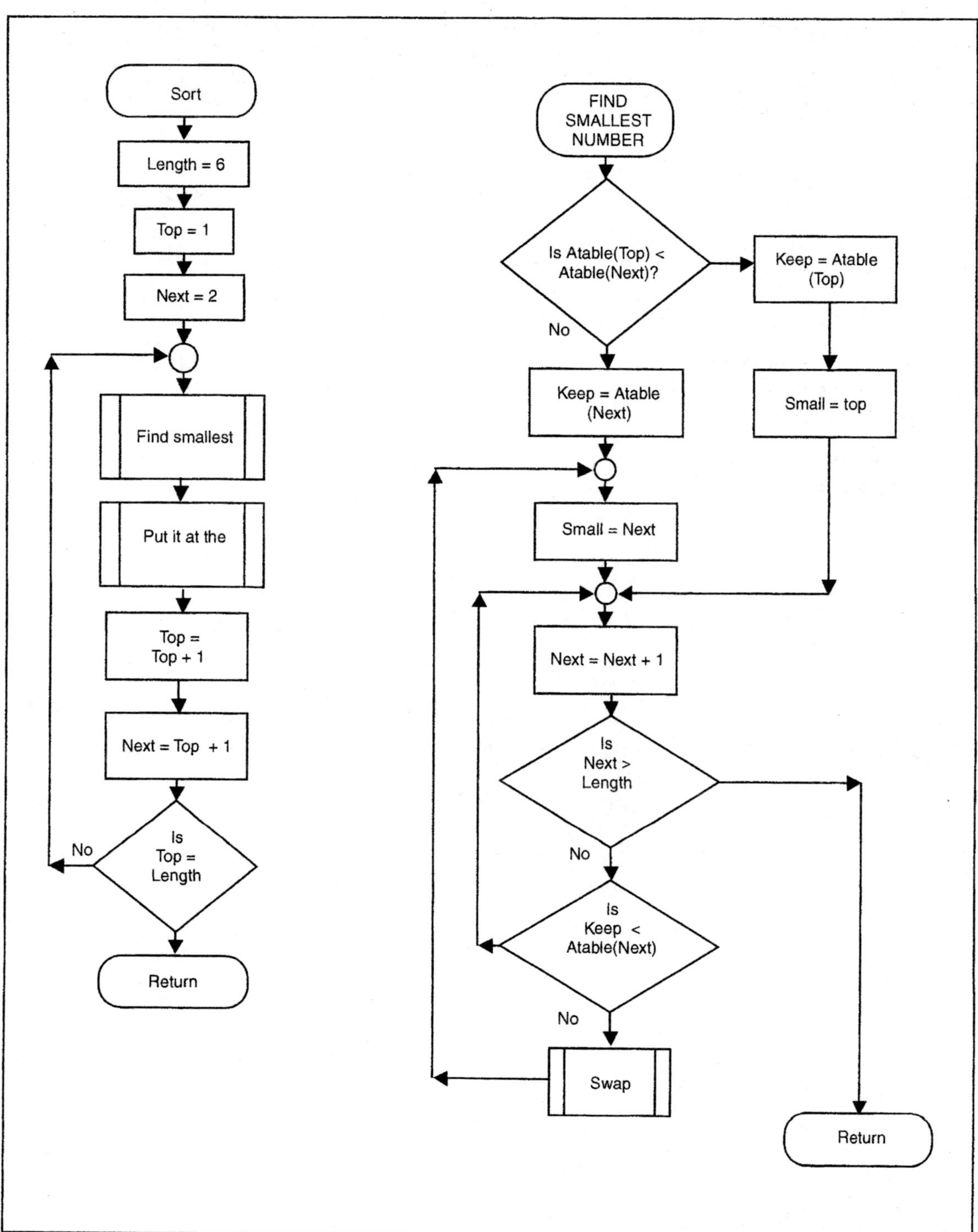

Figure 13.8 Part 1–Objective 1 Exercise 1

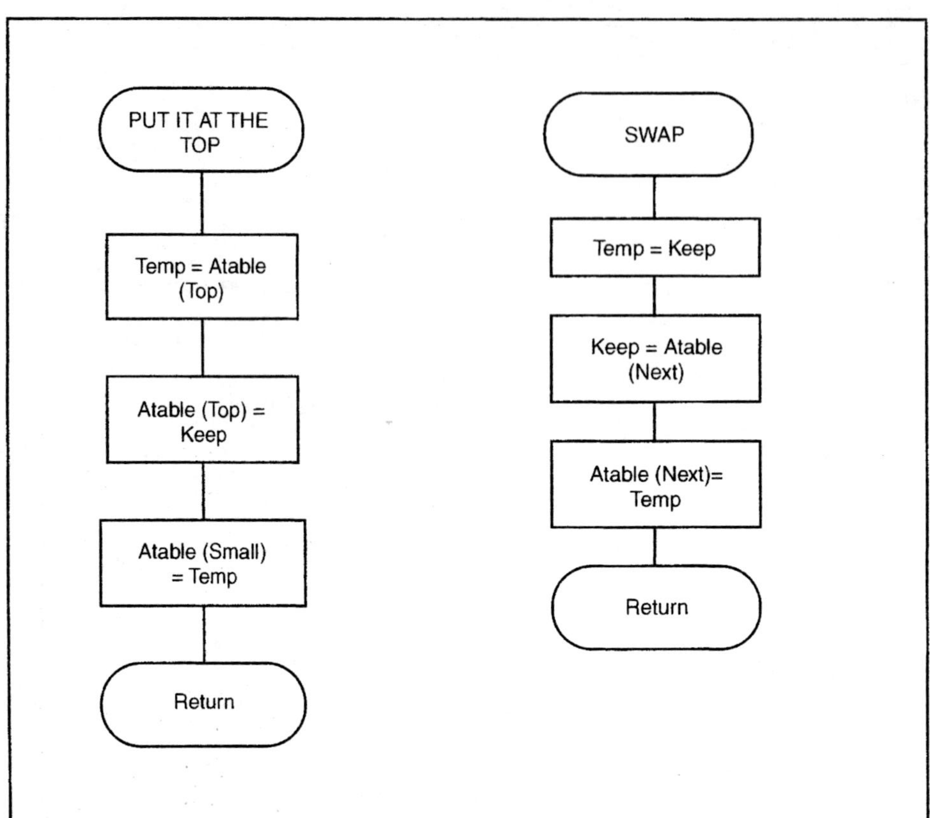

Figure 13.8 Part 2–Objective 1 Exercise 1

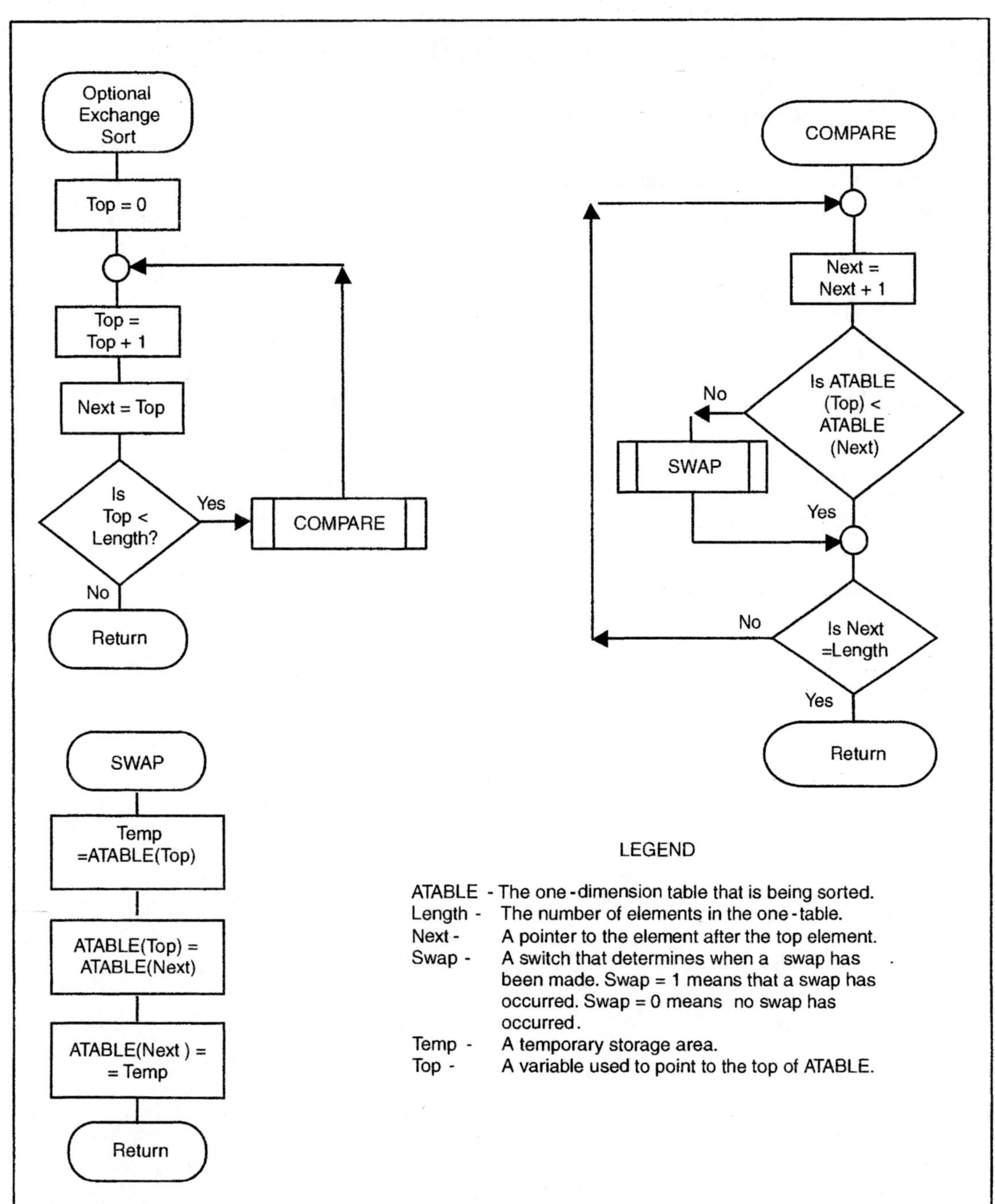

Figure 13.9 Objective 2 Exercise 2

3. The flowchart in Figure 13.10 represents the Shell[5] sort. Examine the flowchart shown. Explain what the sort routine does using a narrative explanation (what things get compared and in what order, how/when things get into sequence, and so on). Using the following six numbers, show how the numbers move during the sorting process of Figure 13.10: 326, 14, 79, 86, 400, 8. Compare these results with the three sort routines in the chapter.
4. The flowchart in Figure 13.11 makes use of an extra table to hold the sorted elements. This sort has the advantage of retaining the original table in addition to the sorted version. Examine the flowchart shown. Explain what the sort routine does using a narrative explanation (what things get compared and in what order, how/when things get into sequence,and so on). Using the following six numbers, show how the numbers move during the sorting process of Figure 13.11: 326, 14, 79, 86, 400, 8. Compare these results with the three sort routines in the chapter.
5. Modify the flowchart in problem 1 to work with a two- or three-dimensional table.
6. Modify the flowchart in problem 2 to work with a two- or three-dimensional table.
7. Modify the flowchart in problem 3 to work with a two- or three-dimensional table.
8. Draw a flowchart for a merge sort routine. (Hint: Research merge sort in the library and/or through the Internet before starting the flowchart.)
9. Select any of the sorting flowcharts from the exercises and write out all of the steps for the sorting process described. Use the techniques shown in the chapter. Create your own table of three numbers to use in the description.

5 Named for D.L. Shell who published it in 1959.

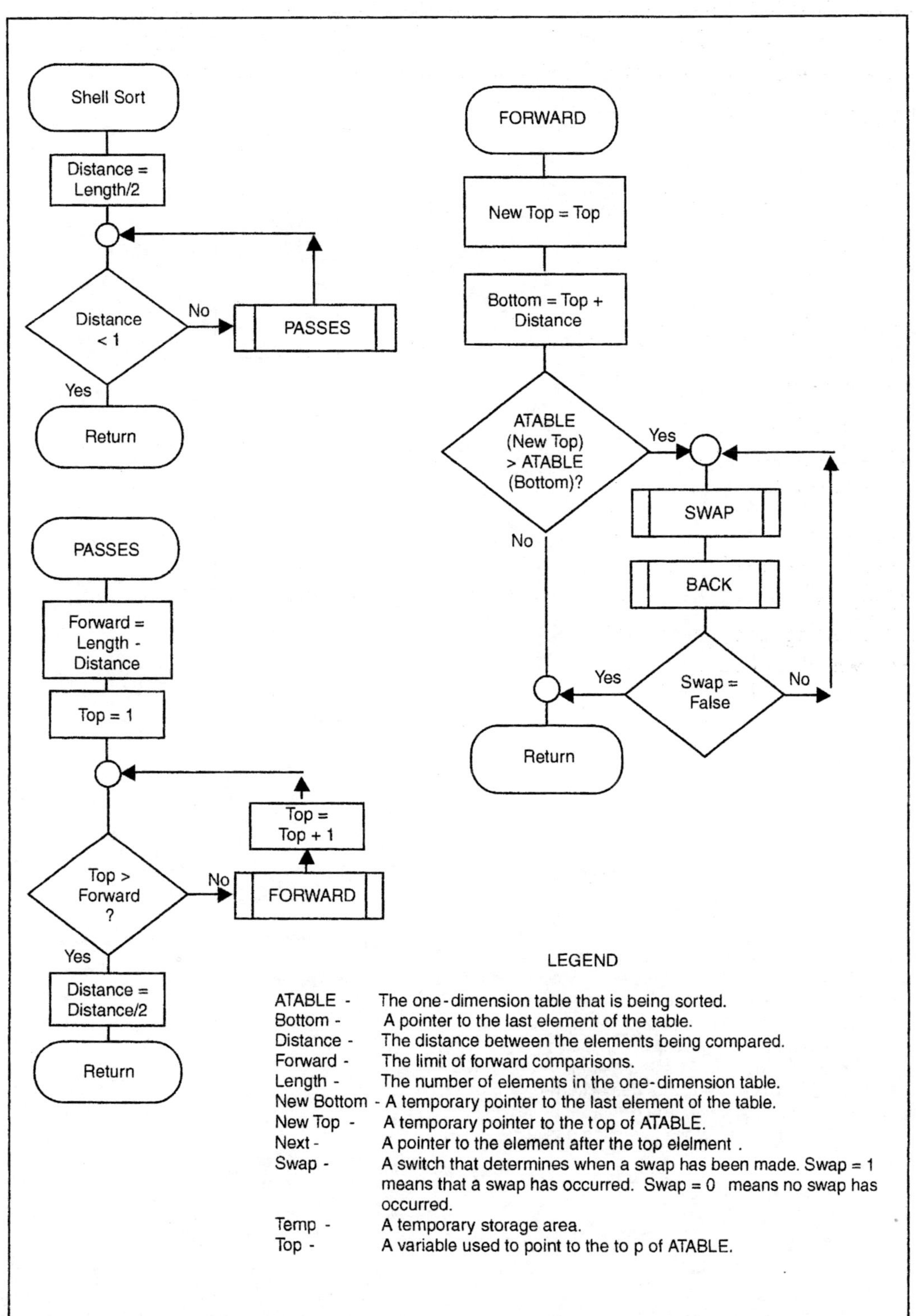

Figure 13.10 Part 1–Shell sort

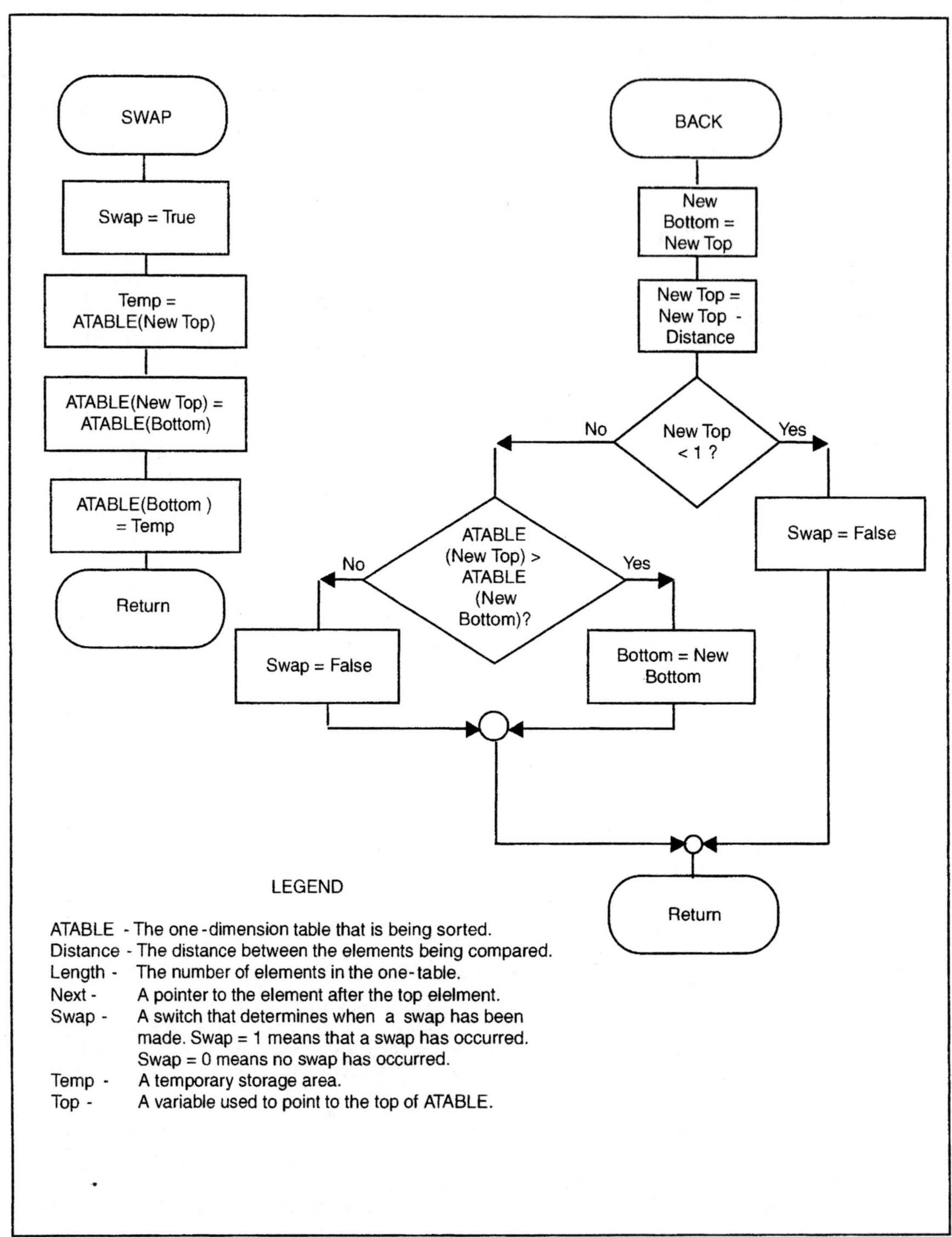

Figure 13.10 Part 2–Shell sort

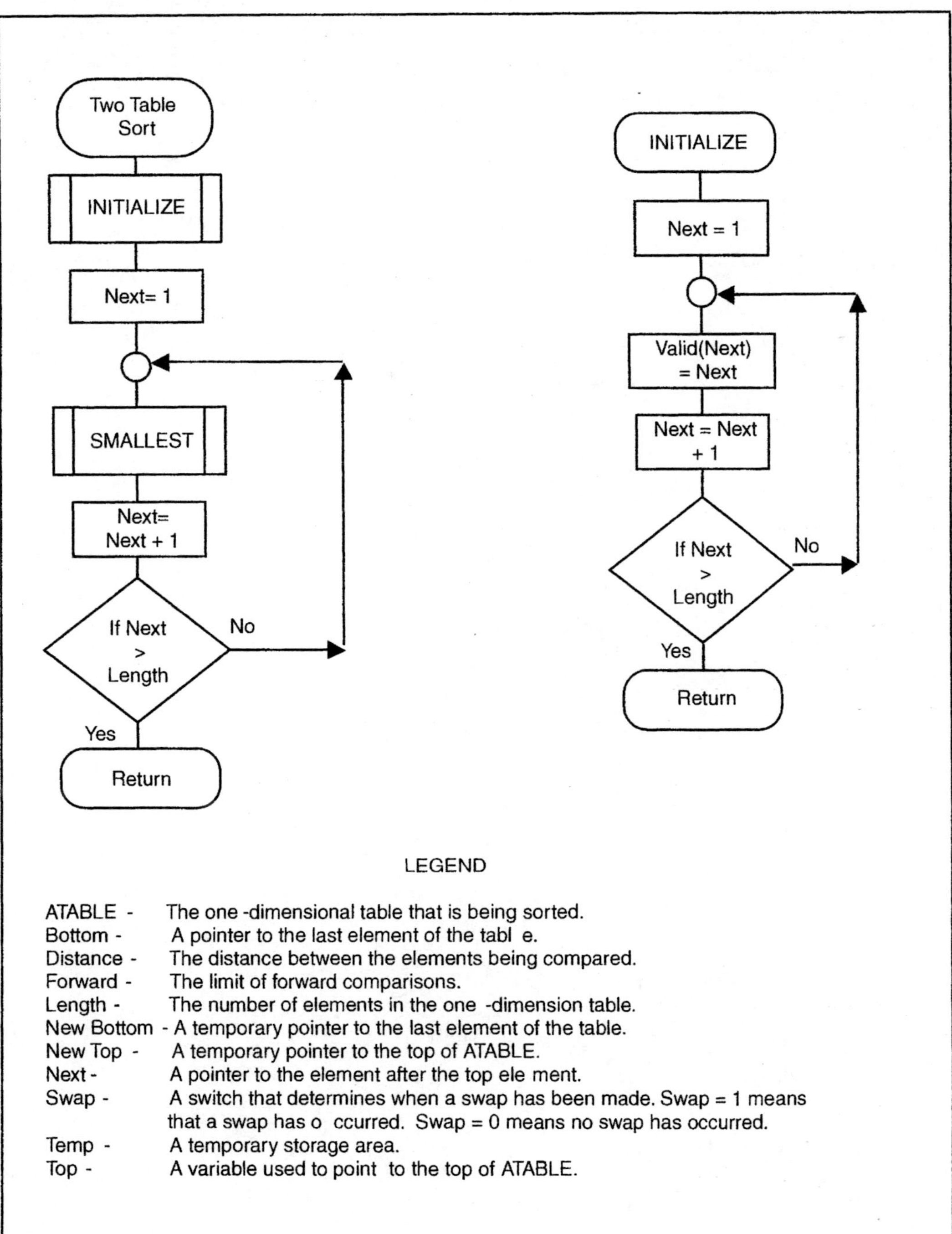

Figure 13.11 Part 1–Two table sort

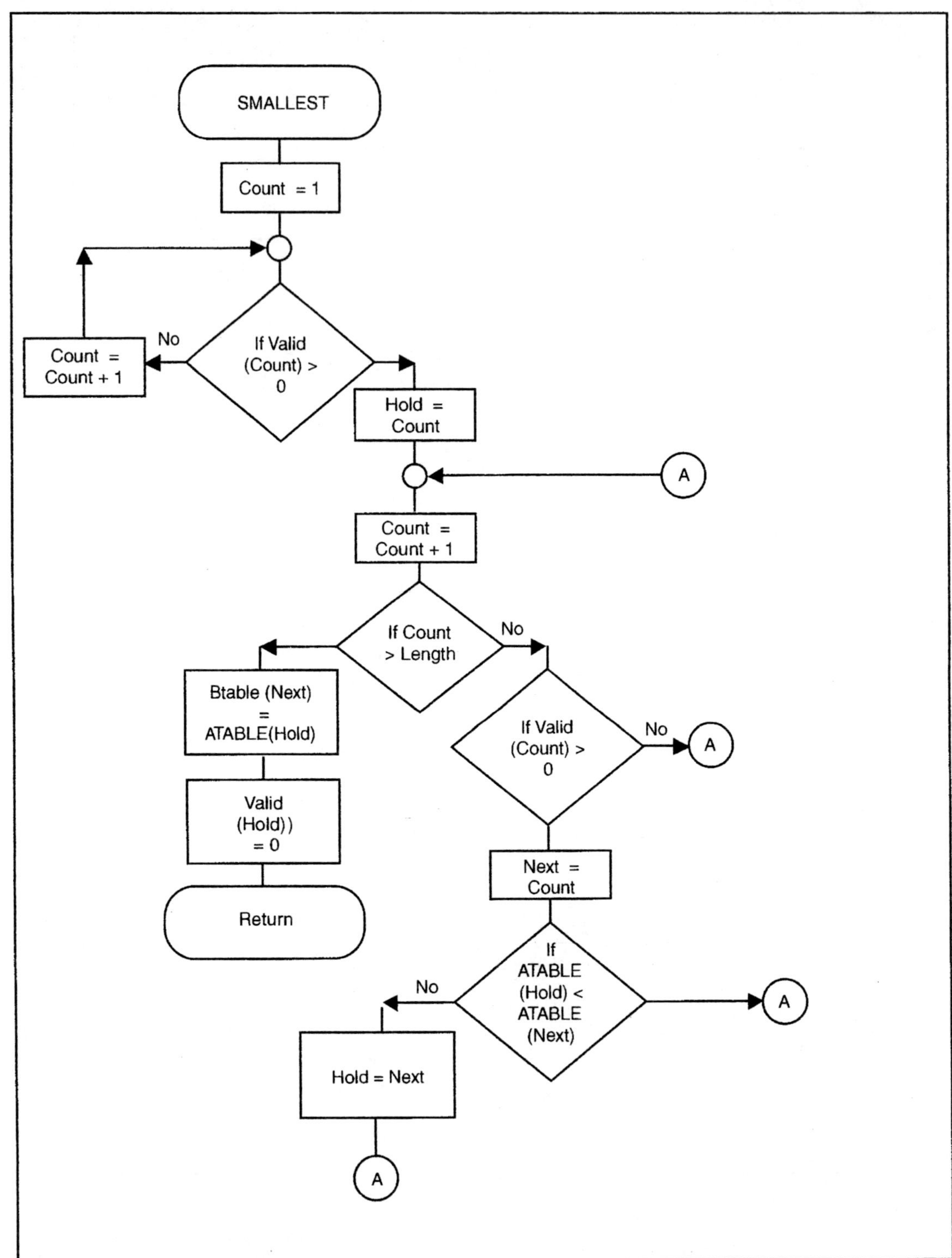

Figure 13.11 Part 2–Two table sort

Objective 2 Read, modify, and analyze pseudocode for sorting algorithms.

1. The pseudocode below represents a simple sorting algorithm. Explain what the sort routine does, using a narrative explanation (what things get compared and in what order, how/when things get into sequence, and so on). Using the following six numbers, show how the numbers move during the sorting process 326, 14, 79, 86, 400, 8.

```
Simple_sort_program
   ATABLE(6)
   Length = 6
   Top = 1
   Next = 2
   Repeat until Top = Length
   Find_smallest_number
   PUT_IT_AT_THE_TOP
   Top = Top + 1
   Next = Top + 1
   Return
   FIND_SMALLEST_NUMBER
         If ATABLE(Top) < ATABLE(Next) Then
               Keep = ATABLE(Top)
               Small = Top
         Else
               Keep = ATABLE(Next)
               Small = Next
         Endif
         While Next <= Length
         If Keep < ATABLE(Next) Then
                     Next = Next + 1
         Else
               SWAP
               Small = Next
         Endif
         Endwhile
         Return
   PUT_IT_AT_THE_TOP
         Temp = ATABLE(Top)
```

```
        ATABLE(Top) = Keep
        ATABLE(Small) = Temp
        Return
  SWAP
        Temp = Keep
        Keep = ATABLE(Next)
        ATABLE(Next) = Temp
        Return
```

2. The pseudocode below represents a modified exchange sorting algorithm. Explain what the sort routine does using a narrative explanation (what things get compared and in what order, how/when things get into sequence, and so on). Using the following six numbers, show how the numbers move during the sorting process of this pseudocode: 326, 14, 79, 86, 400, 8. Compare this process with the exchange sort shown in the chapter and explain how they differ.

```
Optional_exchange_sort
   Top = 0
   While Top < Length
   Top = Top + 1
   Next = Top
   COMPARE
   Endwhile
   Return
   COMPARE
         While Next < Length
         If ATABLE(Top) >= ATABLE(Next) Then
               SWAP
         Else
         Endif
         Endwhile
         Return
   SWAP
         Temp = ATABLE(Top)
         ATABLE(Top) = ATABLE(Next)
         ATABLE(Next) = Temp
         Return
```

3. The pseudocode below represents the Shell sort. Explain what the sort routine does using a narrative explanation (what things get compared, and in what order, how/when things get into sequence, and so on). Using the following six numbers, show how the numbers move during the sorting process of the pseudocode: 326, 14, 79, 86, 400, 8.

```
Shell_sort_program
    ATABLE(6)
    Distance = Length/2
    While Distance >= 1
            PASSES
    Endwhile
    Return
    PASSES
            Forward = Length - Distance
            While Top <= Forward
            FORWARD
            Top = Top + 1
            Endwhile
            Distance = Distance < 2
            Return
            FORWARD
                    New_top = Top
                    Bottom = Top + Distance
                    If ATABLE(New_top) > ATABLE(Bottom) Then
                            While SWAP = True
                            SWAP
                            BACK
                            Endwhile
                    Else
                    Endif
                    Return
            SWAP
                    Swap = True
                    Temp = ATABLE(New_top)
                    ATABLE(New_top) = ATABLE(Bottom)
                    ATABLE(Bottom) = Temp
```

```
                    Return
               BACK
                    New_bottom = New_top
                    New_top = New_top - Distance
                    If New_TOP < 1 Then
                         Swap = False
                    Else  If ATABLE(New_top) >
ATABLE(New_bottom)                          Then
                              Bottom = New_bottom
                         Else
                              Swap = False
                         Endif
                    Endif
                    Return
```

4. The pseudocode below makes use of an extra table to hold the sorted elements. This sort has the advantage of retaining the original table in addition to the sorted version. Examine the pseudocode shown. Explain what the sort routine does using a narrative explanation (what things get compared, and in what order, how/when do things get into sequence, and so on). Using the following six numbers, show how the numbers move during the sorting process 326, 14, 79, 86, 400, 8. Compare these results with the three sort routines in the chapter.

```
Two_table_sort
   INITIALIZE
   While Next <= Length
   SMALLEST
   Return
   INITIALIZE
         While Next <= Length
         VALID(Next) = Next
         Return
   SMALLEST
         Count = 0
         Repeat
         Count = Count + 1
         Until Valid(Count) > 0
         Hold = Count
         While Count <= Length
```

```
            Repeat
            Count = Count + 1
            Until Valid(Count) > 0
            Next = count
            If ATABLE(Hold) >= ATABLE(Next) Then
                  Hold = Next
            Else
            Endif
            Count = Count + 1
      Endwhile
      Btable(Next) = ATABLE(Hold)
      Valid(Hold) = 0
      Return
```

5. Modify the pseudocode in problem 1 to work with a two- or three-dimensional table.
6. Modify the pseudocode in problem 2 to work with a two- or three-dimensional table.
7. Modify the pseudocode in problem 3 to work with a two- or three-dimensional table.
8. Write pseudocode for a merge sort routine. (Hint: Research merge sort in the library and/or through the Internet before starting the flowchart.)
9. Select any of the sorting algorithms pseudocode from the exercises and write out all of the steps for the sorting process described. Use the techniques shown in the chapter. Create your own table of 3 numbers to use in the description.

Other Assignments

SoftSkills

Select one problem from Objective one, two, three, or from the Internet/library research projects. Prepare, and give an oral report to the class on your selection.

Internet/Library Research

A. Research various sorting algorithms and write a paper describing some of the other sorting algorithms available. Include a flowchart description of a sorting algorithm that you found that was different from any in the text.

B. Research various sorting techniques and write a paper describing some of the other sorting algorithms available. Include a pseudocode description of a sort algorithm that you found that was different from any in the text.

Module 1

NUMBERS AND COMPUTER ARITHMETIC

I do hate sums. There is no greater mistake than to call arithmetic an exact science. There are . . . hidden laws of Number, which it requires a mind like mine to perceive. For instance, if you add a sum from the bottom up and then again from the top down, the result is always different.

M. P. La Touche (1878)

OBJECTIVES

After completing this chapter, you will be able to:

1. Identify the ASCII code for any character, given the character and the ASCII code table.
2. Identify a character given an ASCII code and the ASCII code table.
3. Add two binary numbers.
4. Add two hexadecimal numbers.
5. Convert numbers from one number system into another (binary to hexadecimal, hexadecimal to decimal, and so on).

Introduction

In the preceding chapters, we have ignored the use of numbers as much as possible. Indeed, the best computer programs have the least numbers. Numbers are replaced by variable names where possible in computer programs. In Chapter 1 we saw how variable names could help make a program more general and more flexible. Numbers can cause serious problems in computer programs so it's important for designers, systems analysts, and computer programmers to have some understanding of the problems with numbers.

Types of data

All computer languages support at least two types of data: numbers and characters. Numbers can be further classified into integer and real, which we will discuss later. Characters can be classified in three different categories: numerals (0, 1, 2, . . . 9), alphabetic (a, A, b, B, . . . z, Z), and special characters (!, @, #, $, %, ^, &, *, and so on). Special characters are all characters that are not numerals and not letters of the alphabet. All characters must be represented in a computer in the binary number system. (Why?) This representation normally takes place using a standard code. Today, three standard codes are in widespread use: *ASCII* (American Standard Code for Information Interchange), Unicode, and EBCDIC (Extended Binary Coded Decimal Interchange Code). EBCDIC was developed by International Business Machines (IBM) and is still used on some mainframe computers. Unicode is the new 16-bit code system for character representation developed because the 8-bit system, ASCII, did not allow for more than 256 characters. Some languages (Chinese, for example) demanded a larger character set than ASCII allowed. ASCII is a subset of the Unicode system and is the code set that we will explain. Once you have an understanding of the ASCII code, it is easy to understand a variety of coding systems.

Today's computers operate on the binary number system (base 2) because binary computers were easier to construct than computers using our normal base 10 (decimal) number system. Computers are capable of distinguishing two states: current flow (on) and no current flow (off). By assigning numeric values to the on (1) and off (0) conditions, we can develop the mathematics of computer operations.

A bit in a computer can be considered to be a 0 (on) or 1 (off), which gives us two possibilities from which to choose. If we combine 2 bits into a string of bits, how many possibilities are available? We could have the following combinations for 2 bits: 00, 01, 10, and 11. So we see four combinations with 2 bits. How many combinations are available with 3bits? 000, 001, 010, 011, 100, 101, 110, and 111. Do you see a pattern here? Look at Table M1.1.

1 Number systems and their conversion processes are explained in detail in Appendix C. Appendix C is intended to supplement this chapter.

So we see from Table M1.1 that given the number of bits, we can calculate the number of possible combinations of those bits to be equal to 2 raised to the power of the number of bits. For 16 bits we would have 216 possible combinations. How is that helpful?

We need to assign a binary value to every character that we want to store in the computer's memory. If we have about 200 characters that we want to use with our computer, then we will need a code system that uses eight bits. This is how both the ASCII and EBCDIC code systems work. The complete ASCII code table is in Appendix B, and we will refer to it for the next section.

Number of bits	Number of combinations	Pattern recognition
1	2	2^1
2	4	2^2
3	8	2^3
4	16	2^4
5	32	2^5
6	64	2^6
7	128	2^7
8	256	2^8

Table M.1.1 Bit Combinations

ASCII

The letter "a" is represented by the ASCII code 0110 0001. This is a different code then the capital "A"(0100 0001) because the characters are intended to be different. The basic ASCII character set contains 128 characters because the ASCII code was developed using seven bits. The 8th bit was added later, and the ASCII code table can now be expanded to 256 characters. At this stage you might find it easier to use the decimal equivalent to identify the characters so we see that the number 65 is equivalent to "A". Now notice that a "B" is equivalent to 66. This means that A + 1 is equal to B. This is unusual arithmetic to say the least; but when computer operations were being designed, the designers felt that B should be one greater than A. You may also observe that a + 1 is equal to B. Many computer applications take advantage of this fact, and this number scheme is what makes alphabetic sorting possible. Another way to state the rule A + 1 = B is to say that B is greater than A. So when we sort alphabetically, the letters end up in the proper arrangement. Is "{" less than or greater than "!"? Use the ASCII table in Appendix B to find that "!" is equivalent to 0010 0001 (33) and "{" is 0111 1000 (120). So { > ! Most unusual arithmetic, but it is the arithmetic of the computer. Have you ever wondered why the names are in the sequence found in the phone book? How would you sort the following: M & S Inc. and MSM Inc.? Which one comes first? Why? How would you sequence M ~ S and MSM?

Now that you have some understanding of the ASCII code table, let's look at the numerals. In the ASCII code, the numeral "1" is 0011 0001. But if you know any arithmetic at all, you know that the number 1 is just 0000 0001. A glance at Appendix B tells us that 0000 0001 is the SOH character, which tells the computer that we are starting a message. This sounds like a conflict, and it is. We need one additional rule to make these codes actually work along with our numbers. We must tell the computer whether a variable is either a number or a character. In the BASIC language, we do this using a dollar sign ($). A character or string variable is identified to the computer by ending the variable name with a $. COBOL specifies data types in the data division, and Java specifies data types using a declare statement. Each computer language has its unique method of telling the computer whether or not a variable name is associated with a number or a character because we operate on/with numbers differently than we do with characters.

Here's a simple example that you can perform on any computer in any language to see the difference between numbers and numerals (character number). The program shown here is written in QBASIC only because QBASIC is a very simple language to understand.

Program one

```
One$ = "1"
Two$ = One$ + One$
Print Two$
End
```

Program two

```
One = 1
Two = One + One
Print Two
End
```

Translate each of the two programs to any language that you happen to have handy and compare the outputs. Why are the outputs different? Because numbers can be used as numbers or as characters, and they are not the same. Unfortunately, people can't tell the difference between the number 1 and the character 1 so you can't know the correct answer to this problem: 1 + 1 = ?

Numbers

All computers support a variety of numbers. In the previous section, we looked at the category known as integers. Other categories include binary numbers, octal numbers, hexadecimal numbers, real numbers, and complex numbers to name only a few. The number system is far too complex to be examined in any detail here, but some topics need to be introduced in a first course of computer programming. We have already examined one of the most complicated of the problems in the preceding paragraphs, and we will move on to some other simple analyses of number problems in the computer.

To begin the discussion, we need to understand the computer's numbers. Remember that the computer can only distinguish between on and off (1 and 0), and all the other numbers we use are artificial tools that people need in order to understand what the computer is doing. The computer's number system is extremely simple when compared to people's number system, but people have become so accustomed to their clumsy system that they often think it is simple.

Let's do some comparing. People use the digits 0, 1, 2, 3, 4, 5, 6, 7, 8, and 9 to make numbers. The computer uses only the digits 0 and 1. Two digits are simpler than 10. What about addition?

Table M1.2 shows an addition table for people numbers, and Table M1.3 shows an addition table for computer numbers.

+	0	1	2	3	4	5	6	7	8	9
0	0	1	2	3	4	5	6	7	8	9
1	1	2	3	4	5	6	7	8	9	10
2	2	3	4	5	6	7	8	9	10	11
3	3	4	5	6	7	8	9	10	11	12
4	4	5	6	7	8	9	10	11	12	13
5	5	6	7	8	9	10	11	12	13	14
6	6	7	8	9	10	11	12	13	14	15
7	7	8	9	10	11	12	13	14	15	16
8	8	9	10	11	12	13	14	15	16	17
9	9	10	11	12	13	14	15	16	17	18

Table M1.2 Decimal Addition Table

Certainly Table M1.3 is much simpler than Table M1-2. Computer addition (or binary addition) can be summarized into three simple rules:

+	0	1
0	0	1
1	1	10**
** Pronounced one zero or zero with a carry		

Table M1.3 Binary Addition Table

1. 0 + 0 = 0
2. 1 + 0 = 0 + 1 = 1
3. 1 + 1 = 0 and carry 1

Using these three rules and only these three, we can add any binary numbers (and multiply too, but we'll save that for a later course). Let's see a couple of examples, written in human standard form:

	0001	0010	0101	0011	1011
+	0001	0001	0101	0011	1101
	0010	0011	1010	0110	11000

We work these addition problems like any other addition problem, but we use the addition table for binary numbers (or the three rules). In the first problem we add 1 + 1 in the right-hand column and get zero with one to carry. We then move to the second column and add the 1 that we carried to the top 0 (results in 1), then add that to the bottom zero, which gives us 1. The third column is 0 + 0 = 0 and the left-most column is the same. Check the other four problems to ensure that you get the same answers as shown.

You don't need to be an expert at binary arithmetic in order to write/design computer programs, but it is nice to see the computer side of the story from time to time. We'll leave binary arithmetic at this level and move on to integer operations.

Integers

Remember now that when we talk about 7, we're just using a convenient notation for people. The computer version of 7 is 0111. During an earlier discussion of binary searches, we mentioned a difficulty in integer division. Here's the basic problem. What is 7 divided by 2? Remembering that all numbers have to be expressed as integers, the only possible answers would be 3 or 4. The correct answer is 3, but some computer programs will return the answer 4. (To demonstrate this, try entering =7/2 into one cell of a Microsoft Excel spreadsheet and set the cell format to provide zero decimal places). The answer is 4 if we believe in rounding up. Rounding up is an extra step in the division process so without rounding we get 7/2 = 3; this is the "normal" answer that we expect to get from computer integer arithmetic.

What is 15/6? (2). 36/5? (7).

The computer version of integer division is the simplest case of division, where we are accustomed to the more complex version of rounding or worse, resorting to fractions to make things work out. The simple problem works this way: Three cars are in a parking lot to be divided by two people. Each person gets one car. Yes, there is a car left over and that's exactly what it is—left over. The complex version in this problem is silly: each person gets 1.5 cars. How would you do that? (Try dividing 3 children by 2 parents and you'll end up in the same place.)

These real problems and a real desire to allocate items more specifically led to the development of the dreaded fraction, which is discussed in the next section.

Real Numbers

The real numbers (you should have learned something about the real number line in elementary school) are composed of rational and irrational numbers.

Rational Numbers

The rational numbers are just fractions. Any rational number can be written as a ratio of two integers. The word rational was derived from ratio in the definition. So let's divide 3 pizzas by 2 people. Each person gets 1 _ pizzas. Nice, isn't it? Now let's look a little closer at certain fractions.

First, you need to remember that the computer is restricted to the binary number system, and we need to see how that would work with fractions. In the binary number system, a fractional number could be written like this: .111.

The place values for this number are _, _, and1/8, where each 1 stands for the corresponding fraction (in our decimal system .111 is 1/10, and 1/100, and 1/1000)

Our number .111 base 2 then stands for 1/2 + 1/4 + 1/8 or 7/8 (.875) base 10. The base 2 number .101 would be 1/2 + 1/8 or 5/8 (.625) base 10. The math gets a little tedious as we make the fractions smaller.

In the binary number system, we have to use the fractions 1/2 + 1/4 + 1/8 … to represent our number. How would you represent the number .01 base 10 as a sum of the fractions 1/2[2]?[3]? A little work will demonstrate that it is impossible to represent the number 1/10 in the binary number system. No matter how many fractions you add together, you can't quite get to the exact value of 1/10.

The computer cannot represent the decimal number .01 exactly, which means that it also cannot represent the numbers 1/100, 1/1000, and so on. Most people are satisfied with the accuracy of today's computers because programmers have, for the most part, written programs that work around these problems. The problems still exist!

Irrational Numbers

The problems we have demonstrated previously occur with relatively simple forms of numbers. Irrational numbers are fairly complicated even in the decimal number system. In fact, we cannot represent an irrational number exactly in our decimal number system so what chance would we have in the computer's binary system? The very best we can do is to use an approximation for the irrational number and hope that the computer's approximate representation of that approximate representation is close enough to yield a pretty good answer. Pretty good answers work most of the time. As we extend the accuracy of the computer (32-bit processing, 64-bit processing, and so on), we get better answers. If you have an interest in mathematics, this field is wide open to new discoveries.

Hexadecimal Numbers

Before leaving mathematics entirely, we should look at a very interesting number system called hexadecimal. The term hexadecimal means literally 16 (hex means 6), and this number system is based on 16 or has a radix of 16. Remember that the binary system has a radix of 2, and the decimal system has a radix of 10. The radix, or base, tells us how many counting digits we will use. In binary we can use the digits 0 and 1. In the decimal system we use the digits 0, 1, 2, 3, 4, 5, 6, 7, 8, and 9. Therefore, in the hexadecimal system, we must have 16 digits. What might those be? 0, 1, 2, 3, 4, 5, 6, 7, 8, 9, A, B, C, D, E, and F. What comes after F is a combination representing place values like 10 in the decimal system. After F we get 10. Now it's critical to read that as "one, zero" because it is not ten. Just as in the binary system "one, zero" is not 10 (it's 2).

2 In our decimal system, the period before the number is a decimal point; but in other number systems, the period is referred to as a radix point to avoid confusion with base 10. The number system base (base 10, base 2, and so on) is also called radix.

3 The 16-bit radix 2 number .0000010100011111 is equal to the decimal number .009994507. Obviously a 32-bit number would be closer to .01 as would a 64-bit number, and so on. As of this writing, all computers have a limit.

Table M1.4 shows an addition table for the hexadecimal number system. Once you have learned how addition tables work, it's a simple matter to construct a table to use in order to accomplish basic arithmetic. If you continue in the computer programming field or move into the computer hardware field, you will need to know both the binary and the hexadecimal number systems well. This is sufficient introductory material for this course.

+	0	1	2	3	4	5	6	7	8	9	A	B	C	D	E	F
0	0	1	2	3	4	5	6	7	8	9	A	B	C	D	E	F
1	1	2	3	4	5	6	7	8	9	A	B	C	D	E	F	10
2	2	3	4	5	6	7	8	9	A	B	C	D	E	F	10	11
3	3	4	5	6	7	8	9	A	B	C	D	E	F	10	11	12
4	4	5	6	7	8	9	A	B	C	D	E	F	10	11	12	13
5	5	6	7	8	9	A	B	C	D	E	F	10	11	12	13	14
6	6	7	8	9	A	B	C	D	E	F	10	11	12	13	14	15
7	7	8	9	A	B	C	D	E	F	10	11	12	13	14	15	16
8	8	9	A	B	C	D	E	F	10	11	12	13	14	15	16	17
9	9	A	B	C	D	E	F	10	11	12	13	14	15	16	17	18
A	A	B	C	D	E	F	10	11	12	13	14	15	16	17	18	19
B	B	C	D	E	F	10	11	12	13	14	15	16	17	18	19	1A
C	C	D	E	F	10	11	12	13	14	15	16	17	18	19	1A	1B
D	D	E	F	10	11	12	13	14	15	16	17	18	19	1A	1B	1C
E	E	F	10	11	12	13	14	15	16	17	18	19	1A	1B	1C	1D
F	F	10	11	12	13	14	15	16	17	18	19	1A	1B	1C	1D	1E

Table M1.4 Hexadecimal Addition Table

Other Number Systems

If you've been paying attention throughout the course, it should be obvious that there are some more number systems. An infinite number of different number systems exist. Some, like octal (radix 8), are popular in the computer industry. Others are simply interesting studies for mathematicians. The study of number systems is left for you to continue in future courses.

Summary

This chapter was not meant to make you a mathematician, but rather to introduce you to some of the limits of computing numerical answers using a machine. If a person can solve a mathematical problem, it is likely that the person will get a more accurate answer than the machine. At best, the machine will get as good an answer as a human would; and at worst, the computer will get a completely wrong answer. Wrong answers from a computer are unexpected among the general population. Good designers and programmers can avoid some wrong answers, but many wrong answers that cannot be avoided are generated by computers. You will probably never know all the limitations of computers, but you should be aware that they do have limits.

Key Terms

Each number in parentheses indicates the page where the term first occurs in the chapter.

ASCII (294)	hexadecimal (299)	radix (299)
base (299)	integer (294)	rational number (298)
characters (294)	irrational number (298)	real number (296)
fraction (298)	numeral (294)	

Exercises

Objective 1 Identify the ASCII code for any character, given the character and the ASCII code table.

1. Using the ASCII table in Appendix B, determine the binary code for the following characters:

q	blank space	;	^
"	7	0	[

2. Using the ASCII table in Appendix B, determine the binary code for the following characters:

p	null	:	&
/	9	@	]

3. Using the ASCII table in Appendix B, determine the binary code for the following characters:

a	\	>	#
+	4	D	}

4. Using the ASCII table in Appendix B, determine the binary code for the following characters:

,	F	$	%
- (minus)	6	<	k

5. Using the ASCII table in Appendix B, determine the binary code for the following characters:

1	~	E	=
(	!	b	?

Objective 2 Identify a character given an ASCII code and the ASCII code table.

1. Using the ASCII table in Appendix C, determine the characters for the following binary codes:

0010 0000	0011 0000	0010 1000	0011 1000
0111 1111	0011 1111	0010 0010	0011 0100

2. Using the ASCII table in Appendix C, determine the characters for the following binary codes:

0001 0000	0001 1000	0001 0100	0001 1100
0101 1111	0001 1111	0001 0001	0001 1010

3. Using the ASCII table in Appendix C, determine the characters for the following binary codes:

0100 0001	0110 0001	0101 0001	0111 0001
1111 1111	0111 1111	0100 0101	0110 1000

4. Using the ASCII table in Appendix C, determine the characters for the following binary codes:

1001 1101	1011 1110	0111 1010	1000 1111
0010 0001	1001 1101	1011 1111	1100 1111

5. Using the ASCII table in Appendix C, determine the characters for the following binary codes:

1001 1101	1011 1110	0111 1010	0000 0001
0010 0001	1011 1101	1001 1001	0000 1111

Objective 3 Add two binary numbers.

1. Solve the following binary addition problems.

$$\begin{array}{r} 0001 \\ +\ \underline{0010} \end{array} \qquad \begin{array}{r} 0101 \\ +\ \underline{0001} \end{array} \qquad \begin{array}{r} 0011 \\ +\ \underline{1001} \end{array} \qquad \begin{array}{r} 1111 \\ +\ \underline{1111} \end{array}$$

2. Solve the following binary addition problems.

$$\begin{array}{r} 1001 \\ +\ \underline{0010} \end{array} \qquad \begin{array}{r} 1101 \\ +\ \underline{0001} \end{array} \qquad \begin{array}{r} 1011 \\ +\ \underline{1001} \end{array} \qquad \begin{array}{r} 0111 \\ +\ \underline{1111} \end{array}$$

3. Solve the following binary addition problems.

```
  0101     1101     0100     1110
+ 0110   + 0101   + 1011   + 1110
```

4. Solve the following binary addition problems.

```
  1111 0101     1101 1111     1011 0100
+ 0110 1111   + 0101 1011   + 1011 1110
```

5. Solve the following binary addition problems.

```
  1001 1101     1011 1110     0111 1010
+ 0010 0001   + 1001 1101   + 1111 1111
```

6. Solve the following binary addition problems.

```
  1001 1001 1001 1001 1101     0100 0000 1111 1010
+ 0110 1111 1111 1111 1111   + 0101 1011 1110 1100

  0110 1110 0110 01100010      1011 1111 0000 0101
+ 1001 0000 0000 0000 0000   + 1010 0100 0001 0011
```

Objective 4 Add two hexadecimal numbers.

1. Solve the following hexadecimal problems.

```
  000A     0065     00AB     0FFF
+ 0001   + 0017   + 00AB   + 0FFF
```

2. Solve the following hexadecimal problems.

```
  000B     0065     0A1B     0FFF
+ 0002   + 0117   + 00AB   + F1FF
```

3. Solve the following hexadecimal problems.

```
  000C     10F9     1FAB     F123
+ 0003   + 4017   + 00CD   + 0958
```

4. Solve the following hexadecimal problems.

```
  F00C     EDBC     BAF1     CDEF
+ 4321   + 9876   + ABCD   + 1111
```

5. Write the hexadecimal number that follows the given hexadecimal number:

A. 099F	C. FFFF	E. FFF9
B. 0000	D. 9999	F. AAAA

6. Write the hexadecimal number that precedes the given hexadecimal number:

A. 099F	C. FFFF	E. FFF9
B. 0000	D. 9999	F. AAAA

7. Write the hexadecimal number that follows the given hexadecimal number:

A. EEEE	C. F111	E. A349
B. 5BBB	D. CDEF	F. 1299

8. Write the hexadecimal number that precedes the given hexadecimal number:

A. EEE	C. F111	E. A349
B. 5BBB	D. CDEF	F. 1299

Objective 5 Convert numbers from one number system into another (binary to hexadecimal, hexadecimal to decimal, and so on.)

Appendix C has complete instructions for performing the conversions listed here Convert the following:

1. Binary to hexadecimal

A. 1001 1100	C. 0100 0101	E. 1111 1110
B. 1000 1101	D. 0001 0011	F. 1011 1010

2. Binary to decimal

A. 1001 1100	C. 0100 0101	E. 1111 1110
B. 1000 1101	D. 0001 0011	F. 1011 1010

3. Hexadecimal to binary

A. 99F	C. FFFF	E. FFF9
B. 1000	D. 9999	F. AAAA

4. Hexadecimal to decimal

A. 99F	C. FFFF	E. FFF9
B. 1000	D. 9999	F. AAAA

5. Decimal to binary

A. 150 C. 788 E. 4095
B. 32,768 D. 49 F. 16,383

6. Decimal to hexadecimal

A. 150 C. 788 E. 4095
B. 32,768 D. 49 F. 16,383

7. Binary to hexadecimal

A. 0110 0011 C. 1111 1010 E. 0000 0001
B. 1101 1001 D. 1111 0011 F. 1011 1011

8. Binary to decimal

A. 0110 0011 C. 1111 1010 E. 0000 0001
B. 1101 1001 D. 1111 0011 F. 1011 1011

9. Hexadecimal to binary

A. F99F C. AAFF E. BDC9
B. 1111 D. ABED F. BED1

10. Hexadecimal to decimal

A. F99F C. AAFF E. BDC9
B. 1111 D. ABED F. BED1

11. Decimal to binary

A. 8192 C. 164 E. 29
B. 65,768 D. 824 F. 9999

12. Decimal to hexadecimal

A. 8192 C. 164 E. 29
B. 65,768 D. 824 F. 9999

Other Assignments

SoftSkills

Select one problem from the Internet/library research projects. Prepare and give an oral report to the class on your selection.

Internet/Library Research

A. Using library and Internet resources, find another number system not mentioned in this chapter and write a short paper describing its use. Draw the addition table for the number system you find.

B. The ASCII system will soon be replaced by the Unicode system. Using library and Internet resources, research the Unicode system and write a paper describing it. Be sure to include how the ASCII will be incorporated into the Unicode.

Module 2

MODULES: FUNCTIONS AND PROGRAM DESIGN

If you improve or tinker with something long enough, eventually it will break or malfunction.
Arthur Bloch

OBJECTIVES

After completing this chapter, you will be able to:

1. Describe modules, sub-modules, and their use.
2. Read, draw, and modify flowcharts of modules.
3. Read, write, and modify pseudocode of modules.

Introduction

Modules, as used in this text, are defined as a group of related tasks that combine to complete one purpose (function) in a program. A module is self-contained and does not rely on other parts of a program to complete its purpose, except that it may send and receive data to and from other modules and may invoke sub-modules. Modules operate in a hierarchy. Main module maintains the primary control over the program. Control is passed to sub-modules as necessary control is returned to the main module when the sub-module has completed its function. The terms module and sub-module are used in this text in a generic sense and can be applied to many other situations.

Modular Programming

Modular programming is a technique for programming that breaks a problem into parts. Each part can be solved independently of the others so that several people could work on the program simultaneously without comprising the others' efforts. Each part of the solution is called a module, and one of them is the main module which is responsible for controlling the flow of the program. The hierarchy chart is the best picture of the modular concept. Each rectangle of a hierarchy chart represents a module. Every module under another module is called a sub-module. Modular programming is the best method of programming very large programs. This text attempts to illustrate modular concepts even on small projects so that the reader can observe the techniques. Many different terms are used to describe program modules, and the more common terms are described below.

Programs and Subprograms

The main portion of a *program* is usually referred to as the main program. During the execution of the program, modules are invoked by the main program, and they are called *subprograms* because they are subordinate to the main program. These subprograms are sub-modules. The term subprogram is used in some languages to mean a specific type of module, but here it will be used in the generic sense.

Functions and Methods

Functions are subprograms that normally return one value to a program. Many functions began as a result of a need for mathematical functions in computer programs. Mathematical functions like sin, cos, and log were programmed and saved internally to a programming language so that they could be used by simply referring to their name. To get the sin of 30^0, for example, the programmer could state x = sin (30), and the computer would return the answer and save it in the storage location named x. Many hand-held calculators perform these functions with a particular key labeled with the function name. Notice that the value 30^0 is sent to the function. This is an example of passing parameters that will be described in more detail shortly. *Methods* are used in the Java language and are similar to the functions normally described in other programming languages.

Subroutines, Subprograms, and Procedures

Generally, *subroutines*, *subprograms* and *procedures* differ from functions in that they will be used to return more than one value to the main program. They are usually invoked in a different manner than functions. A typical method of invoking a subroutine is by using the command "call." Subroutines and subprograms are usually given names by the programmer. The rules for naming subroutines and subprograms are essentially the same as the rules for naming variables. These types of sub-modules are called *procedures* in the Pascal language.

Objects and Classes

In some Object-oriented languages modules[1] represent *objects*, while other languages use *classes* to represent objects. The generic definition of a module in this text would allow us to define classes as modules as well as objects.

Invoking or Calling

When a program *invokes* or *calls* a subprogram, control is transferred to the subprogram. The instructions within the subprogram are executed and then control returns to the calling program.

Recursive Call

Recursive call refers to the process of a sub-module invoking itself. Some languages do not permit recursive calls and some do. Some problems are more easily solved using recursive techniques; but to be useful, they must be implemented in a language that supports the recursion. The process is best described by an example. Finding the factorial value of an integer (N!) is a common mathematical computation. The factorial of an integer is defined as follows:

If Integer = 1 Then Integer! = 1
If Integer > 1 Then Integer! = 1 * 2 * 3 * … * Integer

If Integer = 6 then Integer! = 1*2*3 = 6

1 In Object-oriented Fortran for example, objects are represented in modules.

A recursive subprogram for calculating N! might look like the following pseudocode:

```
FACTORIAL(Integer, Result)
        If Integer = 1 Then
                Result = 1
        Else    If Integer > 1 Then
                        Result = Integer*Factorial(Integer-1,Result)
                Else
                        Print "Integer out of range"
                Endif
        Endif
        Return
```

Parameter Passing

In general, a module can pass information or data to a sub-module and vice versa. This data transfer is known as *parameter* (or argument) passing. There are specific cases where information can only flow in one direction, and there are also data that are restricted to a particular module. Data or information that is restricted to a particular module is generally known as private (or local) data. Data or information that is available to all modules of a program is generally known as public (or global) data. If you have data in a module that is needed in a sub-module, one method of getting that data to the sub-module is by passing the data in a parameter list. The variables (or constants) in the parameter list or known as *arguments*

As an example, assume that you have a subroutine named BOWLER_AVERAGE. The purpose of this subroutine is to compute the average score for a bowler who has bowled a known number of games. The subroutine would need to know the bowler's scores and how many games were bowled. We'll assume that the scores are in a table called SCORES and the number of games bowled is in a variable named Number_of_games.

To call the subroutine and pass the necessary data to the subroutine we might say:

Call AVERAGE(GAME_SCORES, Number_of_games, Average)

In the sub-module we might find the following:

AVERAGE(TABLE, Quantity, Mean)

1 In Object-oriented Fortran for example, objects are represented in modules.

The sub-module would have the capability to be reused with any program that needed to compute an average for a table of scores. For example, the same sub-module could be used to compute a student's average for a group of tests. That program might contain the following call statement.

Call AVERAGE(TEST_SCORES, Number_of_tests, Mean)

The intent of the previous illustration was to pass a table of scores and a value for the number of scores to be averaged and return the value of the average. The actual results will depend on the programming language being used and what type of variables are being used.

Normally, the parameter lists will match with regard to the number of variables. However, some languages allow calls with fewer variable names than the sub-module list contains. The remaining variables are typically assigned a value of zero. The variables in the call statement and the sub-module must match with respect to variable type or unpredictable results will occur.

Value Parameters

Value parameters are parameters whose values are changed in the subprogram but not changed in the calling program.

Reference Parameters

Reference parameters are parameters whose values are changed in the subprogram and the calling program. In our example above, the value of the variable Mean is set to the average of the scores, and that value is returned to the calling program. In the statement:

Call AVERAGE(GAME_SCORES, Number_of_games, Average)

The value of Mean is stored in the variable named Average as well.

Global (Public) Variables

A variable that is declared as a *global variable* can be changed or observed in any part of a program or its subprograms. The advantage of this type of variable is that the value is accessible at any point in the program. A disadvantage of this type of variable is that the name cannot be reused at any point in the program. These variables should be used for data that is necessary at all points of a program. If a variable is needed in several modules but not the entire program, then it is best to pass the variable in a parameter list.

Local (Private) Variables

A *local variable* is a variable whose value is only available in a specific sub-module. The variable name may be reused in other parts of the program with different values and meanings. An advantage of this type of variable is that the name can be reused. As an example, consider a program with four modules that all have a counter controlled loop. All the sub-modules could use a variable named counter to control their respective loops, and there would not be a conflict in their values. The obvious disadvantage of a local variable is that it cannot be referenced from another module.

Enrichment – Doing it with Pseudocode

For this text we will use the word "call" to invoke a sub-module. The word "return" is used to return control from a sub-module to the calling module. The sub-module names are depicted in all capital letters to distinguish them from ordinary variables. The sub-module names will be presented in capital letters and follow the general rules of naming variables. The parameter list will be included inside parentheses with the variables/constants separated by commas.

As an example, assume that there is a sub-module named SWAP. SWAP is a sub-module whose purpose is to swap the positions of two variables. To do this, we know that we will need the two variables and a temporary storage location. The value of the temporary location is not important in the calling module, but it is important in the sub-module so the temporary location need not be passed in the parameter list.

The calling statement might look like this:

```
Call SWAP (Variable1, Variable2)
```

And the sub-module would look like this:

```
SWAP(First, Second)
            Temp = First
            First = Second
            Second = Temp
End
```

Assuming that the value of Variable1 was 7 and Variable2 was 12 when the call was made, we would find after the sub-module that the value of Variable1 was 12 and Variable2 was 7.

Notice that the variable names are different in the sub-module list. This is to illustrate that the variable names are not necessarily passed to the sub-module, but rather the values of the variables are passed. The programmer can keep the original variable names assigned by the calling module or rename the variables within the sub-module. The two parameter lists in each list must match with regard to types of data, but the names are not required to be the same. One advantage of having different names in the two lists is that the sub-module could be re-used in other programs that might contain different names in the calling module.

Summary

This module was intended to amplify the definition of a module and describe the various types of modules that are available in various programming languages. Various names were identified for modules including main program, subprogram, subroutine, function, method, and class. The process of invoking sub-modules was identified and parameter passing was explained.

Key Terms

arguments (310)
call (309)
class (309)
function (308)
global variable (311)
invoke (309)
local variable (311)
method(308)
module (308)
modular programming (308)
object (309)
parameter (310)
passing parameters (310)
procedures (309)
program (307)
recursive call (309)
reference parameter (310)
sub-module (308)
subprogram (308)
subroutine (309)
value parameter (311)

Exercises

Objective 1 Describe sub-modules and their use.

1. Write the call statement for a subprogram named GPS that is passed five parameters. The first parameter is an earth latitude, the second is an earth longitude, the third parameter is an elevation, the fourth parameter is a time, and the fifth parameter is a result.

2. Write the call statement for a subprogram named MARS that is passed four parameters. The first parameter is distance, the second is an angle, the third parameter is a time, and the fourth parameter is a result.

3. You're writing a module that will convert latitude and longitude coordinates in decimal degree format to degrees, minutes, and seconds. Write the call statement for the module describing each parameter that must be passed to the module. HINT – degrees latitude and longitude are converted to minutes by multiplying by 60. Minutes are converted to seconds also by multiplying by 60..

4. Examine the call statement and subprogram statement below. Assume that the call statement is supposed to call the subprogram statement shown. Describe any problems that you see with the two statements.

   Call POSITION (global, max, min, result)

   POSITION (area, length, width)

5. A friend suggests that you could write a sub-module for a program that reads in the prices of some items, totals the prices, and prints out the results. You consider this and then tell your friend that this would be a proper use of sub-modules or an improper use of sub-modules. Defend your position in writing, describing why this is proper or improper.

Objective 2 Read, draw, and modify flowcharts of modules.

1. Design a sub-module that calculates the sum of bowlers' scores for the season. Pass it three parameters, a table of scores, the number of scores and a variable name to receive the answers. Draw the flowchart for the sub-module.

2. Design a sub-module that calculates sales tax. Pass it three parameters, the price of the item, the tax rate, and a variable name to receive the answers. Draw the flowchart for the sub-module.

3. Design a sub-module that calculates the dollar value of a piggybank full of coins. Pass it five parameters, the number of quarters, dimes, nickels, pennies and a variable name to receive the answer. Draw the flowchart for the sub-module.

4. Design a sub-module that calculates the standard deviation for a list of numbers. Pass it three parameters, the list of numbers, the number of items in the list, and a variable name to receive the answers. Draw the flowchart for the sub-module.

5. Design a sub-module that calculates the value of X^n for integer values of n. Pass it three parameters, X, n, and a variable name to receive the answer. Draw the flowchart for the sub-module.

6. Design three sub-modules for calculating averages. One sub-module will calculate mean, one calculates average, and one calculates mode. Have a module call each of the three in turn and then print the three averages. Pass each module a table of numbers and a value indicating how many numbers are in the list. Draw the flowchart for the three sub-modules and main module.

Objective 2

Enrichment – Doing it with Pseudocode

Read, write, and modify pseudocode of modules.

1. Design a sub-module that calculates the sum of a bowler's scores for the season. Pass it three parameters, a table of scores, the number of scores, and a variable name to receive the answers. Write the pseudocode for the sub-module.
2. Design a sub-module that calculates sales tax. Pass it three parameters, the price of the item, the tax rate, and a variable name to receive the answers. Write the pseudocode for the sub-module.
3. Design a sub-module that calculates the dollar value of a piggybank full of coins. Pass it five parameters, the number of quarters, dimes, nickels, pennies, and a variable name to receive the answer. Write the pseudocode for the sub-module.
4. Design a sub-module that calculates the standard deviation for a list of numbers. Pass it three parameters, the list of numbers, the number of items in the list, and a variable name to receive the answers. Write the pseudocode for the sub-module.
5. Design a sub-module that calculates the value of X^n for integer values of N. Pass it three parameters, X, n, and a variable name to receive the answer. Write the pseudocode for the sub-module. Write pseudocode for the same problem using recursive calls to solve the problem.
6. Design three sub-modules for calculating averages. One sub-module will calculate mean, one calculates average, and one calculates mode. Have a module call each of the three in turn and then print the three averages. Pass each module a table of numbers and a value indicating how many numbers are in the list. Write the pseudocode for the sub-modules and the main module.

Other Assignments

SoftSkills

Select one problem from objective 2, 3 or the Internet/library research projects. Prepare and give an oral report to the class on your selection.

Internet/library research projects

A. Research a programming language and determine how that language supports the features described in this module. Write a report of your findings.

B. Research applications of sub-modules (functions, subroutines, subprograms, etc.). Write a paper describing one of the interesting applications that you found during your research.

Appendix A

SAMPLE SOLUTIONS: MILES PER GALLON

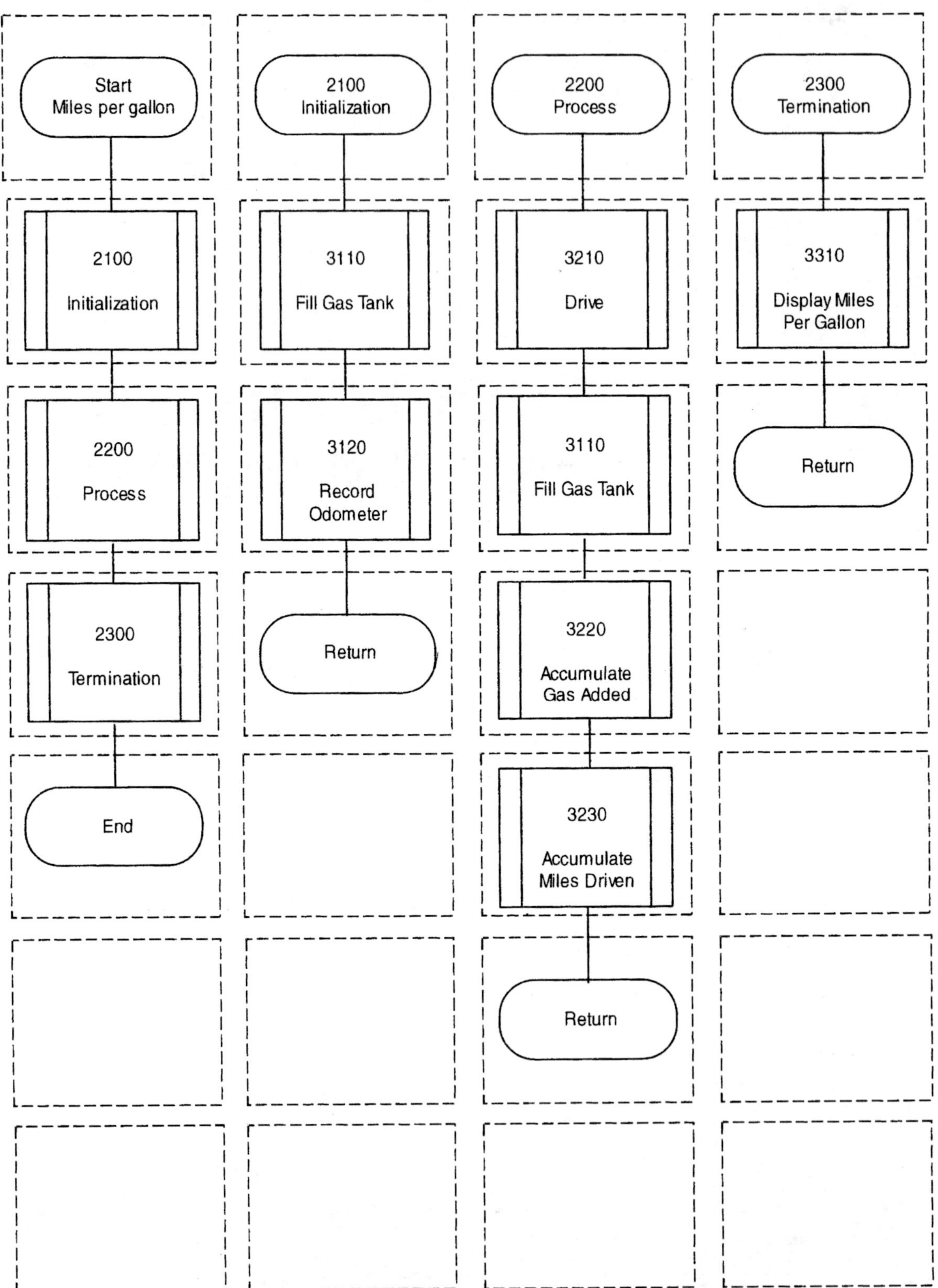
Start
Miles per gallon
2100
Initialization
2200
Process
2300
Termination
2100
Initialization
2200
Process
2300
Termination
End
3110
Fill Gas Tank
3120
Record
Odometer
Return
3210
Drive
3110
Fill Gas Tank
3220
Accumulate
Gas Added
3230
Accumulate
Miles Driven
Return
3310
Display Miles
Per Gallon
Return

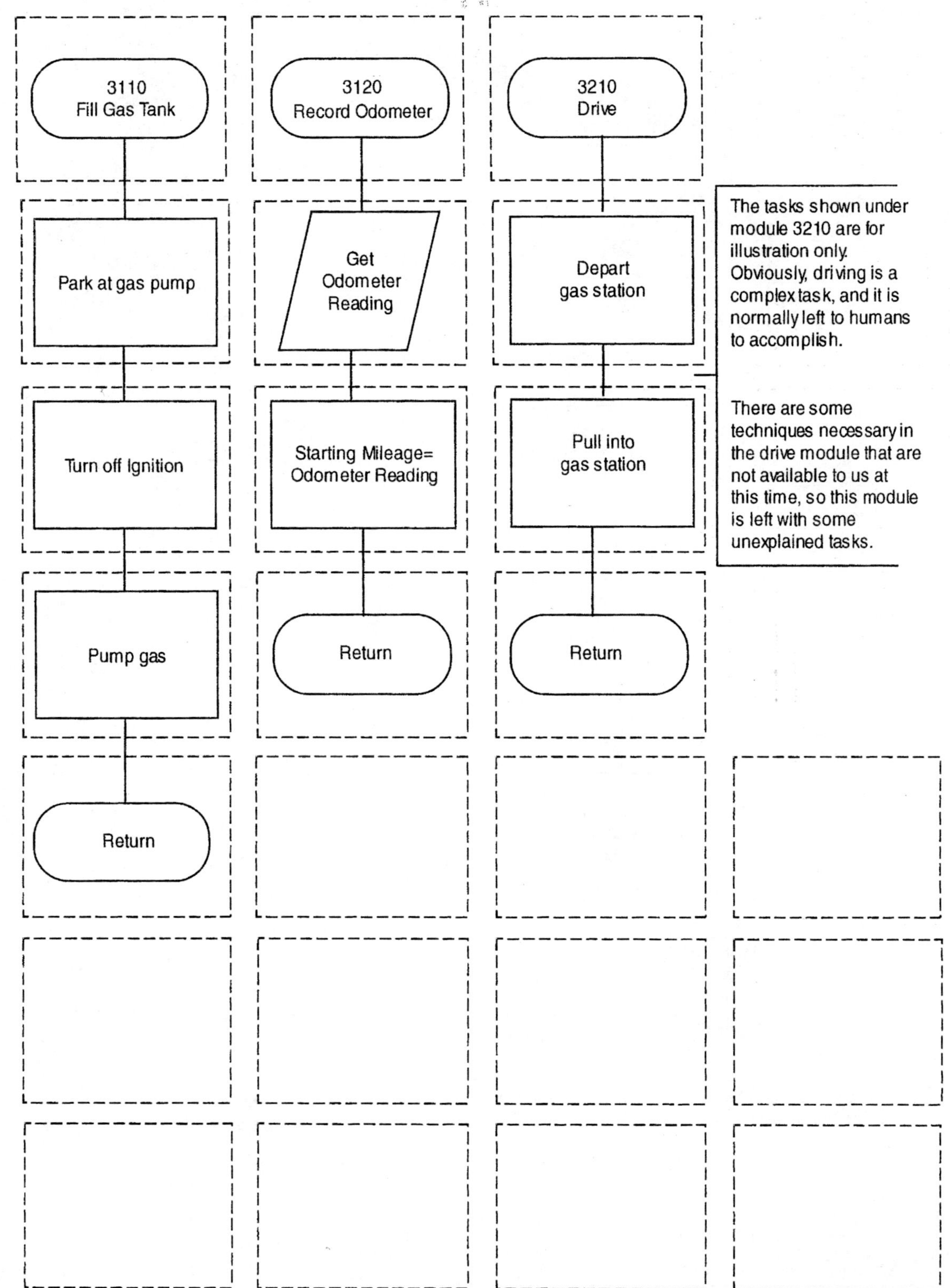
3110
Fill Gas Tank
3120
Record Odometer
3210
Drive
Park at gas pump
Get
Odometer
Reading
Depart
gas station
Turn off Ignition
Starting Mileage=
Odometer Reading
Pull into
gas station
Pump gas
Return
Return
Return
The tasks shown under module 3210 are for illustration only. Obviously, driving is a complex task, and it is normally left to humans to accomplish.
There are some techniques necessary in the drive module that are not available to us at this time, so this module is left with some unexplained tasks.

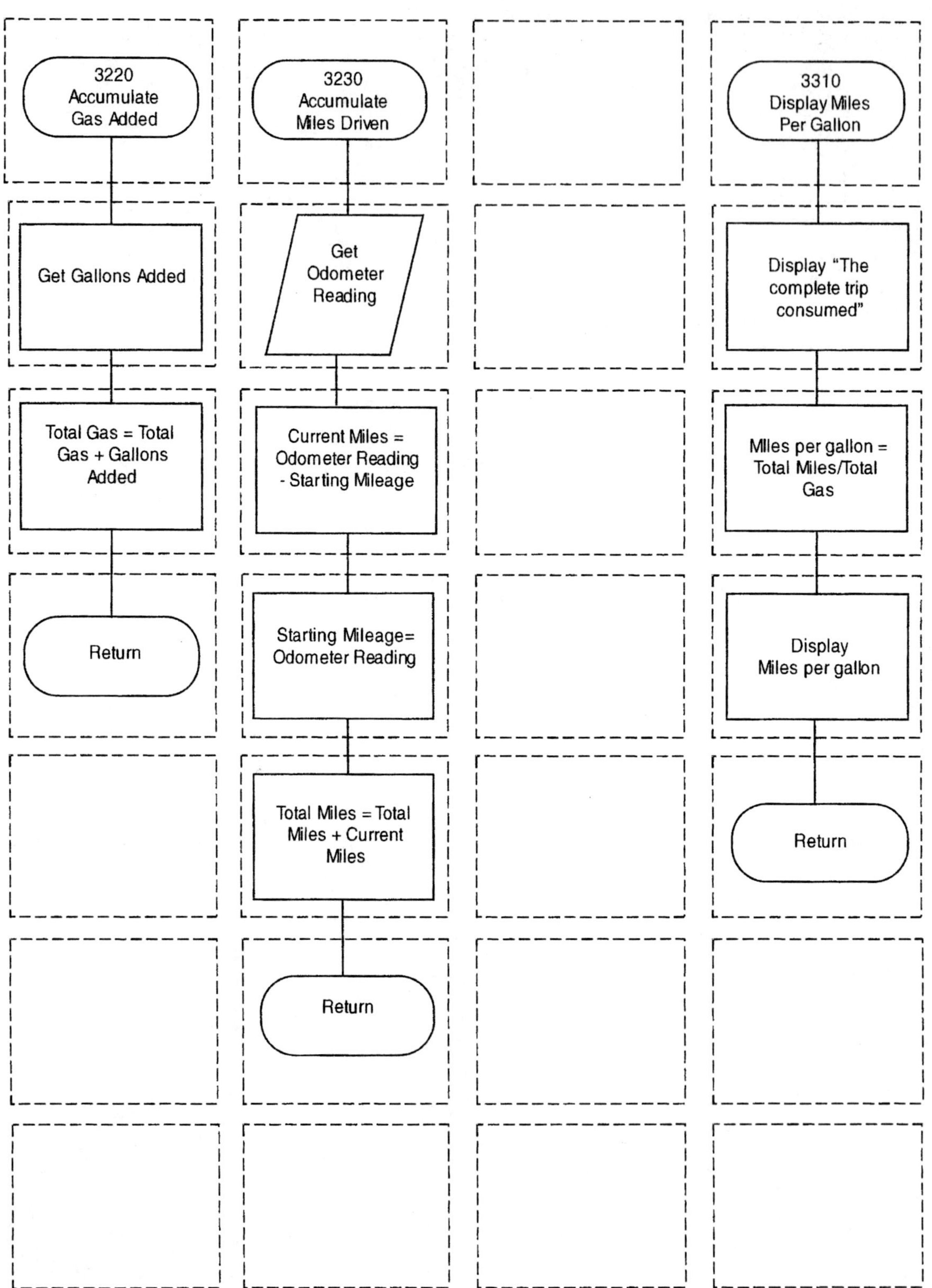

3220
Accumulate
Gas Added
Get Gallons Added
Total Gas = Total
Gas + Gallons
Added
Return
3230
Accumulate
Miles Driven
Get
Odometer
Reading
Current Miles =
Odometer Reading
- Starting Mileage
Starting Mileage=
Odometer Reading
Total Miles = Total
Miles + Current
Miles
Return
3310
Display Miles
Per Gallon
Display "The
complete trip
consumed"
Miles per gallon =
Total Miles/Total
Gas
Display
Miles per gallon
Return

```
      Miles Per Gallon Program

            Initialization

            Process
            Termination
            End

      Initialization

            Fill_gas_tank

Record_odometer
Return

      Process

            Drive

Accumulate_gas_added

            Calculate_gas_used

            Calculate_miles_driven

            Return

      Termination

            Miles_per_gallon = Miles_driven/Gas_used

            Display Miles_per_gallon

            Return

      Fill_gas_Tank

            Park_at_gas_pump

            Turn_off_ignition

            Pump_gas

            Return

      Record_odometer

            Get odometer_reading

            Starting_mileage = Odometer_reading
```

```
        Return
    Drive
        Depart_gas_station
        Pull_into_gas_station
        Return
    Accumulate_gas_added
        Get gallons_added
        Total_gas = Total_gas + gallons_added
        Return
    Accumulate_miles_driven
        Get odometer_reading
        Current_miles = Odometer_reading - Starting_mileage
        Starting_mileage = Odometer_reading
        Total_miles = Total_miles + Current_miles
        Return
    Display_miles_per_gallon
        Display "The complete trip consumed"
        Miles_per_gallon_ = Total_miles/Total_gas
        Display Miles_per_gallon
        Return
```

Appendix B

COUNTER LOOPS

Figure B.1 depicts all the combinations of counter controlled loops.
Figure B.2 depicts the four "unique" counter loops that can be formed.

Proceeding from left to right in the figure B.2, we find that the first flowchart is the standard post-condition logic, and the process always is completed once.

The second flowchart is used to prevent the process from being accomplished even once. This is extremely important if you are processing files that could be empty. If end = 0, this loop terminates immediately. In all the other cases, the loop executes some instructions even though end = 0.

The third flowchart will prevent the process from completing if the file is empty. However, it also terminates if end = 1. The counter is incremented and then tested, so one record will not be processed by this loop. Sometimes that logic is preferred.

The final flowchart always completes one process and avoids the problem of the previous flowchart.

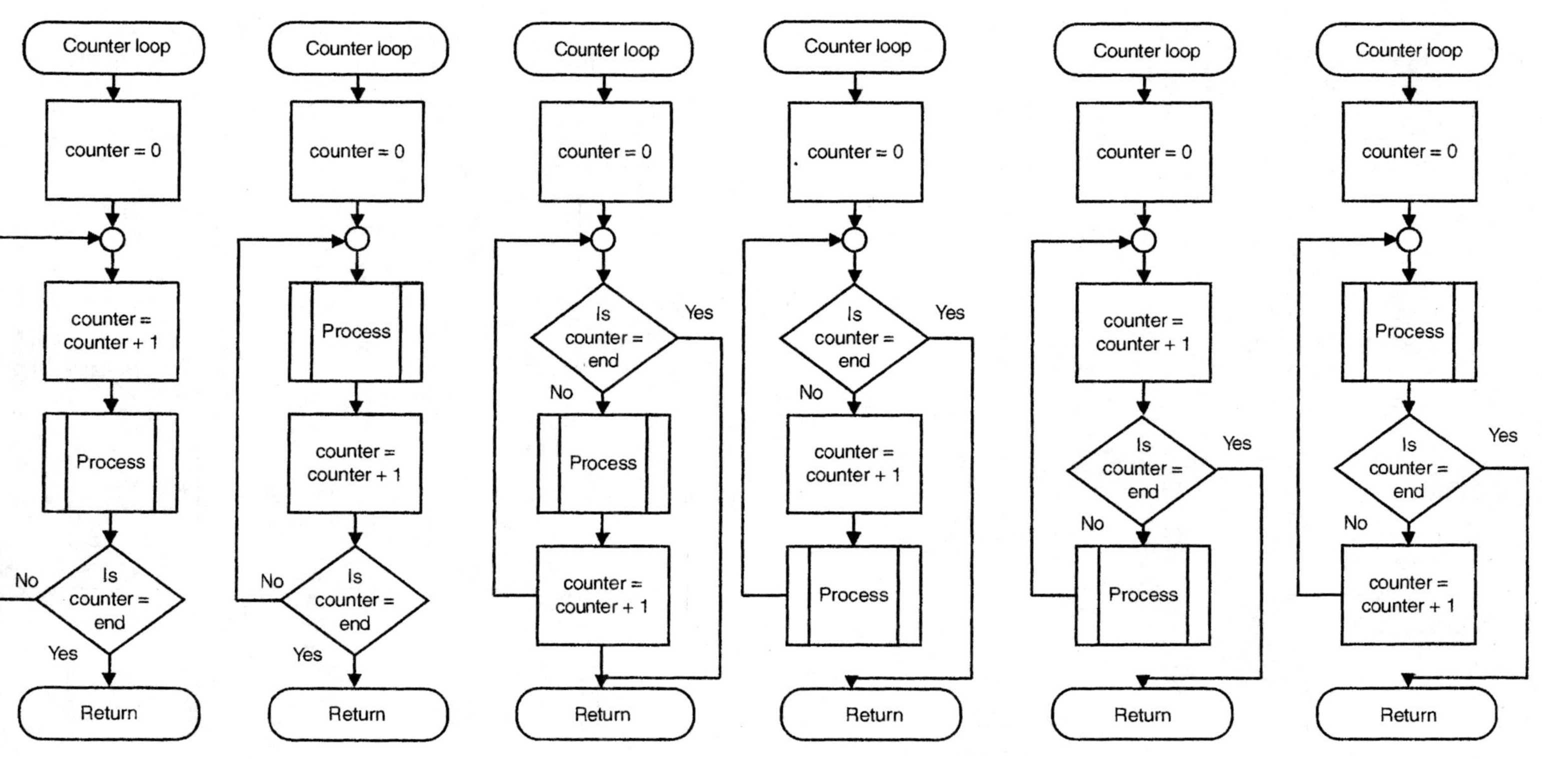

Figure B.1 Counter Loop Combinations

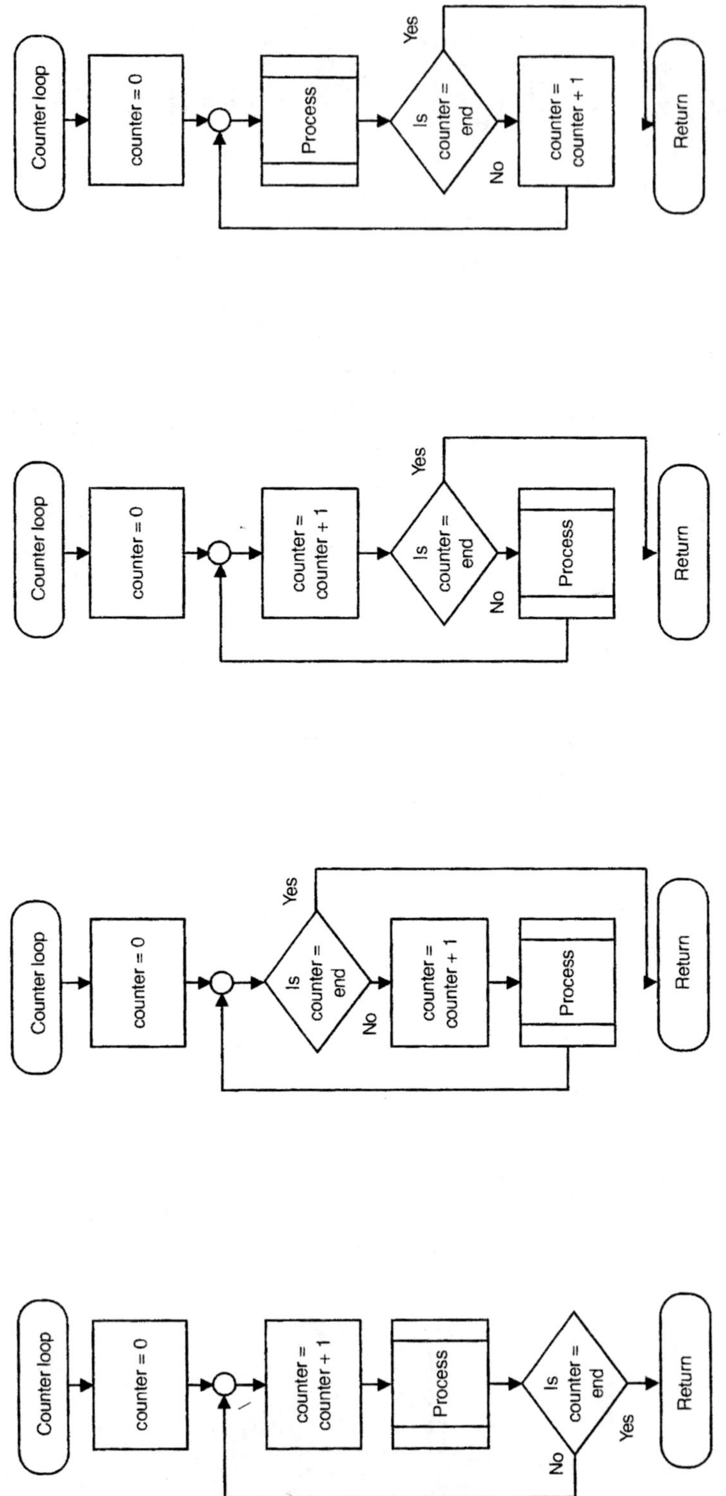

Figure B.2 Unique Counter Loop Combinations[1]

1 Text descriptions of the flowcharts are found on Page 318.

Appendix C

CONVERSION TABLE

128 ASCII CHARACTERS

Decimal	Hex	Binary		Character	Comments
000	0000	0000	0000	NUL	Null character
001	0001	0000	0001	SOH	Start Of Header
002	0002	0000	0010	STX	Start Of Text
003	0003	0000	0011	ETX	End Of Text
004	0004	0000	0100	EOT	End Of Transmission
005	0005	0000	0101	ENQ	Enquiry
006	0006	0000	0110	ACK	Acknowledgment
007	0007	0000	0111	BEL	Bell
008	0008	0000	1000	BS	Backspace
009	0009	0000	1001	HT	Horizontal Tab
010	000A	0000	1010	LF	Line Feed
011	000B	0000	1011	VT	Vertical Tab
012	000C	0000	1100	FF	Form Feed
013	000D	0000	1101	CR	Cariage Return
014	000E	0000	1110	SO	Serial In (Shift In)
015	000F	0000	1111	SI	Serial Out (Shift Out)
016	0010	0001	0000	DLE	Data Link Escape
017	0011	0001	0001	DC1	(XON) (Device Control 1)
018	0012	0001	0010	DC2	(Device Control 2)
019	0013	0001	0011	DC3	(XOFF)(Device Control 3)
020	0014	0001	0100	DC4	(Device Control 4)
021	0015	0001	0101	NAK	Negative Acknowledgment
022	0016	0001	0110	SYN	Synchronous Idle
023	0017	0001	0111	ETB	End Of Transmission Block
024	0018	0001	1000	CAN	Cancel
025	0019	0001	1001	EM	End of Medium
026	001A	0001	1010	SUB	Substitute
027	001B	0001	1011	ESC	Escape
028	001C	0001	1100	FS	File Separator
029	001D	0001	1101	GS	Group Separator
030	001E	0001	1110	RS	(Request to Send) (Record Separator)
031	001F	0001	1111	US	Unit Separator
032	0020	0010	0000	SP	Space
033	0021	0010	0001	!	
034	0022	0010	0010	"	
035	0023	0010	0011	#	
036	0024	0010	0100	$	
037	0025	0010	0101	%	
038	0026	0010	0110	&	
039	0027	0010	0111	'	
040	0028	0010	1000	(	

Decimal	Hex	Binary		Character	Comments
041	0029	0010	1001	)	
042	002A	0010	1010	*	
043	002B	0010	1011	+	
044	002C	0010	1100	,	
045	002D	0010	1101	-	
046	002E	0010	1110	.	
047	002F	0010	1111	/	
048	0030	0011	0000	0	
049	0031	0011	0001	1	
050	0032	0011	0010	2	
051	0033	0011	0011	3	
052	0034	0011	0100	4	
053	0035	0011	0101	5	
054	0036	0011	0110	6	
055	0037	0011	0111	7	
056	0038	0011	1000	8	
057	0039	0011	1001	9	
058	003A	0011	1010	:	
059	003B	0011	1011	;	
060	003C	0011	1100	<	
061	003D	0011	1101	=	
062	003E	0011	1110	>	
063	003F	0011	1111	?	
064	0040	0100	0000	@	
065	0041	0100	0001	A	
066	0042	0100	0010	B	
067	0043	0100	0011	C	
068	0044	0100	0100	D	
069	0045	0100	0101	E	
070	0046	0100	0110	F	
071	0047	0100	0111	G	
072	0048	0100	1000	H	
073	0049	0100	1001	I	
074	004A	0100	1010	J	
075	004B	0100	1011	K	
076	004C	0100	1100	L	
077	004D	0100	1101	M	
078	004E	0100	1110	N	
079	004F	0100	1111	O	
080	0050	0101	0000	P	

Decimal	Hex	Binary		Character	Comments
081	0051	0101	0001	Q	
082	0052	0101	0010	R	
083	0053	0101	0011	S	
084	0054	0101	0100	T	
085	0055	0101	0101	U	
086	0056	0101	0110	V	
087	0057	0101	0111	W	
088	0058	0101	1000	X	
089	0059	0101	1001	Y	
090	005A	0101	1010	Z	
091	005B	0101	1011	[	
092	005C	0101	1100	\	
093	005D	0101	1101	]	
094	005E	0101	1110	^	
095	005F	0101	1111	_	
096	0060	0110	0000	`	
097	0061	0110	0001	a	
098	0062	0110	0010	b	
099	0063	0110	0011	c	
100	0064	0110	0100	d	
101	0065	0110	0101	e	
102	0066	0110	0110	f	
103	0067	0110	0111	g	
104	0068	0110	1000	h	
105	0069	0110	1001	i	
106	006A	0110	1010	j	
107	006B	0110	1011	k	
108	006C	0110	1100	l	
109	006D	0110	1101	m	
110	006E	0110	1110	n	
111	006F	0110	1111	o	
112	0070	0111	0000	p	
113	0071	0111	0001	q	
114	0072	0111	0010	r	
115	0073	0111	0011	s	
116	0074	0111	0100	t	
117	0075	0111	0101	u	
118	0076	0111	0110	v	
119	0077	0111	0111	w	
120	0078	0111	1000	x	

Decimal	Hex	Binary		Character	Comments
121	0079	0111	1001	y	
122	007A	0111	1010	z	
123	007B	0111	1011	{	
124	007C	0111	1100	|	
125	007D	0111	1101	}	
126	007E	0111	1110	~	
127	007F	0111	1111	DEL	

Appendix D

SOME NUMBER SYSTEMS AND THEIR CONVERSION[1]

1 This section of the text was provided by Dr. Colin Archibald. None of the content was modified. It is intended as a supplement to the module on computer arithmetic.

- **The decimal number system.**

  This is the number system that we use every day. Let's consider what it means to be using the decimal number system.

  There are 10 symbols: 0, 1, 2, 3, 4, 5, 6, 7, 8, 9

  Numbers are represented using powers of 10 for the positions of the digits; for example, the decimal number 983 means 9 groups of 100, 8 groups of 10, and 3 groups of 1.

  The digits are written left to right; that is, from most significant digits to least significant digits.

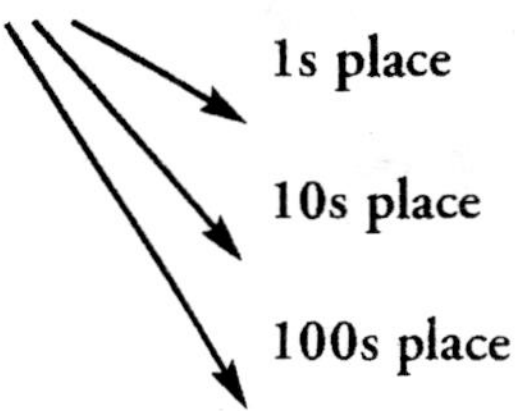

  We can represent the "places" (or positions) in powers of 10.

	1000	100	10	1
...	10^3	10^2	10^1	10^0
		9	8	3

  This continues for as many decimal places as you require; for example, the millions place is 10^6.

Note!

Anything to the power of 0 is 1

- **Internal representation of numbers in computers.**

  Computers are electronic machines. They work with electricity. Although we will not study electronics here, it is interesting to note that all data that is represented inside a computer can be thought of as "there is a voltage present" or "there is no voltage present."

  With these 2 electrical settings, we can represent exactly 2 values, 0 and 1.

The binary number system has grown from this simple concept. (BI—meaning 2, e.g., bicycle has 2 wheels.)

Consider the binary number systems in the same terms as we discussed the decimal number system above.

There are 2 symbols, 0 and 1.

Numbers are represented using powers of 2.

The numbers are written left to right, most significant digits to least significant digits.

Recall from above:

We can represent the 'places' (or positions) in powers of 10.

	1000	100	10	1
...	10^3	10^2	10^1	10^0
		9x100	8x10	3x1

In binary, the places are represented in powers of 2.

	128	64	32	16	8	4	2	1
...	2^7	2^6	2^5	2^4	2^3	2^2	2^1	2^0

How do we represent values in this number system? How do we convert back and forth between decimal and binary?

- **Converting from binary to decimal.**

What is the decimal equivalent of 10011 ?

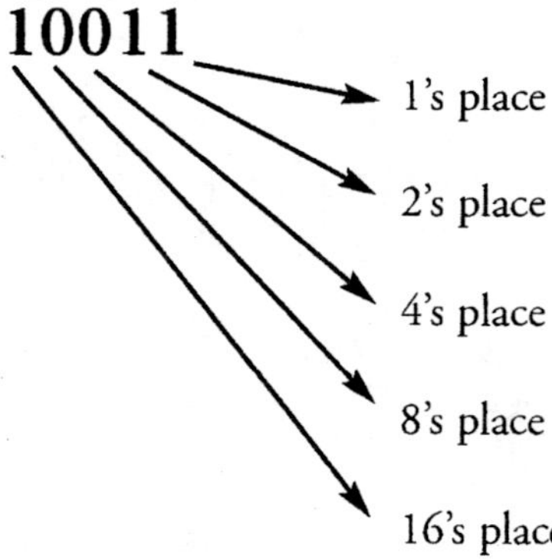

	128	64	32	16	8	4	2	1
...	2^7	2^6	2^5	2^4	2^3	2^2	2^1	2^0
				1x16	0x8	0x4	1x2	1x1

16 + 2 + 1 = 19

The binary equivalent of the decimal number 19 is 10011

When converting from binary to decimal, write the values of the places as indicated above, and think of it as "one group of 16, one group of 2, and one group of 1."

Exercises

Convert the following numbers from binary to decimal:

11

1011

1001

1000

1100101

- **Converting from decimal to binary.**

What is the binary equivalent of the decimal number 27?

The process is similar to the above method@EMDASHjust going in the other direction. Write the values of the binary positions, and start taking the groups out of the decimal number.

	128	64	32	16	8	4	2	1
...	2^7	2^6	2^5	2^4	2^3	2^2	2^1	2^0

Leading 0s are generally not interesting, e.g., we don't write 937 as 0000937. When converting to binary from decimal, locate the first position that will contain a 1. In this case, 27 has 1 group of 16.

	128	64	32	16	8	4	2	1
...	2^7	2^6	2^5	2^4	2^3	2^2	2^1	2^0
				1x16				

Take the 16 out of the decimal number: 27 – 16 = 11

Now we need to represent 11 in the remaining positions.

Since the remaining number is greater than or equal to 8, we can take out one group of 8.

	128	64	32	16	8	4	2	1
...	2^7	2^6	2^5	2^4	2^3	2^2	2^1	2^0
				1x16	1x8			

Take the 8 out of the decimal number: 11 – 8 = 3

Now represent 3 in the remaining places.

There are 0 groups of 4, there is one group of 2, and 1 group of 1.

	128	64	32	16	8	4	2	1
...	2^7	2^6	2^5	2^4	2^3	2^2	2^1	2^0
				1x16	1x8	0x4	1x2	1x1
				1	1	0	1	1

11011 is the binary representation of 27.

Exercises

Represent the following decimal numbers in binary:

4

7

15

37

74

197

- **Bits and bytes.**

  In computing, a single binary position is called a bit. This is the smallest unit of representation possible. Each bit can represent the values 0 and 1. By putting these bits together, we can create larger numbers as described above.

  Suppose we have 3 bits to work with. What are all the possible numbers we can represent with 3 binary bits?

  000 0
  001 1
  010 2
  011 3
  100 4
  101 5
  110 6
  111 7

  We can represent 8 different values, 0 – 7.

  Suppose we have 4 bits. The largest number we can represent is 1111 (decimal 15).

  5 bits – 11111, this is decimal 31.

  Suppose we have 8 bits. This will soon become very difficult, so let's go back to fundamentals and see how to calculate the maximum value for the positions.

  In decimal, what is the largest number that can be represented with 3 digits? 999. With 6 digits? 999999

  $999 = 10^3 - 1$

  $999999 = 10^6 - 1$

  It works the same in binary. The largest number that can be represented in

4 bits 1111 $2^4 - 1 = 15$ (get out a calculator)

8 bits **1111 1111** $2^8 - 1 = 255$

The most common grouping of bits in internal representation in computers is 8 bits. This is called a **byte.**

A byte can represent the values 0 – 255.

Exercises

What is the largest value that can be represented in:

2 bits
5 bits
7 bits
15 bits
a byte
a word

- **Hexadecimal—Intro.**

All numbers represented internally are stored in binary. It becomes very difficult to work with long strings of binary numbers 1110110100100101010101010101

When these are written, we often put spaces every 4 places to make it slightly easier to read.

1110 1101 0010 0101 0101 0101 0101

It's still not easy to work and do arithmetic in this number system. Converting back and forth between decimal and binary is also not convenient. Many considerations are needed that make it necessary to work in these number systems, as you will learn in your advanced courses.

It is common for us to represent internal memory addresses in binary, but the numbers would be so long that a shorter representation is used. This is the **hexadecimal** number system.

- **Hexadecimal.**

  There are 16 symbols. 0, 1, 2, 3, 4, 5, 6, 7, 8, 9, A, B, C, D, E, F
  (Note: a b c d e f are the same – it seems to be a preference to use capitals.)

  Numbers are represented using powers of 16 for the positions of the digits.

  The digits are written left to right, i.e., from most significant digits to least significant digits.

  The letters are used to represent the decimal values as follows:

  A = 10
  B = 11
  C = 12
  D = 13
  E = 14
  F = 15

  Note that in decimal (base 10), there are 10 symbols; in binary (base 2), there are 2 symbols; and in hex (base 16), there are 16 symbols.

  A hex number is commonly written with a prefix of 0x to distinguish it from a decimal number. It may also be written with a subscript after the number to indicate that it is a hex number: $23E5_{16}$ $23E5_{H}$

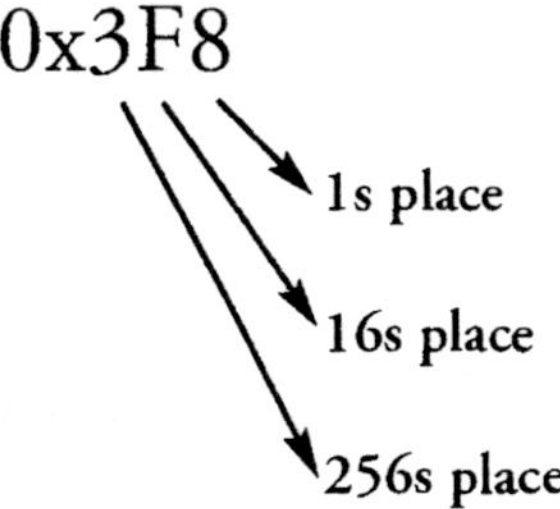

We can represent the 'places' (or positions) in powers of 16.

	4096	256	16	1
...	16^3	16^2	16^1	16^0
		3	F	8

We often write hex numbers starting with 0x to make it explicit that this is not a decimal number.

- **Converting between binary and hex.**

  This is the easiest conversion. Recall that 4 bits can store the values 0–15. It is not a coincidence that a single hex character can store the values from 0–15.

  Convert this binary number to hex: 1010 1100

  It is generally accepted that we convert 4 bits at a time to decimal, and then to the hex.

  1010 is 8 + 2 = 10 (decimal) = 0xA

  1100 is 8 + 4 = 12 (decimal) = 0xC

  so, 1010 1100 = 0xAC

Exercises

Convert the following binary numbers to hex:

1101
1111
0010
1001 1111 0101 0011
1011 0111 0001 1110

Converting from hex to binary works the same way. Each hex place corresponds to 4 bits in binary.

0x4D

4 is 0100
D is (13 decimal) 1101

0x4D = 0100 1101 (the leading 0 is not necessary here, but is included to avoid errors in reading these numbers)

Exercises

Convert the following hex numbers to binary:

0x8
0xD
0x3A
0xFF
0x8E4C

- **Converting between decimal and hex.**

	4096	**256**	**16**	**1**
...	**16^3**	**16^2**	**16^1**	**16^0**
	1000	**100**	**10**	**1**
...	**10^3**	**10^2**	**10^1**	**10^0**

- **From hex to decimal.**

This is about the same as we did in the binary conversions except that now we have letters that represent 10-15.

Consider this example:

0x3D

3 x 16		=	48
D(13) x 1	=	13	
	——		
		61 decimal	

Another example:

0x5D4C

5 x 4096	=	20,480
D(13) x 256	=	3328
4 x 16	=	64
C(12) x 1	=	12
		————
		23,884 decimal

- **From decimal to hex.**

	4096	256	16	1
...	16^3	16^2	16^1	16^0

- **Convert the decimal value 637 to hex.**

Subtracting groups....

2 x 256 = 512   637 – 512 = 125
7 x 16 = 112   125 – 112 = 13
D(13) x 1 = 13

637 decimal = 0x27D

Any numbers larger than this are not calculated by hand. Even numbers this large may normally be done by calculator unless the person is highly skilled and working with these conversions daily.

ASCII Code—Internal Representation of Characters—a b c A B C ....

Until now we have looked at the internal representation of numbers. Computers also do text processing, and a representation of letters is required.

Recall that everything in a computer is based on 1 and 0 (voltage and no voltage).

How will we represent letters using only combinations of 1 and 0? It was decided that a standard code is required that all computers storing characters will use. This is called the ASCII code.

ASCII—American Standard Code for Information Interchange

In the ASCII code, each character is represented as a small integer number. Which letter is represented by which number was decided arbitrarily.

For example, the ASCII code for the character 'A' is 65.

'B' = 66
'C' = 67
...

'a' = 97

All of the characters in the ASCII code are less than 128. This is important. What is the largest number that we can represent in 7 bits?

$2^7 - 1 \quad = \quad 127$

This means that each character's ASCII code can be represented in a single byte—8 bits (with a bit to spare).

Consider the binary presentation of the character A = 65.

64	32	16	8	4	2	1
1	**0**	**0**	**0**	**0**	**0**	**1**

100 0001 is the internal representation of the character A

Exercises

Use the ASCII code chart in Appendix B to find the binary code for the characters:

E
e
*
%
4
9
Z
"

INDEX

Note: numbers in italic indicate tables, figures, or footnotes.

E

F

G

H

I

J

K

L

M

N

O

P

Q

R

S

T

U

V

W